OFFICIAL

Multimedia Publishing
FOR **Netscape**

WINDOWS & MACINTOSH

Make your Web
pages come alive!

An imprint of
Ventana Communications
Group

GARY DAVID BOUTON

Official Multimedia Publishing for Netscape: Make Your Web Pages Come Alive
Copyright © 1996 by Gary David Bouton

Library of Congress Cataloging-in-Publication Data ·

   Bouton, Gary David, 1953-
      Multimedia publishing for Netscape : make your Web pages come
      alive / Gary David Bouton. — 1st ed.
         p. cm.
      Includes index.
      ISBN 1-56604-381-6
      1. Multimedia systems. 2. Electronic publishing. 3. Netscape.
     4. World Wide Web (Information retrieval system) I. Title.
     QA76.575.B69   1996
     006.6—dc20   96-16332
                                                       CIP

First Edition 9 8 7 6 5 4 3 2 1
Printed in the United States of America

Published and distributed to the trade by Ventana Communications Group, Inc.,
P.O. Box 13964, Research Triangle Park, NC 27709-3964
919/544-9404   FAX 919/544-9472

Limits of Liability and Disclaimer of Warranty

Trademarks

OFFICIAL

Multimedia Publishing
FOR Netscape

WINDOWS & MACINTOSH

Make your Web
pages come alive!

ABOUT THE AUTHOR

Gary David Bouton is an author and illustrator whose books share a common theme: that of visualization solutions, a future buzzword meant to encompass digital graphics, imaging, page layout, animation . . . anything that helps to accurately convey a thought through the use of one or more computer art forms. Gary, with his wife and frequent coauthor, Barbara, are owners of *Exclamat!ons*, a firm that "polishes rough ideas" for Fortune 500 companies. Gary has received international awards in publishing and design from Corel Corporation, Macromedia, and the Intergalactic Newsletter Competition, sponsored by NYPC and InfoWorld.

He comes from a traditional background in art and advertising and believes that designers with similar backgrounds can benefit from books like *Official Multimedia Publishing for Netscape*. For traditional artists, the creative process of turning a concept into a finished multimedia product is accomplished through means that can sometimes be less than obvious, and the author's approach is to begin with the familiar, then integrate experience with new technological discoveries.

Among the author's credits are *Inside Adobe Photoshop* and *CorelDRAW Experts Edition*. Gary is the current moderator of the CorelXARA discussion group on CorelNet, and is an active member of the HTML Writer's Guild. The author can be reached through CompuServe at 74512,230, or on the Internet at bbouton@dreamscape.com.

Acknowledgments

The best books you'll find in the genre occasionally referred to as "after market," "third-party," or simply "computer" books, presume that the author knows what he or she is writing about. In this ever-changing field of application software, a good author, then, needs to take one of two routes to writing accurate, timely documentation.

The first route is to spend what seems like 95 percent of one's waking hours researching, and then *updating* the research as manufacturers upgrade a product right from underneath you! This approach, unfortunately, leads to a never-ending tome, and the accompanying stress can result in domestic cacophony.

I was lucky enough to be offered an alternative when writing *Official Multimedia Publishing for Netscape*. To bring the book you hold before you to completion, Ventana surrounded me with the best professionals in their respective fields and allowed me to invite professional friends of my own. I'd like to thank the following kind souls who took the time and care to "navigate" this text to a safe harbor, to steer me clear of dangling participles, and to check the pantry for provisions throughout the voyage:

- Cheri Robinson, Product Manager, who is also the person who gave me my first break authoring what now seems like a CorelDRAW version negative 2 book. Cheri, thanks for the opportunity that *this* book has provided for me to continue the "art lessons" and occasional silliness. Continuity is as important as personal growth, and you've given me the chance to practice both.

- Beth Snowberger, Project Editor, for her work above and beyond the call of publishing. Beth helped keep this tome a focused one—I was actually planning on writing a chapter on "Fun With Alpha Channels" before she gently suggested that I was getting a little off-topic. She also encouraged me to express an idea or technique in user-friendly terms . . . something that is fairly hard to accomplish without making a book pander, stoop, or otherwise condescend to the reader. Thanks for the personal attention, Beth, and I hope I did you proud.

- Development Editor Jim Deegan, for his fine insights, organizational prowess, and spirit of forgiving when the manuscript occasionally disintegrated into

  ```
  <floundering>
  <IMG SRC= "Oh, I don't know! Who cares, for the 40th
  time????!" Height=10 feet, give or take a square acre>
  </floundering>
  ```

  Jim, I appreciate the time and effort you've contributed to make this book easy to read for users of all skill levels.

- JJ Hohn, who did the fishing for the many, many great shareware and special editions of commercial software you'll find on the Companion CD-ROM. All of us involved with the *Official Multimedia Publishing for Netscape Companion CD-ROM* feel it's the right product for independent Web authoring, as well as being a superb resource collection of files for following the examples in the chapters. Thanks, JJ; your work allowed me to keep with the writing throughout the development of this book.

- Allen Wyke, who collated, sorted, and tested the contents of the Companion CD-ROM to ensure that a GIF file is actually a GIF file, and that Windows and Macintosh users can access native file formats. Allen, you took a lot of the pressure off of me through your fine work indexing an extremely complex directory structure.

- Brad King, for his efforts in contacting the many shareware and commercial software creators, whose permission made much of the Companion CD-ROM a reality.

- Amy Moyers and Diane Lennox, for allowing me to edit page proofs and for accepting contributions for cover copy and art. This is *not* Standard Operating Procedure (SOP) in my experience as an author, and I deeply appreciate the courtesy.

- Technical Reviewer and fellow Corellian Steve Bain, a gifted author in his own right, who accepted the responsibility of authenticating Macintosh and Windows techniques shown in this book. Steve, I hope I have the privilege in the near future to pick apart one of *your* books (*onnnly*, kidding, Steve!), and let's go ring the doorbell again real soon, eh?

- Eric Coker, for his technical advice in Chapters 7 and 8.

- Spousal Editor Barbara Bouton, for putting up with the hours and the general condition of our living accomodations that are a direct result of authoring, and for checking my grammar and thoughts before FedEx cheerfully dispatched the manuscripts to North Carolina.

- At Adobe Systems, thanks to Sonya Schaefer, John Leddy, and Peter Card for the use of Illustrator, Dimensions, PageMaker 6, and Photoshop for the Macintosh, and for the continuing kind words about this whole project. Sonya, I've created an AutoText entry in MS Word to thank you because you're always there to provide when I rely upon Adobe's tools to complete a book.

- At Fractal Design Corporation, Daryl Wise and Jon Bass for the use of Painter and Poser in this book. Poser is a completely amazing program, unique in its capability to portray human forms, and I look forward to nothing but the best from it and your company.

- At Macromedia, Rix Kramlich, Brian Perkins, and John Dowdell for the technical support and the early copy of Extreme 3D for Windows and the Macintosh. Much of the artwork shown on the Companion CD-ROM and on the following pages would have been impossible to create without your kind assistance.

- Michael Bellefeuille at Corel Corporation for the use of CorelXARA, used in combination with other software and as a stand-alone application to create the example designs on the Companion CD-ROM.

- Ashley Sharp at Virtus Corp., for the use of Virtus WalkThrough Pro.

- Many, many thanks to Scott Brennan, President of Dreamscape On-Line, Inc., our Internet Service Provider and friend who has demonstrated to the Boutons that personal service is alive and well in the 1990s world of communications.

- Gordon J. Robinson, my childhood chum, who has shared with me over the years everything from brass trio sonatas performed on a loading dock to allowing me to use his name, and quite conceivably his professional reputation, within examples found in books like these. Thanks, Gord! Remember when we shipped Benny to Cortland?

DEDICATION

This book is dedicated to Cheri Robinson, who has always been her best with me, in times that occasionally were less than ideal. Her belief in me as an author has far outstripped my own belief, with regularity, through the writing of seven books. If you benefit from this book, they're my thoughts, but it's Cheri's effort that brings this information to you.

Contents

Introduction

Forget everything you know about traditional publishing! For more than six months now, discussion groups, newsgroups, and mailing lists formerly dedicated to design applications, image-setter problems, and hardware workarounds on the Internet have shifted in topic. If you subscribe to desktop publishing or graphics lists, you've probably seen 20 "How do I create an animated GIF?" questions for every one message asking, "How do I get extended characters, like a copyright symbol, into PageMaker?" Everyone today is passionately interested in publishing to an immediate, global audience—the World Wide Web—and also wants to push the limit of the types of graphically-rich contents contained in Web documents.

Official Multimedia Publishing for Netscape takes a comprehensive, in-depth look at new techniques for creating Web-ready objects such as VRML worlds, animation, and sound, as well as at the keys to porting the skills you may already have with your existing applications to create exciting, attention-getting Web sites. Through step-by-step examples using Windows and Macintosh applications and utilities, *Official Multimedia Publishing for Netscape* also shows you the ins and outs of integrating text, graphics, and media objects to create a professional site with definite commercial possibilities.

If you're coming to the Internet from a background of computer graphics or desktop publishing, this book is designed to help you rethink traditional publishing limitations. Color space and resolution, for instance, are measured differently when graphics are displayed in HTML format, as are font styles. Throughout this book, you'll discover new possibilities for your existing talents when you apply them to the new media of the Web. If you're a newcomer to computer graphics, but you have a firm grasp of HTML and its formatting, *Official Multimedia Publishing for Netscape* will turn you on to the best graphics programs and utilities for both Windows and the Macintosh, to round out your education in Web authoring tools. And even if you just picked up your machine yesterday and want to get into the Web action, *Official Multimedia Publishing for Netscape* can be your guide to basic and advanced techniques for composing documents that can be visited by users of every computer platform.

This book was written from an artist's perspective by an author who has spent many years relearning techniques for new media, as well as discovering the fastest, most effective artistic techniques for visual communications. There are two fundamental tenets for solving communications problems, regardless of the artistic medium a creator uses:

- If the artistic problem cannot be solved with the current set of rules and limitations, it's best to take a holistic approach, to step outside of the "system"—the materials and approach—with which you're working on a solution. Get yourself a larger scope. And frequently a larger, more generalized, productive set of tools!

- Self-definition leads to self-limitation. If you say to yourself, "I can't fathom this HTML stuff. I'm a designer, darn it, not a programmer!" or some such declaration, then you'll be less successful at communicating through the multimedia capabilities of Netscape Navigator and the Web. Don't allow your occupation to become a *preoccupation* when approaching this new avenue of personal and commercial expression. We're all new to this Web stuff, and if you regard yourself as a professional in terms no more specific than a "visualization solution expert," you can then more easily cast off the shackles of past techniques, tools, and experience, free yourself to discover new tools and repurpose existing tools, and get on with the adventure of composing multimedia for the Web.

THE NONLINEAR MULTIMEDIA PUBLISHING GUIDE

To better serve the specific needs you might have regarding Web object creation and integration techniques, *Official Multimedia Publishing for Netscape* is not written in a "page one is for novices, page 500 is for accomplished users" fashion. Instead, each chapter in this book addresses an area of Web authoring. You might choose to plunge into the VRML chapter if this area is of the most immediate interest to you, or you might decide to take the procedural approach, and investigate each chapter's contents in sequential order. *Official Multimedia Publishing for Netscape* is sort of like a subway system; you can indeed get to one area from another, but it's up to you to decide where you want to begin, how many points you pass through, and where you want to wind up. In digital multimedia authoring, you similarly might begin with one art form that leads you to another, and this book contains numerous cross-references to neighboring chapters, so if you don't find a specific solution in Chapter 3, for example, we'll tell you where you can find more comprehensive information about a related topic in Chapter 5.

COMPLETE WORKING EXAMPLES THAT SHOW A PRINCIPLE

Although *Official Multimedia Publishing for Netscape* was written in a modular style as described in the preceding section, you'll notice that the example files referenced in this book are highly structured, complete in their execution, and awaiting your perusal on the Companion CD-ROM. The author has found in his continuing education that there's nothing quite as useless as an example that demonstrates a principle within a vacuum. *Official Multimedia Publishing for Netscape* contextualizes a technique—we show you, for example, not simply how to create an animated GIF, but how the file is embedded in a document, how to resize it and reduce its color capability for optimized display, and we'll even suggest such a file's appropriateness for specific themes of Web sites. All the example sites on the Companion CD-ROM can be copied to your hard disk and played within Navigator, and the files can be modified using NavGold, an image editor, and a text editor so you can better see how something works. Our belief in creating this book is that text can reach a point in communicating an idea at which it's best to *show an example*. And the example sites show how a specific technique can be integrated with a *related* technique, to construct a synergy that Web audiences have come to appreciate and demand.

CONVENTIONS USED IN THIS BOOK

Because the Internet is accessible to all users who have a connection, it follows that *Official Multimedia Publishing for Netscape* was written for users of different operating platforms. The example sites on the Companion CD-ROM were created using a Pentium 133 MHz running Windows 95, and a PowerPC Macintosh 8500 running System 7.5.3. The Companion CD-ROM was mastered to accommodate a few unique file types for each platform, but the real problem in making *Official Multimedia Publishing for Netscape* accessible to the different versions of the Windows and Macintosh operating systems had to do with unique conventions. This book attempts to ford any gaps in documenting techniques by implementing the following conventions and specifications:

- *Biplatform applications use similar, but not identical commands. Official Multimedia Publishing for Netscape* spotlights no fewer than 12 full-featured commercial applications; in every chapter, you'll see how specific programs can produce media elements for Web use. Most of these applications are biplatform, and there is little or no difference in key commands or menu items used to produce an effect. However, we've adopted the convention in this book that if a program, such as Adobe Photoshop, uses key commands that are different in Windows than on the Macintosh, the key commands are given for Windows first, then in Macintosh format. For example, to load the dialog box for the last-used filter in Photoshop, we'd advise users to follow a step written like this:

Press Ctrl+Alt+F (Macintosh: Cmd+Opt+F) to load the dialog box for the filter you used in Step x.

. . .which means that holding the three keys mentioned in the step produces the intended result in Photoshop.

When there is a significant difference in steps used in an application that's available in both Windows and Macintosh formats, we fully explain both sets of steps. Additionally, Windows supports the use of a secondary mouse button. In Navigator, the secondary mouse button is used to display a context-sensitive shortcut menu. On the Macintosh, there is no secondary mouse button support, so Netscape offers a click-and-hold technique to call the shortcut menu. In instances like this one, where it's necessary, we give explicit instructions for both operating platforms in this book.

■ *Nicknames for well-known products are used.*   We'd have a larger book here, and needlessly so, if we mentioned the full brand manufacturer, product name, and version number when referring to specific applications. For this reason, you'll occasionally see Adobe Photoshop 3.0.5 referred to as simply "Photoshop" in the text of this book. Similarly, CorelDRAW!, CorelPHOTO-PAINT!, and other Corel Corporation products are mentioned sans the exclamation mark. Ventana Communications Group acknowledges the names mentioned in this book are trademarked or copyrighted by their respective manufacturers, and our use of nicknames for various products is in no way connected with trademark names for these products. When we refer to an application, it is usually the most current version of the application, unless otherwise noted.

■ *The CD-ROM icon refers to a file on the Companion CD-ROM.* Because we wanted *Official Multimedia Publishing for Netscape* to be a hands-on book, there are many areas in chapters where you'll be asked to copy a file from the Companion CD-ROM to your hard disk to complete an example assignment. The icon next to an example step indicates that you should copy the file(s) and use them within the step. Because CD-ROMs are *Read-Only Media*, you'll need to save completed assignments to your hard disk, and you might occasionally need to remove the write-protection from a CD file, even though you've copied it to your read/write-capable hard disk. Certain applications do not acknowledge a file copied from CD-ROM as editable.

In Windows 95, to remove write-protection from a file, right-click on the file as it is displayed in a folder window. Choose Properties from the shortcut menu, then uncheck the Read-only Attributes check box if it's checked.

In Windows 3.1x, click on a file in File Manager's window, then choose File | Properties, and uncheck the Read Only check box if necessary.

On the Macintosh, click on a file in a folder window or on the Desktop, then choose File | Get Info from the Apple menu. Uncheck the Locked check box if a checkmark is displayed.

Official Multimedia Publishing for Netscape presumes that you're comfortable with the operating system on your machine, that you know how to copy, move, and delete files, and that your system has a few megabytes of hard disk space free to work with the example files.

A QUICK LOOK AT WHAT'S IN STORE

Earlier in this Introduction, the analogy was made between a subway system and this book's organization. What's the second thing you look for on public transportation (the first being a seat)? The following is a *map* of the adventures to come in *Official Multimedia Publishing for Netscape* chapters:

The first two chapters are intended to form a foundation for the advanced HTML and graphics composition that follow in subsequent chapters. If you're experienced with page layout, but can't get a handle on HTML, these chapters are for you. We also take a look at how any design application can be used to produce a graphic that's Web-ready.

Chapter 1, "Composing in HTML & NavGold," discusses how the HyperText Markup Language (HTML) works and how special tags and attributes can be used to define Web page elements. We also show you some of the power of Navigator Gold's WYSIWYG Editor for quickly composing and linking HTML pages while insulating the user from tedious and complex HTML formatting. The example site in Chapter 1 shows how a traditional desktop publishing document can be made Web-ready through rethinking and reworking layout elements to better suit the electronic presentation format.

Chapter 2, "Vector-to-Bitmap Conversions," takes you through the relationship between the format of digital graphics most people can create, and the reserved types of graphics types used in HTML documents. If you use CorelDRAW or Illustrator, there are a number of techniques you can use to convert these vector formats of images to bitmap GIF and JPEG file types. Learn how to make every pixel count in your image, and arrive at the best looking image possible from bitmap or vector applications.

The next four chapters show how different types of applications can be used to create Web objects beyond the humble GIF89a image. Learn how modeling applications can make your site a more dimensional one, learn how to create animation, and explore the virtual worlds of the VRML file format.

Chapter 3, "Bitmap Graphics & Special Effects," gets into the time-honored crafts of Web button making and seamless background texture construction, and takes a look at how other graphics can be integrated into Web sites. Learn the ins and outs of frame-based documents and see how image maps can provide the navigation elements that visitors to your site will want to access.

Chapter 4, "Working With Models," explores the world of 3D applications. You might already own a full-featured modeling and rendering program included when you purchased a software bundle. Learn about the 3D coordinate system, how to create a number of commercial 3D scenes, how to render 3D files to file formats that can be converted to GIF and JPEG format, and how modeling applications can support animation and VRML authoring.

Chapter 5, "Animation & Digital Video Compression," is a resource guide for designers who want to express their craft in an animated QuickTime or Video for Windows file. Navigator supports embedded animations in HTML documents, and Chapter 5 covers animation techniques you can use with applications such as Fractal Design Painter and GIF Construction Set. Also, learn about video compression and how to make a beautiful, yet *small* animated file that visitors to your site can view in an instant.

Chapter 6, "VRML," will show you the structure of the *Virtual Reality Modeling Language*, and how you can author a virtual world with nothing but a text editor and an understanding of VRML specifications for objects, lighting, camera angles, and surface textures. Also featured in Chapter 6 is how to use a modeling application as a VRML authoring tool. Learn how to offer your audience the capability to fly through, walk toward, and experience your 3D Web creations.

The final two chapters go beyond the still —or even moving— image, to include sound, video, and interactive entertainment for visitors to your site. This part of *Official Multimedia Publishing for Netscape* also shows you how to integrate different Web media and includes comprehensive planning strategies to ensure that your site is both full-featured and commercially sound.

Chapter 7, "Working With Special File Formats," is a guide to creative content providers in the basics of sound, video, and Java applets. If you've wanted to include an animated ticker tape on your site, look no further. We enter discussions of VDOLive streaming video, and of how some very full-featured shareware utilities can convert between WAV, aiff, and au sounds digital sound formats, so your message is always heard clear as a bell across the Net.

Chapter 8, "Putting It All Together," concludes our tour of connectivity and presentation of different media objects in *Official Multimedia Publishing for Netscape* with a makeover of Chapter 1's example site. You'll learn a lot through the course of this book, and Chapter 8 shows you the complete integration technique of Web publishing, from concept, to logistics, to the economics of actually posting a site.

You might find the chapters in *Official Multimedia Publishing for Netscape* to be a little longer than chapters written in books concerning a specific application. But, again, this book is about *integration* of media types for the Web. You'll see several ways to approach a design problem in each chapter, and several applications that can help solve a problem. It's recommended that you bring along a handful of bookmarks (those cubes of partially adhesive, fluorescent papers manufacturered by 3M or another company are good), and an idea for a site as you begin to explore with this book.

1 Composing in HTML & NavGold

Congratulations are in order if you came straight to this chapter after reading the Introduction! Although there are a number of really cool tricks you'll learn in chapters to come, Chapter 1 is about Web composition basics. Here we'll provide you with the Internet equivalent of builder's cement and steel, so that your multimedia composition has a solid foundation.

The structure of the HyperText Markup Language (HTML) provides the basis for Navigator enhancements as well as the foundation upon which you can display text, graphics . . . even the products of technology yet to be invented. In the same way that a style sheet in PageMaker provides you with quick formatting of documents, Navigator Gold and other programs offer similar, Web-based authoring tools. This chapter provides the techniques for converting traditional print-oriented layout to its digital counterpart on the Web, and offers several manual procedures for tweaking an HTML document so that it looks exactly the way you intended.

CONCEPTUALIZING FOR THE SCREEN

Perhaps the most fortunate—and unfortunate—individuals currently authoring Web documents are the graphics professionals. It is the computer graphics designer who understands the relationship between a pixel and a PostScript halftone cell and has invested several years working with the various versions of applications shown throughout this book. So where's the unfortunate part of this seemingly useful background?

Simply put, the World Wide Web uses an entirely different medium than traditional publishing: everything is displayed onscreen and not as ink on paper, and a fractional amount of Web documents are actually printed by the recipient to high-resolution imagesetters. Forget about out-of-gamut colors, skip the fine-tuning you'd usually perform to a kerned pair of characters in a headline: HTML was never designed to accommodate the layout artist!

Although it might seem at times that your traditional production experience will not come into play when designing Web documents, the methods you use to *conceive* a design can definitely get your assignment up on the wire more quickly than the competition. And the expertise you might have with drawing, painting, layout, animation, and other applications does indeed fit into the scheme of HTML composition: you simply have to learn a few new rules, and design stuff a lot smaller!

COMPOSITION RULES FOR THE WEB

One of the first things to consider when composing a document for the Web is that fonts, page size, and margins are completely at the mercy of your audience and HTML standards. HyperText Markup Language, a subset of Standard Generalized Markup Language (SGML), is an implementation of a hypermedia system that Tim Berners-Lee spearheaded, commonly referred to today as the World Wide Web. The original specifications for HTML left room for future improvements and innovations, and Netscape's improvements to the original specifications have certainly made the Web a more content-rich, content-diverse place.

However, as long as Web authors are confined to HTML as a transport mechanism for commerce, ideas, and entertainment, there are limitations—some of which *should not* be overcome in future versions—that make composing a Web document a little more challenging than a 32-page magazine. Let's cover the "Big Three Don'ts" before our discussions on how to enhance a Web creation in NavGold and other applications. An artist was once asked how he created a marble sculpture of an African elephant; the reply was, "First, I chipped away everything that didn't look like an elephant." Similarly, let's clear the online artist's loft of unnecessary concerns and notions.

DON'T DESIGN A WEB SITE WITH A SPECIFIC FONT IN MIND

This first "don't" is bound to frustrate users who've spent time and money collecting the best Type 1 fonts for publishing, but the truth is that the HTML standard doesn't provide for the specific declaration of fonts in a document. Font attributes are limited to font color, relative sizing of fonts from a predetermined base font size, and a limited number of special characters (such as trademarks and copyright symbols). Italic and bold attributes are supported by some, but not all, browsers. It is the duty of the Web browser on the visitor's system to provide the most accurate representation of typefaces as specified in HTML.

Think of what PageMaker or Quark documents look like onscreen when Adobe Type Manager is turned off. You can see font size, italic and bold attributes, and color. This is a fair analogy to working with text on the Web. HTML is a reference-oriented tag style of ASCII text; it describes font styles in generalized terms that UNIX, Windows, DOS, and Macintosh machines can decode through a Web browser. A specific font (such as Optima or Palatino) cannot be displayed on a viewer's machine when browsing your document, because HTML wasn't created as a system for displaying page layout down to the type styles.

Nevertheless, you can do a lot of creative things with limited font attributes, and we'll show you some innovative workarounds for the display of text later in this chapter.

DON'T DESIGN CLEAR TO THE SCREEN MARGIN

Because a visitor to your site views your composition on a computer monitor, you cannot predict the size at which your document is displayed. This is an important point: it's a near-universal truth that users dislike scrolling a document that's too big to fit on a single screen page.

So what is the current trend in monitor displays—800 X 600 at 24-bit color depth? Or is it 1024 X 768 at 16-bit color depth? The answer is *no one knows;* graphics professionals tend to have the budget for big monitors and fast video subsystems with lots of RAM, but your audience is probably *not* similarly outfitted.

If you intend to post a single Web page, it's a good idea to use the lowest monitor resolution your computer provides as the resolution in which you first compose the document. Leave room for the document to "play" for the different screen settings your audience might use. For example, a page that looks good at 640 X 480 display pixels will also play well on a monitor running 800 X 600 video resolution. Graphic elements composed to 640 X 480 resolution will shift as the browser adjusts the text for displays running at higher resolutions. But the important point is: *Give visitors a single page that does not require scrolling.* In other words, compose small, and anticipate a viewing audience running big. If you compose to high screen resolution, there is bound to be a visitor who can't see your entire page in a single field of view. And this might be the potential customer who could do you the most good.

Tangentially related to the display "don't" is the need to keep in mind that visitors to your site will also be using different brands of monitors that are connected at various modem speeds, and using different types and generations of processors. We'll address that reality in this chapter and get into the creation of objects for the Web that will appeal to the largest audience. Throughout this chapter, you'll also learn how to provide backups to ensure that the maximum number of people get the most from your work. "Play to the cheap seats" is the motto for the theater—and for the Web.

DON'T DEPEND ON AN AUDIENCE TO BE NAVIGATOR-CAPABLE

Incredible as it might seem, the Web is still browsed by almost 20 percent non-Navigator users. Connections to the Internet that are provided by some online services, and Internet Service Providers who offer a connection bundle, sometimes choose a browser that is incapable of handling documents that contain enhanced HTML elements. Although Netscape is the market leader in Web browsers and Web-browsing technology, you might want to provide alternative document objects that less proprietary browsers can handle. Netscape Navigator Gold allows you to create document links to alternate graphics within a document, and it has other features we'll explore to make your site as accommodating as possible to the general Web audience.

That's about it for the downside of porting traditional publishing to the Web and the end of chipping away those pieces that don't look like an elephant!

If you've been in publishing for a few years, there might be a document on your desk right now that needs to be "Web-ready." If not, the next section provides you with one as an example. And it's a *long* document—if you understand the structure of formatting long documents for the Web, converting short documents will be a snap.

CREATING A WEB E-ZINE ARTICLE

One of the most popular new trends in publishing today is offering an electronic version of a traditionally published article. The *New York Times* has a template into which it daily "dumps" the news for display online, and many magazines also offer an online collection of top monthly articles.

The success of the long document viewed on the Web has to do with formatting, navigation, and accommodation you build into it for speedy, concise online clarity and legibility. In the CHAP01/ DIGITOON folder on the Companion CD-ROM, you'll find all the elements that went into the construction of DIGITOON.HTM, a piece I wrote on digital cartooning. *Digi-Toons* was originally composed in MS Word, and the text and graphics were placed in PageMaker 5 to make the article press-ready. I believe my wisest decision when faced with making the article Web-ready was to discard the publication format and ask myself how this piece would play onscreen.

As typeset on 8½- X 11-inch paper, the article runs about eight pages. Using Navigator Gold, here are the steps needed to produce the coarse composition of a long Web document:

1. Begin with your word processor document. Open the original text file, spell check the file (even if you're certain you already did this!), then strip special characters from the text such as the registered trademarks and copyright symbols. Use a text editor's search and replace feature to find the offending characters and replace them with nothing, or with a blank space to mark the position for the addition of an HTML-type attribute for the character later. Web documents can contain special characters, but they have to be manually added in a style that browsers can decode. For example, applications sometimes automatically enter typesetter's quotes in word processing documents. "Straight" quotes are the standard for HTML documents; em dashes, degree symbols, anything you need to type with a special combination of keystrokes should be replaced with conventional characters and punctuation before continuing.

2. Save a copy of your edited text as an ASCII text file (a.k.a. plain text; *.TXT). If your word processor allows it, save the document with the .HTM or .HTML extension. You can then simply load the document in NavGold's Editor, because NavGold sees the document as already formatted in HTML. The disadvantage to this method is that Navigator will not recognize carriage returns in the document; it will be hard to discern line breaks and paragraph titles.

Alternatively, you can highlight the entire document, and copy it to the system clipboard. You can then paste the text into NavGold's Editor. Choose File | New Document | Blank from the menu, press Ctrl(Cmd)+V, and save the document, if you choose the clipboard route. This might prove to be a better method of porting your plain text because line breaks are preserved; it will be easy to spot a paragraph title within the text.

You've performed the gross composition of the HTML document. Now it's time to gussy it up.

DEFINING FONT SIZES & ATTRIBUTES

As mentioned earlier in this chapter, font sizes are interpreted by Web browsers according to a relative size attribute tag you can assign to sections of text. To make it easy to generate HTML code in NavGold's Editor, push buttons and drop-down boxes reminiscent of word processors can be found on the toolbar. However, it should be noted that Netscape's implementation of tags for text is not 100 percent approved HTML code. The plus one (+1), plus two (+2), and so on attributes you apply to selected text generate tags in the document that cause the visitor's Web browser to display the text onscreen *more or less* the same as you see it in the Editor.

But there are some browsers that fail to see the tags at all. These browsers create the proper text size from the default size specified by the tags that surround the text in question. If no tags such as <h1>, <h2>, <UL>, <address>, and so on surround the text, the text will display at the same size as paragraph or body text. Use the "bulletproof" tag <h1> to ensure that heading one is displayed larger than heading two in a document.

As you'll see shortly, you may never have to see the raw HTML formatting for a document if you use NavGold's Editor, but if your document doesn't appear to your audience the way you wrote it, a knowledge of how things work is indispensable.

The <p> tag is a standard HTML tag that tells browsers that the text enclosed within the tags is a paragraph. It is up to the browser then to display the text in whatever the browser uses as the base, default font, and font size for paragraph text. In Netscape's enhanced HTML tag language, a paragraph title that you want to be a larger size than the default-sized paragraph that follows it would be written as:

```
<font SIZE=+1>This is my headline</font>
<p>Here's the paragraph copy</p>
```

Note that tagged text requires both a beginning and end tag: the end is generally the same attribute (such as "font") as the beginning, preceded by a forward slash; greater than/less than brackets separate the tag from the text.

TIP

Get a handle on HTML tag styles, and you're well on your way to understanding how to author VRML virtual worlds. The tag style is very similar in both authoring languages. See Chapter 6, "VRML," for more on Virtual Reality Modeling Language, and check out Ventana's HTML Publishing on the Internet for Windows *or* HTML Publishing on the Internet for Mac *for advanced documentation of the HTML structure.*

It's time to get your hands dirty with a little example of how to format text and add a little color to the *Digi-Toons* document. The ARTICLE.HTM document in the CHAP01 folder is completely unformatted, with the exception of line breaks added to the text to make sections clearer to see. The need for line spacing before and after paragraphs, headers, and other elements is part of a tag's definition. The amount of space rendered onscreen when a browser interprets the tag depends on the specific browser. Unlike interline spacing in DTP documents, these values are determined by the visitor's browser and can't be set or changed by the author of the document. Authors can, however, manually force a "carriage return" to break a line or insert an extra line of space by using the <br> tag. Capitalization of tags is ignored (so a hard break could also be written as <BR>, which might make the tag more readily visible if you need to proof an HTML document as raw text), and two or more consecutive white spaces in HTML code are also discarded by all browsers. All tabs in a document are ignored, and a Web browser will collapse tabs into a single space because there are no provisions in HTML for defining, using, or recognizing tabs. Load the ARTICLE.HTM document into the Editor, and here's how to apply text styles:

1. Scroll down the Editor window until you see the line, "Two Approaches to Cartooning…"

2. Highlight the entire line.

3. Click on the Font Size drop-down list on the toolbar, then choose +2. Again, most, but not all, browsers will recognize the attribute as meaning, "Display this text as two sizes larger than the default text." "Sizes" is an undefined term here, but Navigator 2.01 and later will display the HTML document exactly as shown in the Editor.

4. To ensure that the audience can't fail to recognize the paragraph title as a header, click on the Font Color icon on the toolbar, and choose a color that stands out against the default background color, as shown in Figure 1-1. Click on OK to exit the Color dialog box.

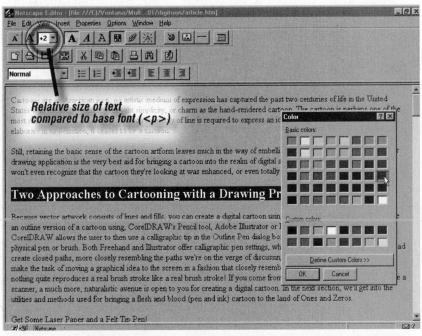

Figure 1-1: *Creating headlines is easy and WYSIWYG (What You See Is What You Get) in NavGold's Editor.*

5. Click on the Center Text button on the toolbar. The paragraph title will now be centered onscreen, regardless of the resolution of the audience's monitor.

6. Play along with me here, and scroll down the document and perform steps 2–5 with the rest of the paragraph titles in this document. There are more advanced formatting procedures to follow, and this can be an experimental document.

7. Save the document as MYTOONS (or whatever you'd like).HTM to your hard disk. You're done.

Although what it looks like you've done is select, format, and colorize text, you've also generated ASCII-based HTML tags in a text document—instructions on how to display this document on the Web. In fact, in a text editor, the colored, bolded, centered headline text appears like this:

```
<center><b><font COLOR="#8000FF"><font SIZE=+2>
Two Approaches to Cartooning with a Drawing Program
</font></font></b><center>
```

In order to find this headline in the document from a Table of Contents at the document's top, the line you highlighted in the previous example now needs to be targeted. We discuss an easy method for composing a hyperlink TOC in the following section.

FONT COLORS IN HTML DOCUMENTS

NavGold's color picker is specific to each operating platform: Windows users can choose from the familiar Windows picker, and Macintosh users can define text color using the Apple Color Picker. However, to achieve platform independence here, it should be noted that there are other ways to indicate colored text.

HEXCOLOR.HTM is in the CHAP01 folder on the Companion CD. If you copy this document to your hard disk, also copy BACKGRD.GIF—it's required to see all the available colors in the chart.

HEXCOLOR.HTM shows all the RGB values for colors that Netscape has defined by user-friendly names. Therefore, if you like burlywood as a color for text, you could in fact type **<font COLOR="#burlywood">** preceding text to get the same effect in a document as specifying this color with the Editor's color picker. The pound sign is required to precede any format of font color attribute, named or hexadecimal. Netscape also uses these reserved, named colors according to the HEXCOLOR.HTM chart in Java applets. The tag name is converted to hexadecimal code when a document is mailed from the Editor or when saved in the Editor.

Do *not* mistake this chart for the Netscape Color Table (as shown in Chapter 5, "Animation & Digital Video Compression"), however. This chart only represents the reserved-name colors Netscape can read and the equivalent values expressed in hexadecimal code. The Netscape Color Table is used to define nondithering colors, of which there are very few in the reserved text color list.

CREATING A TABLE OF CONTENTS

The eight pages that the *Digi-Toons* article took up on paper takes almost 18 screens when formatted without graphics at 640 X 480 viewing resolution. Okay, this is a fair-sized document. There are three options you have for making online documents of this length less tedious for a visitor to your site:

- Cut copy. This is usually not a preferred option, but it's realistic and sometimes necessary as you compose complex sites.

TIP

HTML pages, like traditional publications, often contain widows and orphans, and these stranded words at the beginning or end of a paragraph look as awkward as they do in print. There is no force-justification in HTML standard code, so copy cutting can be an alternative when lines don't flow exactly right and none of the tricks shown in this chapter straighten out a paragraph.

- Break the document into several different HTML pages and create links between them. This method can be a trade-off of speed for ease of access you provide the visitor to your site. If a link fails to produce secondary HTML documents for the visitor, this strategy fails. Additionally, Web search engines might catalog a secondary page without cataloging the *top page* (the page from which the visitor jumps to secondary documents). You have less control of how a complete document is browsed by breaking the document into smaller parts.

- You can keep the document as a long HTML file, create a thorough, hyperlinked table of contents on the first page, and allow the visitor to jump within the document that's optimized for speed through the use of small graphics. This is the strategy we review in the following sections. The added benefit to this HTML structure is that a visitor can download the complete document in one pass, instead of chasing down every linked subpage to the document.

If you'd like to copy the entire DIGITOON folder to your hard disk from the CHAP01 folder on the Companion CD-ROM, you can retrace the steps used in NavGold's Editor to recreate the Table of Contents for the *Digi-Toons* Web page. See Figure 1-2.

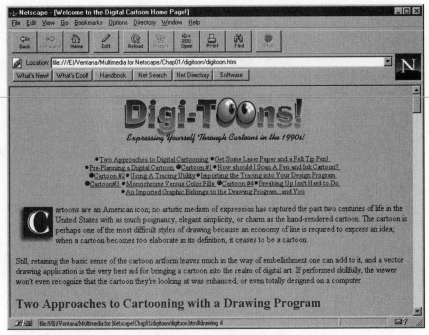

Figure 1-2: *A Table of Contents for a long Web document is a must. Visitors can then hyperlink to a topic of interest without scrolling.*

Alternatively, you can use the document you saved in the preceding example to create the hypertext links:

1. In NavGold's Editor, scroll down to the first paragraph title in the document.

2. Highlight the first few words of the text, or a few words you can associate with this section, then press Ctrl(Cmd)+C to copy this section to the clipboard.

3. Deselect the text, insert your cursor at the very beginning of the line, then click on the Insert Target button on the toolbar.

4. A dialog box appears that has a field for the name of the anchor (the target), as in Figure 1-3. Insert the cursor in this field, and press Ctrl(Cmd)+V to paste the clipboard text in the field, then click on OK.

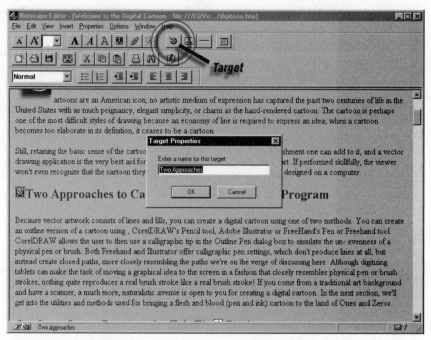

Figure 1-3: *A target name can be anything you choose; it's helpful, though, to name a target with the same name as text found in the target.*

5. Highlight the entire paragraph title and press Ctrl(Cmd)+C.

6. Scroll up to the top of the document. If you're using your own document, put a few carriage returns before the first sentence. If you're following along with a copy of the DIGITOON.HTM document, highlight over the first TOC listing (the identical sentence you copied to the clipboard), and then press Ctrl(Cmd)+V to paste the text in. This step is not obligatory; the point of this example is we're going to show how to *link* the Table of Contents entry to the text in the document.

7. Let's make the TOC font size relatively smaller than the paragraph text to easily distinguish it from the paragraph text and to allow more TOC fields at the top of the document without the need for the visitor to scroll. Highlight the entry, and choose -1 from the Font Size drop-down list.

8. Click on the Link button on the toolbar. Click on the Link tab on the Properties menu (Win95 users can right-click on selected text to access the shortcut menu, which contains the Properties command).

9. Links to named targets can be made to targets within the current document or to any other document that contains named targets. Links can also be made to any file that is on the same system as the document or to the URL of files on remote systems. The Properties tab displays all the named targets for the document you choose. As you can see in Figure 1-4, I've named all my targets before making links, and Two Approaches has been chosen for the link. You might want to use the procedure of naming all targets, then making links, if a document is a long one such as *Digi-Toons*.

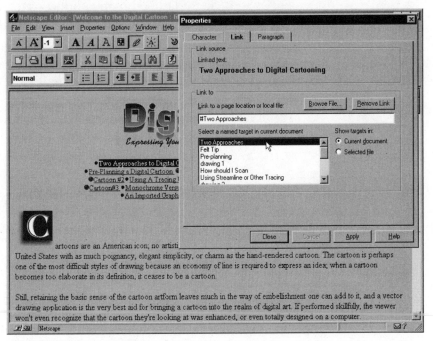

Figure 1-4: *Text linked to a named target location in a document will move the visitor's view to that location when they click on it.*

10. That's how you name a target and make a link. You can continue targeting and linking in this document, or take this knowledge to a real assignment now!

Again, NavGold's Editor has taken the drudgery and possible syntax mistakes out of hand-typing the tags in a text editor. Additionally, you'll notice that the text becomes underlined when it is linked to a target (see the following tip). What you've done is tell NavGold to type:

```
<a href="#Two Approaches">Two Approaches to Digital
Cartooning</a>
```

Links in HTML are preceded with the Anchor tag that includes the *href* attribute (i.e., hypertext reference) that tells browsers what the target name is ("#Two Approaches") for the jump to occur within a single document. For an external link, the name of the document must be included before the pound sign. The text between the opening Anchor tag and the closing Anchor tag (</a>) is displayed as the underlined hypertext link.

Similarly, a target for the link must be preceded by an Anchor tag that uses the NAME= attribute. In this example, the target icon is represented in HTML text as:

```
<a name="Two Approaches"></a>
```

TIP

Users can choose to display text in any font on their system, and can choose to display links and followed links (links you've already accessed) in different colors, or without the underscore. In Navigator, these options can be specified in Options | General Preferences, on the Fonts and Colors tab, and only apply to local viewing of a Web document—every user can define their own display elements.

Great? So why are you going through the fuss to define colors and fonts when the user can turn them off? Because very few users go through the bother of customizing this Navigator option; there are very few fonts as utilitarian and easy to read as Navigator's default of Roman text. And many experienced users choose to leave the options alone, because they realize that changing them can alter display of the

Web author's composition. There are only really two occasions when a visitor might choose to alter their view of your font formatting: if you did something truly obnoxious with the text, such as changing the font size and color every other character, or if the visitor finds the text too small to read at the specified font size.

ALIGNING TEXT TO GRAPHICS

Ironically, as text-based as HTML code is, it is the graphic in a document that governs the placement of text around the graphic. You'll notice in the *Digi-Toons* document that tiny bullets precede the Table of Contents entries. This was done for visual relief, as a design element, and also to allow the visitor a broader target to hit when making jumps. Apple engineers discovered years ago through research on interface usability that users tend to hit the corners of icons, and not square in the center of them. Therefore, take a hint from interface research and give your visitor as much latitude in making a link as possible; make live elements out of areas that are *close* to the intended target.

Miniature bullets can be created in almost any image editing program. Attention to detail is of little concern; the ones preceding the TOC listings are only 10 pixels in height—how much detail can you hope for?

If you peruse the DIGITOON.HTM document, you'll notice that the bullets for the TOC are in two different colors: the purple dots are used as indicators that the link will take them to a graphic in the document, while the black bullets highlight the paragraph links. I tried here to keep with an unobtrusive color scheme through the document and to stay away from matching colors that are also used as default text colors for links. The bullets were created in Paint Shop Pro for Windows. A new document window of 10 X 10 pixels was created, the background was defined as a color I could later define as transparent, and a colored dot was painted on it. You'll notice in the document that the bullets drop out around the edges; see Chapter 2, "Vector-to-Bitmap Conversions," for the steps needed to create a transparent GIF file.

Here are the steps needed to import bullet graphics and link them to the document:

1. Use the SMBULLET.GIF image in the CHAP01/ DIGITOON folder on the Companion CD-ROM in this example if you're fresh out of bullets. Copy the file to your hard disk before continuing; the file needs to be saved, and CD-ROMs are read-only media. Place your cursor in front of the first TOC listing in NavGold's Editor window, then click on the Insert Image button.

2. Click on the top Browse button, then select the SMBULLET.GIF image from your hard disk.

3. To get the TOC listing that goes after this button to align properly, choose the Aligned with Baseline button in the Properties window. In Figure 1-5, you can see that I've worked down the TOC list and have highlighted the bullet for the Cartoon #2 reference; the steps for all the bullets are the same. The trick here is to create a button approximately the same height as the text. But because text is displayed at various sizes according to the audience's browser, you need to "guesstimate" here. I guesstimated that a -1 relative font size would display at about 10 points onscreen, and I lucked out. Build many different bullet sizes: 8 pixels, 10 pixels, and 12 pixels in height are good because a pixel is roughly equivalent to a point in typographic terms with most of today's video subsystems.

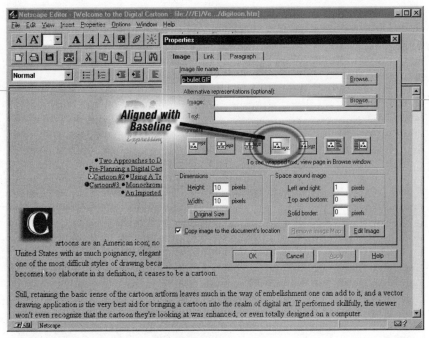

Figure 1-5: *To align text to graphic buttons, choose an alignment for the text that corresponds to the base of your graphic.*

4. Before you leave this dialog box, type **0** in the "Solid border" field, and type **1** or **2** in the "Left and right" field on the "Space around image" panel. By default, a solid border is added around objects for easy identification as graphics links on the Web. Most of the time, but not this time, a border around link objects is the friendly, informational gesture to make as an author. Although this is terrific for large graphics, a border would ruin the composition of this TOC because of the small size of the bullets. The bullet is a kind of obvious link element on the Web.

5. Click on OK, then click on the Link button on the toolbox. Make the link to the same target as the text that follows the bullet. You're done!

The raw HTML code for the linked bullet is:

```
<img src="smbullet.GIF" border=0 height=10 width=10>
```

It's worthwhile to note here, before getting into placed graphics, that an image size, as measured in pixels, should accompany the tag in the HTML code. This lets Navigator know how much space to reserve for the graphic before the graphic is downloaded and where to start placing text. Navigator presumes that a graphic should be displayed at its actual size, but will also go through the process of reading the file, then interpolating the graphic up or down in size, if the height and width instructions don't match the actual image size. For example, you could make the bullet in the last example appear the size of a grapefruit onscreen, simply by editing the HTML file to read:

```
<img src="smbullet.GIF" border=0 height=250 width=250>
```

This is a wonderful trick for scaling images without the use of an image editing program, but this also causes a slowdown on visitors' machines as their browsers scale the image after downloading, but before displaying it. The courteous thing to do with graphics is to always specify the default, original size in the document. This allows Navigator to quickly display the image to your audience.

LINKING A DOCUMENT TO AN OUTSIDE TARGET

As you scroll through the *Digi-Toons* online article, you'll notice that the text is peppered with fairly irrelevant, attractively colored GIF images of cartoons. The original article, as traditionally published, looks similar to the HTML composition, but I could never provide a close-up view of my work on demand the way authors can today through the use of a link to a different document.

At this point in this chapter, we're going to walk away a little from online content publishing and ponder the issues of what it means to present a dynamic, real-time piece to a viewing public. You get one chance to make a first impression online—in this respect, Web publishing is very much like a performing art. Make an offensive mistake, even an unintentional one, and you may lose an audience, a potential customer, for keeps. And this defeats the purpose of multimedia publishing, or any other kind of Web authoring.

Therefore, here's a little secret that can help maintain one's ego as a rightfully proud artist, and still fulfill the commercial, educational, or entertainment-seeking goal of a site: keep the graphics down to a bare minimum with respect to color depth and dimensions, and provide the visitor with a link to a different page that features a larger image that's more faithful to your original work. If you scroll down the *Digi-Toons* document, you'll find the FOTOSMAL graphic toward the bottom. It's a 14K file, it's an interlaced GIF, and the colors are dithered in it so the color palette for the file is only 64 of 256 possible colors. The techniques for shrinking an image down to such a size are documented in Chapter 2, "Vector-to-Bitmap Conversions," but the point here is that this image is a link to the real piece of Web art in addition to its artistic presence within the document. As you can see in Figure 1-6, the button, the cartoon, and a little explanation of what will happen when you click on the area are included.

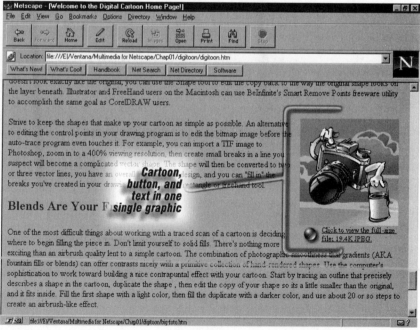

Figure 1-6: *A single GIF file can illustrate a section of a page, indicate that it's a link, and provide information about the file the image links to.*

It would make little sense for this image link to move the visitor to another point in the document: an additional image would increase the file size, and there's no good place to frame a larger image so that the visitor sees only the graphic. Therefore, in the following example, you'll see how to create a *system* for the *Digi-Toons* Web site (create a separate page and link to it), and provide the visitor with a way back to the top document:

1. Copy the FOTOSMAL.GIF image from the CHAP01/ DIGITOON folder to your hard disk. Alternatively, if you have an image of your own, get it into an easy-to-locate place on your hard disk for the next step.

2. In NavGold's editing window, scroll to a good place in the document for visual relief. Insert your cursor, then click on the Insert Image button on the toolbox.

3. Choose the GIF image from the Browse directory box, and specify right wraparound by clicking on the appropriate button in the Properties window. If you look at the DIGITOON.HTM document, you'll notice that the images are staggered: some are to the left of the page and some are to the right. This serves the composition function of breaking up a monotonous layout, but it's also artistically correct from a traditional publication standpoint. When the subject of a cartoon, photo, or other illustration is facing in a direction—left or right—it should "look into the page." The camera cartoon is looking left and therefore should be placed so that it looks into the page, not off the monitor. This draws the interest of the visitor into the text, not away from the page.

4. Add a target to the GIF image. In the *Digi-Toons* article, there are four cartoons; I called this target "drawing 4" to make future reference easier.

5. Pick out a larger image from your collection, or use the BIG-FOTO.JPG image in the CHAP01/DIGITOON folder on the Companion CD-ROM. Also copy the HOME.GIF file if you want to use a graphical link back to the top

document. The BIG-FOTO.JPG file is in *progressive JPEG* format; not all browsers other than Navigator 2.01 support its viewing. More on this shortly.

6. Choose File | New Document | Blank, and then click on the Import Image button. Choose BIG-FOTO or an image of your own. Save the file as BIG-FOTO.HTM to your hard disk before continuing.

7. Click on the "Align text to top of image" button (the leftmost button) in the Properties window, type **4** in the "Left and right Space around image" field, type **0** in the "Solid border" field, then click on OK.

8. Insert your cursor before the image in the Editor window (or use the arrow keys to move the cursor there), then type **Click here to return to the document**. Optionally, you can now place the HOME.GIF image after the text, so that you see (from left to right) the text, the home icon, and the big image in the Editor. The home icon should also have the "Align to top of text" property associated with it. Don't worry about the composition; the Editor is not WYSIWYG 100 percent of the time, and you'll often want to toggle between browser and editor view to fine-tune a page.

9. Highlight the text, then click on the Link tool on the toolbox. From the Properties box, on the Image tab menu, choose the document you saved earlier from the "Link to" browse field, and then choose drawing 4 in the Named Target field as the object of this link. In Figure 1-7, I've already performed this step but am working on the link to the home icon. It's a good idea to provide text in addition to a graphics link; some browsers don't support images, and some computer users aren't gifted with sight—reading machines can decode and pronounce ASCII text as displayed on the Web for their users, but cannot provide a description of a graphics link that contains no text.

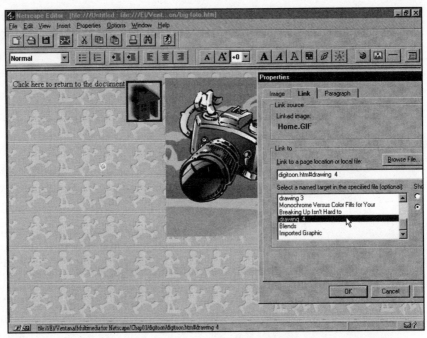

Figure 1-7: *Make a link to a target in a different HTML file to allow a user access back to the top document.*

10. You have half a link now. You can jump from this document to the main document, but the small GIF file back in the larger document now needs a link. In NavGold's Editor, open the main file you edited earlier (MYTOONS.HTM), scroll to the small GIF (or use the TOC links if you made them earlier!), click on it, and then click on the Link button. Choose BIG-FOTO.HTM from the "Linked image" browse field, then click on OK. Because BIG-FOTO is a single-page document, you can call it as a link without specifying a target within the file. You're done!

What you accomplished in the previous example will conserve bandwidth for folks who don't care to see a full-size graphic, and for those who do, you've provided handy navigation back to the exact point where they left off in your article.

Navigation controls are the key to a friendly Web site, one that is recommended to others by visitors. In the next section, we take a look at frames: how to provide navigation for them, when not to use them, and how to make your "picture" suitable for them.

"HTM" OR "HTML": USING THE CORRECT FILE EXTENSION

Although the file extension .HTM is used extensively in this book, if you intend to post your site on an ISP's server, ask the provider which file extensions are preferred and the type of server software they're running. The .HTM and other file extensions on the Companion CD-ROM files were created this way because DOS and Windows 3.1x users also conduct business on the Web.

Both Windows 95 and the Macintosh OS support the use of long file names, as well as extensions that can exceed the DOS limitation of three characters (e.g., MYFILE.TXT). Spaces in the names of files are not used on the Web, but underscores are permitted.

As a rule of thumb, you can be fairly certain that the HTML extension placed after the file name, and separated by a period, can be read by most UNIX, Windows NT, and Apple servers.

TOOLING UP NAVGOLD'S EXTERNAL EDITORS

Before continuing with our page composition examples, there are one or two customizations you might want to take the time to apply to NavGold. Netscape offers some exceptional tools in NavGold's Editor: there's no other authoring tool on the market that offers better WYSIWYG control over HTML composition. But image editing, spell checking, table and frame creation, and a few other Web enhancements are not supported in NavGold's Editor. Instead, Netscape felt it was better to provide *extensibility* through NavGold's interface—a gateway to other applications—rather than to add to Navigator's already substantial file size.

And if we think about it, this was a wise decision. Many business professionals have already chosen, say, an image editor, and you'd probably be most comfortable editing HTML code in the text editor you're experienced with.

Editor Preferences can be found on NavGold Editor's Options menu. Click on this menu item, and you'll see two fields at the top of the General tabbed menu. In the HTML Source field, you can path your way to the text editor of your choice, or click on the Browse button to select the application from your hard disk. In the Image field, you can choose the image editor of your preference. The image editor can be any make or version, but it must be able to handle bitmap format images, specifically GIF, JPEG, PNG (a new bitmap format that is quickly gaining popular acceptance on the Web), or formats that will become available as technology offers them.

For text editing, my personal favorite is TextPad by Helios software. TextPad is a shareware application that's available on the Companion CD-ROM, and it's a Windows-only editor. However, when I swivel around to the Macintosh at our place, BBEdit Lite works like a charm with plain text, and the version on the Companion CD-ROM is freeware.

TIP

If its text-handling capability alone weren't reason enough to try out BBEdit Lite (and perhaps swing for the full-size shareware version), this program also sports an open architecture for which third-party programmers have written extensions. You'll find extensions on bulletin boards and on the Web that help format HTML documents and perform a number of other automated tasks. Additionally, BBEdit Lite can unlock self-running text files on the Macintosh and convert copies to regular plain text, so you can save and copy READ ME files that previously required running.

On either operating system, there is little doubt that Photoshop is the image editor of the pros. Photoshop can be specified as NavGold's External Image Editor. I realize that I'm recommending a Cadillac here, and if you can't make the investment at this time,

NavGold will allow you to specify Paint Shop Pro, GraphicConverter, or other bitmap-type editors in the Image field.

The important point here is that you want a text editor, not a word processor, and a paint application, not a drawing program, as external editors. Word processors hide their own code for text styles in documents, and this ruins HTML code. You want a monospace, ASCII editor. Similarly, GIF and JPEG are presently the only two image types that Web browsers can display without requiring a helper app or plug-in. Illustrator, FreeHand, and CorelDRAW are great design programs, but they are vector drawing programs and cannot edit bitmap-type pixels. Be sure to check out Chapter 2, "Vector-to-Bitmap Conversions," for a more complete description of Web design tools and techniques.

FRAMES: THE NEXT GENERATION OF TABLES

Frames are an innovation of Netscape Communications. Netscape wrote the tag styles, yet very few browsers other than Navigator 2.x, as of this writing, can read the tag style—and every really hip site on the Web uses frames!

The proper name for the elements you might see on a Web site that look like ledges or subwindows is frames, and all the frames displayed in one browser window collectively represent a *frameset*. Frameset is also the name of the tag that creates the collection of frames. The <FRAMESET> tag must be manually written in a text editor or entered in the Editor's Insert HTML tag dialog box (Insert | HTML tag). Frames are not that hard to create, but they can present something of a headache to choreograph because each element in a frame is its own HTML document or other Web object type (such as a VRML file).

When a visitor accesses a frame-based document, conventional navigation rules for Web documents don't always apply. For example, in version 2.01 of Navigator, when you want to go back to a previous page that was displayed in one of the frames in a frameset document, you do *not* click the Back button on Navigator's toolbar. Doing this would display the document or site you viewed in the entire browser window *before* you went to the frameset document. The *correct* method for viewing forward and backward in a frame is to right-click (Macintosh users: click and hold) in the frame to access the Back in Frame and Forward in Frame commands from the Shortcut menu. Navigator 2.01 does not log each window's history, only that of the main frameset document that controls the entire window, because you can have two or more URLs displaying different content from different locations in the same browser window.

This sort of advanced, but atypical, Web enhancement should therefore be treated with more than a little seriousness; have a sound game plan before embracing it as a Web author. You have the responsibility to provide easy, straightforward navigation for a frameset document, or visitors will get lost and bear a grudge against you or your client.

CD-ROM

In the DIGIFRAM folder in CHAP01 on the Companion CD-ROM are all the component files that make up a frame-based version of the *Digi-Toons* document. As you can see in Figure 1-8, the TOC has been broken into a separate frame—it is actually a separate document, DIGI-TOC.HTM—and the article itself is DIGITEXT.HTM, playing in its own frame. The parent document, DIGIFRAM.HTM, makes up 100 percent of the browser window's contents, and this file contains very little besides the name of the HTML files to be played in each window.

Before we take apart the DIGIFRAM document to better see the links and construction, there are a few layout considerations and cosmetic effects that should be discussed. For example, there's a typesetting effect that's called out in Figure 1-8. The links in the TOC to various parts of the text document are flush-left, yet the second line of some of the longer TOC listings have a hanging indent from the bullet that precedes them on the first line. There is *no* hanging indent or other tab format in HTML code, however. This effect was accomplished through the use of a nonbreaking space. In NavGold's Editor, you enter nonbreaking spaces by pressing Shift+Enter. The nonbreaking spaces, however, need to have styles cleared from the text format in order to become invisible as the document is viewed. So after I played with the correct number of nonbreaking spaces in this example, I highlighted the spaces, chose Properties | Text from the menu, then clicked on Clear Style settings. This removed the link associated with the nonbreaking spaces, too, but chances are the visitor won't click on apparently empty space to make a hypertext jump!

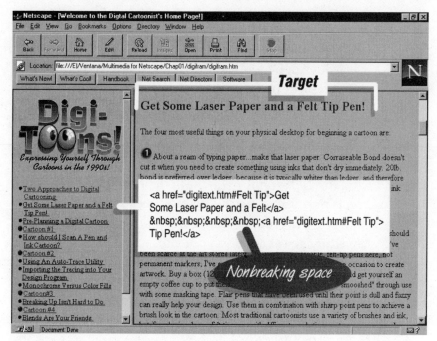

Figure 1-8: *You can create indented lines within a paragraph of HTML by using the nonbreaking space tag.*

The <pre> tag can also be used to force HTML code to accept two or more spaces in text to display as spaces. For example, a line written like this:

```
<pre>     five spaces before this line begins.</pre>
```

would appear in Navigator's browser as a line indented by five monospaced empty spaces. This is a wonderful trick if you want to create table data without using tables (discussed later in this chapter). However, text tagged with the <pre> style will appear in a monospaced font; most browsers substitute Courier for <pre> tagged text. If you don't mind the appearance of the font, the <pre> tag is your ticket for text formatting.

USING MAILTO: INSTANT WEB SITE FEEDBACK

Another point to consider when creating a frameset, or any other type of document, is how you can get direct feedback from your site. Forms require Common Gateway Interface (CGI) scripts, and CGI scripts can be accepted or refused by your Internet Service Provider, depending upon the provider's previous experiences with them. An ill-behaved CGI script can bring down a server, and then *every* site on the server is out of touch, not simply yours.

The Internet services of *mailto:* can provide a mailing address that's only a click away for visitors to your site. In Figure 1-9, you can see how a mailto: URL is placed in a hypertext link Anchor tag on the *Digi-Toons* page. Both the button and the underscored text will pop up an e-mail dialog box (in non-Netscape browsers, a helper mail reader might be specified by the browser), and the visitor can respond to your site.

The Anchor text in a mailto: link should usually be accompanied by the full-text name of your e-mail address. In this example, my address follows the text string that declares the mailto: link. If you should decide to reference a button instead of text, visitors with graphics turned off in their browsers will not be able to discern that this is a mailto: link or read your address.

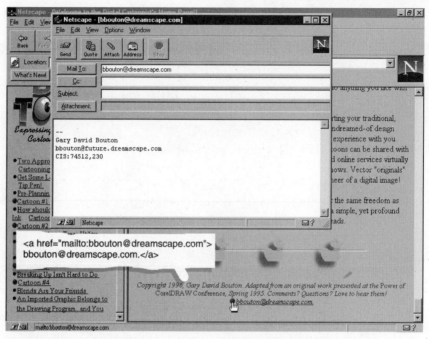

Figure 1-9: *You can provide copyright information, credits, and a mailto: address as part of the closing to your document.*

THE STRUCTURE OF A FRAME-BASED DOCUMENT

Framed-based documents are actually nested HTML documents. To create a frame document, you first need to decide how many frames should compose the opening document. More than two frames will require that the second frame serves as a different frame "container" within the frameset document, and this can get quite confusing to choreograph if you plan on using three or four frames.

Basically, after the title of the document (you'll find the <TITLE> tag when viewing the source code in a document, but not in NavGold Editor's window), you must specify the number of COLS (columns) or ROWS the container frameset document displays. Generally, because the monitor is landscape in orientation, and Navigator's toolbars make the browser windows even wider than high, it's good to compose the frameset document as columns. You can then break the columns up into rows of subframesets.

Frameset columns and rows can be specified either as percentages of the browser window screen, in pixel dimensions, or as a relative size (not recommended). For example, the FRAMESET tag:

```
<FRAMESET COLS="25%,75%">
```

is a percentage attribute; the frameset will display as one-quarter window width on the left, and three-quarters of the browser window width on the right.

It's helpful to use pixel values instead of percentages to define column widths if you have a graphic in a document to be displayed within a frame. In the DIGIFRAM.HTML document, the width of the left frame is defined as follows:

```
<FRAMESET COLS="235,*">
```

The graphic at the top of the TOC listing in the left frame (DIGI-TOC.HTM is the document displayed within the frameset) is a little less than 235 pixels in width. Always build a little padding into the width of a frameset that will contain a document with graphics, and always make a note of a graphic's width before writing the frameset tags. If a graphic exceeds the width of the frameset column or row attribute, scroll bars will appear in the frameset window—and a scroll bar will hide some of the graphics and text you want to present in the frameset as the document opens onscreen.

The asterisk written into the frameset COLS attribute tells the browser to give the remainder of the screen to the other document called within the frameset document. You could therefore define a three-column frameset as

```
<FRAMESET COLS="33%, 33%,*">
```

or write the whole attribute out as

```
<FRAMESET COLS="33%, 33%, 33%">
```

Directly following the <FRAMESET...> tag should be the <FRAME SRC> tag, which points the browser toward the document with the content in it, which is to be displayed within a frame.

TIP

Be warned that the <BODY> tag, used to describe the content of the document following the <HEAD> tag, has no place in a frameset document. A frameset *.HTM document is only a container for other HTM documents. Sometimes, an HTML authoring program will put BODY tags in the document by default. Strip these tags out of a frameset document; otherwise you could crash the browser, or at the very least, the frame-based document will not load correctly.

In the DIGIFRAM.HTM example, the Table of Contents document and the text portion of the article are called as follows:

```
<FRAME SRC="digi-TOC.htm" NAME="TOC" NORESIZE>
<FRAME SRC="digitext.htm" NAME="text">
</FRAMESET>
```

You'll notice that the documents are also named; the NAME tag is essential to allow the user to navigate back to the top frameset document. Names for HTML documents are easy to write, and they follow the same convention as the target names for high-lighted text and graphics within an HTML document. We'll show how the implementation of targeted documents works shortly.

The NORESIZE attribute can be used when you don't want visitors to adjust the frame sizes in a document they're viewing. In the DIGIFRAM.HTM example, I decided that the Table of Contents frame was wide enough without a visitor dragging the frame to widen it, which would create a narrow, hard-to-follow neighboring text frame.

To call subsequent frames within a frameset document, you need to create additional frameset tags. For example, a two-column, frame-based document whose right frame contains three equal-sized frames is written as:

```
<FRAMESET COLS="50%,50%">
  <FRAMESET ROWS=100%,*>
  <FRAME SRC="long_tall_left_frame.htm">
  </FRAMESET>
  <FRAMESET ROWS="33%,33%,33%">
    <FRAME SRC="tiny_top_right_frame_1.htm">
```

```
    <FRAME SRC="tiny_top_right_frame_2.htm">
    <FRAME SRC="tiny_top_right_frame_3.htm">
  </FRAMESET>
</FRAMESET>
```

TIP

It's usually a good idea to indent HTML code to create a visual nesting order for frames as you write them; the indented example above shows the hierarchical nesting of frames as written to a frame container document.

In the following section, you'll see how to add a cutting-edge navigation element—the imagemap tag—to frame-based documents. It's client-side image mapping; it requires no ISP intervention of CGI scripts, and authoring tools for image maps are becoming more and more available.

THE IMAGEMAP TAG

Image mapping is the reference of many different URLs to a single bitmap image. If you've ever wanted to create a number of navigation buttons for a Web page, but have problems neatly aligning many bitmap graphics to the text, the imagemap tag is your ticket.

Although the authoring tools available today make it *appear* as though they write special instructions into a bitmap to define different URL areas, this is not so. In actuality, image map utilities provide text-based local coordinates for a referenced image in an HTML document. The URL for a specific location assigned to an area of the bitmap graphic is located in the host HTML document, not in the bitmap graphic that is the image map.

CD-ROM — If you open the DIGIFRAM.HTM document from the DIGI-MAP folder (not the DIGIFRAM folder) in CHAP01 on the Companion CD-ROM, you'll see the same frame-based document as appears in the DIGIFRAM folder, with a slight enhancement. In Figure 1-10, you can see that the Table of Contents frame includes options for viewing the document. Users who want to speed through the text without the graphics can click Text Only. Art enthusiasts can gander at a picture-only document by clicking on Cartoons Only. And the same content, without the frameset structure, can be viewed by clicking the appropriate image map button.

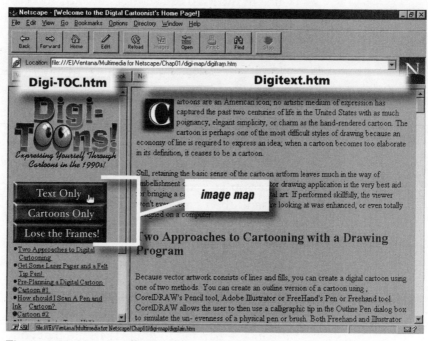

Figure 1-10: *You can offer the visitor a choice of viewing formats for your document by providing links on the top document.*

To illustrate how this particular Web system is built around image map links and magic targets, here's a walk-through of the steps needed to enhance the DIGIFRAM document. Mapedit is a shareware utility for Windows (you can find it on the CD-ROM or at http://www.boutell.com/mapedit/) used to define image area coordinates. We'll also show how Fractal Painter 4, a biplatform design program, can handle image mapping.

CD-ROM

1. Create the HTML document in which you want to place an image mapped graphic. Mapedit can use images in JPG and GIF format (the current version cannot open a progressive JPEG image).

2. Create the HTML documents to which you want to link the image map in the main HTML document.

3. Launch Mapedit, then choose File | Open/Create.

4. Click in the Map or HTML File field, and type in the name of the document which contains the graphic to which you want to assign multiple URLs. Alternatively, you can click on the Browse button. The NCSA and CERN Standards option is not relevant here: these are the two types of *server*-side mapping you can perform in Mapedit. It should be pointed out here that some browsers will fail to recognize client-side mapping, as we're showing here. When in doubt as to your audience, provide text links in addition to an image map to ensure navigation controls for everyone.

5. Once you've specified the HTML document, click on OK. Mapedit then provides you with a list of graphics referenced in the HTML file. Choose the image you want to Mapedit, then click on OK.

6. A window appears that contains the image. This is a proxy window; although it's a convenient graphical metaphor for the image you want to map multiple URLs to, *no* information will be written to the graphic. Mapedit instead writes the imagemap tag to the HTML file that contains the *reference* to the graphic.

7. Choose Tool | Rectangle, then click, drag, and make a final click to define an area in the image. When the Object URL dialog box appears, you should type the name of the URL in the top field. In the bottom field, provide an alternative, text-based description for the URL (in case a visitor's browser doesn't support client-side image mapping, or the user specified that the graphics for a site should not load).

8. Repeat step 7 with other areas of the image you want to link to a URL. Although Mapedit offers different shapes for image map areas, it's best to stick with simple rectangles. The more complex the link shape, the more complex the coordinate description will be in the HTML

document . . . which is another opportunity for your
visitor's browser to fail to decode the imagemap tag.

9. Test your links before closing and saving; choose
   Tools | Test+Edit, then click on the areas you've defined as
   links. When the area of the image onscreen is presented in
   reverse video colors, the Object URL dialog box pops up,
   as shown in Figure 1-11, and the URL you specified is
   displayed. If this information is correct, you're done. If not,
   you can retype the URL, or click on Cancel, and redefine
   the shape of the URL link.

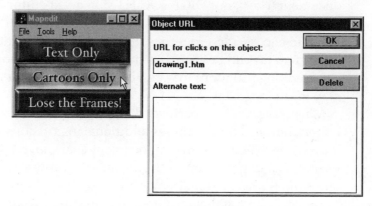

Figure 1-11: *Keep image map regions simple in shape; the coordinates have
to be written as text to your HTML file.*

You're done with the image map, and your top document
should now link to other documents when the audience simply
clicks in the zones of the bitmap graphic that you defined as links.

However, if you use an image map in a frame-based document,
you will run into the same hitch that the author did with displaying links in a full-sized browser window. You need to use the
magic target tag to make the link display in a frame which contains
the HTML document that contains the imagemap tag.

IMAGE MAPS, FRAMES & MAGIC TARGETS

Because frames in a frameset document are seen as discrete content windows, the image map in a frame will move the visitor of your site to the linked document, but the linked document will play in the *same frame*. You can imagine how awkward it would look in the DIGIFRAM document if the visitor linked to a full-size cartoon graphic which plays in the narrow Table of Contents frame!

Imagemap tags are text, but the Editor displays them as tiny tag icons. They appear at the bottom of the document because this is the location of the image map text coordinates in the HTML document (check out DIGI-TOC.HTM in a text editor to see this). If you right-click (Macintosh users: click and hold) on one of these tags and choose Tag Properties from the shortcut menu, the imagemap tag can be seen. It is in the HTML tag dialog box (or in a text-editing program) that you can turn the target for the image map into a magic target.

Magic target names perform the same function as regular targets, but the name includes additional instructions for the browser as to how the linked document is displayed within frames. The target="_top" attribute tells the browser to display the linked image in the full-size window, not in a frame within the frameset. Additional magic target names can be used to override the default action of Navigator to display linked documents within the frame from which they are called. All magic target names are preceded with an underscore:

- **Target="_blank"** This target moves the visitor to a new, fresh window. This is great for getting the visitor out of nested frames, but also calls another Navigator window. In theory, the visitor could have a dozen open windows left after they quit the current document when you use target="_blank"—and they might not thank you for your efforts!

- **Target="_parent"** This magic target displays the link in the FRAMESET parent of the current document. You might never need to use this target, except when you want to provide navigation out of deeply nested framed documents.

■ **Target="_self"** This target loads the link document in the same window as the document which contains the link.

In Figure 1-12, you can see the DIGI-TOC.HTM document displayed in NavGold's Editor after Mapedit assigned imagemap tags to the document. You can turn an imagemap target into a magic target in this window, or perform the magic in a text editor, which is most likely the place where you'll create frameset documents.

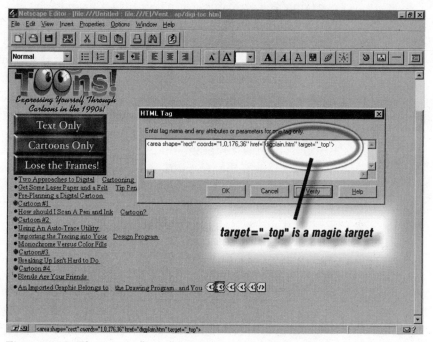

Figure 1-12: *The target="_top" attribute will take the visitor to a full-window view of the document linked to the document within a frameset.*

USES FOR IMAGE-MAPPED FRAME NAVIGATION

If you understand how Netscape's extensions to conventional HTML work, new creative doors of opportunity become wide-open for the multimedia publisher. The DIGIFRAM.HTM document in the DIGI-MAP folder calls the top page containing the DIGI-TOC and DIGITEXT HTML documents, but from there, the site branches out to 10 other HTML documents, each of which contains text, graphics, or a combination thereof.

There is a complete "slide show" subsystem to the DIGI-MAP site; if the visitor chooses Cartoons Only, a full-screen presentation of each of the article's illustrations appears in the browser window. Navigation controls are provided for going back in the slide show, moving forward, or escaping back to the TOC and article frameset. The navigation on each full-screen cartoon document (BIG-WEB.HTM, BIG-FOTO.HTM, and so on) is accomplished through the use of image mapping, and magic targets are not needed to keep the presentation full-window, because each of the full-screen cartoon documents needs to be referenced only by document name—the full-screen documents aren't called to screen within frames.

As a side note of interest here, you'll probably want to keep both NavGold's browser and a separate editor window on your desktop as you compose HTML documents that contain both text and graphics. As mentioned earlier, alignment of text to graphics is accomplished through the graphic, and not the text. In Figure 1-13, you can see what the editor displays onscreen as the image map graphic, the alternate text link, and the cartoon are arranged. Although from left to right, clockwise, you see the cartoon, the navigation controls, and then the alternate text link; the composed document, when viewed in the browser window, appears in a different clockwise order. NavGold informs you in the Properties dialog box that wrapping text doesn't display as WYSIWYG in the editor. Although text wrapping to the right of both images provides the wanted composition, you'll need to toggle back and forth between the browser and the editor to assure yourself of this.

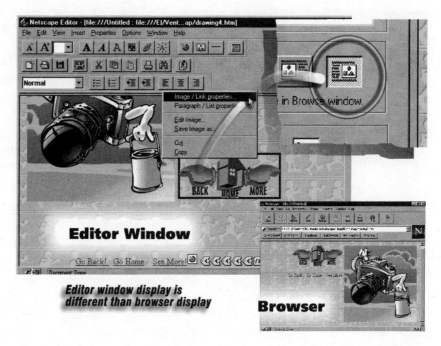

Figure 1-13: *Work between editing and browser windows to make sure the tags and alignment are what you intend to display to visitors.*

FRACTAL DESIGN PAINTER & IMAGE MAPS

Like many of the examples in this book, the greatest help to your Web-authoring suite of tools are your own manual skills and talent, gleaned from inspecting and emulating HTML code schemes that produce the graphical "look" you're after. In the following example, you'll see how to add the coordinates of an image map file to an HTML document, and in the process, understand what makes up this tag code.

Fractal Design Painter 4 writes a map file (the Windows version adds the *.MAP extension to this text file) but doesn't add this coordinate information to your HTML file for a very simple, very good reason. Map text files are frequently accessed by CGI scripts to provide server-side image mapping on sites. But because Navigator's understanding of enhanced HTML allows *client*-side image maps (Internet Service Providers get a lot less nervous when the visitor's machine requires fewer exchanges between server and client to make image map links), Painter can provide the data you need for *either* client- or server-side mapping.

In the following example, a new Web document, an advertisement for the fictitious MegaBurger chain of fast-food palaces, is in need of an image map that can change the apparent resolution of documents viewed on the Web. Many times, an HTML document offers guidelines for the visitor to adopt to "view this image as it was created and intended." I don't have a high regard for sites that ask the visitor to make changes to their system to accommodate a document in this way. It's easy enough to accommodate viewers running 640 X 480, or even 1024 X 768 with the click of an image map, if you compose your document to two or more different screen resolutions. It's a little more work, but it'll impress and please visitors.

If you'd like to skip ahead to Figure 1-16 to see the site, now's a good time. What we're going to do is create an image that will serve as an image map that links to different documents composed to different screen resolutions.

Here's how to perform image mapping in Painter, and what to do with the image map coordinates, depending upon your method of mapping:

1. In Painter, create the buttons you need within a single-image window. The image will ultimately be saved as a single GIF file, but Painter will assign different URLs to *floaters* in a Painter file, so make a floater for each link you want to provide to a different URL.

   Making floaters in Painter is easy: select an area with the Rectangular Selection tool (you can use the Oval tool, also), then drag the selection. The selected image area then becomes a floater, and you can see its name on the Objects: Floater List (click Ctrl(Cmd)+4 to display it if the palette isn't already onscreen).

2. Double-click on the floater title on the Floaters list that you want to define as an image map area. The Floater Attributes dialog box pops up. Click on the WWW Map Clickable Region check box, and select Rectangle Bounding box.

3. In the Name field, you're provided with a target name for the floater. You can change this to anything you like, but this is the name that the HTML document provides as a link name for the area within the image map.

4. In the URL area, type the name of the link document. As you can see in Figure 1-14, I'm creating option buttons for links in a frameset document: the 800 X 600 floater will call the MEGA800.HTM document (a page composed to 800 X 600 viewing resolution) when clicked on.

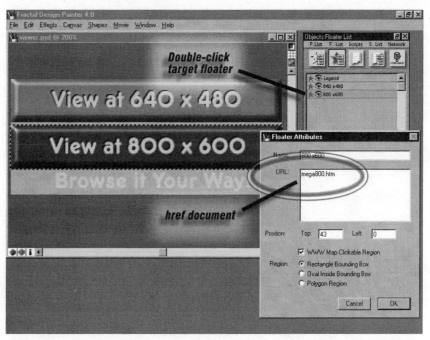

Figure 1-14: *Fractal Design Painter 4 can provide coordinates for client- or server-side image mapping.*

5. You can save a copy of the image file in Painter's RIF format or Photoshop's PSD format at this time to preserve the floating image area property for later editing work. Having done that, choose File | Save As, then choose the GIF format.

6. Painter will remind you that the GIF format doesn't support floating image objects, but this is okay, because you've saved a copy already. Click on OK in this box, and the Save as GIF Options box displays in the workspace.

7. Click on the Interlace check box, choose a type of color reduction and amount from the Number of Colors and Imaging Method fields (hint: output to 64 colors, and allow Painter to dither the image instead of quantizing it), then click on one of the Map Options: NCSA or CERN. Painter will not write an image map text file with the floater coordinates if you don't choose one mapping type or the other. If you want to perform server-side image mapping, you'll need to speak with your Service Provider, who can tell you which type of mapping the site will use. But if you intend to perform client-side image mapping, click on either mapping type to get the text file you need. You'll see how to graft this information into an HTML document shortly.

8. Click on OK, and you're done. Close Painter, and we'll examine and use the image map text file Painter produced shortly.

MANUALLY EDITING AN IMAGE MAP

Again, Fractal Painter 4 generates a text file with the coordinates for image map locations, but it is up to you as to how this file is used: client-side or server-side mapping can both be performed from the data Painter creates.

If you performed the previous example, you should have two files in the same location on your hard disk. One is the GIF file, and the other is a text file that should have a label something similar to MYFILE.gifNCSA.map. Open the file in a text editor, and let's see how this file can be manually entered into an HTML file so it functions as a client-side image map.

Image map links to graphics within the syntax of an HTML file need to be tagged with an <IMG SRC...> tag that names the file, defines any size and border attributes, then uses a target name for the USEMAP image. The USEMAP target can then be specified anywhere in the document following the <IMG SRC...> tag; I copied the coordinates Painter provided to the bottom of the M800T document, because the image map GIF image and all the surrounding text and graphics are in a table (an enhancement covered shortly). It's easier to edit the image map coordinates (if necessary) without messing up the table tags when the table information contains only the <IMG SRC...> tag and not the complete data for the imagemap tag.

If you open the M800T.HTM document from the MEGAMEAL folder, you'll see

```
<IMG SRC="viewer.gif" border=0 usemap="#viewer">
```

nested between <TD> and </TD> tags. These are table tags, and the location of the <IMG SRC...> tag places the GIF buttons in a cell within the table. In context, the <IMG SRC...> line above means, "The image source in this table cell is VIEWER.GIF; it shall display with no default border around it (indicating a link), and when the browser hits this line, it is to use the target information named "viewer" to see what regions of the GIF image contain links."

If you then scroll to the bottom of the M800T document, you'll see the target, the coordinate references, and the href (HTML reference) to the documents the GIF image map links to. In Figure 1-15, you can see in the bottom pane of TextPad the document that Painter provided. In the top frame is the target for the image map, and the coordinates have been copied into the correct places for the COORDS attribute.

In English, from top to bottom, the target is telling the browser, "You know that USEMAP target ("#viewer") you read when you displayed the GIF image in the table earlier in this document? Well, here's the link. The first area shape in this image at coordinates "0, 43, 259, and 83" represents a link area. Specifically, the "MEGA800.HTM" document should be displayed onscreen if anyone clicks in this area of the map."

The second area maps outside of the system to the MEGA640.HTM document, and undeclared areas in the GIF image link to nowhere (<area shape="default" noref>). The map tag ends with </map>, and the areas you need to copy and edit are highlighted in Figure 1-15.

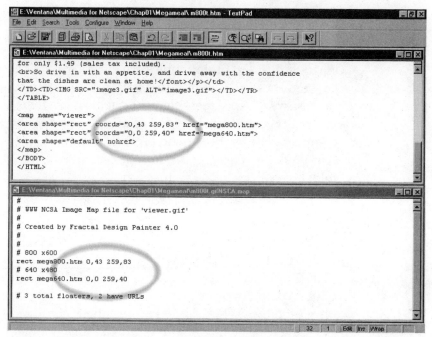

Figure 1-15: *The coordinates for image maps are the hardest part of creating an image map link; let an authoring tool do the work for you.*

Let's get to the reason why the target and href links were broken into different areas of the document. In the next section, we'll discuss the use of tables, when a table is more appropriate than a frameset, and how to use the two together to fine-tune page layout.

ACHIEVING A "CORPORATE LOOK" ON THE WEB

It seems to be a preoccupation of people who design Web sites for a living to attempt the impossible using HTML code. One of the best tools to format an HTML document—which by definition should not be formatted (!) is a proposed HTML 3 standard that Navigator presently supports called *tables*. Although tables were conceived to hold column-and-row data (the HEXCOLOR.HTM document in the CHAP01 folder is a good example), as designers we can bend the unofficial rules somewhat and "brute force" other Web content into HTML tables. Misuse of an enhancement might cause the document to fail to display in some browsers (but *any* non HTML v. 2 standard element can do this), and the table example to follow is provided as a technique, although not necessarily one you could depend on with an important business client.

The MegaBurger home page(s) are constructed in a workaround fashion to faithfully reproduce what is known in advertising as a checkerboard layout. Although it's easy to alternate text blocks with graphics on a printed page, there are a number of obstacles to overcome when porting a magazine design to screen format.

NavGold's Editor does not provide the tag style for tables; it's up to this chapter, you, and a good text editor to create them.

TABLE ATTRIBUTES

Tables must begin and end with the <TABLE></TABLE> tags. You can define as many columns and rows as you like, but to keep your work on a single width of the visitor's monitor (i.e., requiring no horizontal scroll bars), use the <TR> tag when you want to begin a new cell row. Tables must begin with this tag, and the </TR> tag ends a line of cells. If you want to write a table that has two columns and two rows into a Web page, the code would look like this:

```
<TABLE>
<TR><TD>Put something here</TD><TD>and here</TD></TR>
<TR><TD>and here</TD><TD>and something here!</TD></TR>
</TABLE>
```

As mentioned earlier, a table can be a container for anything you like: graphics, text, and, when future plug-in support is offered in Navigator, objects such as animations will be able to play within a cell in a table.

The CELLPADDING attribute can be used after the TABLE tag to specify the amount of distance between the contents of a cell and its border from other cells. And the CELLSPACING attribute can specify the distance between neighboring cells.

However, table attributes must apply to an *entire row* of cells—you cannot, for example, choose the third from the left cell in the middle row, and apply special text formatting or spacing using table attribute tags. With present HTML standards, you also cannot adjust the "play" between the browser window edge and the beginning of the table.

So how do you present a "bleed" ad, as they call it in publishing—a page whose edges end at the browser window edge? You link the table document to a frameset document consisting of a single frame. This is a down and dirty trick, and certainly someone who inspects your HTML code would never credit you with a tidy solution . . . but it works. In Figure 1-16, you can see the MEGA800.HTM document displayed onscreen, with the content document M800T.HTM in the background. The M800T.HTM document, played as a stand-alone document, must display padding between the table and the upper and left edges of the browser window. In contrast, when the MEGA800.HTM frameset document is used to display M800T.HTM within its single frame, the upper left edge of the content document is practically touching the browser window. Frameset contents display at different proximities to the browser window edge according to the system the document is played on. But overall, you can count on this solution to ensure accurate measurements down to a pixel or two when displaying highly structured Web sites.

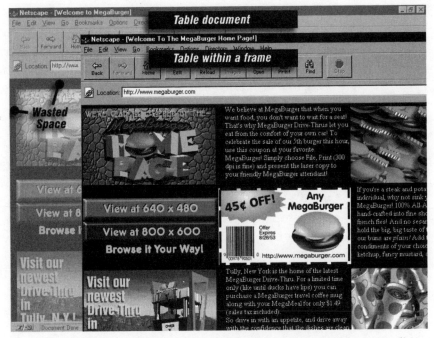

Figure 1-16: *Designs within frameset containers can ensure that document display fills the browser windows as completely as the visitor's video system allows.*

TIP

The MegaBurger Web site was carefully planned, but there's one other attribute that's missing that could help it, or your own assignment, achieve pixel-perfect element placement. The TABLE tag supports the ALIGN and VALIGN attributes, of which there are several values. Adding the ALIGN=left, right, or center attributes to the beginning of a table row controls the horizontal placement of elements contained within the cells, until the </TR> tag is made. Additionally, vertical placement can be specified using the VALIGN=top, middle, bottom, or baseline attributes.

In context, vertically aligning the contents of a row to the bottom of each respective cell would be made like this:

```
<TR VALIGN=BOTTOM><TD>text</TD><TD>more text</TD></TR>
```

I was primarily concerned that the text didn't touch neighboring table cells in this document, so instead of taking the time to write the cells with ALIGN tags, I placed a 7-pixel wide, 140-pixel high transparent GIF file at the front of each table cell, to keep the text indented slightly. For more information on using GIF transparent "spacers," see Chapter 3, "Bitmap Graphics & Special Effects."

The MEGA640.HTM document is a frameset that is linked to the mega800 document by the image map, and both frameset documents serve to keep the respective content documents, M640T.HTM and M800T.HTM, displayed onscreen as edge-to-edge compositions. It should be noted that the dimensionally smaller of the documents—the one that's displayed when visitors click on the 640 X 480 image map button—needed to be composed differently than the 800 X 600 document. If you view the document in Navigator's browser window, you'll see that a vertical scroll is permitted, and that the checkerboard composition is staggered into 3 screens. The images would be too small, even at 640 X 480 viewing resolution, so instead of a 3-column, 3-row table, the 640 X 480 document sports 2 columns and 5 rows; a block of copy was eliminated in the larger version of this advertisement. Compositionally, however, the text color, images, and layout style are common to both documents, and a visitor would probably be thankful that accommodations were made up front in the document for different viewing resolutions.

PLAN FOR MISTEAKS!

For all of our discussions in this chapter on how to present a document on the Web as close to original concept as possible, there are a few things that you have no control over. The Web is not the same as a captive audience, and you can't possibly preview your masterpiece on all the system configurations possible of users visiting your site. A good case in point (and a lesson here) is the MegaBurger ad when displayed on our Macintosh system. The MegaBurger document was composed on a Win95 system, and wouldn't you know it, it might have served the author well to preview, as he worked, on *both* systems.

Figure 1-17 is a view of Navigator 2.01 for the Macintosh, with the MEGA640.HTM document playing inside. As you can see, although Roman is specified for both the Macintosh and Windows screen font, the Mac displays a slightly broader bitmap rendering of a Roman font. This causes the lines of text to break slightly differently, and to ride up in the table more than intended.

Figure 1-17: *HTML ensures document consistency, but not uniform identity, when played on different platforms and different systems.*

Even if you test a site on five different machines, there will be a sixth out there somewhere that'll make nonsense out of displaying your highly-tuned document. That's the biggest reason for displaying documents in several different formats, using links to offer the visitor alternative arrangements of your composition. The message here is that if you create a checkerboard design using the steps in this chapter, don't count on everyone seeing it as you intended because it's good to be single-minded in concept, but perilous to execute the concept in a single style. The checkerboard example could be redesigned a half-dozen other ways, beginning with a little cell padding, to allow for slight variations of display on different systems.

ACCOMMODATING DIFFERENT BROWSERS

Some of the enhancements to basic HTML that Netscape Communications has offered authors have to do with *trip switches*. These are small elements you can write into a page to give browsers that can't decode frames, special image formats, and other elements a way to gracefully display a limited view of the document—instead of displaying nothing at all.

The <NOFRAMES> tag was specifically designed as a container for an alternative document or a message informing users that their browsers can't handle the enhanced HTML code. The <NOFRAMES> tag should go directly after the <FRAMESET> tag, and end with </NOFRAMES> before the <FRAME SRC> tag calls any HTML documents.

One possible technique is to place between the <NOFRAMES> and </NOFRAMES> tags the contents of a document that is generic, by-the-books HTML code. The disadvantage to this technique is that the document loads very slowly—it no longer simply calls the HTML documents for display, but is a true content-driven HTML document.

An alternative that's popular and also *extremely* insulting is the message, "Sorry! Your browser is *frame-challenged!* Go download Navigator and try again." Imagine your own feelings toward such a blatant "have/have not" declaration. "Oh, yeah? Whatever you were *trying* to sell, chum, forget it" would be a fair response.

Instead, let's try the gracious approach. Yes, you would like the visitors to go and get Navigator so they can see your site as intended in the future, but your first offering should be an alternative way to browse the document. In Figure 1-18, you can see the display of the DIGIFRAM.HTM document (from the DIGI-MAP folder on the Companion CD-ROM) as viewed in Microsoft's Internet Explorer version 2.0.

CD-ROM

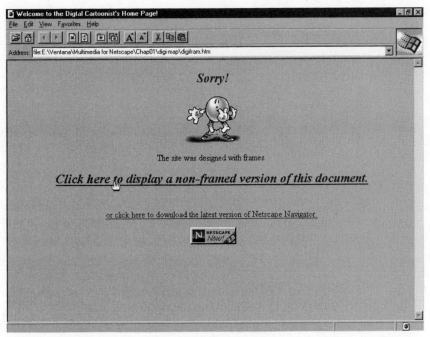

Figure 1-18: *Offer visitors that run browsers without enhancement capabilities a graceful, friendly alternative to viewing your work.*

If you look at the source code for DIGIFRAM.HTM, you'll see that very little had to be added between the <NOFRAMES> tags to make the apology and offer alternatives. You're allowed to snag the Netscape Now! button off Netscape's home page, and use it in your own NOFRAMES addendum to documents; a copy can also be found on the Companion CD-ROM. When viewers hit the NOFRAMES message within the document, they can click on the nonframed version text, which is an href link to DIGITOON.HTM, a version of the article shown at the beginning of this chapter. So you can repurpose documents as you create variations and improvements to Web sites.

USING THE ALT ATTRIBUTE

Although the World Wide Web has become a graphically sumptuous place in cyberspace, experienced surfers occasionally exceed the speed of light on the Web by turning graphics off in Navigator. This action keeps the user from becoming bogged down on a site that has too many graphics, or wonderful graphics that are simply too large in file size, but it also puts *your site* out of business even though *your* wonderful graphics are *small*!

Additionally, reading machines for the blind cannot pass along information to their users about graphics unless you provide an alternative caption for graphics that might not be displayed to all of your audience.

This is where the ALT attribute comes into play. Adding an alternative text description of a graphic takes no more time than naming a file and finding the correct field in NavGold's Editor. In Figure 1-19, you can see the result of adding an ALT attribute to a JPEG file that was compressed in progressive format. As of this writing, only LViewPro and a few other shareware utilities can generate JPEG images that increase image resolution over time (like interlaced GIF images "rez-up" onscreen). Navigator 2.01 reads progressive JPEG images perfectly, and the images in the BIG-BUX, BIG-FOTO, and other full-page HTML link documents in the *Digi-Toons* Web system were created with progressive JPEG compression.

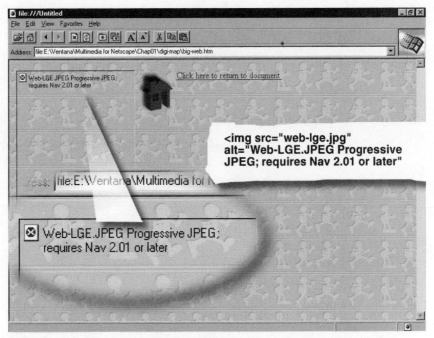

Figure 1-19: *The ALT attribute will display a text message in areas of your document where graphics cannot be accessed or viewed.*

Although the images look better than indexed color GIFs, and store at a size much smaller than their GIF counterparts, if you use this compression scheme, you should offer a text-based description as an ALT attribute. Here's how to add an ALT description to act as a placeholder when a user's browser doesn't load the graphic:

1. In NavGold's Editor, start a new document (File | New Document | Blank), then save the file as MYTEST.HTM.

2. Click on the Insert Image button on the toolbar, then browse for an image you can place within the document. Any GIF or JPEG will do in this example.

3. In the "Alternative representations (optional):, Text" field, type:

    MYIMAGE.GIF (or **MYIMAGE.JPG** if it's a JPEG file): **requires Navigator 2.01 or later to view.**

Also, you could provide a little advertisement here if you feel that visitors to your site might simply have chosen not to load graphics with pages they browse.

`Really cool image! Win $1,000 if you can find the mistakes in this picture`

. . . might be a misleading, adolescent use of the ALT attribute, but it would get visitors to come back to your site with graphics capabilities turned on in their browser.

4. Click on OK, and you're done.

It's easy enough to manually add this feature to an existing HTML document, and it's only four steps in NavGold's Editor. The alternative text display for graphics shows your audience that you're a good host.

TIP

The Alternative image option in the Editor's Properties box isn't intended for the display of a different file format. Instead, it can be used to gradually replace the first image that downloads from your site. See Chapter 8, "Putting It All Together," for some innovative uses of this graphics property in your multimedia presentations.

But don't use the field to specify a different file format of the same image.

PROTECTING YOUR WORK

No discussion of Web content structure is complete without first addressing how we should go about protecting our work from piracy.

The short answer to "How can I ensure that individuals who visit my site don't rip off my ideas or graphics?" is . . . "You *can't*." The World Wide Web belongs to a global community, a community where laws are self-imposed. If Netizens are lucky, it will stay this way, too. Unfortunately, copyright laws are as hard to enforce as is the dispensing of papers from an unattended newspaper box on the corner—you'll have the honest types who drop quarters in the slot and others who leap at the opportunity presented by an unlatched box. There are all types in this world, and more and more are populating the Web.

Fortunately, Web sites are becoming public places, and really popular sites that have a look of their own are hard to imitate, or appropriate from, without people noticing. Additionally, common copyright laws in the United States are being observed more and more as traditional publications spin off electronic versions for the Web.

There is not much you can do to protect the written word on the Web beyond making a clear copyright statement at the bottom of the document. The best defense, however, from someone stealing a *graphic* for their own use from your site is to *sign your work*. In Figure 1-20, you can see a graphic that I've added a copyright line to. In Photoshop, you can type text, then use the Image | Effects | Rotate 90° command to place the copyright statement in the image, but in a location that doesn't ruin the artistic content of the graphic. If you keep the signature slightly inside the image content, it becomes harder to deface the signature or crop it off the image.

Figure 1-20: *Signing your work shouldn't interfere with the composition, but it should make visitors think twice about repurposing (ripping off) the piece!*

Adobe Photoshop 3.0.5 also features an information standard developed by the Newspaper Association of America to identify transmitted text and images; you can embed up to 2,000 characters in an image in TIF or JPEG format, invisibly. The File | Get Info command is your ticket to completely documenting the ownership of a JPEG image you'd like to post on your site (the GIF format doesn't support File Info). In Figure 1-21, you can see the five entry fields in File Info for specifying an assignment, the owner, the creator, and other image details.

Figure 1-21: *Photoshop's File Info can encode text strings in a JPEG image that can only be decoded using Photoshop and other proprietary software.*

Having received this tip, you can now rest assured that a JPEG image you post can only be altered by *other* owners of Photoshop! To be fair, the File Info was originally intended as a documenting device and not a security feature; and yes, other Photoshop owners can access and change the data you've saved to this special implementation of JPEG formats. We are at the very first step of initiating Web security; this need for protection of intellectual and artistic property has only begun to be considered as content—and visitors—have densely packed the bandwidth over the past two years. Already, many software manufacturers have prototype versions of encrypting software that puts an invisible "finger-print" of user-defined information into the header of *any* type of graphics image, animation, or sound file.

Ownership of a Web-published piece will soon become as easy to prove as any traditionally published story or work of art. In the meantime, to thwart content piracy, the surest method is (to paraphrase the villagers' advice concerning town gossip): "Don't post anything you wouldn't want to see on the front page of the morning newspaper." Don't become paranoid about piracy, but also don't post pieces that you can sell. Keep the images too small to reprint, and sneak your name or other identification in there somewhere.

Moving On

Although most Web browsers are limited to displaying bitmap format images and designs, other digital art forms are being supported by Navigator plug-ins at the rate of about one every other day. If you have skills in drawing programs, but can't wait for the browser support required to display Illustrator, FreeHand, CorelDRAW, or other formats, don't sweat it. Chapter 2, "Vector-to-Bitmap Conversions," shows the ins and outs of file format conversion, and provides valuable insights on how to make copies of your original art that'll look great on the Web, without the need to learn a new design application.

2 Vector-to-Bitmap Conversions

The term *computer graphics* has evolved to a point where the uninitiated use it to describe special effects in television commercials. The same phrase, when tossed at today's graphic designer usually elicits the response, "What app did you do this in?"

If you prefer to use a vector drawing application such as Adobe Illustrator, CorelDRAW, or Macromedia FreeHand to express a concept, stay tuned, because this chapter shows you the ins and outs of converting graphics for use in Web documents. But even if you prefer a different digital medium and are an expert in a painting program such as Photoshop, for instance, there's still a lot in store for you here. The applications used to create a design have branched into different formats, file types, and structures, but you'll soon see that computer art, like technology itself, is converging. The point of convergence for the designer is the Web graphic, and in this chapter you'll see how to squeeze the best quality out of the humble pixel!

Extending Web Graphics Within Navigator

Until recently, there were really only two formats for graphics that were practical to use on a Web page—GIF and standard (baseline) Joint Photographic Experts Group (JPEG) images—both of which are bitmap formats. Netscape Navigator 2.0, however, sports native support for viewing an additional bitmap format—progressive JPEG. Progressive JPEG images, which display faster and have a smaller file size than baseline JPEG images, can be viewed within Netscape Navigator without the assistance of a helper application. As of this writing, there are only a few applications that can read and write a progressive JPEG, and applications that only offer baseline JPEG read/write support *can't* display this proprietary use of the JPEG format for images. A progressive JPEG is a streaming type of image—it immediately begins to build on the visitor's monitor. In contrast, a baseline JPEG needs to be completely downloaded before it displays.

JPEG Files & Lossy Compression

Unlike color channel images and indexed bitmap images described in this chapter, a JPEG image (Windows users identify this file type with the *.JPG extension) is a compressed image that uncompresses on the fly as a viewer opens the file in an image browser or application.

Unlike LZW compression and proprietary formats that compress image data, JPEG discards image information during the compression process. The consortium of businesses that established the JPEG file format used an artistic eye to evaluate image data that can be lost from an average image without discernable loss of image quality. It should be noted, however, that successive recompression of an image in JPEG format continues to erode image quality. You therefore should not save a JPEG image after editing it; instead, save the image in TIF or other file format that does not recompress the image in a lossy fashion. If you need to edit an image and save it as a JPEG, it's usually best to work with the original file, and not a JPEG copy.

Additionally, Corel Corporation and Macromedia have released plug-ins and helper applications for Netscape Navigator that allow the display of *vector*-based, inline graphics from within a Web page. Because Netscape Navigator is "plug-in friendly," you can expect more companies to follow Corel's and Macromedia's lead, and as a result, you'll have a wider range of software and formats you can use to create Web graphics.

But before you relegate the trusty bitmap image to the trash icon in favor of recently supported vector formats, read on and you'll discover that, as with most innovations, there are tradeoffs you'll have to make in composing your Web document.

ADVANTAGES & DISADVANTAGES OF VECTOR WEB GRAPHICS

Every digital file format has its unique strengths and weaknesses, whether they be color capability, size, proprietary features, or other factors. Even though vector graphics are supported now in limited formats for the Web, *any* new image type viewed in Netscape Navigator places an additional requirement on your audience. Visitors must install the plug-in before they can see your work.

If you only use GIF and JPEG graphics in your pages, you reach a larger audience than you do when you use graphics that need plug-in support to display. But you may decide that what you gain—a greater audience—may not be enough to compensate for the design limitations you encounter when you reject vector formats and confine yourself to using only bitmap graphics. Both kinds of graphics can have their place in Web documents depending upon your audience and the type of graphical idea you want to convey.

Although this chapter primarily covers the conversion techniques for translating vector information to bitmap, we'll begin with a brief excursion into including vector images in a Web page. Vector files have two basic advantages over their bitmap equivalents: vector images can be scaled up or down without loss of design content, and vector images are typically smaller than bitmaps, so their saved file size allows them to be loaded into a viewer fairly quickly.

In the following section, we take a look at an existing vector standard, that of the CMX file, how it works, and how you can make it a Web element.

Corel's CMX Vector Format

A Macintosh version of CorelDRAW is promised by July of 1996, but currently this design application is a Windows-only program. Note that the Corel CMX Netscape Navigator plug-in, which is necessary for viewing CMX (*Corel Media eXchange,* or more commonly written as *Corel Presentation Exchange*) images in Web documents, is available only in a Windows version at present. Therefore, the audience you'd have when designing a Web site containing Corel's CMX vector design format would be a Windows-only audience. This might be a determining factor in your design—many Web designers prefer to reach the widest possible audience with their presentation.

The CMX format of graphic also can only be created using a Corel product. CMX images are usually created by exporting a graphic from CorelDRAW and choosing CMX as the type of file you wish to export. The specifications for the CMX format might be thought of as a generic vector file format. Unique CorelDRAW object properties such as linked blends and editable shapes created with version 6's Polygon tool can be accurately exported, but lose their special properties should you—or a visitor who's downloaded your work—try importing them again to CorelDRAW.

Also, because a vector image needs to be drawn as pixels on a monitor every time you move it or resize it, the number of objects in the illustration is directly related to the time it takes to be completely redrawn and visible. If you were to draw a scene with a foreground object and a thousand background stars, the CMX file would actually take much more time to display than an equivalent bitmap image. Always consider your content before you choose your medium!

Despite the CMX's limited attraction, and some limitations on what you can include in a CMX graphic, everything changes over-night with the Internet, and the vector format of graphics might indeed rise to popular acceptance more quickly than you know.

VIEWING A CMX VECTOR GRAPHIC

Before members of your audience can view a CMX vector graphic, they must install the CMX viewer, which can be downloaded from ftp://ftp.corel.com/pub/misc/Corelcmx.exe, and the agreement with Corel Corp. permits you to put this file on your own FTP server for download. The viewer can also be downloaded directly from Corel's http://www.corel.ca Web site.

Because the CMX viewer utility is a helper application, you must place the NPCMX32.DLL file in Netscape Navigator's plug-ins directory (run the setup program after downloading the CORELCMX.EXE to extract this file); in general, you should *always* check to make sure a helper application has been copied correctly to this location. Additionally, to be able to view a CMX image within a document in Navigator, you must go to the Helpers tab in Options I General Preferences, specify a new MIME type (Image) and MIME subformat (x-cmx), and choose the NPCMX32.DLL file as the application used to launch the CMX viewer.

CREATING & EMBEDDING A CMX GRAPHIC

After installing the CMX viewer, you are ready to create and embed the CMX graphic. In CorelDRAW, create your graphic on a standard portrait page (8½ X 11 inches). At present, you should distort the graphic when you're done to make it fill the entire page. This procedure makes the graphic look funny, but when you specify the size of the graphic within the HTML document, it becomes undistorted. We are hopeful that Corel Corp. will eliminate the necessity for this step in future releases of the CMX browser.

The graphic should not contain a fountain fill that's offset—that is, a fill composed of several transitional colors (also called a *gradient fill* in other applications) whose relative center of the blend is off center. The CMX format doesn't support this custom feature. Nor does it support PostScript fills. However, you can use Lens objects, bitmap fills, vector fills, PowerClips, and Powerlines in your graphic, and the CMX export supports these.

To embed the graphic, choose File | Export, then choose the CMX version 5 or 6 format from the Export dialog box in CorelDRAW versions 5 or 6. You might want to create a new folder in which you'll put exported graphics and your HTML document to test the Web page; you can right-click in a directory window to add a new folder any place you like on your hard disk in Windows 95.

You can treat your vector-based CMX graphic exactly like a GIF or other bitmap graphic when it comes to using it in your HTML document. For example, you can put a CMX graphic in a table or frame, wrap text around it using HTML ALIGN attributes, and specify the display size of the graphic using the HEIGHT and WIDTH attributes.

If you have the CMX viewer properly installed on your system, and would like to view a CMX image in an HTML document, drag the COFFEE.HTM document from the Companion CD-ROM (found in the CMXEAXAM folder in the CHAP02 folder) into Netscape Navigator to load the file. If you view the source code for COFFEE.HTM you will see that the CMX graphic was inserted into the document using the following EMBED command. Notice that, in the example, the attributes of WIDTH and HEIGHT are used to set the display size of the graphic to 150 pixels wide by 150 pixels high.

```
<EMBED SRC="coffee.cmx" width=150 height=150>
```

One of the perks of using the CMX browser is that you can enlarge your view of the embedded graphic. If you right-click on the graphic and choose PopUp from the shortcut menu, a larger version of the image will display in a new window (see Figure 2-1). Another perk is that if you choose Save this Image as from the Shortcut menu, you can save the CMX graphic to your hard disk and then later open it and work with it using the same tools you'd use with a native CorelDRAW design.

Figure 2-1: *A PopUp box is the next best thing to a zoom tool when viewing a document with a CMX graphic.*

Although support for the CMX vector format is limited to Windows at present, a scalable graphic could be very useful if you needed to specify a technical illustration or a map to visitors to your site. The visitor could access the PopUp box to view, in detail, parts of a graphic that a bitmap equivalent would fail to display.

Bitmap images are of fixed resolution, and many designers brought up on vector drawing applications wouldn't think about switching, but the reality of designing for the Web is that you need to be flexible to keep in touch with current and prevailing technology. And this is why the next sections show you how to make your vector designs look as handsome as possible . . . after converting a copy to bitmap format.

PIXELS & RESOLUTION

When I finally put my physical drafting table into the background as a tool, and adopted a vector drawing program, I was amazed at this new *resolution-independent* graphics format. I'd immediately sprawl my design ideas over the default $8\frac{1}{2}$ -X 11-inch page (a luxury never thought of with $45 bond ledger pads!), knowing that I could then scale a design to fit on a trading card or the Astrodome, without ruining the focus, content, or detail work of the original.

If you come from a background in drawing (rather than painting) and you're proficient with DRAW, Illustrator, FreeHand, or other commercial drawing programs, your ticket to the next big attraction, that of designing Web graphics, begins here with examining a pixel.

A pixel is a unit of measurement for both screen display and for artwork created in paint-type, or *raster* art programs, such as Photoshop and Fractal Design Painter. The equivalency of pixel-unit measurements to the more conventional inch, pica, or point is not very straightforward, however. The shape of a pixel is usually rectangular (or even perfectly square). Most monitor manufacturers offer precise alignments such as pin-barrel and parallelogram adjustments, because the personal computer has a knack for creating and displaying things best that contain right angles.

It might come as a surprise to some designers who insist upon doing all their work in a vector drawing program, that even drawing applications depend upon pixel units. Every vector application today draws a bitmap preview onscreen—the information is taken from the vector math saved and loaded within the application, but it is in the picture element format—a halftone dot on a physical page, or a screen pixel—that a vector image is displayed *and* printed.

How Pixels Correspond to Inches

The pixel unit can be compared to a printed dot from a laser printer; without contextualizing a pixel with a denominator (usually expressed in inches), the pixel is amorphous. In the same way "75 miles" describes a distance, while "75 miles per hour" expresses a speed,"pixels" describes a unit, while, for example, "pixels per inch"(ppi) describes a *resolution*—the frequency with which samples in a bitmap-type image exist.

"Pixels per inch" must be further contextualized before this measurement can be used to calculate the absolute, resolution-dependent size of a file.

The linear dimensions of a bitmap image, the height and width, are inversely proportional to the resolution of the image.

Therefore, a 1- X 1-inch bitmap image of 300 pixels/inch resolution can also be expressed as a 2- X 2-inch graphic at 150 pixels/inch without changing a pixel, but only if the viewing/editing utility you use has the capability to change the resolution of the image. This truth about resolution-dependent bitmap graphics can be used to calculate the exact dimensions an image will have when viewed in a Netscape Navigator window.

An image with a specific number of pixels will always display at the same height and width on monitors running the same screen resolution. But there's a hitch to this formula: the Macintosh and IBM/PC machines have established a *slightly* different method for displaying an image's dimensions (in inches) because the resolution—the number of screen-display pixels per inch—isn't always the same. And this can become an important issue, because inches (or points or picas), not pixels, are usually used when specifying the size of an object in a vector drawing program.

Here's what happens: Most programs running on the Macintosh will tell you that a full-screen capture taken at a 640 X 480 (pixel) monitor resolution is 8.89 X 6.67 inches, but this is as incomplete a description of a bitmap graphic as when Window's Paintbrush program tells you that the same full-screen capture has Image Attributes of 6.7 X 5 inches. In either case, you have information only about the linear distances of the image's edges. In *neither* case do the measurements indicate how many pixels there are in each inch.

Fortunately, both screen-capture measurements are "right"; both captures contain the same number of pixels, but Windows prefers the 96 pixels/inch standard for measuring screen pixels. Therefore, the linear measurement, in inches, is smaller than the same Macintosh capture, which measures monitor resolution at 72 pixels/inch. Whew!

Therefore, the vector designer should take more than a little caution when describing the size of a bitmap image (such as the one found in this chapter's walk-through example) merely in inches without a specific resolution. This is important stuff if your employer runs a cross-platform enterprise, or if someone's specified a design for the Web in inches, but didn't tell you which platform the measurements were taken from!

CREATING A TEMPLATE FOR A WEB PAGE

The example that follows is based around an imaginary assignment: Your client wants a bitmap (GIF or JPEG) graphic for a Web site that targets collectors of antique recordings—The Virtual Marconi page. Your client also wants the home page to fill one screen so that the Macintosh and Windows visitors to the site (who will be running different screen resolutions) will be able to see the entire page without having to scroll.

To follow along with this exercise, you will need a bitmap editor in addition to a vector drawing program. For our purposes, the ones you use don't really matter. On the Macintosh as well as Windows, Adobe Photoshop (shown in this chapter) and Fractal Design Painter are perfect for bitmap editing. If you work in

Windows, Corel Photo-Paint is a fully functional bitmap editor and is up to this chapter's task as well. If you don't have a bitmap editor installed, you should check out the shareware bitmap editors Paint Shop Pro (Windows) or GraphicConverter (Macintosh). Paint Shop Pro is found on the Companion CD-ROM.

CD-ROM

If you'd like to try out the "math" here for measuring the live space from within Netscape Navigator, it's really quite simple to begin: adjust your monitor resolution to the lowest possible (to compose for Web site visitors who might be running 640 X 480 monitor resolution), take a screen capture of Netscape Navigator, then save the file to hard disk in BMP, PICT, TIFF, or other format.

In Figure 2-2, you can see the interface for Netscape Navigator for the Macintosh. The live space within which you have to compose, within a single nonscrolling area, is about 600 pixels by 300 pixels. At 72 pixels per inch (ppi) screen resolution, this translates to about 8.3 inches wide by 4 inches high.

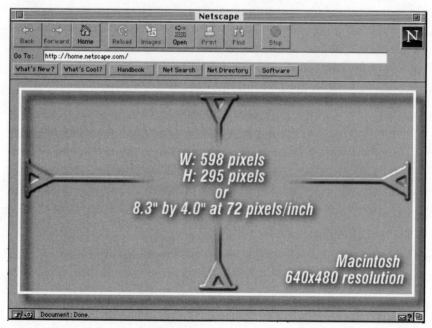

Figure 2-2: *If you use a drawing application on the Macintosh, keep your graphics within 8.3 X 4 inches.*

In Figure 2-3, you can see a Windows screen capture of Netscape Navigator, with a live area cropped inside. Although the pixel count is identical, the dimensions within which you should compose in a vector application are slightly smaller.

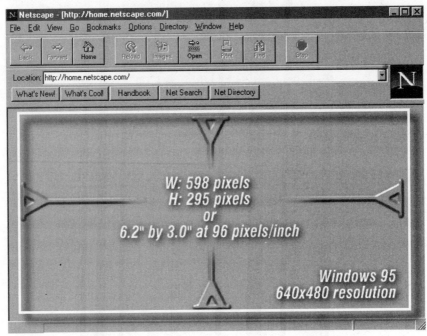

Figure 2-3: *In Windows, keep your vector graphics inside the 6.2- X 3-inch limit.*

Adobe Photoshop, Corel Photo-Paint, and many other imaging programs offer information palettes that can tell you the height or width of a cropped image area in inches or the equivalent number of pixels. This is how the author arrived at the pixel values in the previous two figures. But, using the following equation, you can easily make the calculation manually to create Web graphics from pixel images that are exactly the size you intended them to be:

```
Pixel(#)/resolution of image = Inches
```

Therefore, a 640-pixel width onscreen at 72 pixels/inch measures 8.89 inches (640/72 = 8.89).

In case you don't have an appropriate vector graphic program handy to continue the vector-to-bitmap adventure here, the Companion CD-ROM contains sample files written to several common vector formats for Windows and the Macintosh. Bring along your drawing application to the next section!

THE VIRTUES OF RESIZING WORK BEFORE EXPORTING

Many experienced users of programs such as Photoshop are aware of the perils of resizing bitmap artwork. Because there are a finite number of pixels in a bitmap graphic, when you change the dimensions *while maintaining the same resolution*, you distort the image content. This is because you've changed the number of specified pixels in the image, and even an application as good as Photoshop can't really fill in the missing pixels in a completely aesthetically pleasing way because it's a program, not an artist.

Pixel-based artwork, unlike vector art, is entirely dependent upon a grid of pixel units for image content. A collection of pixels represents color, outlines, fills, shading . . . everything within an image that makes up a recognizable scene. So when you respecify the number of pixels that should make up the grid that's the framework of a pixel-based image, color pixels are added or removed in places that might not make the overall image look so swift. When you're converting a vector image to bitmap format, therefore, you should always size the image in the vector drawing program to the final dimensions that you want the finished bitmap to be. By doing this, you've spared yourself the frustrations of rearranging pixels in your export.

To gain firsthand experience in converting a graphic from a *resolution-independent* vector format to a *resolution-dependent* bitmap format, and to put the previously mentioned pixel-to-inches equation to work, look on the Companion CD-ROM, in the CHAP02 folder. In this folder you will find the vector design MARCONI, which has been saved in CorelDRAW's CDR format, Adobe Illustrator's AI format, Macromedia FreeHand's FH5 format, and CorelXARA's XAR format. The FreeHand and Illustrator files

CD-ROM

are binary compatible (can be opened with either the Macintosh or Windows versions of these programs). If you are using some vector drawing application other than CorelDRAW, CorelXARA, Free-Hand, or Adobe Illustrator, try importing the Illustrator file into your application.

ILLUSTRATOR: THE LINGUA FRANCA OF VECTOR FILE FORMATS

Adobe Illustrator was the first widely used commercial vector design program, and as such, the format for its stored file information became a standard among users on both the Windows and Macintosh operating platforms. The Illustrator format uses a subset language of PostScript, also an Adobe invention, which is a platform- and device-independent page descriptor language.

Not to be mistaken for the Encapsulated PostScript (EPS) file format, the Illustrator format (which appears with the .AI file extension under Windows) can often be imported by applications which can translate the vector information to their own formats; CorelDRAW and FreeHand can read a file that was saved in the AI file format.

In contrast, an EPS file uses a slightly different set of PostScript descriptor language, and can include bitmap and vector information within the same file. EPS images are generally noneditable when imported to a vector program without using special conversion utilities. EPS files usually are created for placement within a desktop publishing document—at printing time, the EPS file sends the specific PostScript printing code directly to a PostScript output device—and EPS images frequently contain low-resolution bitmap headers within the file so you can accurately place this file within a document.

Basically, there are two ways to output a vector design to bitmap format after it has been scaled by the vector drawing program to the optimal dimensions for display. Some drawing programs, such as Illustrator 6 for the Macintosh and CorelXARA for Windows, can directly write a file to TIF or other bitmap formats, while others can write to a format that an image editing application can then rasterize to bitmap format.

Each of the following sections features the way a procedure is done in a specific application, and the examples are presented using different approaches. The first approach is that you own XARA or Illustrator, and these programs convert vector designs to bitmap format automatically. The second approach assumes that you're using an earlier version of Illustrator, FreeHand, or CorelDRAW: these applications can write AI files that Photoshop can convert to bitmap better than the applications' native capability to transform the design. While it is unlikely that you will always have the same application as the one featured, you will find that the steps you need to take in your application are very similar to those performed in the featured application. Only the names and the exact locations of the tools and commands will differ, for the most part. Therefore, if the example tells you to use the Pick tool, your application may call the tool the Selection tool.

EXPORTING A VECTOR DESIGN FROM CORELXARA

CorelXARA must be mentioned in a discussion of vector-to-bitmap conversions because this unique Windows program handles bitmaps and vectors in the same way. You can trim a bitmap-imported image with a vector shape, create transparent vector objects to use as shadows on top of bitmaps, and export your design as a *seamless*, production-quality file in several bitmap formats.

Here's how to use CorelXARA to export the MARCONI.XAR file to its final image resolution:

1. In XARA, choose File | Open, then choose MARCONI.XAR from the CHAP02 folder on the Companion CD-ROM.

2. In XARA, ruler position and units of measurement should be part of the saved file's information, and the file was saved with the zero origin in the upper left of the design. If it isn't, click and drag the zero origin there using the Selector tool. The units displayed on the Info bar should also be set to inches. If this isn't the case, press Ctrl+Shift+O (Options), click the Units tab, then choose inches from the Page units drop-down list.

3. To make this a trouble-free example, all the objects have been grouped in MARCONI. Click anywhere on the design to select it, then click on the Lock button to the right of the size fields on the Info bar to proportionately scale the image.

4. Insert your cursor in the H(orizontal) box on the Info bar, type **3.1**, then press Enter. See Figure 2-4.

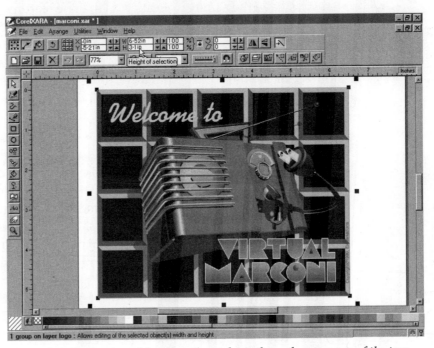

Figure 2-4: *Resize a graphic proportionately, and use the narrower of the two dimensions for scaling it to fit in the Netscape browser window.*

5. Choose File | Export, then choose CompuServe GIF (*.GIF) from the Save as Type drop-down list. Give the file an eight-character (or fewer) name (sorry, the convention for file-naming on the Web is the lowest, 8.3 denominator), followed by a period and the GIF extension. Click on Save.

6. In the GIF Export Bitmap Options dialog box, type **96** in the dpi drop-down box, click on the Selection radio button if XARA didn't preselect it, check Interlaced in the GIF Export Type field, then click on Export.

That's it! Your exported graphic will have no stair-steppy, aliased edges, and it's ready to load into Netscape's browser for previewing.

ANTIALIASING & METHODS OF EDGE SMOOTHING

What *is* antialiasing? It's the result of a process by which pixel areas of color contrast are smoothed out to create a more lifelike, less "computer-looking" digital image. There are several techniques programmers adopt to create an antialiasing effect; however, antialiasing is not, strictly speaking, a "feature" of an application, but instead is the outcome of a series of calculations a program makes.

The visual appearance of *aliasing* can look like harsh, stair-steppy edges around bitmap image areas where, say, a blue circle meets a green background. Screen artifacts, or "screen trash" are also a result of aliasing, and most often either of these unaesthetic image qualities is due to the application's inability to properly resolve an image at any particular viewing dimension.

Let's use a modeling and rendering application as an example of how antialiasing can spell the difference between a photorealistic image and one that looks as though it were written to a primitive Color Graphics Adapter (or *CGA*, one of the earliest color formats for PC monitors) display. Modeling programs pass the finished information about a scene to a rendering engine. It is then the responsibility of the rendering engine (or program) to calculate the color for each pixel in the finished image. Vector wire frame models are very much like the vectors you design in drawing applications. Curves are generally *approximated* as they pass through control points (it's a fast, efficient way to define a curve, mathematically speaking), and the curves only have a fixed position and color value when they're displayed onscreen, or when the curve information is written to a file format.

However, it's *how* the application evaluates the color of each pixel written to file or displayed onscreen that determines the final appearance of your design. CorelXARA is the only vector drawing application at this time that antialiases screen display of vector information.

Back to our hypothetical modeling and rendering scenario: Suppose a model in a scene was texture-mapped with a material that has seven or eight different colors. However, this model is positioned so far back in the scene that its entire surface will only be rendered to finished file format as an area of a single pixel. Logic tells us here, then, that the resulting color pixel representing this texture-mapped model in the finished image can only be one color; it cannot contain all the colors because the imaging window in this example is confined to a single pixel.

This is where the term *aliased* comes from. If this textured model were simply written to file with no filtering performed, the color pixel written to represent this tiny model in the scene would be an "alias" for the information you created in the original modeling file. In short, because you can't sample the texture at a size that can hold *all* the texture colors, the single pixel's color misrepresents the intended information.

Antialiasing can be used in this example to average—to filter—the raw, resolution-independent data in the scene to resolution-dependent bitmap format. In Figure 2-5, you can see side-by-side close-ups of an aliased (unfiltered) bitmap image of the MARCONI design, and the same image when it's been antialiased.

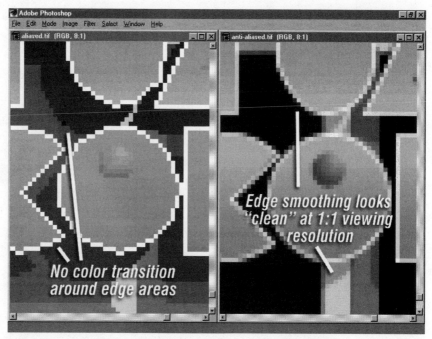

Figure 2-5: *Pixels that are of an average color between neighboring pixels can antialias the harsh color contrasts.*

The qualitative result of antialiasing an image as it's converted to bitmap format is one of slight blurring. However, the amount of blurring, and the blurring of only selected areas of the image through antialiasing can generally be controlled by the user. The most common method for "brute force" antialiasing is by resizing a bitmap; that is, by creating more or fewer pixels in the image by changing image dimensions *without* changing image resolution.

This is a fairly crude form of inducing antialiasing, however. Resizing is completely ineffective as an antialiasing scheme if the host application doesn't also support *resampling*. Resampling, in this usage, means the averaging of pixel color values (called *interpolation*) to make color values for new pixels while resizing the image up, or for assigning new colors to existing pixels when some are eliminated through the sizing-down process. Figure 2-6 shows a simple graphic at bottom left, and from left to right on top: an enlargement of the original, an enlargement of a resized, noninterpolated copy, and finally an enlargement of a resized copy whose resulting pixels have been interpolated.

Figure 2-6: *Resizing without averaging pixel colors simply increases areas of the same color; interpolation creates new pixels with an average of existing color values.*

You'll notice in the last figure that although the interpolated, resized image doesn't contain stair-steppy, aliased edges, it also lacks the focus, the smoothness, and the detail quality one expects from photorealistic bitmap images.

To bring this discussion back to the MARCONI example, in Figure 2-7, the left copy of the design was simply screen captured from Adobe Illustrator, then resized and resampled through basic *linear interpolation*. The figure on the right was rasterized (converted from vector to bitmap information) using Adobe Photoshop: the specific, final dimensions for the image were specified, and Photoshop then used *bicubic* interpolation to antialias the image *without* resizing it in the process.

Figure 2-7: *Pixels can still retain colors that are a harsh contrast to neighboring pixels if you resize an image to create antialiasing.*

You'll also notice in the previous figure that an indiscriminate amount of antialiasing is applied to the resized graphic. The best, most refined method of smoothing edges within a bitmap design is to allow a rasterizing filter, such as the one found in Photoshop or Corel Photo-Paint, to create color transition pixels in only the area of an image that suggests curves or diagonal lines—artistic embellishments that computers have a tough time representing because graphics are right-angled in nature when they're digital.

NEIGHBOR PIXELS, BILINEAR & BICUBIC INTERPOLATION

In the previous section, a few terms were thrown out that should be explained a little. In a nutshell, your vector design will *not look* exactly as you created it when it's been converted to bitmap form: vectors and bitmaps are two different media, so it's helpful to understand all methods available to you to create the most eye-pleasing bitmap rendition of your masterpiece:

- *Nearest-Neighbor Resizing* is the simplest of calculations a bitmap editing program can perform to create or delete pixels from an image when you scale it up or down. Nearest-neighbor resizing is also, typically, the way a vector design program displays images onscreen. When no antialiasing calculations need to be performed, images redraw quickly onscreen to update editing changes. This form of resizing and conversion simply adopts the color of a neighboring pixel in an image when more pixels need to be created through resizing of the image. It's also the least aesthetically pleasing transformation. The top, left window in Figure 2-6 is a result of nearest-neighbor resizing.

- *Bilinear Interpolation* is the averaging of pixel colors sampled across lines of pixels converging upon a target pixel. The target pixel gets its color information from an average of other neighboring pixels and the target pixel's original color when the image is resized, or rasterized to pixel format from vector information by an application such as Photoshop.

- *Bicubic Interpolation* is also the averaging of pixels surrounding the new, target pixel, but the additional mathematical step of *weighting* the average of the sampled colors is performed by the application. Photoshop owners will notice that these three methods are offered in the General Preferences as interpolation methods. Bicubic interpolation involves the most calculation of the three methods, but also ensures that color transition areas in a graphic are smooth and exhibit the least amount of blurring of image detail.

Of the three processes mentioned above, only linear and bicubic interpolation result in antialiasing. To show you a graphical example of the process of interpolation, imagine a logo you've designed in a vector drawing program that consists of nine different colored squares, three each in three rows. Your final size for the image as a bitmap is only one pixel, however. (This is an *example*, okay? Work with me on this one!) With nearest-neighbor calculations, the resulting logo could be any of the nine different colors—you'd have no opportunity to decide which one of the nine colors prevails.

Bilinear interpolation would produce a single pixel of unusual color as its result: the color would be an average of each of the nine original squares' colors. It might look like mud, but it would be an accurate approximation of the original content of the image given the limited size of the finished image, and that's what antialiasing is all about.

Bicubic interpolation would average all nine squares to produce the final pixel's color, but would give preference to the predominant original color value in the finished pixel. In other words, if several of the nine original squares displayed heavy green characteristics, the pixel would have more of a greenish cast to it than if the pixel color was a straight average blend of nine discrete color values.

Figure 2-8 is a graphical representation of the math process used to create bicubic interpolation. When nine color squares must be represented as a single square, interpolation is used to average all the color qualities of the original image, then the final square takes on the color that is mathematically weighted to represent a combination of all colors, with emphasis upon the most common color value.

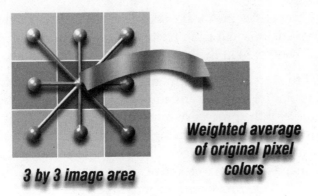

3 by 3 image area

Weighted average of original pixel colors

Figure 2-8: *An example of how interpolation calculates a new pixel, based on an average of surrounding pixel colors.*

On a slightly grander scale (a bitmap with a much larger number of pixels than nine), bicubic interpolation results in smooth color transitions around image detail edges, while areas that do *not* portray a detail edge are not averaged. The overall process creates a soft, photographic image while retaining image focus.

The following section describes how to convert the MARCONI image from Adobe Illustrator 6 for the Macintosh. Illustrator 6 has a new feature—the capability to convert vector graphics to bitmap format from *within* the application. We'll also show in following sections how to make the vector-to-bitmap conversion within a bitmap editing program, in case your drawing application doesn't support internal conversions to bitmap.

EXPORTING DESIGN WORK

Even if a drawing application is your main design resource, you'd be well served to invest in a professional-level bitmap image editing application. Why? Because an image editor gives you the freedom to perform correction work on a design that's been converted to bitmap format; you can't always trust a vector program to convert a copy of a file to bitmap format with accurate color specification.

And you can correct a 24-bit color image before it is transformed to an 8-bit color GIF file, but not using Illustrator, CorelDRAW, or a host of other popular vector-based design programs' native features.

ILLUSTRATOR

Here's how to use the new Rasterize feature in Illustrator 6 to convert the MARCONI drawing to bitmap format:

1. Open MARCONI.AI from the EXAMPLES/CHAP02 folder of the Companion CD-ROM. There are no layers in this file, and all objects have been grouped, to make selecting it easier.

2. Choose the Selection tool, and click on the design to select it.

3. Choose Window I Show Control Palette.

4. Click on the lower, right dot on the centering box on the Control palette. Now, scaling will occur relative to the selection's lower, right corner. Guidelines have been added to this file to indicate when you've scaled the image to its final, intended dimensions.

   The Control palette indicates that the original size of the graphic is 6.41 inches wide by 5.12 inches high. As we've shown in Figure 2-2 earlier in this chapter, the maximum size of the graphic should be a little fewer than 300 pixels (on a 640 X 480 display), or a tad less than 4 inches at the Macintosh monitor resolution of 72 pixels/inch. Four divided by 5.12 is 78 percent.

5. Try 77.5 percent to be conservative when resizing the graphic; type **77.5** in the Scale field, then press Enter to scale the graphic, as shown in Figure 2-9.

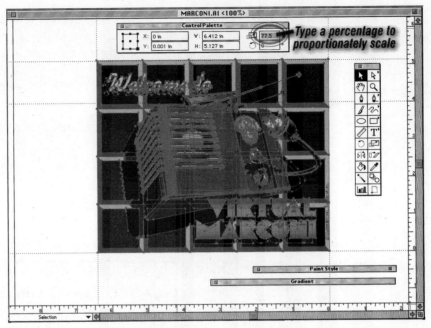

Figure 2-9: *Scale a vector graphic to accommodate the resolution and dimensions of the Netscape browser window.*

6. Choose Object | Rasterize. On the Rasterize palette, choose RGB from the Color Model drop-down list. Although Illustrator compositions are written in CMYK (Cyan, Magenta, Yellow, and Black) color space, images for the Web definitely need to be exported to the color space (a fancy term for the volume of available colors for a specific device) native to monitors: RGB (Red, Green, and Blue).

7. Click on the Screen Resolution radio button. As you can see in Figure 2-10, the dpi field now displays 72. Don't change this number; it's right for Macintosh displays, and if you're a Windows user reading this step, please *ignore* it, because as we mentioned earlier, IBM/PCs use smaller dimensions and higher screen resolution.

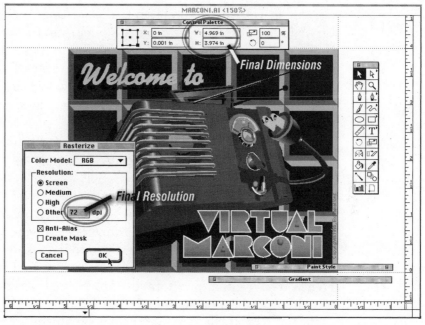

Figure 2-10: *3.974-inch height at 72 dpi will yield a bitmap image that's less than 300 pixels in height.*

8. Check the Anti-Alias check box, then click on OK. Illustrator will now use interpolation to average the best pixel colors from the vector design, and a bitmap will replace the vector design on the Illustrator page in about 10 seconds.

9. Choose File | Save As, then choose Targa Format, or TIFF Format from the Format drop-down box, and name this document MARCONI to your hard disk in the "Save this document as" field. Click on OK.

10. Illustrator will flash you an attention box warning that the format you've chosen will not allow you to edit the image when it is read back in. Don't fret, and click on OK; you have an editable original on the Companion CD-ROM. Choose 24 bits/pixel in the Targa Options dialog box, then click on OK.

11. Close Illustrator, and you're finished.

A file in TIFF format or Targa is a *color channel* image—its color capability and structure is quite different from that of the GIF 89a format, a format unfortunately not offered in Illustrator. And this means converting the exported graphic one more time before you have a Web graphic; but it's actually good to keep a TIFF or Targa image around, because editing one, if needed, is easier than editing an *indexed color* GIF image.

FREEHAND & CORELDRAW EXPORTS

At the time of this writing, Macromedia FreeHand is the only biplatform drawing application whose versions are in synch: the features you'll find in the Macintosh version are the same as the Windows version. Moreover, the steps we'll walk through in the following example are roughly equivalent in CorelDRAW 5 or 6. So if you have either program, the procedure is basically the same for scaling and exporting the MARCONI image.

It should be noted here that the Adobe Illustrator format is recommended for export. That format does not convert the design to bitmap format, but instead converts the design to a structure that can be directly imported into Photoshop, Corel Photo-Paint, or Micrografx Picture Publisher, the three leading image editing applications. What these programs share is the capability to rasterize vector images stored in AI format while applying antialiasing. Neither FreeHand nor CorelDRAW directly supports antialiasing for bitmap formats, as CorelXARA and Illustrator 6 do.

Here's the quickest way to scale and export a file from FreeHand or CorelDRAW version 5 or 6:

1. In either program, choose File | Open, then open MARCONI from the EXAMPLES/CHAP02 folder on the Companion CD-ROM. The file extension .CDR refers to the CorelDRAW file, while the .FH5 extension means that either a Windows or Macintosh FreeHand designer can open and edit the design.

2. You'll notice that there is a guideline at the 3.1-inch mark on the vertical ruler. This is the target height for the MARCONI design export. In FreeHand, choose View | Snap To Guides from the menu. In CorelDRAW, choose Layout | Snap To Guidelines.

3. In FreeHand, click on the (grouped) objects with the Pointer tool to select them, then hold the Shift key (to constrain proportions) while you click and drag the upper, right-corner point of the selection left and down toward the guideline at the 3.1-inch mark. In CorelDRAW, with the Pick tool, click the grouped object to select it, then click and drag the top, right selection handle toward the guideline; the proportions are automatically constrained because you chose a corner selection handle. Figure 2-11 shows what this looks like in FreeHand.

Figure 2-11: *Use a guide for the image's final height, then proportionately scale a graphic.*

In either program, you've successfully resized the design when your cursor snaps to the guideline.

Alternatively, you can use the Transform Palette in FreeHand to precisely scale the selection to its final height and width. If you're in Windows, the proper percentage to enter in the Scale Factor field is 59 percent. 3.1 inches divided by the original height of 5.1 inches is about 60 percent, so our target size is a little conservative, and the 3.1-inch height was arrived at by dividing the maximum Netscape browser window height of 300 pixels by the screen resolution of the PC, which is 96 pixels/inch (300/96 = 3.125).

In CorelDRAW, you can choose Effects | Transform (in CorelDRAW 6, it's Arrange | Transform | Scale and Mirror) to display the Transform Roll-Up, where you can type identical values in the Horizontal and Vertical fields to proportionately resize the MARCONI design.

4. In FreeHand, choose File | Export, then choose Adobe Illustrator 3, 4, or 5.x from the List Files of Type drop-down box, name the file, find a target folder on your hard disk, and click on OK. In CorelDRAW (with the graphic still selected), choose File | Export, check the Selected Only check box, choose Adobe Illustrator from the List Files of Type drop-down box, make certain that the file is named with an .AI extension and not .EPS, specify a folder on your hard disk for the export, then click on OK (in version 6, click on Export). Choose Adobe Illustrator 3.0 format in the final dialog box, then click on OK.

5. You're done! Close your application, and let's get into some facts, limitations, and tricks you can use to turn your Illustrator file into a bitmap.

USING AN IMAGE EDITOR TO CONVERT VECTOR GRAPHICS

Artists who have spent years perfecting a relationship with commercial printers and service bureaus have become adept at converting designs to a different color model used in printing. CMYK color (for Cyan, Magenta, Yellow, and Black) uses an entirely different color space than the RGB display color you must save a bitmap image in for display on the Web. CMYK colors appear duller because this model has a different color *gamut* than RGB color. A color gamut is a portion of the color spectrum or the range of colors that can be expressed by any particular device.

Because Illustrator was designed as a production tool for commercial printing and not for creating RGB images, you may find that an Illustrator design looks a little duller than its RGB counterpart. However, many advanced image editors such as Photoshop and Corel Photo-Paint can bring out brilliant colors in a vector-to-bitmap converted design. If you have an Illustrator design ready to convert to bitmap, or if you'd like to use the example image on the Companion CD-ROM, the following steps can be used for importing the file into Adobe Photoshop and color correcting it:

1. In Photoshop, choose File | Open, then select the MARCONI.AI file in the EXAMPLES/CHAP02 folder of the Companion CD-ROM. The Rasterize Adobe Illustrator Format dialog box pops up.

   Because vector files are resolution-independent, you can specify almost any resolution and dimension you like in this dialog box; it depends upon your system's RAM and available space on your hard disk. For this example, however, let's think small—specifically, the target size for the Web graphic, which must be less than 300 pixels in height. In Figure 2-12, you can see that you can split the units of measurement in the dialog box. Therefore, if you didn't complete the example in this chapter where you resized the Illustrator graphic, here's a second chance to modify the file before it becomes a resolution-dependent bitmap.

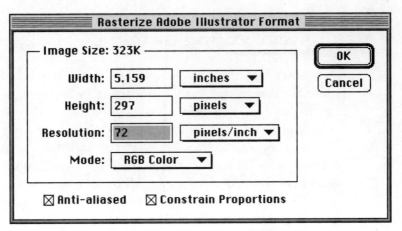

Figure 2-12: *You can choose the final size of an Illustrator conversion in pixels or inches.*

2. Aim for 298 pixels in height, and 373 pixels in width; the Resolution field becomes unimportant, because you're not measuring pixel count per inch, you're simply measuring the number of pixels in the rasterized image. You might want to leave this at Photoshop's default value, though, if you intend to use this import filter a lot.

3. Choose RGB Color Mode from the Mode drop-down box. Even though an Illustrator import might display colors within CMYK color space, you don't want the resulting bitmap image to be in CMYK color mode because this makes editing and color-correcting the image harder.

4. Check the Anti-aliased check box to ensure that filtering calculations will be performed while the vector image is converted to bitmap format, then click on OK.

The process of calculating each pixel color in the Illustrator import might take up to 30 seconds or so, but when the image does appear, you should save this image as MARCONI.PSD—the Photoshop version 3 format—to your hard disk. This image needs to undergo some minor transformations, as we'll describe in the next section.

MANIPULATING COLORS IN A BITMAP IMAGE

As stated earlier, pixels in a bitmap image account for 100 percent of the image's recognizable qualities. Unlike a vector path, which has a shape you can edit independently of its fill or outline (stroke) property, an area of a bitmap image represents shape, fill, shading, width of an outline, and other properties entirely with the color of the pixel, the grid unit.

This apparent limitation of the bitmap format of graphics, however, leads to some possibilities that cannot be accomplished easily with a vector drawing program. For example, to globally lighten a vector design, you'd need to reassign each object in the composition a lighter value; in contrast, a pixel image can be lightened with a mouse click or two. In the following example, you'll see how to adjust the color and tone of the MARCONI image to push the colors and contrast of the image more toward the lush RGB colors, and to diminish the perception that the graphic falls within CMYK printing color space:

1. If you didn't import the MARCONI graphic, that's okay—use the MARCONI.PSD file in the EXAMPLES/CHAP02 folder on the Companion CD-ROM for this example. Choose File | Open, then load the image into Photoshop.

2. If the image doesn't appear to have enough contrast or color, you can correct both of these problems by choosing Image | Adjust | Color Balance.

3. Uncheck the Preserve Luminosity check box on the Color Balance palette, begin with the Midtones radio button, then click and drag the middle slider toward green by about +6. The Color Balance palette allows you to move specific tonal areas in an image toward their color opposite. By unchecking the Preserve Luminosity check box, you can change the tonal values (the brightness, the neutral color component of a color) in the image in addition to shifting the color values. This action is similar to what a photo lab does to color correct an image that was taken outdoors with indoor film. But in this case, you're moving

the tones in the image away from cyan, magenta, and yellow values (printing ink values) toward the red, green, and blue values of an RGB image. See Figure 2-13.

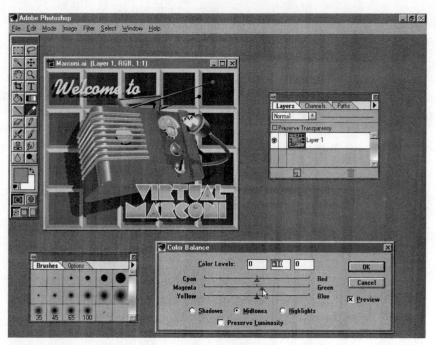

Figure 2-13: *Changing color values away from CMYK and toward RGB often creates a more exciting composition.*

4. Play with the other ranges of tones—the Highlights and the Shadows—click on a radio button, then move any of the color sliders in either direction, and watch the colors in the MARCONI image change.

5. Once you're happier with the colors, you might want to change the amount of color versus the amount of neutral grayscale information within the colors (the tone). This is accomplished by saturating the image or only selected areas. Saturation is the amount of distinct hue a color displays; when a color has equal amounts of all different hues, the image becomes grayscale. Press Ctrl+U to display the Hue/Saturation palette.

6. Click and drag the Saturation slider up to about +20, and see what you think about the results. Remember, there's no such thing as an "out-of-gamut color" with images bound for the Web, because of WYSIGTAP, What You See *Isn't* Going To A Printer! Try not to oversaturate the image, however. If areas begin to block in, you're adding an excess amount of pure hue to the pixels and ruining the contrast in the image. Click on OK after you're happy with the image.

7. Finally, the contrast of the image and the range and influence of neutral tones can be corrected in the image. The changes you've made to the image so far have addressed the value and amount of color, but the image might not display the punch you'd like onscreen. This has to do with the amount of black ink added to a CMYK color composite image. Generally, the preset colors in Illustrator are carefully constructed to avoid *coverage;* black is used to add contrast and "body" to colors, but too much black in addition to the C, M, and Y inks can cause puddles in areas on printed paper.

   However, too much ink is of no concern in the example here; it's not going to be printed. Press Ctrl+L to display the Levels palette, then click and drag the middle slider slightly toward the right. This increases the contrast in the midtones of the MARCONI image without changing the Black or White Point. Generally, the midrange of an image contains the most visual information, but always trust your own eyes, because every image is different in composition, tone, and color. Try dragging the slider so that the midpoint is at about .86, then click on OK when you're happy with the preview.

We added a little more information in the preceding steps about color theory because you might not use Photoshop, but the principles of changing color cast, saturation, and tonal content can be put to use in most professional quality image editors. The same adjustments can be made in Picture Publisher or Photo-Paint; the controls might be labeled differently, but they perform the same functions.

THE PERK OF USING ILLUSTRATOR FORMAT

Tangentially related to our discussion on converting Adobe Illustrator format images to bitmaps through Photoshop is the capability of the GIF89a format to include a transparent color. A "dropout" color in a GIF file is how Web designers float a graphic upon a color background or a different, tiling image. (See Chapter 3, "Bitmap Graphics & Special Effects.")

Let's suppose for a moment that your client likes the foreground elements in a design, but doesn't care too much for its background. Instead, he'd like an image to float upon a colored background when the document is displayed in Netscape Navigator. The solution is simpler than one could imagine. Illustrator files, regardless of whether they were created in Illustrator, are imported into Photoshop as an image layer, and empty areas of a design—those that do not contain paths—aren't converted to bitmap format, but instead appear as clear areas.

Now, "clear" is an unusual condition to occur within a bitmap image, and pixels can only appear invisible within a special format of bitmap file. Only certain applications can understand file header information that says, "This explicit color value shouldn't appear onscreen." Nevertheless, if your drawing application can write a legitimate Illustrator file and you own Photoshop, you can make separating foreground elements from the background a breeze, and you can define a dropout value for the final GIF image in lightning time.

Here's how to work with an Illustrator file in Photoshop to create a transparent GIF:

1. Make sure you're using Photoshop 3.0.5 on the Macintosh, or that you have downloaded or otherwise acquired the Windows patch file that adds the GIF89a export filter to the application.

2. Choose File | Open, then choose the DROPOUT.AI file from the Companion CD-ROM. This design does not include a background; it only contains some 3D text that was created in Adobe Dimensions and then exported in the AI format.

If you'd like to try your own drawing here, use one created in FreeHand, Illustrator, or CorelDRAW that contains no background objects. Select the objects, then choose File | Export. (CorelDRAW users should check the Selected Only check box.) Choose the Illustrator (*.AI) format—unless of course, you're *using* Illustrator—choose version 3 or higher for the export format, then save the export to your hard disk. Then open the image in Photoshop.

3. In Figure 2-14, you can see that the way Photoshop handles an Illustrator image with no background objects is to leave these areas clear on an image layer. The checkered pattern indicates that this is clear space.

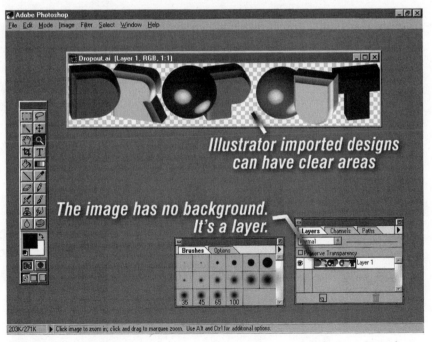

Figure 2-14: *Photoshop makes it easy to drop out a converted vector image's background in the final GIF image.*

4. Choose File | Export | GIF89a Export after you've made color and tonal corrections, if any.

5. In the GIF89a Export Options box, you have your choice of dropout colors—the color within the special GIF format that Netscape Navigator "sees" as being transparent. Unless your drawing has a lot of shades of gray, the default color is a good choice, and you don't need to change it. Additionally, the default method of *color reduction* to GIF's 256-color format is Adaptive. This, too, probably doesn't need to change, because Adaptive color reduction to a fixed palette offers 256 of the closest matches to the original artwork. Other methods for "palette-izing" an RGB image depend upon a predetermined *color palette*, which might not match up well to the colors used in your unique image.

6. Check the Interlaced check box. This makes the exported GIF begin to display as soon as it is received by Netscape Navigator. Click on Preview now to see how greatly Adaptive color reduction affects your work.

7. In Figure 2-15, you can see the Preview box, with a window you can zoom and scroll. The background isn't transparent in the preview (it's the default color from the previous dialog box), but this color will indeed drop out when the graphic is viewed in Netscape Navigator. Beneath the window is the exact color palette to which Photoshop will reduce this copy of the original. It might be hard to see in this black-and-white figure, but you can expect to see very little image *dithering* (a topic covered in the next section, "Color Modes & Color Reduction"), and the antialiased edges will blend smoothly into your client's background image on his Web page.

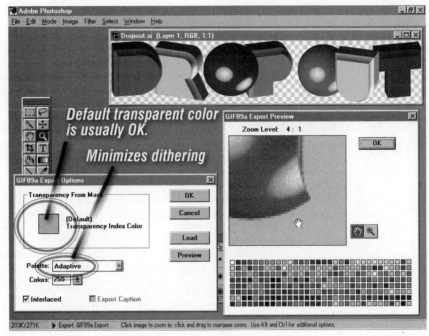

Figure 2-15: *Photoshop offers a preview of how faithfully the color-reduction method you use portrays the original image.*

8. Click on OK, then click on OK in the Export Options box. In the Export GIF 89a dialog box, name the file and save it to your hard disk. Done!

Use of colors is of critical concern to the Web graphics artist, because the bandwidth of the World Wide Web dictates that everything shall be small in order to download quickly. And color capability is one property of a bitmap graphic that determines the overall file size that must be passed from server to viewer. In the next section, we'll cover some topics relating to the GIF format's color depth. A vector design doesn't need to be overly concerned with such onscreen artifacts as dithering, but when you convert an image to bitmap, understanding the best methods to choose is a must.

Color Modes & Color Reduction

If you've ever accidentally loaded a 4-bit (16 colors) or 8-bit (256 colors) video driver, then opened an RGB 24-bit (millions) color image in a viewing program, you witnessed a process called color reduction. Good image editing programs will automatically dither the number of colors in the image to those colors available with the current video driver, while other programs will display the closest match to the current system's colors.

Dithering is a process that creates patterns of color within an image as a process of "faking"—approximating—the colors that cannot be displayed within a limited video palette. Most of the time, you'll want to convert a vector drawing to a bitmap image in RGB (also called *TrueColor*, *24-bit*, or *millions*) color mode. RGB color is also called *channel color* because of the way color is stored within the file format. Let's examine the difference between RGB color and indexed color, the format in which the GIF type of image is structured.

RGB Color

RGB color is called channel color because every pixel within the image is calculated by the mixture of presence of red, green, and blue additive light, presented to the user in a separate view—a *channel*—of the RGB image. Many programs, including Photo-Paint and Photoshop allow you to view and edit discrete channels of each component color according to the brightness—the presence—of each of these components. For example, if you look at an RGB image of a woman wearing a turquoise sweater, the RGB image will display various intensities of what appears to be grayscale information if you view each of the color channels separately. The red channel will most likely appear to be black in the sweater area; red makes no contribution to turquoise, and therefore no brightness will or should appear in the red color channel. However, the green channel will display lighter tones, and the blue channel will be very light in appearance, because green is present in the color turquoise, and blue is a very large contributor to the overall turquoise color.

Because each color channel in an RGB image can hold up to 256 brightness values for each of the 3 component colors, an RGB image is also called a 24-bit color image. Each color channel can hold 2 (bits) to the 8th power of brightness values (equal to 256 unique tones), and with 3 color channels, the image equals 2 to the 24th power, for 16.7 million possible colors. It's usually best to keep a copy of your converted vector image in RGB format, even though its destiny is to become an indexed GIF image. You may want to edit the bitmap image in the future, and indexed images have no discrete color channels—and advanced image editing programs don't work so well with a limited color palette within an image.

Common file formats for saved RGB images are TIFF, Targa, usually native application formats such as Photoshop's and Photo-Paint's, and occasionally, a specific type of PCX format (ZSoft's creation).

INDEXED COLOR

Indexed color images contain one-third as much color information as their RGB counterparts, and because of this, they can load quickly, and are ideally suited for Web graphics. As opposed to RGB images, indexed color images organize colors in an image according to referenced color slots. An indexed color is assigned an index value, such as red=223, green=128, and blue=49. When the indexed color is loaded, the application quickly reads the index for the color, references the number according to the image's color table (a.k.a. color palette), and this table provides the color information for display. Indexed color images are usually not created, but instead are a product of performing color reduction on an RGB image. An indexed color image is typically confined to 256 unique color indices; if the table were larger, the table and the lookup process would become ungainly, making the file size large and inefficient. Applications such as Photoshop simply consider an image with greater than 256 color capability to be a color channel image.

Common file formats for indexed color images are GIF, PCX, PICT, and BMP. These formats can efficiently store the limited data. TIFF and Targa formats can also store an indexed color image, but it's not economical because you have a large color capability in these formats, and a limited number of stored colors. Storing an indexed color image in the TIFF format is like carrying a pair of socks around in a steamer trunk.

DITHERING

As mentioned earlier, dithering can simulate colors in a copy of an image with low color capability, most of the time effectively conveying the same feel and content of the original RGB image. In Figure 2-16, you can see a graphic of a house in the upper left corner, with examples of *diffusion* dithering, *ordered* (or *patterned*) dithering, and no dithering ("nearest color") performed on the original. We've exaggerated the examples here to convey the visuals a little better on this black-and-white page: the color reduction was from RGB color to a palette of 16 colors instead of the usual GIF 256 color capability.

Figure 2-16: *Diffusion dithering usually provides the most eye-pleasing effect when an image cannot contain the original's complete color palette.*

Diffusion dithering is accomplished by calculating the error with which a pixel represents original pixel color. If the application determines that the error is enough to totally misrepresent the original pixel color, the color is moved to an adjacent position. And this process is calculated sequentially for the entire image. The effect is fairly pleasant, and many viewers don't recognize a diffusion dithered image as such when compared to the original, because the error in color when compared to the original is scattered—diffused—across the entire image.

Patterned, or ordered dithering, creates a weave of pixels that, if looked at quickly, blend to create an approximate color value close to the RGB image original's. Because of the relatively small size of Web graphics, patterned dithering is not really recommended for color reduction; the weave begins to dominate over the content—the detail—in the design. Photoshop users cannot perform pattern dithering unless System color is chosen when you switch between RGB and indexed color modes.

No dithering is often an option in image editors, but should only be chosen when color reducing to 256-color GIF format if the original image contains fewer than 256 unique tones. In Figure 2-16, the house image looks awful, because there is an excess of colors, most of which can't be represented using the indexed palette. What images would look okay if you applied no dithering? Grayscale images, for one; image map buttons that only have a border and some text would convert straight to a limited, indexed palette; and occasionally you might take a very monochrome photograph—a snowfall in evening light might fit within 256 possible unique colors.

ADAPTIVE PALETTES: SPECIFYING YOUR OWN 256 COLORS

Although an indexed color image in a format such as GIF can only contain 256 unique colors, they can be any colors you wish. This opens the possibilities for the designer—especially the vector graphics designer. With the exception of gradient blends, most elements in even a sumptuous vector design contain fewer unique colors than you'd imagine. If you know in advance that your design is bound for the Web, you can deliberately limit the palette of colors within the design and ensure that the bitmap version contains accurate information about the original.

On the other hand, if you want the creative freedom to design a Web graphic any way you please, you can still come out of this a winner when converting a copy to a fixed palette of 256 colors. The trick is to use an image editing application's capability to seek the most commonly used colors in an image, map these colors to the indexed palette of a GIF image, and apply dithering to the remaining areas of color that'll become unavailable in the fixed GIF color palette.

Here's how to perform optimized dithering in a number of different applications for the PC and the Macintosh. The examples that follow assume that you have an RGB image in TIFF, Targa, or another format ready to go:

- **Fractal Design Painter (v. 3 or higher for Windows or Macintosh)**   Choose File I Save As, then choose GIF files (*.GIF) from the drop-down list; choose a target location for the saved file, then click on OK. In the Save As GIF Options box, choose 256 colors from the Number of Colors list; click on the Interleaf GIF check box; under Quantizing Options, choose Dither Colors; then click on Preview Data to see what the export will look like. If you're happy with the results, click on OK, then click on OK in the Options dialog box, and you're done. You've used the maximum number of colors available in the GIF format, and Painter only offers diffusion dithering for a smooth-looking graphic with limited colors.

■ **Corel Photo-Paint 6 or later**   Open the target image of
your choice, then choose Image | Convert to | 256 Colors
(8-bit). In the Convert to 256 Colors dialog box, choose
Optimized (*not* Adaptive) as the Palette type, and Error
Diffusion as the Dither type, then click on OK. The palette
for the new indexed image will display on the color palette
on the bottom of the screen. Choose File | Save As, then
choose CompuServe Bitmap (GIF) from the Save as Type
drop-down list. Pick a hard disk location for the file, then
click on Save. In the Transparent Color dialog box, click on
the 89a Format radio button, check the Interlaced image
check box—do not check the Transparent color box—then
click on OK.

■ **Adobe Photoshop 3.0.5 or later**   Choose File | Export, then
choose GIF 89a Export. If the Palette drop-down box offers
you Exact as an option, this means that the target RGB
image contains fewer than 256 unique colors and no dithering will be performed. Chances are, however, that your
image will exceed this number of unique colors, so choose
Adaptive if Exact doesn't pop up by default. Make sure
that the Interlaced box is checked, and click on Preview if
you'd like to look at the color palette for the GIF export and
at how much, if any, visible dithering will be performed. As
you can see in Figure 2-17, the MARCONI converted
graphic looks pretty good at 3:1 viewing resolution, and
therefore will display nicely at the fixed 1:1 viewing resolution offered in Netscape Navigator. Click on OK, click on
OK again to confirm the export, then name the file and
choose a location for it on your hard disk.

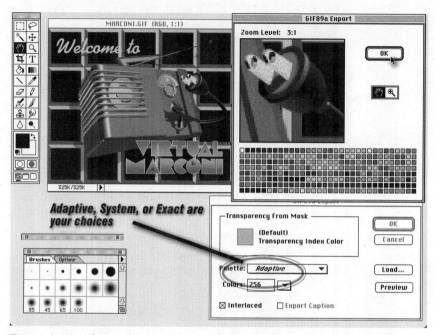

Adaptive, System, or Exact are your choices

Figure 2-17: *Advanced image editing programs offer an adaptive or optimized palette based on frequency of color values in the original picture.*

- **Paint Shop Pro for Windows v. 3 or later**   Choose File | Open, select your graphic, then choose Colors | Decrease Color Depth, then choose 256 colors (8-bit). In the Decrease Color Depth dialog box, click on the Optimized radio button and click on the Error Diffusion radio button; you also might want to use the (optional) Reduce Color Bleeding feature. This option limits the amount of dithering "spread" when the colors are reduced. Click on OK, then choose File | Save As, and choose GIF-CompuServe from the List Files of Type drop-down list. Choose Version 89a-Interlaced as the File Sub-Format. Click on OK and you're done.

- **GraphicConverter for the Macintosh**   Drag an image you've converted to bitmap format using any of the steps in this chapter onto the GraphicConverter icon (or alias) to launch the application and load the file. Choose Picture | Colors | Options, then click on the Optimize Color Table radio button, then click on OK. Choose Picture | Colors | Change to 256 Colors (8-bit). In File | Save As, choose GIF from the Format drop-down box, then click on Options. In the GIF box, click on 89a, Interlaced, then click on OK. You'll notice that GraphicConverter also offers the option to Optimize the Color Table in this dialog box; this radio button should be selected only when you have an image you're certain contains a handful of unique values. The color table of a screen button image, for example, could be only 4 bits. The smaller the color table within the GIF format, the more quickly it can be loaded as a visitor browses your Web site.

Click on OK, name your image, then click on Save, and you're done.

Regardless of which operating system you use to compose documents for the Web, you probably should use the DOS file-naming conventions. This will ensure that everyone, and every device, on the Web will be able to read the file name correctly. Stick to eight characters and a period separating the file name from the file extension—in this example, MARCONI.GIF.

PREVIEWING YOUR WORK

We've covered a lot of methods and theory in this chapter, but the real proof is in the publishing! If you've completed the MARCONI image conversion, you might want to see what it looks like within a document viewed with Netscape Navigator right now.

The Macintosh and Windows versions of Netscape Navigator make connections a little differently. While you can indeed drag an image Netscape can read into Netscape Navigator's window to view it, this action will alert the system that you want to establish a Web connection—and you don't! You simply want to preview your work.

In Netscape Navigator for the Macintosh, double-click the Netscape icon (or an alias) to launch it, then *quickly* cancel the connection by clicking on Stop in the PPP Connection Status box. A second attempt will be made, so click on Stop in the box a second time when it appears, then click on OK when Netscape tells you that it can't find the DNS entry.

Once the Netscape Navigator window appears, drag and drop your test GIF image into the window, as shown in Figure 2-18.

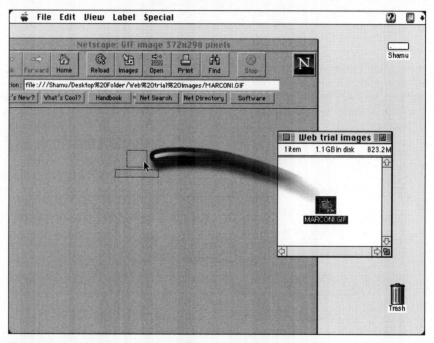

Figure 2-18: *Netscape Navigator allows you to view an image type the browser recognizes by dragging the file into the window.*

In Windows 95, launch Netscape Navigator. By default, Netscape Installer will put a shortcut on your desktop; if for some reason you don't have one here, you can create a shortcut. The desktop is a very convenient place for your communications programs, in Windows or the Macintosh, because it's easy then to drag a file from a folder window to launch an application.

After the Netscape interface opens, click on Stop to prevent Netscape from loading its home page, and click on Cancel when the Connect to dialog box pops up. Then find your graphic, and drag it into Netscape's browser area.

In Figure 2-19, you can see the MARCONI graphic displayed on a screen running 640 X 480 resolution. At less than 300 pixels in height, the browser window doesn't scroll, and your client is happy because the visitor can see the artwork from edge to edge.

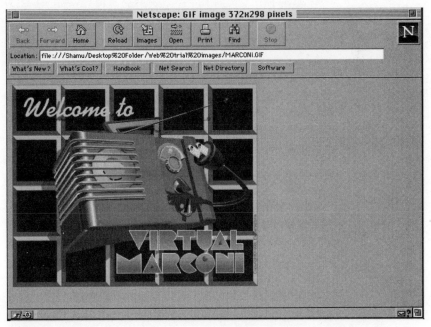

Figure 2-19: *If you understand resolution, color depth, antialiasing, and conversion methods, your artwork will always look its best on the Web.*

MOVING ON

Whether it's vector or bitmap you choose as your primary format for computer designs, this chapter has taken you through the basics of making the design look its best as a bitmap on the Web.

In Chapter 3, "Bitmap Graphics & Special Effects," we'll extend our exploration of materials to compose multimedia Web presentations a little further. We'll also get into some special effects you can create for buttons, other navigational elements, and graphics themselves. So bring along an idea or two from this chapter, and let's see how the process of multimedia authoring is one of integration.

3

Bitmap Graphics & Special Effects

After you've worked with HTML documents for a while, you'll discover that the proposed and approved HTML standards for tag styles are simply a different medium than WYSIWYG document formatting tools such as DTP or word processor. But designers intuitively make the distinction between oils and charcoals and don't attempt the same techniques used with one medium with the other. Professional communicators adapt to different media and make the most from each medium's strengths. Although it's a natural reaction to get a little frustrated when you can't seem to perform the same desktop publishing feats within an HTML document, it's important to remember that HTML is simply a different structure for a document. HTML is not inferior, it's not excessively limited, it's simply . . . different.

This chapter takes a look behind the scenes of several HTML pages to show you how to achieve some effects that can make a Web page look every bit as exciting and graphically sumptuous in Navigator as it might be on the printed page. You'll learn how the HTML format can accept wonderful artistic enhancements, and occasionally how to "trick" a document into displaying what you've envisioned. To take full advantage of how Web elements integrate and to see how the graphical elements work together, we'll reverse-engineer a number of sample documents in this chapter.

In Figure 3-1, you can see the Web site of a fictitious group of investors called The Monde Group. If you'd like to "visit" this site, copy the MONDE folder in the CHAP03 directory of the Companion CD-ROM to your hard drive, then load the GROUP-M.HTM document into Netscape Navigator. The Monde Group site consists of two frame-based pages. Therefore, each frame displays a different HTML document to compose the entire site. A client-side image map links the first frame document to the second frame document, and an ordinary HREF links from the second back to the first document.

Figure 3-1: *You can divide a page into columns to resemble a traditional printed document through the use of frames.*

There are two things we'll examine here in The Monde Group site: layout and content of the graphics and the best way to create them. If you're going to create graphics of the correct size to fit within frames, it is necessary to take a look at how the frames are defined in this page.

FRAMING YOUR ARTWORK

Framing a physical painting usually proceeds in this order: you buy (or create) a painting, then find or build a frame of appropriate dimensions. However, framing, Navigator-style, operates in reverse. That is, you need to measure the frame *first*, then tailor a copy of your graphics to fit inside.

THE FRAMESET TAG

In Figure 3-1, you can see that the frames for the first page of The Monde Group's site are divided into two columns, with the left column containing two rows. This feat is accomplished in the HTML document by first declaring two columns right after the TITLE tag, like so:

```
<FRAMESET COLS="*,275">
```

The FRAMESET tag replaces BODY in frame documents, and the COLS attribute is specified either as a comma-separated list, or in relative sizing (a comma separating values, followed by a percent sign). The asterisk in the above tag tells Navigator to display the nonspecified frame column in the remainder of the screen. Therefore, the right frame—the one containing the graphic of The Monde Group's corporate headquarters—will always appear at 275 pixels wide, regardless of the viewer's screen resolution.

So this tag allows us to create a graphic whose width we can be fairly certain of. If you open HQ.GIF in a bitmap editor, you'll notice that this graphic is 287 pixels wide (because I wanted to slightly crop the graphic), and there is an additional vertical space at the bottom of the graphic that features an embossed title. The reason why this was done is that at 640 X 480 viewing resolution, the title beneath the building is out of frame and doesn't show (Figure 3-1 *doesn't* show the embossed title), but visitors to this site who are running higher screen resolutions *would* see the additional embellishment of the embossed title. Without the additional graphic area, visitors to the site would see only Navigator's default background in this area at 800 X 600 and higher monitor resolutions. And this would spoil the document composition.

The trick here is to play to the strength of the medium's limitations, and to accommodate as wide an audience as possible within your Web composition.

The left column of this Web page is divided into two rows: the text box on top contains a scroll bar, while the frame containing the navigation buttons does not. This was accomplished by the use of another FRAMESET tag within the HTML document directly following the FRAMESET COLS tag, as follows:

```
<FRAMESET ROWS="75%, 25%">
```

We've used percentages in the ROWS attribute, and this works because of a compositional preference here. In other words, 75% text box and 25% button box happens to fit the compositional scheme—and there are no "magic numbers" here if you like the layout and would like to use it in a Web document of your own. Directly following the FRAMESET ROWS tag is the SRC attribute, which provides the name of the file or link to be displayed in the first frame. The line:

```
<FRAME SRC="about-us.htm" NAME="Corporate Profile">
```

places the ABOUT-US HTML document in the upper left scrolling frame, and the NAME attribute allows the document, as displayed in the frame, to be targeted by links (usually frames) in other documents. Therefore, in this instance, it's good to name the text frame, because if you decide later to create a link to the other document in this site by clicking on one of the buttons, you'll have a reference to a named frame to jump back to from the other page.

SCROLLING

Let's suppose that The Monde Group has commissioned you to build this site, and you can't get a straight answer in advance as to how much copy will need to go in the ABOUT-US HTML document. This poses no problem if you allow the frame to scroll. A scrolling frame is accomplished by *doing nothing* in the HTML document: the SCROLLING attribute is, by default, always on. The marble texture you see in Figure 3-1 behind the text will go on forever without visible tiling because it is defined in the HTML code as a background image. Therefore, it will support as much copy as The Monde Group throws at you. Creating nontiling patterns is a topic we'll get into later in this chapter.

The buttons in the bottom left frame are contained within the BUTTONS.HTM document, and again, because viewers might see this page at different resolutions, the button graphic contains "bleed" to the right and the bottom of the image. Viewers of this page at 1024 X 768 won't see additional buttons, or larger buttons, but *any* viewing resolution will display all three buttons. Because a percentage of the frame was specified in the ROWS attribute, the button frame can never be a fixed dimensional value; the building graphic is of fixed (pixel) width, which leaves us with only the option of specifying the remainder of the screen width for the buttons. However, there's no need to scroll the button window (there's no area of foreground interest other than the button faces), so the

```
SCROLLING="No"
```

attribute directly follows the reference to the BUTTONS.HTM document. The tag for the button frame closes with

```
NORESIZE>
```

which prohibits viewers from manipulating the frame edges with the cursor to change the dimensions of the frame. Actually, the NORESIZE attribute in this example stops *all* the frames from being resized because the frame with the NORESIZE attribute touches the other frames, so if one frame can't move, the others can't. The attribute therefore only needs to be used once within the document—a very economical way to maintain consistency of the site when viewed by visitors running different screen resolutions.

The left column is closed with the </FRAMESET> tag, and

```
<FRAME SRC="building.htm" NAME="1 Monde Plaza"
```

is the next line in GROUP-M.HTM. BUILDING.HTM is a document that contains the building graphic, and the NAME attribute here allows it to be targeted by other links. Finally, the GROUP-M document is closed with </FRAMESET> and the close HTML tag.

This is the structure of the HTML document; in the following sections, you'll see how to create the most exciting *content* for the frames!

> ### TIP
>
> *Images used as background "wallpaper" such as the buttons image in this example, cannot be image mapped. So how do you create the links? MOND-MAP.GIF rests on top of BUTTONS.GIF in the BUTTONS.HTM document, and MOND-MAP.GIF is completely transparent. That is, the image is entirely one flat color, and this color was defined as the transparency value when the GIF was created. The "clear" image was then client-side image mapped. See Chapter 1, "Composing in HTML & NavGold," for details on how to do this.*

CREATING NAVIGATION BUTTONS

Before we get into the various methods and programs you can use to create navigation elements for a Web page, it's important to understand that buttons are composed of a completely nonunique material. This material consists of pixels, the building block of bitmap images. Something that looks like a button onscreen only becomes a navigation button when it's linked in an HTML document to a URL. The point is that *any* image—an image of a knob, an airplane, or your boss's face—can be a button; it helps the visitor if your image *looks* like a conventional button, but we'll show you how to stretch your imagination *and* the appearance of a button in this section.

Although you can illustrate a button in programs such as Illustrator or CorelDRAW (see Chapter 2, "Vector-to-Bitmap Conversions," for information on converting vector graphics to bitmaps), it's far quicker, easier, and more fun to seek out automated applets to accomplish the task. There are a number of Adobe standard plug-ins that can make button creation a charmed task, and I've created a font on the Companion CD-ROM to serve as a template for creating scores of different navigation buttons in a flash.

THE ALIEN SKIN BUTTON APPROACH

Alien Skin Black Box version II filters are biplatform plug-ins that come in both 16-bit and 32-bit versions, so these filters can be used on the PowerMacintosh OS, the 68K Macintosh OS, Windows 3.1,

Windows 95, and Windows NT. Plug-ins that follow Adobe's specifications can be used in the following programs:

- Fractal Painter
- Photoshop
- Paint Shop Pro (Windows only)
- Illustrator 6 (at press time it is Mac only)
- ColorIt (Macintosh only)
- Adobe PageMaker 6 (believe it or not!)
- PhotoStyler v. 2
- Corel Photo-Paint (Windows only)
- Picture Publisher (Windows only)

Plug-ins can also be used with other bitmap editors that can read Adobe's plug-in standard.

So what does the Black Box suite of plug-ins do? The Black Box filters "illustrate" a selection area you create in any of the programs that support the filters. These illustrations look like buttons, torn paper, whirls of color, drop shadows, and more. A demo version of the Cutout filter is included on the Companion CD-ROM, and of particular interest to anyone who makes Web graphics for a living is the Inner and Outer Bevel filter. We use this filter in the following example of building your basic button.

We need to acknowledge at this point that everyone who is interested in designing for the Web isn't necessarily an accomplished artist. For example, creating an elliptical selection area in a bitmap image to represent a button isn't artistically challenging, but the Web's a graphically competitive place, and sometimes you need to express an idea that your skills can't execute. This is why the WebKnobs font is included on the Companion CD-ROM. Web-Knobs is a collection of basic—and not so basic—geometric shapes, bundled in font format: TrueType and Type 1 versions for Windows and the Macintosh are included in EXAMPLES\CHAP03. There is no reason why a character from a typeface can't be used as a button: after the character's outline has been converted to pixel format, it then becomes a graphic like any other Web element, and loses its unique, proprietary font quality. Additionally, if you find that the following example suits your design needs, symbol fonts are easy to come by, and a Zapf Dingbat character can also become a handsome Web-page button.

If you have the Alien Skin II filters installed in an application on your machine, here's how to create instant "Web Knobs":

1. Load the Companion CD-ROM into your CD-ROM drive.

2. For Macintosh users, open the EXAMPLES\CHAP03 folder, then drag the WebKnobs folder on top of the System folder. Click on OK in the Attention box to allow the font information to be copied to the Fonts folder, and you're in business.

   Windows 3.1 users need to open the Fonts Utility in Control Panel and select WebKnobs from the EXAMPLES\CHAP03 directory on the Companion CD to copy the TrueType font to system. Windows 95 users can click on File | Add New Font in the Fonts Utility in Control Panel. If you'd like to install the Type 1 version instead of TrueType WebKnobs, you need to do this through Adobe Type Manager's control panel . . . and you need to own a copy of ATM version 3.02 or later.

3. Launch the application in which you use Alien Skin plug-ins. We're showing Photoshop in this section as the host application, but you can use the same steps in different, plug-in-capable applications.

4. Navigation buttons should be small. Therefore, choose a new file within the application that's no more than 100 pixels high or wide, at 72 pixels/inch resolution.

5. Choose the foreground color for the button from your application's color picker.

6. Choose the Type tool, and depending upon your application, choose the font size and type before or after making an insertion point for the text in your new file. In Figure 3-2, you can see Photoshop's Type Tool dialog box. We chose 72 points for the size of the text, because 72 points approximately equals 1 inch (a point of text is approximately equal to a pixel of screen resolution). Choose WebKnobs from the list of installed fonts, then type a character or two until you find a character that will suit your needs as a button.

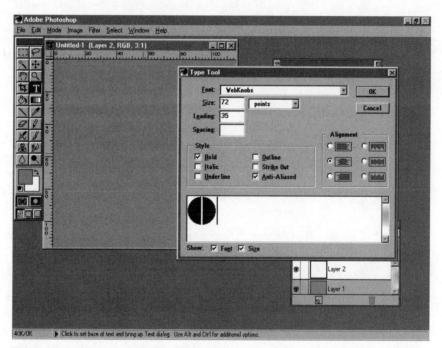

Figure 3-2: *Choose a foreground color for your button, then use the WebKnobs font to create the geometry!*

TIP

If you'd like a quick, graphical representation of a character in a symbol font, without the fuss of trial and error, there are utilities on the Macintosh and in Windows that eliminate guesswork. On the Macintosh, you can use the Apple Menu's Key Caps to look at a font character. However, Letraset offers a free Macintosh Character Chooser utility at http://www.esselte.com/letraset/productshowcase/typereference/CharacterChooser.hqx. Character Chooser's character window is large enough to get a good idea of the character you need, and Macintosh and Windows users can download a free "Font of The Month" when you visit the site, to boot!

Windows users can choose the Character Map utility in either Windows 95 or Windows 3.x to find a character you'd like to use as a button.

7. Once you've specified the character, *don't* deselect it! In Photoshop, Photo-Paint, and a few other applications, you can save selection information (the area inside the "marching ants") to a selection channel, often called an alpha channel. This selection information can then be recalled as often as you wish, and more importantly, the Alien Skin filters depend upon selection information to create their magic.

8. Choose Alien Skin from the Filters menu, then choose Inner Bevel 2.0.

9. As you can see in Figure 3-3, the Inner Bevel plug-in provides a preview window and a handsomely stocked preset list, in case you don't want to create a custom effect the first few times out. In this figure, the Highlight brightness is being tuned. This control is useful depending upon the foreground color you've chosen for the button—darker colors can take an increased brightness, while paler colors need less Highlight brightness to appear less washed out.

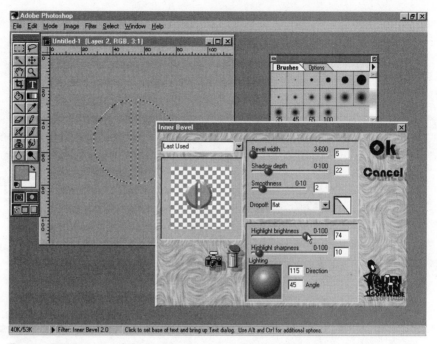

Figure 3-3: *Inner and Outer Bevel are two plug-ins that take an embossed effect to the level of photorealism.*

10. Click on OK, and you've got yourself a button like the pros use. In fact, many experienced graphic artists who've turned to the Web as a publishing vehicle have been using Alien Skin filters for button and headline elements for almost two years.

If your image editing application supports saved selections in channels, there are a number of refinements you can make to buttons created as this example demonstrates. Drop shadows and textured buttons are only two of the enhancements we'll cover in this chapter.

In Figure 3-4, you can see an entire page of buttons created using the Inner Bevel plug-in and WebKnobs. The drop-shadow effect will be discussed a little later in this chapter. The whole process took about 30 seconds, and the finished file, WEBKNOBS.GIF, is in the CHAP03 folder and can be edited to suit your Web graphics needs.

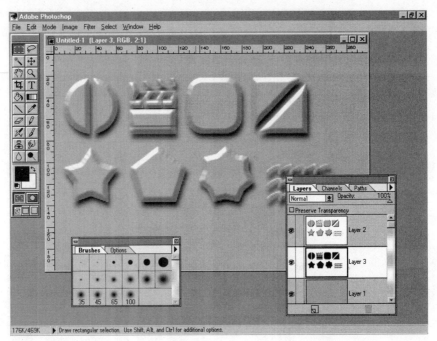

Figure 3-4: *Alien Skin filters should be in your arsenal of Web graphics tools if you need to create navigation buttons.*

Basically, the navigation buttons for The Monde Group's site were created the same way as the buttons in the previous example. A texture from Kai's Power Tools was used as a fill to simulate brushed metal, the Inner Bevel was applied, and then text was added after the emboss effect.

In the following section, we'll take a look at how scanned or other natural-looking textures can be edited so that a small sample can be seamlessly tiled across a background of any size.

Generating & Editing Textures

Because Netscape Navigator supports background images in HTML documents, you're no longer confined to specifying a uniform background color for your documents. However, it's a fundamental mistake to take any image you like based upon composition and define it as your Web page background. Backgrounds are usually (though not always) subordinate in their contribution to an overall piece. This strongly suggests that for most design purposes, a background image should be of muted tones and content that can be ignored without too much trouble. A background should support, not dominate a Web composition.

The format for background images supported by most browsers is GIF, and the chosen image will repeat as many times as necessary to fill the document window. JPEG format is supported by Navigator 2.0, but if a visitor doesn't use Navigator 2.0, they'll see a default color background instead of your graphic. You should therefore bear two things in mind when creating a background texture:

- The image should be small—50K should be the maximum; 35K would be better. The final size depends upon how happy you are with the load time for the image.

- Unless you're striving for an unusual artistic effect, the source image should repeat seamlessly; it should display no visible edges when it's tiled across the background of the document.

Using 2.5 inches by 2.5 inches by 72 ppi would yield a file of about 32K when saved to GIF's indexed color format, and this is a comfortable size to scan to or paint within. However, preventing an image from showing seams when it is tiled requires some thought and a trick or two.

INSTANT TEXTURES FROM TEXTUREMAKER

There are many outstanding texture-creation utilities and programs on the market today, but we're going to single one out in preparation for an upcoming example of how to remove the seams from a texture image. Adobe TextureMaker for the Macintosh (an OEM version for Windows is expected Fall 1996) creates extremely lifelike organic textures such as wood, marble, and other stones. The reason why we're showing TextureMaker here is that this program generates images quite like physical textures you'd scan: realistic and uncooperative when you need an image that seamlessly tiles!

Part of the trick of creating a natural-material background tile for a Web page is to increase the size of the visible details within the texture, where possible. If you're scanning an image of, say, some linen, set the sampling resolution to twice the finished image size, and use half the dimensions you'd planned on. The resultant image will have less visual content but more *detail* within the content. Exaggerating the texture helps the viewer recognize the texture, and presumably there will be enough *foreground* compositional interest to obscure the fact that this small sample is repeated across the page.

CD-ROM   The following example is an optional one: If you own TextureMaker, we'll walk you through the steps for creating some marble for the background of the ABOUT-US.HTM document for The Monde Group. If you don't have this app, MARBLE.TIF is provided in the CHAP03 folder of the Companion CD-ROM, or you can bring along a texture of your own when we get to the section on how to edit a texture into a seamless tile.

Here's how to generate some marble for the background image:

1. Launch TextureMaker, then choose File | New.

2. In the Standard Gallery dialog box, choose Green Marble from the Marbles list, then click on OK.

3. Choose File | Image size, then type **300** in the (pixels) Width field, type **150** in the (pixels) Height field, then click on OK. These dimensions, at 72 ppi, will create a 132K file, that when reduced from 3 color channels to a single channel indexed color GIF, will be about 44K. This is larger than the recommended 35K but still a size that will load fairly quickly when sent from a server, and the pixel dimensions make the math easier when we edit the texture.

4. You'll see in Figure 3-5 that the marble texture is made from five fractal algorithms (the Spots, Wood, and other icons toward the bottom left of the interface). Each of these components can be scaled. Click on Granite, then click the pull-down menu for Magnification, and choose 4x bigger (2x bigger is the default for this texture layer).

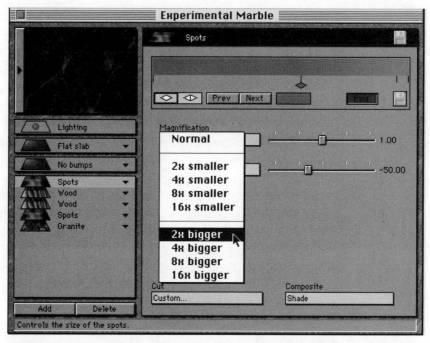

Figure 3-5: *TextureMaker offers controls for scaling image detail. Make the detail larger for a tiling Web background.*

5. Perform the previous step with the remaining layers. The layers are rendered from fractal calculations (*algorithms*), and fractals increase in image detail as you zoom in, so overall quality isn't sacrificed by increasing the layer resolution.

6. Choose Render | Render to File, then name the file, and save it as an uncompressed TIFF file. Click on OK. On a PowerMacintosh 8500, the rendering of the marble at 132K will take about a minute; 68K machines will render the image in less than 5 minutes. Close TextureMaker now, and open the image editor you use.

As mentioned earlier, regardless of how handsome a Texture-Maker file—or a scanned natural texture—appears, chances are that it will display its edges as it tiles across your Web-page background. The following section describes in detail how you correct this.

CREATING A SEAMLESS TILING GIF IMAGE

The secret to making a texture into a seamless tiling texture is to literally turn the image inside out. This is the first step; when the image's center becomes its outside edges, you're assured that repeating tiles will not display a seam. The second step is covering the areas currently on the *inside* of the edited image—this is where the former edges now lie, and usually the edge areas don't align with one another.

Creating an image whose areas have been shuffled inside out is not complicated if you have access to Corel Photo-Paint version 6 or later, or Adobe Photoshop. Both these programs feature the Offset command, which wraps an image within the image window in either a clockwise or counterclockwise direction. If you don't own either program, you can still perform the necessary first step of making a tiling image in any bitmap editor that offers a selection tool.

Here's how to turn the marble image (or one of your own) into a seamless tiling background texture:

1. In Photoshop, open the MARBLE.TIF image, then choose Filter | Other | Offset.

2. In the Offset dialog box, type **150** in the Horizontal field, type **75** in the Vertical field, and click the Wrap Around radio button. The MARBLE image is 300 X 150, so the values here for the Offset box are exactly half the original dimensions. It's important to measure your image prior to using the Offset command. In Figure 3-6, you'll notice that the inset illustration shows how the four quarters of the image are being rearranged. If you don't use Photoshop or Photo-Paint, you can create your own offset image by copying the four quarters of your original image to the locations numbered in Figure 3-6.

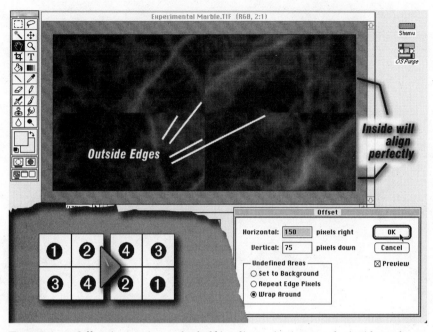

Figure 3-6: *Offsetting an image by half its dimensions turns the inside to the outside edges, and vice versa.*

3. Click on OK. Here comes Part 2 of the transformation.

4. With the Rubber Stamp tool (sometimes called a cloning brush in other applications), sample a point of clear area in the image that displays some of the same qualities as an area where there's an edge you need to retouch. In Photoshop, you Alt(Opt)+click over the sample area.

5. Brush over the edge with the Rubber Stamp tool. In Figure 3-7, you can see that a duplicate of the original marble has been created (Image | Duplicate) prior to the Offset command. The sample is taken, then the Rubber Stamp tool is applied to edge areas in the offset image.

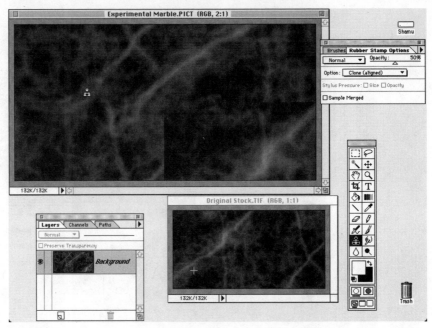

Figure 3-7: *By cloning original image areas over the edge marks in the texture image, you effectively remove visible seams when the image is tiled in Navigator.*

6. When you're through, choose File | Export | GIF 89a Export, and export a copy of the texture to GIF format. You're done!

The ABOUT-US document framed within the GROUP-M.HTML document contains "dummy text" (*greeking*) that forces the window to scroll by an additional frame's height when viewed at 640 X 480 monitor resolution. If you open this document in Navigator and scroll the window, you'll see that the marble tile (TILE.GIF) doesn't appear to have any edge marks, even though we know that the image is much smaller than the frame. Additionally, the marble was made darker, so that the text reverses off the marble more clearly.

You may choose to play with the tonal quality of a background so text is more legible, and we have a section in this chapter that addresses this issue.

If you check out the ABOUT-US.HTM document, you'll see that directly following the BACKGROUND attribute is the BGCOLOR tag, which specifies a dark blue as 004000 in hexidecimal code: it's Red:0, Green:64, and Blue:0 on a 256-shade color brightness scale. It's always a good idea to specify a color background even when you're tiling a background image; in this way, you have control over the composition if your images don't download properly. See Chapter 1, "Composing in HTML & NavGold," for more information on color as specified in an HTML document.

CREATING A "FLOATING" BUTTON

Alien Skin filters are not the only way to make navigation buttons for your Web site (they might be the *easiest*, however!). The WebKnobs font can be used in any application that uses system or Type 1 fonts, and to conclude our examination of The Monde Group's Web site, this section is devoted to the methods used to create the jump page from the home page. If you click on any of the buttons on the home page of The Monde Group, you'll notice that the button bitmap image is an image map (see Chapter 1, "Composing in HTML & NavGold"), and the jump page is under construction, regardless of the button you click on. The button in the center frame is referenced to return to the main document, as shown in Figure 3-8.

Figure 3-8: A link back to the page from which the visitor has jumped can be anything: hypertext or a graphic are most common.

The 3D button shown in the previous figure was created in Adobe Dimensions, a vector-based Macintosh product that comes with Illustrator 6 or can be purchased separately for under $100 street price. Chapter 4, "Working With Models," covers some of the more advanced techniques for adding rendered models to a Web page, but Dimensions makes the world of 3D graphics accessible for designers who feel more comfortable with 2D designing. Another vector-based 3D program that's made for both Macintosh and Windows is Ray Dream Inc.'s AddDepth. AddDepth goes for less than $50 street price and comes as CorelDEPTH in the Corel version 6 suite of applications.

In Figure 3-9, you can see that two symbols from the WebKnobs font have been combined, then extruded in Dimensions. The finished artwork is saved in Illustrator format and then imported to Photoshop to become a bitmap image. The BUCKBUTN.AI file is in the CHAP03 folder on the Companion CD-ROM, so you can follow the next example that covers background color mapping and the creation of a Gaussian drop shadow.

Figure 3-9: *Extruding a simple shape or text symbol can make a Web graphic leap off the page.*

As you'll see in the next section, a transparent GIF is not used as the button element on the Web page. Instead, the background color of the GIF image matches the background color defined for the HTML document within the center frame.

MATCHING COLOR BACKGROUNDS

It's most useful to have Photoshop handy for merging layers of image information, as the following example demonstrates, but if you understand the *principles* of what's going on here, you can use almost any image editor to get the same effect. In addition to the

Illustrator file of the button, BUCKBUTN.CDR, a CorelDRAW version 5 file is provided in the CHAP03 folder, and a very similar set of steps can be performed to create the button effect.

Here's how to make the drop-shadow dollar bill sign button:

1. In Photoshop, choose File | Open, then select the BUCKBUTN.AI file from the CHAP03 folder on the Companion CD-ROM.

2. The Rasterize Adobe Illustrator Format dialog box pops up. By default, the dimensions of the imported image are the same as they were in the application used to create the image. Therefore, leave the Height and Width fields alone (1.4 X 1.4 inches is a good size for the button); choose 72 as the pixels per inch Resolution, choose RGB Color Mode, then click on OK. It will take a moment or two for Photoshop to convert the vector information to bitmap format.

3. Once the image appears in the workspace, choose Image | Canvas Size, then enter **150** in both the Height and Width (in pixels) fields. You need some "play" around the foreground button to add a background and a drop shadow. Click on OK after changing the Canvas Size.

4. Double-click on the Layer 1 icon on the Layers palette, then type BUCKBUTTON in the Name field, and click on OK. Doing this will make the button layer easier to reference in the upcoming steps.

5. On the Layers palette (press F7 if the palette isn't onscreen), click on the new layer icon on the bottom left. Choose Multiply as the Mode in the New Layer dialog box, then click on OK.

6. Drag the new Layer 1 icon on top of the BUCKBUTTON icon on the Layers palette to move this layer behind the BUCKBUTTON layer.

7. Click on the BUCKBUTTON layer to make it the active layer.

8. Press Ctrl+Alt+T (Macintosh: Cmd+Opt+T) to select the opaque areas of the BUCKBUTTON layer.

9. With any selection tool (the Rectangular marquee tool is fine), hold Ctrl and Alt (Macintosh: Cmd+Opt), then drag

the selection area down by about 1/8 screen inches. The selection marquee moves, but not its contents (the button). You're repositioning the marquee to create a drop shadow.

10. Choose Select | Feather. Windows users of Photoshop version 3.0.4 or later can right-click to access the Feather command from the shortcut menu. In the Feather dialog box, type **3** in the Pixels field, then click on OK. See Figure 3-10.

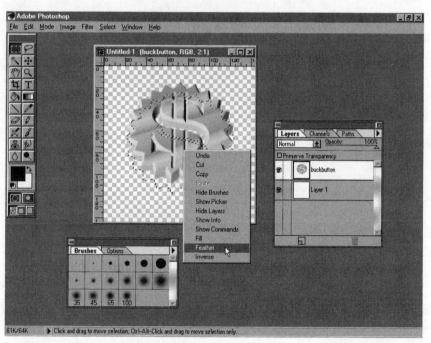

Figure 3-10: *Feathering the selection border will create a soft shadow edge for the button.*

11. Type D; this restores the foreground/background current colors to black foreground and white background.

12. Click on the Layer 1 icon on the Layers palette.

13. Hold Alt (Opt), then press the Delete key. This floods the selection area on Layer 1 with foreground color, and you now have your drop shadow.

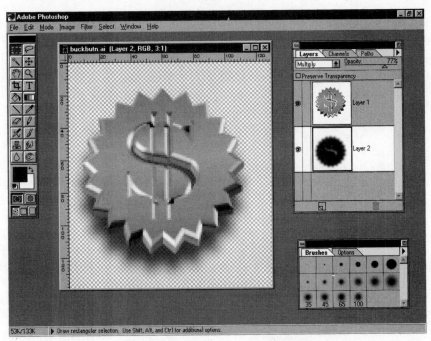

Figure 3-11: *You can create a soft, Gaussian-type drop shadow for your buttons by feathering and filling an outline on a layer in Photoshop.*

14. Press Ctrl(Cmd)+D to deselect the selection marquee, then save the file to hard disk as PANIC.PSD. Then close Photoshop.

The advantage to using Photoshop for this button-construction assignment is twofold. First, Illustrator files that contain no background elements are interpreted by Photoshop as being clear. You therefore can specify a background color for the button image at any time in the future. Second, you can maintain separate elements, exactly as you can in a drawing program, by the use of layers. Corel Photo-Paint and Picture Publisher also support layered bitmap images.

SCOUTING FOR A BACKGROUND COLOR

As mentioned earlier, Navigator supports the use of background colors, but the specification for colors within an HTML document is expressed in *hexadecimal* numbers. Hexadecimal code is based on a 16-digit system and include values 0, 1 through 9, and characters A through F. It's a more efficient method for storing data that would otherwise need to be written as straight binary, ones and zeroes . . . neither system, though, is the most intuitive of color specs for the graphics designer. For example, our target color here for the background is #8080FF—which is not exactly the way you'd usually spec pale violet. Fortunately, Navigator Gold's Editor allows you to choose from a color picker to define the background color of the document, and it's the RGB values, not the hexadecimals, that need to be defined in the PANIC.PSD image, because Photoshop doesn't speak hexadecimal.

Here's how to apply the same background color to the "panic button" as the background of the GO-BACK.HTML document, which is displayed in the center frame of the POUND, BUCK, and OTHER HTML documents in this Web site:

1. Open Navigator Gold and make sure you don't have a live connection going (close out of PPP connections if you're on the Macintosh, or click on Cancel in the connection dialog box in Windows).

2. Choose File | New Document. A blank document appears in Navigator Gold's Editor.

3. Choose Properties | Document. On the Colors/Background tab, click on Use Custom Colors. In Windows, the system color picker appears. On the Macintosh, the system color picker pops up.

4. For this example, let's assume that The Monde Group wants a pale violet background surrounding the frame that holds the return button (what the PANIC.PSD image will become). In Windows, click on the sample swatch shown in Figure 3-11. Now click on the Define Custom Colors button, and write down the RGB value for this color (R: 128, G: 128, and B: 255). Macintosh users will have a little tougher time matching a Navigator background to the background of the button image here, because the system color picker doesn't correspond to the same increments of

RGB values as measured in Netscape's hexadecimal calculations, or in Photoshop's own color picker. To define the same pale violet used in this example, choose the Apple RGB color space, then enter **50**, **50**, and **100** in the respective RGB percentage fields.

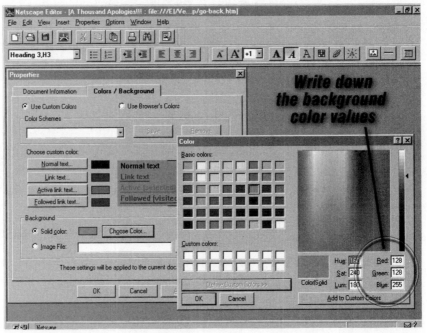

Figure 3-12: *Write down the component colors of a Web-page background for use later in defining an image background color.*

TIP

If you're composing a Web page on the Macintosh, to attain the freedom to choose any color value for backgrounds, Photoshop is invaluable. Pick the color you want from the color picker within Navigator Gold, write down the percentages, then when defining a color in Photoshop for an image background, choose File | Properties | General, and select the Apple color picker for use in Photoshop. You can then easily match the Navigator background color to any image.

5. Exit the document without saving, then launch Photoshop, and load PANIC.PSD.

6. Add a layer to the bottom of this file, using the method described earlier for the drop shadow.

7. Click on the foreground color on the toolbox, then type in the values you wrote down in the RGB color area of Photoshop's color picker. See Figure 3-13. Macintosh users should choose the Apple color picker from File | Preferences | General, then enter the values you wrote down from Navigator Gold's Editor window.

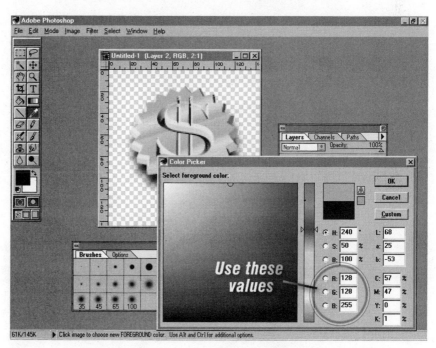

Figure 3-13: *Match the numeric RGB values in Photoshop to the values you specified in Navigator's Editor.*

8. Click on OK, then press Ctrl(Cmd)+A to select the entire new layer.

9. Press Alt(Opt)+Delete to fill the area with foreground color, then press Ctrl(Cmd)+D to deselect the area.

10. You might want to perform a little tweaking to the image at this point. First, if you select the drop-shadow layer and drag the Opacity slider to the left on the Layers palette, you can change the opacity of the drop shadow. Also, it might be a good idea to add some text below the button to indicate that this is indeed a button that sends you back to the parent document. Fancy buttons are nice, but if they interfere with the navigation of the document, it's wasted effort.

11. Choose File | Export, then choose GIF89a Export. Make sure the Interlaced box is checked, then click on OK. In Figure 3-14, you can see the Preview window for the export, which is a nice feature to access before clicking on OK: it allows you to see how a multilayered image is flattened for GIF format and how much, if any, dithering is applied due to color reduction.

Figure 3-14: *A layered image is flattened and color-reduced to meet the file re-quirements of the GIF format.*

12. You're done! You can use Navigator Editor's Insert | Image command to see how well the exported image's background matches the color you specified. It should be flawless.

CREATING BUTTONS IN DRAWING PROGRAMS

If your experience with computer graphics is more toward the vector drawing program than bitmap editing, you can still create a button graphic as in the preceding example, and it'll work exactly the same as the version described in this section.

Start with a button shape, then use the drawing program's blending capability to create the drop shadow. Begin with a shape identical to the outline of your button, then duplicate the shape. Fill the first outline with black, then fill the duplicate with the same color value as the background you'll decide upon. In this example, the pale violet is R: 128, G: 128, and B: 255.

Slightly offset the two shapes, position the black one directly beneath the button, and position the pale violet shape to the right and bottom of the first by about a half-inch. Use the Blend feature to create intermediate shapes containing transitional colors. Then create a rectangle slightly larger than the group of shapes, and place it to the back of all objects. Fill the rectangle with the background color, then export all objects to GIF format. Remember to pay attention to the size of the graphic (keep it small), and choose 72 ppi as the resolution. Depending upon the capability of your drawing program, you may need a program such as GraphicConverter or Paint Shop Pro to make the GIF image an *interlaced* GIF image.

TIPS ON ALIGNING GRAPHICS

We need to address the tag styles and attributes—parts of the integration process required when composing a Web site—that went into The Monde Group's site. The BUCK, POUND, and OTHER HTML documents are structured with three vertical frames of fixed width (FRAMESET COLS=33%,33%,*). The SCROLLING attribute didn't need to be used here, because the documents displayed in the frames were constructed to contain elements that fit into the frames at 640 X 480 viewing resolution without scroll bars. The left and right frames don't scroll because they contain only a background GIF image (SORRY.GIF in SORRY.HTM). However, the GO-BACK.HTM document could sprout a vertical scroll bar if there were an excess of text in the document, or if the PANIC.GIF file were any larger. So the trick here was to limit the amount of text and the size of the graphic to fit inside a frame displayed on the smallest video resolution.

There's another interesting characteristic of the FRAMESET command that you can use in your own documents. Notice that there is no ROWS attribute in the FRAMESET to BUCK, POUND, or OTHER. By manually adding breaks (<BR>) to the headline in the GO-BACK document, the width of the text is always kept inside of the frame column width, and the <DIV ALIGN=CENTER> attribute surrounding the text keeps the text centered relative to the button image. The only thing that could spoil this neat arrangement is if the viewer has defined a huge base font size for *their* copy of Navigator. However, the chances of this are slim, because doing this displays *most* documents at a size that's extremely irritating.

MAKING TIDY JUMPS

If you've been surfing to graphically rich sites, occasionally you'll notice that jumping from one page to another leaves the original copy of Netscape loaded on your desktop. It's possible that if you jump, then return, too many times within a site, you could in theory have as many instances of Netscape on your desktop as your system memory allows! The occurrence of multiple instances of Navigator is mostly a result of frames being targeted to new windows instead of reusing the current window or a different window. As the designer/creator of an HTML document, you can use different TARGET attribute commands to specify how and when document windows are created or reused.

The problem with jumping from an HTML document contained in a frame is that the document you are jumping to, by default, is displayed in the same frame and replaces the document you were viewing. This is because the frame is only the *container* for the document's linked page—Netscape interprets this as, "show me the link I am going to in the same location (document window)"— and the window in this case happens to be a frame.

Therefore, to avoid linking a document you want to display full-screen to a small frame, and to avoid littering the viewer's desktop with multiple Navigator windows, you can use the TARGET attribute. In the BUTTONS.HTM document (which displays in a tiny frame), TARGET="_TOP" is appended to the referenced document. TARGET="_TOP" is called a *magic target name*; all target names preceded by an underscore perform "magical" things. This magic target name tells Navigator to replace the contents of the current Navigator window (which in the example used here holds the entire frameset of documents described by GROUP-M.HTM) with the new document you are calling. If you check out the BUTTONS.HTM document, you'll see that its usage is:

```
<area shape="rect" coords="26,13,137,86" href="buck.htm"
TARGET="_top">
```

The hyperlink reference, BUCK.HTM, when modified with the TARGET="_TOP" attribute, jumps the visitor to a full-screen view of the BUCK.HTM document; it would get pretty cluttered if the three-frame window displayed within the BUTTONS.HTM frame! The AREA SHAPE attribute in the preceding line is a reference to an image map's coordinates; we explain the use of client-side image maps in Chapter 1, "Composing in HTML & NavGold."

Additionally, the TARGET="_parent" attribute is used in the POUND, BUCK, and OTHER documents, and this is another handy magic target name. This is a reference to the immediate FRAMESET parent of the document, which is the GROUP-M.HTM document.

TIP

"_PARENT" and "_TOP" are only two of the magic target name attributes. See Chapter 1, "Composing in HTML & NavGold," for more information on magic targets.

The material covered so far should give you a good beginning to more advanced Web-page composition, from both an HTML and an artistic viewpoint. However, we realize that every Web page is as unique as its creator's personality, and we have suggested rather than shown you precisely how to create a specific element. Therefore, the following bonus sections continue the special effects flavor of this chapter, and give you the how-tos for *incredibly* advanced, strange, and wonderful stuff!

SPECIALIZED BITMAP ELEMENTS

You already know the fundamentals for creating tiling Web-page backgrounds and buttons, and the following sections detail how to perform variations on a theme.

CREATING A "SIGNATURE" BACKGROUND

This effect is commonly seen on designer luggage and handbags, but its use as a graphical element anywhere can provide visual reinforcement of the sponsor of a document. To create a diagonally cascading logo, signature, or symbol, you'd want to follow the same techniques as those shown for creating seamless textures earlier in this chapter. In Figure 3-15, a simple logo has been created on a layer in Photoshop. The canvas area measures 316 pixels wide by 80 pixels high; and the logotype is positioned in the center, toward the top of the canvas, one or two pixels from the top edge. You can find the example source-image in the CHAP03 folder on the Companion CD-ROM if you'd like to play along in this example.

Figure 3-15: *MY-BIZ.PSD contains the configuration for a logo you want to cascade as a Web document background.*

You'll notice that the logo is on a layer on top of a neutral background, and that there is a saved selection channel in the image that describes the location of the logo within the image window. The trick here is to use the Offset command on only the logo, then create a second logo after the Offset command has displaced the original. Here's how to do this:

1. Divide the dimensions of the image window by two. In this example, the width would then be 158, and the height would be 40.

2. Choose Filters | Other, then choose Offset.

3. Type **158** in the Horizontal field, and type **40** in the Vertical field. Make sure that Wrap Around is checked, then click on OK, as shown in Figure 3-16.

Figure 3-16: *The Offset command only affects the current layer. The background layer and alpha channel won't shift.*

4. Press Ctrl(Cmd)+D to change the current foreground color to default (black), Alt(Opt)+click on the channel #4 title on the Layers palette, then hold Alt(Opt) and press Delete. This fills the saved selection area, loaded on the top layer of the image with foreground color. See Figure 3-17.

Figure 3-17: *Fill the saved selection area above the logo layer with foreground color. Only the foreground image moved during Offset, and not the saved selection.*

5. Press Ctrl(Cmd)+D to deselect the marquee, and you're basically done!

This is a good checkpoint before you invest too much time in this logo creation. Ask yourself, "Am I going to use light or dark text as the foreground to my Web page?" You see, black or dark text really won't be legible when placed above this image, because it's too dark; being a neutral color, it's also too light to support white or lighter text.

It's a serious mistake to provide artwork or post personal creations that fight with the text content of your document. This is when all designers, including the author, must take the perhaps unwelcome step of editing the background creation—it has to take on less contrast and become either lighter or darker to support text. In this example, we'll go with black text, and therefore we need to make the background lighter. In Photoshop, and most other image editors, you can either choose the Brightness/Contrast controls, or go with a tone map command, if offered (Photoshop calls this the Levels command).

In Figure 3-18, you can see that some greeking has been typed on a new layer on top of the logo, and that the current editing layer which contains the cascading logo is being targeted with some tonal adjustments. By increasing the Black Point in the image, you're specifying that the darkest shades in the design are actually lighter than the darkest possible tone—you're selectively removing contrast from the design. Click on OK when the text above the image is legible.

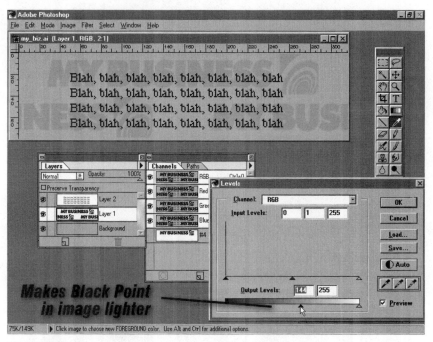

Figure 3-18: *Test the brightness and contrast of your background image before you finalize it.*

You can use the GIF89a Export filter now to export the logo. If you'd like to load MY-BIZ.HTM from the CHAP03 folder on the Companion CD-ROM, you'll see a single-page Web document similar to that in Figure 3-19. The logo will cascade endlessly, for as much text as you need to place in the document.

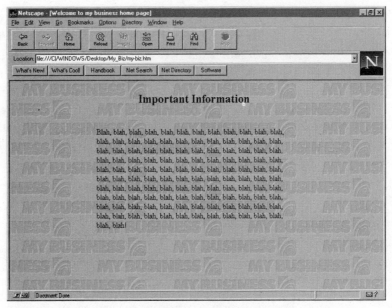

Figure 3-19: *Reinforce your company name, without overstating it, by using a faint wallpaper-background image.*

You'll also notice that a slight emboss was applied to the logo in the preceding figure. This effect can lead to some visual distraction from the foreground content of your document unless you apply a very small amount of embossing. You should perform the emboss effect *before* tonally adjusting the image (most image editors support this effect).

TIP

You'll also notice in the MY-BIZ document that the text is confined to a narrow, justified column. How do you do this?

Create a transparent GIF image of a single color (you can use black), whose transparency value is the same color. In other words, create a clear pixel image. The text is within a table in the MY-BIZ document; the table is 3 columns, and the GIF image (SPACER1.GIF in this document) is placed in the left and right columns. SPACER1.GIF is 150 pixels wide, and 2 pixels high.

➡

You need to experiment a little with the width of the GIF image to shrink or expand the text cell in the middle column of the table. If you load a low-resource image editor such as Paint Shop Pro or Graphic-Converter, you can fine-tune the width of the transparent GIF in the background while you view changes to the document. However, NavGold's Editor initially writes the correct size for the graphic into the HTML document, and you might need to change the width and height attributes for the image in the HTML document before reloading the document and viewing the changes.

BUILDING A TEXTURE ON A BUDGET

Applications costing hundreds of dollars are frequently referenced in the examples in this book, and although we feel they are common applications for graphics designers, we also realize that not every Web author is a graphics designer! There are several graphics applications for both Windows and the Macintosh that can do amazing things if you're just getting into graphics software. Paint Shop Pro (for Windows), for example, is an inexpensive shareware program that's feature rich.

Here's a short example of how to create a nice, professional texture using only the features found in the shareware version of Paint Shop Pro version 3.12 (included on the Companion CD-ROM):

1. In Paint Shop Pro, open a new file, specify 100 pixels in Width, 100 pixels in Height, and choose 16.7 million colors (24-bit) as the Image Type. Click on OK.

2. Use the Flood Fill tool to color the image any color you'd like. You can change the overall color later.

3. Choose Image | Special Filters, then choose Add Noise.

4. Increase the percentage spin box value to about 38, click the Random radio button, then click on OK. See Figure 3-20.

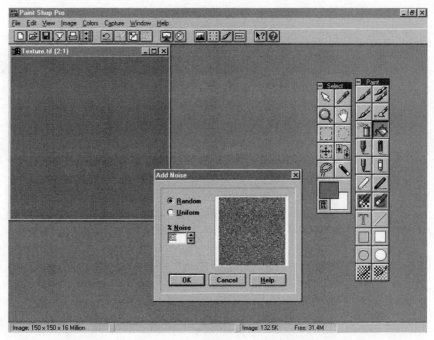

Figure 3-20: *Noise added to a solid background can help create a texture.*

5. Choose Image I Special Filters, then choose Emboss. There is no preview or way to specify the emboss effect, but as you can see in Figure 3-21, the Emboss filter definitely adds visual interest to noisy pixels.

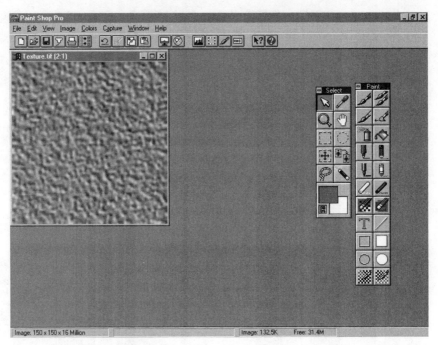

Figure 3-21: *Embossed noise can take on the appearance of rough stone, sandpaper, or other real-life texture.*

Optionally, you can blur the resulting image to make the texture appear like leather or an aerial photograph, and you can use the Colors|Colorize command in Paint Shop Pro to give the texture an even hue.

Or, if you're *really* on a budget, the Companion CD-ROM contains many sample textures created by the author for playing with in documents of your own. Check out the BOUTONS/TEXTURES folder; the documents are all in TIF format, which is platform-independent, and these images can be easily converted to GIF89a interlaced format.

EFFORTLESS SEAMLESS TEXTURES

Two programs—one biplatform and one Macintosh-only—are inexpensive solutions to creating out-of-this-world textures. And besides the modest price for either (under $130 street price), these programs can generate seamless textures that can benefit from your artistic taste, but are not demanding on your artistic talent.

Alien Skin TextureShop is a stand-alone Macintosh application that can also install into Photoshop as a plug-in, and its strong suit is that it can create textures that look, well . . . *alien!* TextureShop might not be appropriate for a Fortune 500 company's Web site, but if you want to get attention in a very colorful way, Texture-Shop provides everything you need in one package. In Figure 3-22, you can see the interface for TextureShop. Many preset bins of textures come with the program, and by dragging a texture from the Preview window (at bottom) into the Mutate window at top, then clicking on the Mutate button, 15 variations on the fractal algorithm that defines the texture are created.

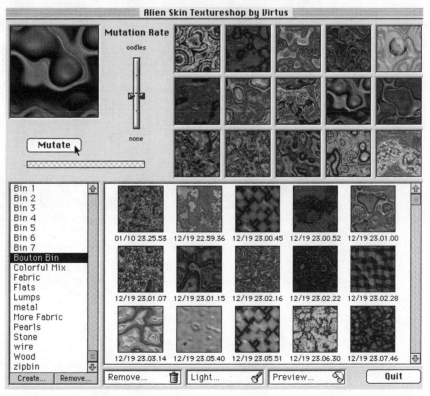

Figure 3-22: *You can create mild or wild variations on a texture preset by adjusting the Mutation Rate slider.*

If you drag a texture thumbnail into the Preview field, you move to a full-screen view of the texture. And you can save the texture to PICT or TIFF format from this window view. In Figure 3-23, you can see the cropping box being dragged to choose the area of the texture to be saved to bitmap format. By holding down the Shift key, you constrain the cropping box to equal dimensions (you can also type values in the X and Y fields), and by decreasing the Feature Size percentage, you can include more detail in the saved selection.

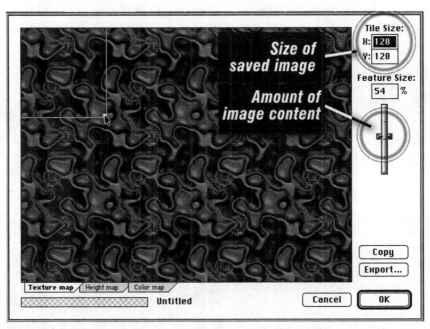

Figure 3-23: *A variation of a texture can be saved to almost any size as a PICT or a TIFF file.*

The beauty of Alien Skin TextureShop is that the saved file seamlessly tiles when used as a Web background; there's no need to offset or clone in edges—the fractal algorithms that produce the textures make every texture seamless.

KPT TEXTURE EXPLORER & OPTIMAL COLOR PALETTES

Although Metatools (formerly HSC Software) has released Kai's Power Tools version 3 for both the Macintosh and Windows, you might want to check out version 2 of the Texture Explorer as a resource for seamless tiling textures. KPT 3's Texture Explorer features a new enhancement: you can generate a nonrepeating texture of almost any size (depending upon your system RAM). Although this is a wonderful feature for desktop publishing people, you need an image that's small and seamless for use as a Web background image.

Version 2 of Texture Explorer is included with version 3, and if you've upgraded, chances are that Texture Explorer 2 is still somewhere on your system. Kai's Power Tools work with a number of image editors that accept Adobe standard plug-ins, and here's how you can create a seamless tiling texture for a Web graphic:

1. In the host application, create a new file 256 pixels in Height and 256 pixels in Width, and 72 pixels/inch resolution. Canvas color is not important here.

2. Choose KPT 2.0 Extensions, Texture Explorer 2.0.

3. Choose from the preset list, or click on any of the mutation tree balls to create texture changes. The center texture window (nested within the smaller 12 preview windows) displays the current texture.

4. When you've decided on a texture you like (this may take several clicks on the mutation tree), click and hold on the center texture window. Choose 256 X 256 from the drop-down menu, as shown in Figure 3-24.

Figure 3-24: *To create a seamless texture image, choose the tile size that corresponds to the image size.*

TIP

If you find a texture shape you like, but are unhappy with the colors in Texture Explorer 2.0, click on the color strip below the Help button. The drop-down menu features Gradient Designer 2.0 as the first menu item. Select it, and you'll open the Gradient Designer window, where you can choose a different color scheme. Click on OK, and you'll be transported back to the Texture Designer.

   5. Click on OK. The texture fills the new image window. This texture will seamlessly tile as a background image.

Fractal Design Painter, shown in this example, has an interesting native feature under the Effects menu called Apply Surface Texture. This filter creates shading in an image to emphasize lighter image areas and add shadows to darker image areas. In effect, the Apply Surface Texture creates a simulated 3D relief to any image. In Figure 3-25, we're adding this embellishment to the image created in KPT Texture Explorer 2.0. The Apply Surface Texture command (under Effects), does not alter the seamless tiling quality of the texture.

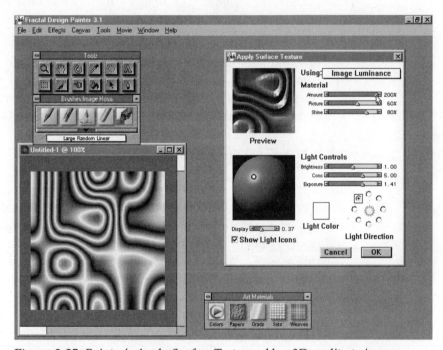

Figure 3-25: *Painter's Apply Surface Texture adds a 3D quality to images.*

TIP

Adobe Gallery Effects, volume I, and Photoshop can also apply a 3D quality by mapping lighting effects to an image based on the image's original tonal qualities (luminance). The Gallery Effects plug-in is called Emboss. Photoshop's Lighting Effects filter (under Filters\Render) can be used to produce an engraved look: To use the Lighting Effects filter for the purposes of embossing, copy a color channel to a new (alpha) channel in the original image, then in the RGB color view of *the image, choose the Lighting Effects filter. Choose #4 from the Texture channel drop-down list, and adjust the default light so it illuminates the image in the preview window but doesn't cast shadows in any direction (which would spoil the seamless tiling effect). A good choice of light for "flat" lighting is the Directional Light type.*

Adjust the Height slider from Flat to Mountainous, then click on OK. Instant 3D texture!

Now that you have your texture, it's important to decide whether it's going to be lighter or darker than the text that goes in front of it; and there's another consideration to keep in mind: how many colors does the texture need to be when it is saved in the GIF format?

COLOR DEPTH OF GIF IMAGES

In Chapter 2, "Vector-to-Bitmap Conversions," we discussed the indexed format of GIF images: how they differ from color channel images, and why they have a color limitation of 256 unique values. However, simply because the upper threshold of color capability is 256, does not mean that you are obliged to fill every available color slot. Here's where you have the chance to make your Web page load more quickly and not sacrifice image quality.

Photoshop, GraphicConverter for Macintosh, Paint Shop Pro (Windows), Corel Photo-Paint, Fractal Design Painter, and other image editors allow the user to specify the color depth as well as the number of pixels in the single indexed channel of GIF, TIFF, and other bitmap formats. What you gain by reducing the color capability of the saved file is a smaller color palette.

As an example, the MAZE.TIF image created with Texture Explorer and Fractal Painter is in the CHAP03 folder on the Companion CD-ROM. The image, although saved to the TIF format which can hold 16.7 million unique color values, only contains 42 unique colors. Synthetic images, even realistic-looking ones, often contain far fewer colors than you'd imagine. In Photoshop, if you convert the image to Indexed color (Mode | Indexed Color), the dialog box offers 42 as the value to which the file format will be reduced, and the Palette is set to Exact, which means no dithering will occur. This means that a GIF file saved to a 42-color palette can be read by Navigator more quickly than an image with a 256-color palette, with no reduction in color quality.

You can obtain the same savings from Paint Shop Pro. Choose Colors | Decrease Color Depth, then choose X colors (8-bit). In the Decrease Colors dialog box, enter **42** in the Number of Colors field, choose Error Diffusion as the Color Reduction method, then click on OK. You'll note that Paint Shop Pro produces a *slightly* dithered pattern in the saved image, because Paint Shop Pro depends upon the Windows color palette, and cannot perform adaptive resampling of colors the way Photoshop does. Photoshop does not depend upon the system color model for color calculations.

Fractal Painter will not tell you how many unique values are in an RGB image, but it does offer two very sophisticated ways of color reduction that are so subtle, the viewer probably will not notice any dithering. Choose File | Save As, then choose the GIF format from the Save File as Type drop-down list. In the Export box, you can choose from the unique number of colors in the saved palette, choosing multiples of 2 (16 colors = 4 bits/pixel, 32 colors = 5 bits/pixel, and so on). You can also choose either a color-reduction method of Quantization (which produces no dithering, but can cause harsh color transition areas if the image has many colors) or Dithering. Additionally, both Painter and Paint Shop Pro can save to Interleaved GIF format, so the background immediately begins to appear in Navigator's browser window.

In Figure 3-26, you can see GraphicConverter for the Macintosh in action. The MAZE image will be reduced to what GraphicConverter detects to be the minimal number of unique colors in the image.

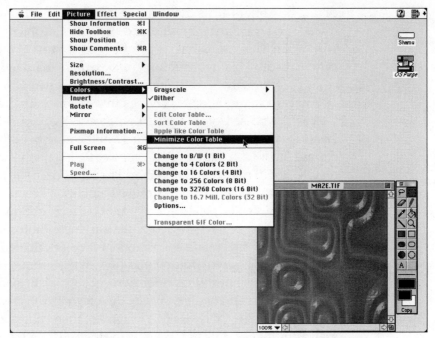

Figure 3-26: *GraphicConverter and other applications can shrink the size of the color table of an image saved in GIF format.*

TIP

If you believe that your foreground content in a Web page will far outweigh the background interest, you might try reducing a background image's unique colors to 16, or 4 bits/pixel. Use dither diffusion as the method of color reduction, and see how it looks on a copy of your file. You'll pick up more download speed and knock a few bytes off the stored size of the image.

In Figure 3-27, you can see the MAZE image loaded as a background in the BY-BIZ Web page. It's not intrusive; it definitely tiles without visible seams; and it's a small file that loads into the browser quickly (23K saved to disk).

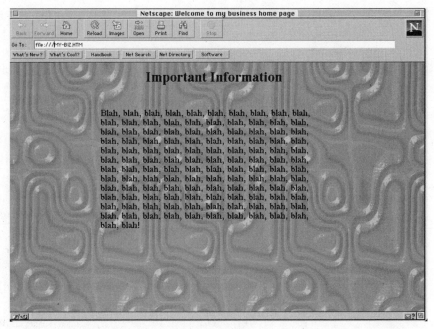

Figure 3-27: *KPT's Texture Explorer is a good choice of filters for producing exotic, seamless tiling images.*

MAKING A HUGE GRAPHIC INTO A TINY FILE

We've emphasized a method or two for paring back the file size of several graphics in this chapter for a reason. There's nothing sadder than building a masterpiece, only to find that you can't get it out the studio door because it's too large! However, there will be an occasion when you'll want to make a graphic large, dimensionally, to create a special effect, and this is where your new understanding of color reduction can really come into play.

The example that follows is a real-life assignment. Carter Downer, a gifted programmer and HTML author, came to me with a stumper: He needed to place text on a graphic for a Web site. But the text had to be text, not a graphic, because the site was frequently being updated. So making text a bitmap element of the underlying graphic was out of the question. Additionally, Carter had a *specific* graphic in mind; and not a pleasant background tiling texture that hinted at wood or marble. The concept was to let the viewer see virtual store goods on a placard, not unlike an illustration of a menu.

CD-ROM

The solution was to build a 1024-pixel wide by 600-pixel high graphic, and use it as a background tiling image (load SPECIALS.HTM in the CHAP03/SPECIALS folder to see the document). This solves the problem of getting the image to begin at the top of the page (placed images don't start at the top of the browser window, but background images can), and the size ensures that even visitors running 1024 X 768 resolution won't see the image tile horizontally.

Now, an RGB image of this size weighs in at 1.75MB, so visitors would probably never patronize the virtual store due to impatience. However, I found that dithering the image down to 4 bits/pixel reduced the image's size to 34K, which loads at an acceptable speed. In fact, visitors wonder why the huge graphic fills the browser so quickly.

Use of contrasting colors in the original image helped pull off the illusion. There were actually very few original colors in the illustration, but they display contrast against one another, and this subtly suggests that there's a lot of color in the image. Also, you'll notice in Figure 3-28, the clipboard for "Today's Specials" is fairly squat when compared to an actual clipboard. Another trick: viewers will never see the entire clipboard, even at 1024 X 768 viewing resolution, because Navigator's browser window is only 596 pixels tall at 1024 X 768 viewing resolution.

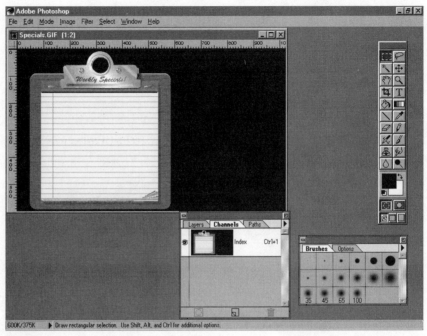

Figure 3-28: *Because the color palette for SPECIALS.GIF is only 16 unique values, this large image loads as quickly as a smaller one of higher color capability.*

Because the clipboard image tiles as a background element, the transparent GIF spacer trick was used in the same way as for MYBIZ Web page. A completely transparent 110-pixel wide by 2-pixel high image is inserted in the left of three table columns in the SPECIALS.HTM document. This pushes the text 110 pixels further from the left of the screen than the table padding specifies. The 110-pixel amount was arrived at by trial and error: the width of the image was changed, and the document was reloaded until a satisfactory centering of the text against the background was achieved. Inline bullets were added before every menu item, and a hard break (<BR>) was placed between each line.

If you'd like to create text that floats on top of a graphic, you might want to create a three-column table and insert a spacer graphic in both the left *and* the right columns. A right column spacer isn't required in this document, because the text was carefully measured to fit within the width of the underlying clipboard graphic. Long text lines without breaks will most likely run off the right of the graphic if you don't use either breaks or a transparent image as a spacer in the right column.

In Figure 3-29, you can see what happens when the clipboard tiling background repeats. It creates a second menu on the page, because the text is longer than a single screen. This potential problem was solved by a number of hard breaks between the first and second block of copy. The exact number of breaks depends upon the height of the background graphic.

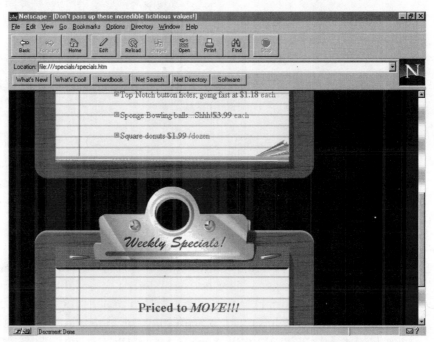

Figure 3-29: *A menu can contain an endless supply of items if the menu is a tiling background graphic.*

MOVING ON

In Chapter 4, "Working With Models," we continue our search for the perfect pixel image for the Web, but we explore a new dimension, specifically that of modeling and rendering programs. Modeling applications have reached the price point where you can indeed afford to create your personal edition of *Toy Story*, and the current crop of 3D programs have a shallow learning curve. As an extra perk, many modeling programs can generate animations and VRML, so a peek into modeling applications before Chapters 5 and 6 will be time well spent. The world is round, cyberspace is deep, and Chapter 4 adds the Z-axis to your Web graphics vocabulary!

4 Working With Models

Although the verb "modeling" might bring architectural CAD work to mind, software manufacturers and enhanced processing capabilities have brought power entertainment industry tools into common use. Realistic dimensional objects, landscapes, even human figures that once required a RISC-based graphics workstation (such as an SGI or SUN mini-computer) can now be created on the Macintosh or Windows platform. Modeling applications operate a little differently than more conventional paint or draw programs, but there is a definite connection between the two. So, if you're ready to take the next step in visualization techniques for documents, this chapter shows you how to navigate, create, and convert models in the world of 3D computer graphics for use on the Web.

3D: A NEW DIMENSION OF COMMUNICATION

A distinction must be made at the outset of your modeling adventures in this chapter between "dimensional" objects and "3D." As popularized in the late 1950s, the term *3D* referred to motion pictures that were produced using two cameras slightly offset to record a parallax view of scenes. The film was then taken from each camera and encoded in such a way that one film strip contained graphical information blocking information from the other strip. The audience of the resulting 3D movie would then don cardboard glasses with special lenses that provided a view of only one film projection for each eye. Then, if you were lucky, the two film projectors would converge the film strips on a screen, and a monster, a knife, or some other object meant to provoke a reaction would appear to come out of the screen.

Today, the technology of projecting encoded, separate views of a scene then letting the viewer decode the information to produce "stereo vision" is still alive and well. But "3D" in this traditional sense has nothing to do with creating dimensional, lifelike designs. We'll use the term *3D* in connection with modeling throughout this chapter, but it does *not* refer to bad science fiction movies or the use of red and blue cellophane in cardboard frames.

Modeling applications are intended to give the graphics designer near-total control over conveying an idea in physical form to the audience. It's helpful to think of modeling programs as a virtual world in which you work creating scenes filled with objects, atmosphere, and lighting. This virtual world within a modeling application is a proprietary one, however; very few modeling applications can create a finished file that can be shared with others who don't own the same application. But most modeling applications allow you to *render* a view—from almost any viewpoint—and you can then share this "snapshot" of your virtual world with anyone who can view a .GIF, .TIF, .JPEG, Targa, or other graphics file format on their machine.

The author is a self-confessed "modeling freak," but my inspiration for creating dimensional designs comes from a frustration with which perhaps you too can identify as a professional who presents concepts to an audience through graphics.

Although its original intention was to provide hyperlinks between text-based documents, the World Wide Web has become a multimedia showcase. And a large part of new plug-in support for Navigator has to do with multiple views of data: spreadsheets can be viewed graphically, and VRML documents can be flown through. New plug-ins meet the demand from professionals for expressing an idea that goes beyond text-based or flat-plane graphics. As a designer, I haven't given up my "2D" draw and paint applications but instead use the dimensional aspect of modeling applications *in combination* with text, paintings, and drawings to create a multimedia experience.

As a Web designer, you've already made the commitment to learning a new form of expression. The following thoughts are made as a precursor to "thinking in 3D"—the first step needed to make modeling a rewarding and productive task.

MULTIPLE RETURNS ON A
SINGLE MODELING INVESTMENT

The simple reality is that if you're going to invest time creating something, your returns on an assignment can be greatly enhanced if not one but *many* different views of your creation can be generated. This is the primary, compelling reason to add modeling to your repertoire of computer graphics tools.

When you draw a scene in a 2D drawing or painting program, modifying the audience's viewpoint of the scene requires that you illustrate the scene an additional time for each new view. In contrast, a simple scene containing models can be manipulated to present a different viewpoint with *no* need to create additional artwork.

BETTER COMMUNICATION TO THE AUDIENCE

Designers frequently "overillustrate" a piece, adding embellishments in an attempt to visually communicate a very precise thought. In a lot of these situations, what the designer is *actually* doing is trying to wring something out of the application that it's simply not capable of offering. If you want to convey photorealism to an audience, the right tool is one that offers built-in photorealism!

In Figure 4-1, the inset image is a collection of paths intended to represent a still life of some fruit. As you can see, it lacks something and requires a moment or two to recognize as the image of a bowl of fruit. On the other hand, the main illustration in Figure 4-1 has been shaded, and because a source of light has now been suggested within the picture, we can recognize the image as a collection of fruit more quickly because the qualities of roundness and shape definition have been filled in. The main drawing looks more realistic because more of the properties of the fruit are included in the drawing to visualize the concept.

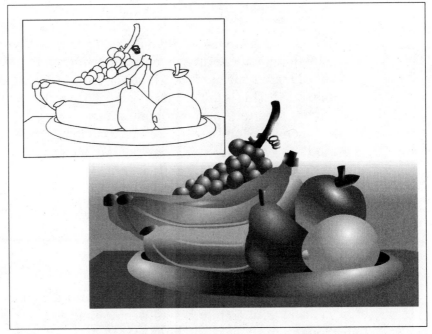

Figure 4-1: *The more real-world properties you can suggest in an illustration, the quicker the audience can recognize the image.*

To draw a parallel between 2D drawing and 3D modeling, most of the time spent on this illustration was in creating its defining geometry—the path outlines—of the fruit shapes. Coloring the individual paths with gradient fills to bring the bowl of fruit to life took a fraction of the time spent designing the outlines.

In most modeling applications, you'll find that constructing a wireframe of an object is most of the task, and covering the wireframe with a surface—marble, chrome, anything you can imagine—is a minor investment of time. Conveniently, building a 3D wireframe object can usually begin with a 2D path: if you're experienced with Adobe Illustrator, CorelDRAW, or some other drawing program, most modeling applications will let you import paths and calculate a third dimension for the path in a mouse click or two.

Let's examine for a moment what's missing from the gradient-filled illustration in Figure 4-1. Although the suggestion of highlights on the fruit immediately communicate to the viewer properties of lighting in the scene and roundness of the fruit, the fruit has no *texture*. Surface detail is a property that immediately registers with the viewing audience; it's what separates the image of a cloth doll from that of a plastic doll.

Usually, the *material* an object is filled with is visually more important than its actual outline, or *shape*. This means that with a modeling application and the right collection of textures, you can create amazingly lifelike designs that would take hours in a drawing or painting program. Figure 4-2 depicts the same subject as Figure 4-1, but the scene has been modeled and rendered, not drawn. The basic outline shapes were created in CorelDRAW, imported to a modeling program, covered with appropriate textures, then rendered. Rendering is a completely automated process. As noted later in this chapter, rendering is a time-intensive task, but it's completed by the software, not you. So you don't have to learn rendering to become experienced with modeling!

Figure 4-2: *This scene required a little more time to complete than an equivalent 2D illustration, but the payoff is a more realistic, more quickly recognized scene.*

As a bonus for investing time in creating a useful model, surface textures, like fills in a drawing program, can be easily changed. Figure 4-3 is a rendered scene—identical to Figure 4-2 in its wireframe model structure—but the fruit is now surfaced with whimsical (as opposed to accurate) textures. The investment of user time to transform the scene was about five minutes.

Figure 4-3: *Surface detail is a key element in 3D modeling creations; the right texture can register more quickly with the viewer than an object's shape.*

Noteworthy here is a simple technique for getting the viewer's attention. In their paintings, surrealist artists have frequently played with inappropriate textures on the surfaces of objects. If you take the time to build, say, a wonderful model of a train, you can render variations of the same object in a glass texture, or brick, or a 2D illustration. Because it's the function of a modeling program to add realistic lighting to a scene, you can wind up with multiple surrealistic scenes by investing in a single session to create the original model.

TIP

Even if you've convinced yourself that modeling isn't your avenue of artistic expression, you can purchase clip objects from third-party manufacturers that will work with a number of modeling programs. Macintosh System 7.5 and later supports the 3DMetafile (3DMF) data structure, which makes it easy to paste a 3D object into application documents; and Microsoft has announced support for Direct 3D, a similar technology, for Windows 95 in mid-1996.

Many modeling/rendering applications also come with a collection of premade clip objects, so you aren't required to be a modeling expert to get in on the new wave of dimensional visual communication.

EXTENDED USE OF MODELS

Among the many reasons why modeling can be the next logical step in your artistic expression, there's one relating to the Web that can give you incentive. Virtual worlds, text files that spring to life when viewed through Netscape's VRML plug-in, can very easily be created from a modeled scene using a number of existing applications. Visual Software's Visual Reality (Windows), Virtus WalkThrough Pro (Macintosh and Windows), and others can generate the *.WRL file that describes a scene which can be linked to an HTML document. The file extension .WRL indicates that a file was written to VRML specifications. The VRML version 1 specifications include support for declaring basic geometric shapes such as spheres and cylinders by using *shape nodes*—an object class that defines materials, lighting, or in this case geometry—in a WRL document. See Chapter 6 "VRML," for more information on VRML nodes. However, more complex shapes—those that will captivate your audience—require a modeling program . . . or incredible mathematical skill!

Additionally, many modeling programs can write an animation file that can be included in your Web site. 3D animation is one of the easiest ways to add motion to your site. Chapter 5, "Animation & Digital Video Compression," discusses the more popular methods of creating animations your audience can view in Navigator's browser.

Do You Already Own a Modeling Application?

Naturally, the discussions that follow will be less useful to a professional who doesn't have access to a modeling application. But if you check the documentation for the mega-programs that have shipped in the past year, you might find that a modeling program *came* with the main program you licensed. You may not have installed it, or the application might not have a name as blunt as "XWare's Modeling Application."

If you've made the move to Adobe Illustrator 6 for the Macintosh, there's a very nice full-featured vector modeling program, Dimensions v. 2.0, included on the Deluxe CD. Dimensions is shown throughout this chapter, because it provides very straightforward, basic modeling functions. It should be noted here that although Dimensions can generate QuickTime movies, it cannot produce models with the 3D geometry required for use in a VRML file. It cannot export objects to 3DMF (the Macintosh system's 3D metafile format) or .DXF format either, which prevents you from moving a scene to a rendering application or other 3D modeling program. DXF (*Data eXchange Format*) is a near-universally accepted format for modeling applications; most modeling programs allow the designer to export a scene to this platform-independent format. Nevertheless, Dimensions can produce some stunning photorealistic 2D artwork you can place in a frame or on a Web page.

The CorelDRAW! version 6 bundle comes with three modeling programs, all of which were originally licensed from manufacturers who produce a Macintosh version.

CorelDEPTH, originally AddDepth, is a handy tool you can use to *extrude* (create a third dimension by projecting a path forward or backward in space) text or outline paths you import in Adobe Illustrator, Windows Metafile, or other platform-specific file types. Although the Depth product cannot perform any operation other than extrusion on a 2D path, you can rotate and add vector textures to the extruded artwork. Depth saves to vector format so that, like

Dimensions, you cannot export a 3D wireframe model to other applications and Depth cannot write a VRML file. But if you need a dimensional logo for a Web page, Depth exported files can easily be converted to bitmap format and used as GIFs or JPEG images.

CorelMOTION 3D is a slightly different version of Specular International's LogoMotion program for the Macintosh. MOTION is a true modeling application that can import .DXF files as well as 2D paths from other applications. Motion's primary use is as an animation renderer, but you can generate still frames for use as a Web graphic. Unlike Dimensions and AddDepth, Motion is a bitmap modeling/rendering program: it doesn't calculate the finished scene as a collection of filled paths. Because Motion's output is bitmap, the surface textures on objects are more photographic than textures produced by vector modelers. LogoMotion can export 3D objects to Specular Infini-D format but cannot generate a DXF file for use with nonproprietary modelers or rendering applications. Similarly, CorelDEPTH 3D provides no gateway from the program other than a finished animation or still frame. Specular LogoMotion can be purchased separately and has been bundled with many different products, including Adobe Premiere upgrades to version 4.2 for the Macintosh.

CorelDREAM 3D, based upon Ray Dream Designer version 3, is a full-fledged modeling and rendering application. Although CorelDREAM 3D was created prior to the interest in or need for Web animations and virtual worlds, it can import 2D graphics and export 3D objects to other programs in the .DXF format. You can also import bitmap textures for use in DREAM 3D scenes, and the rendering quality approaches that of photographic. Designer is biplatform, and version 4 now supports animation of your creations.

If you have any of these programs, this chapter will take you through a basic understanding of dimensional navigation and creation of objects in a virtual world. And if you currently use a stand-alone modeling program, this chapter shows you how to get the most out of it for creating Web graphics.

Navigating 3D Computer Space

My first experience with a modeling program was one of initial confusion and disorientation. Yes, the TV commercials looked really neat, and I *wanted* some of this same magic in my own work! But in the same way that you'd define a page size before composing a DTP document, you need to size up the 3D virtual world in a modeling application before littering it with objects.

First, there's the matter of relativity to consider, which is not unlike how a submarine or space shuttle might define its coordinates. The most tangible way to "think in 3D" is by representing space as a container. When you open a modeling application, the view through your monitor's window is that of the program's *universe* (sometimes referred to as a *world*). You can't see the extent of the modeler's universe any more than you can see the extent of the real universe through your living room window; however, it is this universe that is the container for all objects you might create or import. Because this container universe is dimensional and can contain as many objects as you like, there are *global* and *local* coordinates you can use to position objects. Objects can be moved relative to their original position (*local* movement and/or rotation), or objects can be moved relative to their position in 3D space within the universe—these are *global* coordinate movements.

Your modeling application most certainly will have different names and conventions for application space, but 3D modeling space is usually measured along three axes: an X (or horizontal) axis, a Y (or vertical) axis, and a Z (or depth) axis. Think of a page layout's Cartesian coordinates: there's an origin, with the horizontal measurements extending left and right (this is the X-axis), and vertical measurements extending up and down (the Y-axis). Now, if you visualize a straight line from yourself to the back of your monitor, you've added the Z-axis. These three coordinates can be used to define a point for an object anywhere in the modeling application's universe, as you can see in Figure 4-4.

Figure 4-4: *Modeling space is defined using three axes of dimension: width (X), height (Y), and depth (Z).*

Although all modeling programs offer you three axes of dimension, it's important to check the documentation, because all programs do not use the same reference axes to define an object's orientation toward the user. For example, Visual Software's Visual Reality points the Z-axis up and down, and the Y-axis is used to measure the distance from the front to back of an imported 3D object.

There's a reason why Figure 4-4 displays a hand, specifically a left hand, with legends for the 3D axes. The left-hand coordinate system was developed to allow engineers and users to define the direction of rotation of an object. Rotation is what gives a modeling application object visual interest: very few real life objects look dimensional when viewed absolutely perpendicular to their front facet.

The left-hand coordinate system is a mnemonic you can use to visually tell which axis of rotation affects the side of an object that is facing front. If you point your left hand's thumb straight up, your index finger to the right, and curl the rest of your fingers into your palm, you've made a handy reference chart for positive rotation values along the three axes. Not all modeling applications use these rotation references, but most do.

If in your modeling application you can specify a number of degrees of rotation around the X-axis, look down the X-axis (your index finger), and look at the way your thumb curls. It curls in a clockwise direction, right? This *should* be the positive rotation direction value for an object in your modeling program. Similarly, if you're into a little contortion, each view of your left hand, down each axis, offers a direction and perspective of which facet of an object turns toward you or away from you when rotated along a specific axis. Figure 4-5 is a graphical representation of how the three axes of rotation relate to each other using the left-hand coordinate system. Most modelers allow entry of numerical parameters for rotation and movement of a selected object.

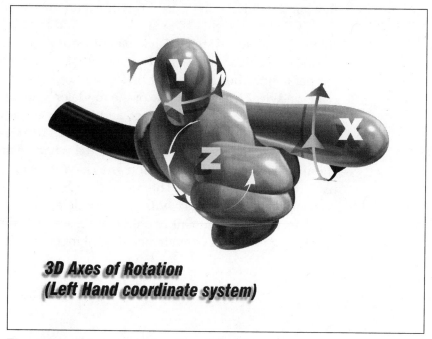

3D Axes of Rotation
(Left Hand coordinate system)

Figure 4-5: *Objects rotate along an axis but do not rotate in the direction of a specific axis.*

TIP

The specifications for VRML 1 use the right-hand *coordinate system. This doesn't change the placement of X-, Y-, and Z-axes in the virtual world, but rotation is specified in the opposite direction as rotation using the left-hand coordinates system. If you intend to write a WRL file instead of allowing an authoring tool to define rotation and object placement, use the direction of your fingers on your right hand, not your left, as a device for quickly seeing how objects rotate in a positive direction.*

Rotation direction is not a straightforward concept, although we practice it daily with real-life objects. It's also the reason why many users grow frustrated with a modeling application and give up. It helps to envision a shish kebab skewered and perched above a picnic grill. The skewer is the X-axis of rotation, and if you're facing the grill, you see front-to-back rotation of the shish kebab. Similarly, if you have a weird cookout that uses a vertical skewer, Y would be the axis of rotation, and you see views panning from left to right of the meal object. And if you don't want to change your view of the shish kebab but simply want to turn it upside down, it's the Z-axis of rotation that would make the peppers on the bottom appear on top without changing *your* view.

Best advice? Choose a view of the modeler's universe—don't change the view. Create an object, and then try to move and rotate it using either the numerical entry fields or a virtual trackball, a graphical feature that almost every modeler has. Visual feedback should give you some orientation as to how a specific modeler's navigation controls work. The point is, *do* get comfortable with your orientations in space within the modeler *before* creating a complex scene. Alignment of objects is critical if you're to create something beautiful or even meaningful in a modeling program.

THE CAMERA'S ROLE IN MODELING

Besides local space and global space, there's a third, relative measurement of space you have control over in a modeling application: your own viewpoint. Objects that are aligned from the limited view provided through the viewport known as your monitor do not portray the position of objects from all three axes. Although many fancy implementations have been designed as user controls for manipulating objects in 3D space from a single 2D position, it is the user view, often called the camera view, that affords the most control over aligning objects. Alignment is perhaps the most critical user task in a modeling application beyond the creation of objects. And as in real life, the best way to align two objects along three axes is to use one view of the scene, then a *different* view.

Overall, the modeling application market is split 50/50 on the issue of whether your monitor view *is* the camera, or whether the camera—the viewpoint from which a finished rendering is made—is a separate entity within the modeler's universe. The advantage of making the camera a unique entity is that, detached from the virtual camera, you can view other perspectives of the scene without changing the framing of the final camera view. However, this also leads to some confusion and the possibility that your finished rendering will contain empty space, because while you viewed and arranged the scene, you didn't look "through" the camera—which was posed at a blank wall or something.

In this chapter we'll use the visual metaphor that you *are* the camera—that is, your view onscreen is the same as the camera that frames the finished picture. Most programs offer at least three views of the universe: the front, the top, and the left or right. It's no coincidence that these perspectives correspond to the X-, Y-, and Z-axes of modeling space. The use of different views is intended mostly for aligning objects and secondarily for selecting objects that are hidden from view at any given perspective.

Rule Number One in creating a scene is to align everything you can in one view, then switch views to make sure the axis of alignment you *can't* see among the objects is also aligned. *Do not* rotate or move objects from a single point of view. An example of this wisdom in practice might be a scoop of ice cream you've built and another object which is the ice cream cone. From a front view, you have control over the X- and Y-axis movement of the ice cream scoop, and you can easily align it so it appears to sit upon the cone. However, you have no information from a front view that would lead you to believe that the ice cream scoop is *depthwise* centered to the cone: it could be closer to you or more distant than the cone.

This lack of Z-axis alignment might be of no consequence, because indeed if you're rendering the model from a viewpoint of the front, the finished 2D rendering won't reflect any Z-axis misalignment. But if your modeling application can render shadows, you won't get the shadow beneath the scoop of ice cream as it slightly overhangs the cone, because the scoop is actually in front of the cone by several inches. Or the bottom of the scoop would be hidden because it's way behind the cone. It's by changing views to the right or left, then moving the scoop along the Z- and Y-axis, that you can ensure alignment of the composite object from any perspective.

The additional benefit of spending a little extra time and working between camera views is that *every* view of this cone example will display perfect alignment. This means that if you decide to pick a different camera view in the future, your modeling work is already completed. And if your application supports linking objects (called *hierarchical linking*), you can then freely rotate the group of objects to create new views.

Changing the camera view is always better at creating new object views than rotating objects from a fixed view to achieve similar results. It is a *big* mistake to start rotating objects before you're certain they're aligned and linked.

PRACTICAL EXAMPLES OF MODELING

Many advanced modeling/rendering applications support various ways of projecting a 2D path in a direction that then becomes the third dimension of an object. Two common methods supported by most entry-level modeling programs are *extruding* and *lathing*.

Extrusion is the creation of a depth surface from a height- and width-only (2D) path along a direction perpendicular to the surface of the path. Depending upon your application, an object might be extruded toward the user or away from the user, but the result is the same: a cookie-cutter object that contains no new information except depth, based upon the original path. A pair of dice, a tube, or a cookie are all obvious examples of what can be created by extruding a path.

Lathing is a process by which the modeler takes a 2D path and rotates it about an axis to create the third dimension for an object. In the lathing process, an object that is symmetrical across its depth axis is created. The resulting 3D object is determined by the axis of lathing and the orientation of the path at the time you perform the process. For example, a half-circle with its flat side traveling up and down and to the path's left can be lathed to create a sphere. In this example, the axis of lathing would be directly upon the flat side of the half-circle; the right side—the curved side—is spun 360 degrees around the Y-axis to define the 3D surface. Candlesticks, chair legs, and urns are examples of the objects that can be created through lathing a 2D path. A tube like the one produced by extrusion can also be created, but you'd rotate a rectangle around an axis to produce the tube, whereas a circle would need to be the path extruded to produce the same object.

Using only the extrusion and lathing features of a modeling program, the next sections take you through the creation of mini-worlds. Although the 2D paths used in these examples can be easily created, the resource files are provided on the Companion CD-ROM in Adobe Illustrator format. Chances are good that your modeler supports the import of Adobe Illustrator (AI) format files.

ASSIGNMENT 1: A MAILBOX

In Figure 4-6 is a scene intended to communicate visually that your Web site welcomes reader response. I painted in a little background to flesh out the image, but the main attraction is the mailbox with the letter flying into it. One of the big advantages of computer art over photography is that modeling programs don't believe in gravity—any object can float!

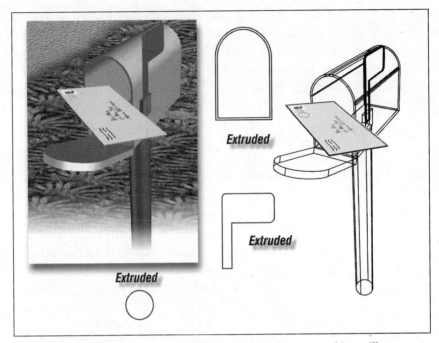

Figure 4-6: *Extrusion is the modeling method used to create this mailbox scene.*

Adobe Dimensions is the application used to create all the scenes in this section, but you can use most any modeling program to achieve the same effect. Here's how to assemble a virtual mailbox:

1. In a drawing program, import or open the MAILBOX.AI file, located in the CHAP04 folder on the Companion CD-ROM. Copy each object to a separate file, save it in the vector format your modeler supports (Illustrator usually works), and name the files something you'll remember later.

2. Import the main path—the mailbox path(s)—into your modeling application. You'll notice that the inner wall of the mailbox is defined as a subpath of the outer path, not unlike a distorted letter "O." You can use an application
   • such as CorelDRAW, FreeHand, or Illustrator to combine two paths so that your modeling application will carve a

negative space when the composite path is extruded. Make sure the direction of the inside path is the opposite of the outer path, or the path will not extrude with an opening to the mailbox.

3. Take a look at how tall the combined path is. If your modeling program doesn't support rulers, it usually offers a grid. Count the grid markers along the height of the combined path, then specify 2x the amount of depth for the extrusion.

4. Import the flag path for the scene. The path was carefully scaled in the drawing program, so you shouldn't need to resize it in your modeling application; it's proportionately correct to the mailbox.

5. Extrude the flag by a fraction of an inch (or grid marker).

6. Import the circle path that will be the mailbox pole, and extrude it by about 3x the value you used for the mailbox.

7. Import the path to be used as the letter, then extrude it by about the same value as you used for the mailbox flag.

8. Now that all the objects are 3D, pick a view for the modeler's universe; lock it if your program supports view locking.

9. Click and drag the flag so that it meets the right side of the mailbox, then rotate it 90° counterclockwise along the Y (vertical) axis. Many programs define the center of rotation as the absolute center of an object, so rotating the mailbox flag here will move it away from the mailbox. Click and drag the flag toward the right side of the mailbox until it's flush against the surface.

10. Click and drag the mailbox pole so that it's centered beneath the mailbox, then rotate the object 90° along its X (horizontal) axis. It doesn't matter whether the rotation angle is positive or negative: the pole is symmetrical.

11. Click and drag the pole so that its top side appears to touch the bottom of the mailbox.

12. Change your view of the scene to the right side. If your program doesn't offer a right side, it most likely will offer a left view. If this is the case, change views and change your viewing quality of the scene to wireframe (if offered); in wireframe view, you can select and move objects "through" other objects.

13. In this side view, align the pole to the center of the mailbox (if necessary), and move the flag along the Z- and Y-axes so it is positioned appropriately on the side of the mailbox.

14. Click and drag the letter object to the front of the mailbox, a distance about equal to the mailbox's depth. You can then rotate the letter from the front view of the scene to any angle without the worry of the letter intersecting the mailbox. Solids can collide and intersect each other in the land of modeling. The effect is artistically interesting about once in a career.

15. Switch back to your original view. You'll notice that the mailbox doesn't have a back facet. Here's the trick: you don't *need* to build something the audience won't *see*. If you look back at Figure 4-6, you'll notice that the final rendering angle for the mailbox scene is posed so you cannot see the back side of the mailbox.

16. At this point, you might want to go through the additional step of importing and extruding the front of the mailbox. This is only an example, but you can extrude the *outer* path of the mailbox compound path by about 10 percent of the height of the path, then rotate it and align it to the front of the mailbox. I'd suggest about a 30° angle of rotation around its X-axis to give the mailbox a partially opened look.

17. Click on the letter to select it, then rotate it so it appears to be flung from the user's point of view into the mailbox.

18. You're done aligning the objects, so you can use the modeling program's grouping feature (if offered) to make your scene a single composite object that can be freely rotated without things becoming unaligned. Then, you can either rotate the composite object to a view of your liking (that doesn't show the missing back of the mailbox), or create a different view of the scene by rotating your own view instead of the objects.

19. Use the rendering capability of the modeling program to create a "snapshot" of your view. You're done!

There are one or two points that are glossed over in this first example. Most modelers offer light sources you can manipulate. If something doesn't look right in a preview of your scene, try adjusting a light—or adding or eliminating one—before you move your objects. You'd be surprised how intuitively many modelers present you with lighting options. Usually, a light is an object in the scene, and you point and position it as you would a physical stage light. Alternatively, programs such as AddDepth, Dimensions, and Extreme 3D offer a trackball panel where the iconic representations of scene lights are moved around a sphere which *represents* world space in the scene.

LIGHTING TIPS

It's impossible to know all aspects of *every* field of art, but a little practical lighting as used in theater and by photographers can enhance the dimensional quality of your modeling work.

Begin your scene with a single, main light, and label it with a unique name. As you progress to complex scenes, it's always a good idea to label everything for future reference.

Position the main light at either 11 o'clock or 2 o'clock facing you, and make it point into the scene at about a 25° angle (rotate it along its Y-axis in a counterclockwise direction). See how you feel about the strength and color of the light, where an application has this feature. This main light position should create highlights on shiny objects on the surface facing the light at either 11 or 2 o'clock.

➡

Next, add a weaker, secondary light 180° opposite the main light; point it up from below the scene, and position it *behind* the scene, so it illuminates objects from the rear and opposite angle of the main light's direction. This is sometimes called a kick light or "catch lighting," and its purpose is to add a visible edge to objects whose main source of illumination is from above. You'd be surprised at how much more apparent detail you can then see in your scene. Shadows are gently interrupted at object edges, and the shape as well as the texture of objects become immediately apparent to the viewer.

More than two lights tend to wash out a scene and make it appear flat. Unless you need additional lights to create a special effect, don't overdo lighting in your scene.

We've also ignored somewhat the use of *textures* in the mailbox example, because we'll get to textures later in this chapter. Another piece of vector artwork is used to make the letter object appear more realistic in the mailbox scene. Adobe Dimensions has the capability to add texture (to *map*) to any facet of an object's surface quite easily, because a template view is offered of any object facet. You simply position an imported piece of artwork anywhere Dimensions indicates a surface is visible to the viewer, apply it, and you have a scene that's more detailed through the use of object texture, not model detail.

Assignment 2: The Corporate Logo

It's a common practice of logo designers to incorporate an iconic representation of a business's specialty in the lettering of the logo. For example, an automotive repair shop might have a logo that contains a wrench where the "i" in "automotive" should be. When you think and work in three dimensions, you have the same opportunity to mix text with graphics, but the net effect can be much more attractive than if created in a paint or drawing program. In Figure 4-7, you can see a logo for a fictitious online creative firm. The "O" in "Online" has been replaced with a light bulb object, and the view has been angled to display all three axes of the composite scene.

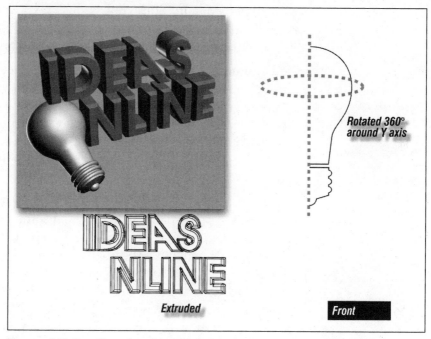

Figure 4-7: *Specify a view for your finished 3D scene that displays many angles of visual interest; rotate your view to include partial views of the side and top of your creation.*

Here's how to recreate the Ideas Online logo:

1. Copy the ONLINE.AI file to your hard drive from the CHAP04 folder on the Companion CD-ROM.

2. Open or import the file in a drawing application, and copy the base, the bulb, and the text objects to separate files. Save these files to AI format or whatever format your modeling application can import (CorelMOTION users can use the CMX file format, and CorelDREAM users can use the CDR or CMX file format).

3. Establish a front view for the new scene in your modeling application.

4. Import the text object, and extrude it by about ⅓ to ½ of the character height of a line of the text. Avant Garde was the original font used to create this text, and generally it's important to stay with a "clean" font when extruding text. The dimensionality of the finished 3D text carries the visual interest, and an ornamental font such as one from the Fraktur family becomes hard to read when extruded.

5. Many modelers offer the option to apply a bevel to the front, back, or both sides of extruded objects. In Figure 4-7, you can see that a straight edge joins the front and side of the extruded text object. Bevel sides help dimensionalize extruded objects, because chances are that one facet or another will catch a light source and contrast it against flatly lit object areas.

6. Import the bulb file, then lathe the path 360° around the flat, vertical side of the path. Note here that some modeling programs require that a path is closed to perform a lathe operation. Dimensions, Dream 3D, and LogoMotion require that a path be open, so the resource paths used in this chapter for objects that are created by lathing have been left open. Be sure to close the paths in the AI files before exporting them if your modeler requires closed paths.

7. Import the base of the light bulb and lathe the path 360° around its flat, open vertical side.

8. Align the base and light bulb objects.

9. Switch to a side view of the scene, then align the depth axes of the base and light bulb. Group the light bulb and base objects.

10. Align the light bulb so it's centered with the depth of the extruded text (the Z-axis).

11. Switch back to your original view, then drag the grouped light bulb to a position where the light bulb substitutes for the missing "O" in the text object. In this example, I've rotated the bulb so that the base extends closer to the viewer than the text or the bulb objects. Get creative with positioning objects; if it looks compositionally correct, then it *is*!

12. Choose a viewing angle for the scene, add lighting, and you're done. In Figure 4-7, the off-axis front preset angle was used in Dimensions, because it provides a view of the top, front, and side of the scene. In short, the view shows all the interesting aspects of the objects.

There was a trick to creating the base of the light bulb that's not exactly technically correct, but it works. A thread on a bulb, a screw, or even the grooves on a vinyl record (the media that the Beatles used to record on) form a spiral, not a series of concentric circles that lathing the path of the light bulb base created. However, at the present angle at which the base is tilted and viewed, chances are slim that a viewer will point out or criticize you for this error. Toward the end of this chapter, there is an example of how to use a specific modeling program to accurately create this fairly complex object. The lesson here is to go with what time allows, and what you can artistically get away with, when designing models.

ASSIGNMENT 3: THE RESTAURANT GRAPHIC

One of the creative twists you can perform with most modeling programs' lathing operation is to revolve a path *less than* 360°. Doing this creates a cutaway view of your geometric solid, and the possibilities can lead to more interesting shapes.

In Figure 4-8, you can see what is called *tabletop photography* in the trade: a simple still life of a wine bottle, some cheese, and a carved apple. All the objects in this scene were created by lathing.

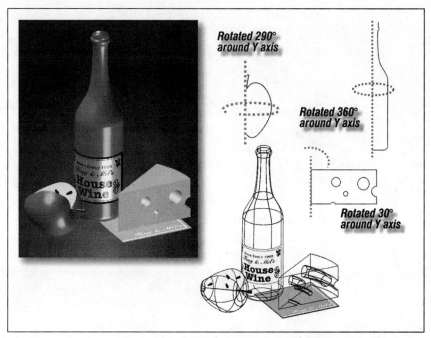

Figure 4-8: *By revolving a path around an axis in an incomplete turn, you can create complex, natural-looking objects.*

Here's how to create a simple food scene:

1. Copy the TONY-MEL.AI file from the CHAP04 folder on the Companion CD-ROM to your hard drive, then open or import the file into a drawing application.

2. Create separate files for the bottle, the cheese, the apple stem, and the apple, and save them to the appropriate format for importing to your modeling application.

3. Define a front view for the scene, then import the bottle into the modeling application.

4. Lathe the bottle path along its vertical, flat axis by 360°. You'll notice that the top of the path doesn't meet the axis of rotation, because it's farther from the axis than the bottom side of the path. This construction allows most modeling applications to leave the top of the model open, creating a hollow shape. Dimensions offers the option to auto-close a path, or not, on the Revolve (Lathe) palette.

5. Import the cheese path, then lathe the path around its left side (the side without the "hole") about 30°.

6. Import the apple path, and rotate it around its vertical, flat side by about 290°. This creates a slice missing from the apple.

7. Import the stem path, and lathe it, vertically, by 360°.

8. Align the stem with the apple from this front view.

9. Align the bottom of the cheese object with the bottom of the bottle.

10. Change to the side view, align the stem with the center of the apple if necessary, and then group the stem to the apple.

11. Switch back to the front view, and rotate the apple so that it lies on its side, with the missing slice area facing up.

12. Align the apple object to the bottom of the bottle.

13. Switch back to side view. Click and drag the apple, then the cheese, to a position slightly in front of the bottle. Make sure the volumes of the apple and the cheese don't intersect the bottle.

14. Switch to a top view of the scene to confirm that objects aren't touching one another.

15. Switch to the front view and make minor tweaks to the scene, as your eye tells you to.

16. Rotate your camera view, *not* the objects, by about 16° in a clockwise direction along the camera's X-axis. This provides a "viewer superior" view of the scene, which is common for scenes where the viewer is taller or larger than the scene. For some *really* interesting virtual worlds, you might want to rotate the camera in the opposite direction, to make the simple food scene seem 10 times larger than the viewer!

17. Point your light source(s) into the scene, display a preview of the scene, and if you're happy with it, render it and you're done.

In the preceding example, we once again "faked" a real life image detail that will go unnoticed by the viewer. The lathed cheese wouldn't, in real life, have holes that also are lathed 16°. But no one can see this goof, because the angle of the final view doesn't allow the viewer to see completely through one of the cheese holes; the audience assumes that the hole ends where one might expect it to end in real Swiss cheese.

The label on the bottle in this example is a surface map placed on top of the default surface color of the bottle. Modeling programs can correctly distort a flat label, across three dimensions.

TIP

To make text appear to float and twist in three dimensions, try creating a surface texture for an object that is text only. Then give the surface of a cylinder or sphere an invisible property. In the world of computer graphics, it's possible to have a texture showing on an object that's mostly invisible.

The slice in the apple displaying pulp and seeds in the preceding example depends somewhat on your modeling application's capability to define different surface maps on an object. You'll notice in Figure 4-7 that the surface of the apple object displays two different textures—of the pulp and of the outer skin. In Dimensions, this effect is easy to achieve, because facets of an object—distinctly different sides—can all have separately mapped artwork. CorelDREAM 3D can also map different images to different sides of the same object using the 3D Paint tool. If your application doesn't support this feature, there's an easy workaround. Create a very thin slice of apple (extrude the apple path by the smallest value allowed), then add a surface of apple pulp, and place the object *within* the missing apple area.

PHOTOGRAPHERS' TRICKS

If a scene such as that shown in the tabletop of the bottle, cheese, and apple doesn't seem to come together—for instance, the foreground prominence of one element isn't strong enough—here's a trick professional still photographers use.

Move any of the objects above the plane which defines the base, or floor, for the objects. Photographers frequently stock a supply of small, wooden blocks to place objects upon when they want to increase the height of an object whose base is hidden by other objects. Because there's no gravity in a modeling application's scene, you don't need wooden blocks, but in reality a tabletop photo frequently contains hidden risers that elevate a background object so the scene looks compositionally correct.

This trick won't work if you're animating the scene by moving around a complete view of the scene. A VRML document based upon your world won't look quite right either, but you can shave hours off a still image composition if you play with the baseline of individual objects.

ASSIGNMENT 4: THE BAGEL LOGO

Our final assignment in this section demonstrates the flexibility of modeling applications that create complex models by stretching the underlying math somewhat. Many modeling programs offer preset geometric shapes that are called *primitives*: the name comes from the fact that you cannot break down one of these shapes to a more basic 3D form. Most modelers offer cubes and spheres as primitives, but you already know how to build them through extrusion or lathing. Another type of primitive, a *torus* (a technical term for a donut), is not offered in all modeling programs, thereby giving the author an opportunity to show how to create it.

When lathing was first described in this chapter, emphasis was placed on making the axis of rotation coincide with one side of the path being lathed. However, there is no reason why an axis of lathing *has* to be located on the path: it can be off the path by an inch or a mile, and this is how a tire, a breakfast cereal morsel, or a bagel can be modeled. Figure 4-9 is an effective use of off-path lathing. Some of the visual interest in the Brewster's Bagels logo lies in camera angle and positioning of the text elements. It's a preposterously overwhelming composition; the elements fairly leap off the page at you, and this is part of the power of dimensional renderings.

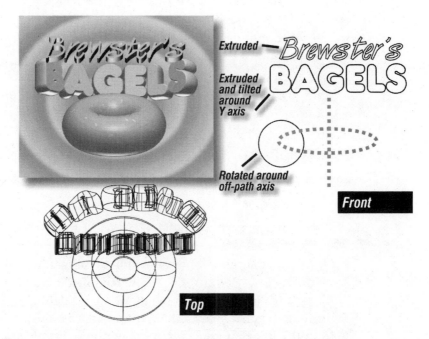

Figure 4-9: *Even simple extruded text can look more dynamic when you break the text into individual characters and make the characters follow a curved, 3D path.*

Here's how to construct the bagel signature:

1. Copy the BAGEL.AI file from the CHAP04 folder on the Companion CD-ROM to your hard drive, then open or import the file in a drawing application.

2. Copy and save the BAGELS and the Brewster's lettering to separate files, then close the drawing application and open your modeling application.

3. Because the shapes we've extruded and lathed so far have been fairly complex, we haven't discussed the native drawing tools in modeling applications. Even experienced modeling professionals tend to prefer a drawing application's tools, simply out of conditioning. But in this example, let's use your program's native tools to create the circle to be lathed into a bagel. Import the BAGELS and Brewster's lettering, then with your program's ellipse (or circle, or closed shape) tool, make a circle a little larger than the cap height of the BAGELS lettering.

4. Define an axis of lathing for the circle that's a distance a little less than the circle's diameter away from the bagel. In LogoMotion, you drag the circle to the right of the Y-axis in the Workshop window. In Dimensions, you create a verti-cal path line with the Pen tool, move it to the left of the circle you created, then while the path is still selected, choose Make Guide from the Artwork menu. Other pro-grams offer similar conventions.

5. Lathe the circle by 360°.

6. Choose the Brewster's lettering, then extrude it by half the amount of the cap height. No bevel is chosen for this lettering because of its somewhat delicate and ornate structure.

7. Choose the BAGELS lettering, then extrude it by about ¾ of its cap height. If your application offers it, try a bevel edge that is rounded. This makes the lettering (Frankfurter by Bitstream was the font used) look like plump baker's dough.

8. Group the objects into a BAGELS and Brewster's hierarchi-cal nest. Modeling programs sometimes break linked paths into separate components, and you want to be able to move the text as groups, not individual 3D characters.

9. Place the Brewster's object over the BAGELS object, and then place the bagel beneath the BAGELS object.

10. Because the bagel was lathed, the bagel's hole should be pointed upward right now. Rotate the bagel toward the viewer, counterclockwise, along its X-axis until you see some of the hole. When the viewer can see more than one side of a rounded object, it helps define the geometry and makes a more photogenic bagel.

11. Rotate the Brewster's lettering clockwise along its X-axis by about 12°. You might notice here that because the Brewster's lettering and the bagel are rotated in opposite, outward directions, a wide-angle lens effect is simulated. Mark this one down the next time you need a special effect!

12. Move to a top view of the scene, then align the two lettering groups and the bagel so that BAGELS is toward the back of the scene (the universe), the Brewster's lettering is in front of it, and the bagel/torus is the frontmost object when you return to the front view of the scene.

13. Ungroup the BAGELS lettering, then rotate the B about 20° in a clockwise direction from your top view (this is rotating the object along its own Y-axis).

14. Select and rotate the A by about 12° in a clockwise direction. Leave the G and E alone, but rotate the L by 12° counterclockwise, and the S should be rotated by 20° in a counterclockwise direction. You've created an arc out of the letters. Align them now so they look like the wireframe shown in Figure 4-9.

15. Group the BAGEL lettering again, then switch to the front view of the scene.

16. Rotate the BAGEL group in a clockwise direction by about 10° along its X-axis so you can see some of the bottom of the lettering.

17. Position lights, and render the scene. You're done.

If you worked through the four preceding examples, you now have a pretty good handle on defining the geometry of the players in a modeled scene. And model-building is the hardest and most time-intensive part of the modeling process. However, as noted earlier, the defining shape of an object often plays a secondary role to the surface texture of an object. The following section explores a different use for textures you might have created for Web site backgrounds.

SURFACE MAPS: PLACING DATA ON DATA

In the land of reality, or at least photoreality, light strikes objects and makes them visible, and light interacts with the surface of an object to reflect its characteristics in the form of *modified* lightwaves to the viewer's eye. In this way, light and surface properties depend upon one another to make up the object your eye sees. The applications that render models (sometimes modeling and rendering are parts of the same application) treat illumination of scene objects in a very similar fashion. A light source needs to be defined to see an object, and if the object is shiny, the reflection of the light falls in the appropriate place on the object.

This brings us to how a user can define a surface for the 3D wireframe model. Basically, there are two things you can specify to a model's surface to cause it to appear the way you like:

- *Surface reflectance.* This option, which is available in many modeling programs, specifies how smooth the surface is—how it directs light that bounces off the surface toward the viewer. Three light reflectance properties can usually be specified using sliders, push buttons, or value fields in a modeling application: *specularity* (the magnitude of a "hot spot" on a smooth surface); the absorption of light indirectly bounced off the object from the environment (*ambient* light); and the amount of diffuse (scattered) light that an object reflects, often called surface *roughness*. With a combination of these three attributes, you can define almost any natural surface's reflectance properties. For example, the bark on a tree contains almost no specular reflectance, but it displays a high degree of diffuse lighting, because light strikes its rough surface and reflects toward the viewer in many directions. But even a tree trunk's most shaded areas also receive illumination from its surroundings (natural sunlight does this), so the tree trunk's surface also sends a certain amount of ambient light back to the viewer from its point of illumination.

However, this first surface property is an incomplete description of a tree trunk's characteristics because the trunk also displays visual patterns *within* its shape. Which leads us to:

- *Surface detail.* Modeling applications have adopted *texture mapping* as a means to place visual patterns across the surface of an object. Although Dimensions and AddDepth rely upon vector artwork to display visual interest on a surface, most modelers allow the user to specify a bitmap image as the source for surface detail.

Surface mapping, or the wrapping of an image around the surface of an object, can be accomplished in several ways. In Figure 4-10, you can see a sphere that has been cloaked with a bitmap image in five different ways to produce five different kinds of objects. We'll make recommendations and offer explanations of these mapping types shortly.

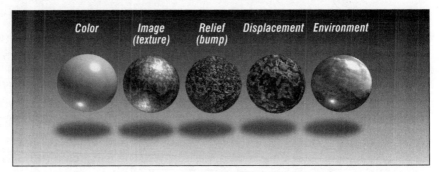

Figure 4-10: *Depending upon the type of surface mapping, an object can take on several different looks.*

COLOR MAPPING

The most basic service a modeling/rendering program provides is color mapping. Color mapping generally involves no additional bitmap image but instead depends on the application to provide a color for a surface. Color mapping by itself offers no photorealistic surface property for a model, but in combination with surface reflectance properties, it can be used to suggest shiny plastic or a rough piece of paper.

IMAGE MAPPING

If you've ever wanted to visualize a brick made of sponge, or a marble pineapple, image mapping allows you to show a bitmap image, not a color, around the surface of a model. It's usually a good idea to build a *seamless* tiling texture (see Chapter 3, "Bitmap Graphics & Special Effects") as the resource for an image map, because images used as textures tend to repeat across the surface of an object when the object is large and the image is small. By tiling an image, you can control the size of the detail across the surface. Many software manufacturers employ special operations within their modeling programs to decrease "smearing"—an unwanted visual effect when a 2D image is projected upon a highly irregular surface. (Try accurately mapping an image of the Empire State Building onto a model of a starfish!) By keeping your images to be mapped simple and capable of tiling without edges showing, you decrease the amount of visual distortion as the image covers the model's surface.

Many, but not all, modeling programs allow you to choose both the orientation of the image map and how the modeler interprets the image as the surfaces meet and change on the model. If you're unhappy with the way a surface looks, use the modeler's features to rotate the image or define a different geometric mapping type for the object. For example, trueSpace offers planar, cylindrical, and spherical mapping types for objects. Your modeling work might go beyond these simple primitive types of objects, but one of them will definitely describe the overall shape of an object better than another. Look under a submenu in your modeler for mapping geometry for objects.

Image maps can also receive surface reflectance properties. Therefore, with an image map of some linoleum, you can add specular lighting to the overall characteristic of a surface to simulate household tiling.

Relief Maps (Bump Maps)

Bump map images are used primarily to enhance the surface characteristics of a model by simulating elevations across a modeled object. For example, a blank sheet of paper contains only surface detail about color, but a relief map applied to a sheet of paper model could transform it into a *crumpled* sheet of paper. In other words, a relief map can help add detail about the actual geometry of an object, without the need to build an extremely complex model, as in the example of a sheet of paper.

Modeling applications use a grayscale image as a relief map. Instead of showing you the image itself displayed across an object's surface, the modeler interprets the brightness values of the relief map image to correspond to the distance of a surface area away from or toward the actual wireframe model. Modelers also can render shadow areas on the surface where a darker portion of the relief image is mapped and, in a similar manner, can add highlight details to the surface where the relief map is brighter. Programs such as Alien Skin TextureShop can produce image maps and corresponding relief maps simultaneously, and they can be used to produce startling results when used in combination on a surface. The sphere in Figure 4-10 is an image map of a sidewalk combined with a relief map that creates bumps and recesses. Both Extreme 3D and CorelDREAM 3D offer splendid features for mixing and blending image and relief maps.

It should be noted that relief and image maps simulate, but don't accurately reproduce, the quality of a rough surface. All but a few high-end modeling/rendering applications take a look at the surface facing the viewer (called the object *normal*) and produce a surface map that only addresses the front side. An object can look slightly unrealistic, because in real life the entire *volume* of an object contains visual detail around its surface, not simply the side facing the viewer.

DISPLACEMENT MAPPING

Displacement mapping is offered in applications that can cost upward of $1,000, and this type of mapping is discussed here as an educational point, not an endorsement to burn a hole in your wallet. Like relief mapping, displacement mapping uses a grayscale image to plot the elevations of an object's surface, but the modeler/renderer sees the object as a geometric solid, not simply a surface. What displacement mapping does, therefore, is *perturb* the wireframe, actually change the geometry as mapped to the finished, rendered image, according to the displacement map. If you look carefully at the sphere in Figure 4-10 that shows displacement mapping, the edges of the sphere are rough, and the elevations on the surface appear more realistic. This example uses an image map in combination with a displacement map.

A way to achieve the same realistic look as displacement mapping with any modeling program is to use an image editor such as Photoshop to erase small areas of the edges of a finished rendered object.

ENVIRONMENT MAPPING

Extremely shiny, mirrorlike objects tend to have no surface details except those reflected from the environment. The classic chrome effect on objects is often achieved in one of two ways: an environment map is calculated by the application, or an image map of an environment is substituted for the "reflection." The main difference between using an environment map and using a "fake" image map is that modeling programs offering environmental reflections can also add an image map to the overall surface of an object. For example, a sphere with an image map "decal" of blue stars on a white background can also reflect an environment of the ocean. Objects in real life often display an intrinsic surface detail in addition to reflected detail.

> **TIP**
>
> *Macromedia's Extreme 3D and Visual Reality are both medium-budget 3D visualization tools that offer very good environment mapping, in case you want to create exceptionally realistic chrome lettering and other Web attractions.*

RAY TRACING

Ray tracing deserves a mention here as a type of surface property; however it's not offered in all modeling/rendering applications, and its effectiveness in making a scene look realistic is somewhat limited. Ray tracing is the visual description of a completely smooth surface using reflections of the object's environment. Ray tracing calculates light onscreen (and in the finished image) as reflected by a surface, which is illuminated from a light source.

However, ray tracing is processor- and time-intensive. Depending upon the surface of a model, the distorted fragments of the surface's environment could be "faked" using an environment map or an image map to detail the surface instead of ray tracing. Your images for the Web need to be small, and the lush detail you might gain through ray tracing will amount to only a few pixels in a 60K or smaller file. Figure 4-11 is an image created in Ray Dream Designer. As you can see, the ray-traced environment in the chess pieces is stunning. However, as an image that would fit in a Web frame, you're never going to see the detail: an image map of some spots and a checkerboard could easily simulate the ray tracing effect.

Figure 4-11: *Accurate reflections are of limited use when the level of detail in an image is quite small.*

Shadows, Opacity & Alpha Channels

As we travel from the shape of an object to its surface properties, we arrive at how a modeler can complete the description of objects in a scene by considering how they interact with the environment. Shadows, opacity, and alpha channels don't relate to each other in a real world sense, but we discuss them together in this section, because your control over each element directly affects the quality of your finished rendering.

SHADOW-MAKING

Shadows are a visual guide to the audience as to where an object is located in the scene. Because it's attention-getting and just plain fun to have objects floating in a scene, shadows can help tie such a fantasy scene to reality. You always need an element of reality in a rendered model: shadows can be the element that the fantasy composition plays against. Figure 4-12 was rendered from models created in Extreme 3D. On the left, the shadows option was turned off; on the right, shadows were rendered into the finished bitmap image. Which image conveys a sense that the yo-yo is on top of the piece of paper?

Figure 4-12: *Shadows help the viewer establish a depth for the finished, rendered image.*

Modeling programs use at least one set of calculations for distributing light—and the absence of light—on the surfaces of objects. *Self-shading* is commonly supported by almost all modeling programs. What self-shading means is that areas within the volume of an object are exposed to different amounts of light. Areas turned away from the light appear darker than areas facing the light.

Off-surface shading is offered by the more expensive modeling programs and is usually accomplished through a technique called *shadow-mapping*. The user never sees the shadow map (it's usually a text or binary file); instead the viewer sees the *effects* of the shadow mapping in the finished image. Shadow mapping calculates points in the finished image that the viewer can see, and whether light strikes these areas or is hidden from them.

It's not uncommon that shadows produced by shadow mapping don't "land" in areas that are artistically pleasing. The author has allowed a modeling program on many occasions to spend hours rendering an image containing a shadow map, only to receive an image that had no shadows! This is because shadow maps are very literal and precise, and a particular light angle might illuminate a surface nicely but cast a shadow way out of view.

If you don't have shadow mapping or another technology to produce shadows in your modeling/rendering program, there's always the manual approach—one the author uses to create convincing shadows and to save rendering time. Here's the trick: create separate image files for the foreground and background objects, then spend a moment or two to visualize what a shadow should look like. In Figure 4-12, the shadow-mapped shadow on the paper simply looks like a silhouette of the yo-yo that's been skewed to the left. Therefore, you could create a copy of the yo-yo, fill it entirely with black, soften the edges a little (Gaussian Blur filters in bitmap editing programs are good for this), then place the shadow object behind the yo-yo in the finished, composited image.

You might want to reduce the opacity of the shadow object before melding the three images—Photoshop, Photo-Paint, Fractal Design Painter, and Picture Publisher all allow objects to be partially transparent when you blend bitmap objects together. Shadows in real life tend to show some surface detail from the object upon which they're cast.

OPACITY

Opacity is not a surface property of an object but a property of the volume of an object. Many applications, including Visual Reality, Extreme 3D, and CorelDREAM 3D, allow you to specify how much light passes through an object. Opacity settings are great for creating glass and liquids, which leads us to another detail in a finished, rendered file that can help you compose a completed bitmap image for the Web.

ALPHA CHANNEL MASKING

What do you call the unoccupied space surrounding a scene? It's blank space; there is no content, unless you've specified a bitmap background or a background color. LogoMotion, Dream, Extreme 3D, trueSpace, Visual Reality, and other programs allow you to specify a rendered file format, and many bitmap image formats allow the inclusion of an alpha channel. Alpha channels are used in programs such as Photoshop and Corel Photo-Paint as a place to store a mask—a grayscale image channel whose brightness values define a saved selection area. Modeling programs often offer the option of writing an alpha channel that describes the contents of a scene: TIF, Targa (*.TGA), and Photoshop's proprietary PSD format are the ones to look for in your modeling application's Save Image As dialog box.

Separating the foreground scene from the finished image's background color then becomes an easy task. Once the objects have a selection marquee protecting them from editing, you can fill the background with an image, a texture, or a color you can define as transparent when the image is copied to GIF format.

One of the fascinating things about the modeling/rendering programs that write this alpha channel is how they treat transparency. Alpha channels can contain 256 unique shades of grayscale brightness. Therefore, if a glass you created in your scene is 50 percent opaque, the modeler/renderer can write a corresponding value of gray to the alpha channel, and a program such as Photoshop will *partially* select the glass. In other words, the glass, as a rendered image, will still contain transparency values, and whatever you decide to place behind the glass as you embellish the finished bitmap image will partially show through.

WILL THE REAL "TRANSPARENCY" PLEASE DISAPPEAR!

In any discussion of computer graphics, it's important to under-stand that "transparency" means different things, depending on the context. Transparent GIFs, the staple of HTML documents, *do not* display the traditional quality of transparency; Navigator reads the GIF file header information and drops out the specified color in the image to make a GIF image's surroundings seem invisible. But if you take a look at the same GIF in an image editor, you'll see a flat colored background in areas that Navigator doesn't display. Yes, it's a transparent GIF, but the transparent areas only exist within the context of an HTML document viewed in Navigator.

Conversely, objects that are semitransparent as a result of par-tial masking in an image alpha channel, or because you gave an object a semitransparent surface in a modeling program, *always* look this way. It's because the image information is constructed in a certain way, not because a predefined background color notifies Navigator that this color should drop out of view.

We've taken you through the navigation, construction, and surfaces for building dimensional scenes. Now it's time to run through the process from beginning to end. How do you add a 3D graphic to a Web document? Extreme 3D and Photoshop are the tools used in the following example. If you don't use these products, the fundamental techniques covered in this chapter can lead to similar results with almost any modeling program and an image editor. Resource 2D paths for this assignment are in the ASSEMBLY.AI file in the CHAP04 folder on the Companion CD-ROM.

CD-ROM

The fictitious "Some Assembly Required" Home Page needs a graphic that indicates what this site is all about. It's an online reference that provides assembly instructions for products most people can't assemble, like an integrated component stereo, or the toy in the cereal box. Here's how to make the graphic shown in the following figures:

1. Import the paths to Extreme 3D. The "parts" include two blocks of lettering ("HOME" and "PAGE"), a profile of a nut, a bolt head, and the outline of half of the bolt threads.

2. Establish a default front view of the scene, then select the "HOME" lettering. Click and hold on the Extrude tool to switch modes to the Bevel Extrude tool.

3. The fields on the status line in Extreme 3D can help make extruded objects of precise measurements. In this example, now that the Bevel Extrude tool has been chosen, you can simply type a value in the Extrude Depth field (.4 is good in this example), type **.1** in the Bevel Width field (the Bevel width value cannot be more than 50 percent of the depth of the extrusion), then press the Enter key on the keypad.

4. Select the "PAGE" object, then perform step 3 on this path.

5. Marquee select the nut paths, then extrude them with a Depth value of .2, and a Bevel Width of .08.

6. Select the bolt head path, and perform step 5 on it.

7. This leaves the bolt thread to be dimensionalized. If you're not using Extreme 3D for modeling, you should lathe the path to make a rounded, somewhat threaded object, similar to that shown in the Ideas Online example earlier in this chapter. But if you want accurate threads, here's an advanced modeling trick that can be done in Extreme 3D and CorelDREAM 3D. Create three duplicates of the thread path, then on all four paths alter the side of the path with the bumps to offset the bumps in a downward direction. Now, decrease the size of the top bump in the four paths from path to path, and do the same with the bottom bump, so the four paths look like the inset image in Figure 4-13.

   This is less work than it seems.

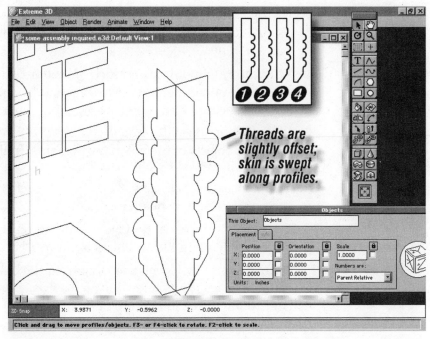

Figure 4-13: *The four paths need to be arranged so their flat sides meet at 90° from each other, when each is rotated around its Y-axis.*

8. Select the profiles one at a time, and give a multiple of 90° rotation around the Y-axis to each, so that the four paths represent a wireframe of the shape of a bolt thread.

TIP

CorelDREAM 3D users can build the threaded bolt in a slightly different way than described in these steps. Click the Freeform tool in the Perspective window, then use the Draw Oval tool to create a circle on the first cross-section plane. Choose Freeform from the Geometry | Extrusion Envelope menu. Four lines then appear, each pair of lines surrounding a direction path line. Click on one of the lines, then choose View | Type | Drawing Plane. Use the Convert Point tools to add points to the envelope line to recreate the first of the four paths shown in Figure 4-13. Repeat the process with the other three extrusion paths, and you've got yourself a threaded bolt.

9. Change views to Three-Quarters (on the View menu), then use the Zoom tool to zoom into a close view of the four paths.

10. With the Skin tool, click on each of the four paths, in a clockwise or counterclockwise direction (sequence of selection is important here; the Skin tool must follow a 3D direction for skinning the paths), then double-click on the first path you clicked on to instruct the Skin tool to close the surface at the beginning of the skinning operation.

11. Switch back to front view, zoom out, then click and drag the bolt thread to beneath the bolt head.

12. Switch to Left view and move the thread object again if necessary to align the bolt head and thread objects.

13. With the Link tool, click and drag from the bolt thread to the bolt head. The bolt head is now a *parent object* (the controlling object in a group of linked objects), and the thread object will move along whenever you move or rotate the bolt head.

14. Use the techniques described in the previous example (see Assignment 4: The Bagel Logo) to compose your scene. In Figure 4-14, you can see that the nut and bolt have been rotated and positioned around the extruded lettering, and the legibility of the lettering is unhampered even though the nut partially obscures your view of the letter "A."

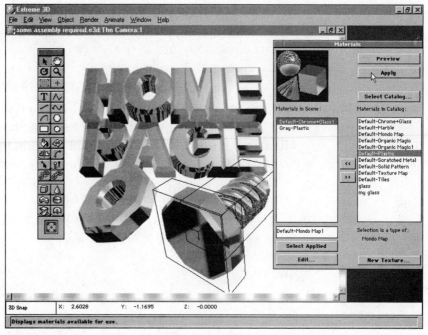

Figure 4-14: *Compose your scene so that objects interact with one another but don't completely obscure text objects.*

15. Applying materials to objects in Extreme 3D is a matter of loading a texture from a collection, selecting an object in the scene, then clicking on Apply. In Figure 4-14, the Window I Materials menu item was chosen to display the Materials palette, and an environment map was used, Chrome+Glass, to make the surfaces of the objects look like smooth metal. The detail work in the surface is a simple checkerboard and sky, but it gives the objects the appearance of hovering above a (checkerboard) surface.

16. After lights are positioned (Window I Lights), it's time to render the scene to 2D bitmap format. Choose Render I Render to Disk, to display the options for rendering.

17. In Extreme 3D, regardless of the dimensions of the viewport (the document window), you can specify a finished rendering size in the Render to Disk dialog box.

Because we'd like this graphic to be viewed without scrolling in Navigator, type **275** in the last field (the horizontal measurement) in the Rendered | Final field, then click in the first field to adjust the height of the finished render. Make sure the Constrain Aspect ratio box is checked.

18. In the Output field, select Targa 32-bit from the drop-down list. Targa images are like the TIF format; they contain three 8-bit color channels for the red, green, and blue components, but an additional 8-bit channel is added for alpha channel masking. Hence, 32-bit is an informational capability, not an enhanced color file.

19. Click on Render, name the file ASSEMBLY.TGA, and choose a directory on your hard disk for the finished file. You're done.

CD-ROM ASSEMBLY.TGA is available in the CHAP04 folder on the Companion CD-ROM in case you'd like to check it out and perform the following steps to make the graphic Web-worthy. It's worthwhile to note here that the example TGA image has additional, 2D text added to it; Photoshop's Text tool was used prior to converting the image to GIF format. Dimensional text is wonderful, but a graphic of only 3D text becomes hard to read, and lacks compositional diversity. Here's how to convert a rendered graphic with an alpha channel to GIF format:

1. You'll need Fractal Design Painter, Photoshop, Photo-Paint (version 6 or later), or other special bitmap editor to work with the alpha channel Extreme 3D has written to the ASSEMBLY.TGA image. Open the image in the bitmap editing application.

2. In Photo-Paint, the alpha channel automatically loads a selection marquee around the background of the image. In Photoshop, you need to Alt(Opt)+click on the Channel #4 icon on the Channels palette to load the selection based on alpha channel information. In Painter, you must hold on the selection mask icon (the middle of the icons on the bottom of the image window), then choose the selection marquee icon (the one on the right) to make the selection marquee appear.

3. In Photoshop and Photo-Paint, the selection marquee might be inverted—the marquee encompasses the foreground objects, not the background. If this is the case, press Shift+F7 to invert the marquee before continuing in Photoshop, and in Photo-Paint, click on the Invert toolbar icon.

4. Click on the foreground color swatch, and choose an RGB value. Write this value down, because you might need it later, depending on your bitmap editor. I've chosen a dark color here, because the background tiling image in the HTML document will be dark. If you choose a similar color, possible fringing (aliasing) around the selection edge will be disguised when the image is converted to transparent GIF format.

5. With the Paint Bucket tool, click inside the selection. See Figure 4-15 for an example of what you should be seeing onscreen.

Figure 4-15: *Fill the background of the image with the color you'll specify as a transparency in the exported GIF copy of the file.*

6. Use your bitmap editor's GIF export capability to export the image to GIF 89a format:

- In Painter, click on the background color swatch on the Art Materials: Color palette, then use the Eyedropper tool to sample the fill color in the image. This sets the background color in Painter to the same background color as your image. Choose File | Save As, then choose GIF from the List Files of Type drop-down list. This displays the Save As GIF Options dialog box. Click on the Background is BG color, click on the Interlace GIF file dialog box, then click on OK.

- In Photoshop, double-click on the Background title on the Layers palette. Doing this displays a dialog box: you're converting a normal image into a layered one—Photoshop won't assign a transparent GIF color to a standard RGB image. Accept the default name for the layer by clicking on OK. Choose File | Export | GIF89a format, then click in the Transparency Index color box. This displays the color picker, and you should enter the RGB values of the foreground color you've chosen in the RGB fields here. Click on OK, then name the file and save it to your hard disk.

- In Photo-Paint, the image needs to be converted to 256 (or fewer) colors before it can be saved as a GIF. Choose Image | Convert to, then choose 256 colors (8-bit). Choose Optimized as the Palette type and choose Error Diffusion as the Dither type. With the Eyedropper tool, click on the background color area, then note the index number for the selected color on the status line. Click on OK, then choose File | Save As, and choose CompuServe Bitmap GIF from the Save as Type drop-down list. An alert box will notify you that masks cannot be saved in this format; click on OK, you don't need the mask Extreme 3D rendered to the alpha channel. Click on the 89a format radio button in the Transparent Color dialog box, then type the index number in the Index field. Check the Interlaced check box, then click on OK.

You're done! Figure 4-16 is a view of the ASSEMBLY.HTM document in the CHAP04 folder on the Companion CD-ROM. As you can see, a frameset was used to display the text and the graphic HTM documents. The 3D graphic's frame has NORESIZE and SCROLLING="no" attributes, so it's always onscreen. The background tiling GIF image is dark enough that it contrasts nicely with the bright chrome lettering.

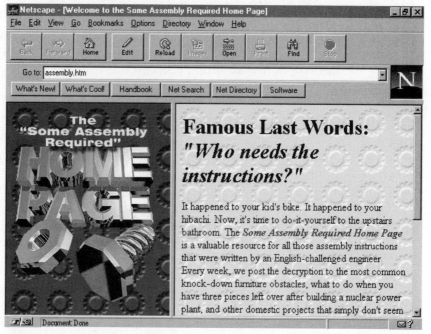

Figure 4-16: *Modeling programs can, literally, add an extra dimension to your graphics.*

MOVING ON

This chapter has not dwelt upon how objects can be manipulated in an HTML document, but instead has concentrated upon how you, the HTML producer, can add a new art form to your profession and your pages. But modeling is only the beginning of the 3D possibilities for Navigator graphics. If you feel confident that you can piece together an interesting virtual world, you can *animate* this world's contents and link a movie to your HTML page.

Animation is Chapter 5's focus, and we'll show you how to use models, paint and draw programs, and some specialty software to add motion to anything you can imagine.

5

Animation & Digital Video Compression

Including digital animation in your multimedia Web document can provide an irresistible attraction for the potential audience; but, because of the present limited bandwidth of the Web, effective movie presentations (like still images) demand succinctness, compactness, and more than a little ingenuity. Getting the audience's attention is easy through the use of animated illustrations or video captures: *keeping* their attention as a clip loads and plays is the *real* trick!

This chapter, therefore, serves a twofold purpose: We'll take you through several methods for making a collection of stills move. We'll also provide treatments of how to ensure cross-platform compatibility with your animated presentation, how to optimize animations for Web use, and how to retain image quality as you compile, convert, and compress your work. The examples in this chapter carry you from concept to completion of an animated file, and the resource images and files can be found in the corresponding folders in the CHAP05 folder of the Companion CD-ROM.

Digital Animation

With all the different formats of animation available for viewing on the Macintosh and in Windows, it's natural to ask whether a specific animation file format can be chosen over another to present the best onscreen video. Fundamentally, Apple QuickTime movies, Microsoft AVI files, Macromedia Director and Shockwave animations, AutoDesk FLI files, Virtus WalkThroughs, and other moving computer images are created in the same way. It's the file *format*—the arrangement of digital information—and the playback requirements that make the real distinction between animated file types.

Animation Tools

All digital animation shares the common "flipbook" approach to displaying moving pictures. That is, a sequence of still images, each containing slightly different visual information, is compressed and then played back in the same screen space to convey the sense of real motion. If you're serious about including animation in a multimedia piece, there are four components, each with corresponding software/hardware requirements, that you should have access to:

- *Some sort of still capture or creation utility.* Although this chapter was written with the graphics designer in mind, video captures that are written out to a sequence of single image files can be treated exactly like a collection of paintings or drawings when you plan an animation. Some graphics software actually comes with an animation-compiling engine (the third item in this bulleted list). Basically, if you have a method for previewing the progression within the still images you create as raw resources for the animation, you can use almost any commercial graphics package.

  The following is a list of applications that you may own or have heard of that can be used to produce uncompiled animation files. Many of these programs are featured in this chapter, and a dagger after the name of a program indicates that that program comes with an animation-compiling utility. Prices of these programs range from shareware to under $400 street price:

- Paint Shop Pro, v. 3.2 or higher (Windows)
- Corel Photo-Paint, v. 6 or higher (Windows) †
- Adobe Photoshop
- Fractal Design Painter, v. 3 or higher †
- Ray Dream Designer Studio †
- Macromedia Extreme 3D †
- Visual Software's Visual Reality, v.2 or higher (Windows)†
- Adobe Dimensions, v. 2 or higher (Macintosh)
- The Valis Group's Flo' †
- Kai's Power Tools, v. 3 or higher †
- Adobe TextureMaker (Macintosh) †

The list could go on to include virtually *every* drawing, painting, and modeling application, but this is a good starting place for your shopping if you need an application within which to design animation frames.

- *An editing utility.* You'll most likely be able to use your image creation program to make minor changes to rendered still frames, except if you use a modeling or texture-creating program for the animation. A good image editing utility should offer paint and/or drawing tools, resizing capability (in case you need to make the overall animation frame smaller), the capability to copy a design area precisely into a selection in a different frame, and batch conversion features such as dithering down to a common palette (covered later in this chapter). Adobe Photoshop is excellent for image dithering, resizing, and retouching; GraphicConverter (Macintosh) and Brenda the Batch Renderer (Windows) can make an easy task of color reducing and changing the format of multiple images. We've included Brenda the Batch Renderer on the CD-ROM.

- *A compiling engine.* Generally, the programs that advertise the capability to create an animation include their own compiling engine. A good animation package will also offer a compressor/decompressor (or *codec*) within the compiler, with options as to the amount and type of codec used. A truly superb animation package allows you to render still images out to sequentially numbered files, so you can compile later—like overnight or after you've added special effects to the still frames. We'll get to the types of codecs and recommendations for animation file types later in this chapter. If your chosen application for creating or capturing raw still images can't compile the images, here are some additional programs worth looking into:

■ Adobe Premiere. Premiere is more expensive than, say a home accounting software package, but it's also a complete video and animation editing suite.

■ Macromedia Director. Director, like Premiere, is a complete graphics solution, and it is similarly priced. You cannot save an animation in QuickTime or Windows AVI formats, but you can distill a Director project down to a Shockwave file that will animate on the Web through a Navigator plug-in.

■ MotionWorks CameraMan, v. 2 or later.

■ PIXAR Typestry's MovieMaker utility. Typestry has been discontinued, but if you can still get a copy through a mail-order house, or if you already own it, MovieMaker will compile a series of still images in BMP, TIF, or PICT format.

■ Dave's Targa Animator (Windows/DOS).

■ Video for DOS (Windows/DOS).

■ MovieStar Maker, by Intelligence At Large (Macintosh), which can bring still images into its workspace and generate an animation that can be played on the Web through the use of a Navigator plug-in for the Macintosh or Windows.

■ Avid VideoShop, which comes free with many models of the Performa and PowerMac 8500. VideoShop can import QuickTime movies and can compile still frames.

■ *Image Playback.* Anything that will require your complete attention as much as creating an animation should be reverse-planned so that you know what the final format of the animation will be. Currently, Navigator 2.0 supports animated GIFs without the use of a plug-in (you'll see how to create one later in this chapter). Navigator 2.0 also supports the CoolFusion plug-in (Windows) for AVI movies and Sparkle (Macintosh) for QuickTime, and there are helper apps for QuickTime available for both Windows and the Macintosh. Additionally, Shockwave files and other proprietary animation types are supported through third-party helper applications; you cannot display these animation types as inline objects in an HTML document as of this writing.

Before you design frame one, ask yourself who your audience will be, then design in an application that allows playback for the widest audience with the least inconvenience downloading an animation player.

CEL ANIMATION & ANIMATED GIFs

Traditional animation usually begins by painting *key frames* on clear acetate (*cels*); a key frame describes a key event in the time line of the animation, such as a character's arm in a fully extended position. How the character's arm *gets* from his side to the fully extended position is the work of *tweeners*—animation studio artists whose responsibility it is to draw on acetates to fill in sequential action *in between* the key frames. The total animated length of this key event depends upon how many frames of acetate are compiled into the animation. Generally, animations for traditional projection contain 12 unique drawings per second; because film travels at 24 frames per second, duplicate animation cels are used to fill out the 24 frames, and the animation is said to be done "in twos." Because traditional animation needed to be accomplished manually, Walt Disney Studios once hired almost every professional (and novice!) tweener in California to help complete the now-classic *Snow White*.

Let's presume that, like the author's, your business *doesn't* consist of hundreds of skilled animation artists, but instead it is you alone who are in charge of authoring an animation element for a Web document. Let's further presume that an animation assignment you've landed is a simple one: illustrate a ball bouncing to get the audience's attention on the opening page of a Web site. Before you dip a virtual pen in the inkwell, let's take a look at the requirements of this assignment. There are basically three ways at present that you can easily add a small animation to a Web document—animated GIFs, embedded QuickTime movies, and Java scripts.

We'll choose the first method—animated GIFs—because, unlike a QuickTime movie, an animated GIF can be exceptionally small in file size, and doesn't require a helper app to run it for the audience. JavaScripting an animation requires that you distribute a class of Java applet to animate the file, and that you have the experience or an authoring tool to facilitate Java programming. We'll touch upon Java applet special effects in Chapter 8, "Putting It All Together."

The action of a ball bouncing can be most easily accomplished through tweening a small number of frames manually. You don't need a modeling program with advanced animation features to accomplish the assignment here.

Every good animation has a *plot;* a ball bouncing up and down might seem like poor commercial entertainment, but let's take a serious look at the plot of a Web animation.

CREATING RESOURCE FILES FOR AN ANIMATED LOOP

From the early days of animation, there has been a technique called *looping* an animation that effectively captures an audience's attention for far longer than the sum total of frames you put into an animation. A loop, as the name suggests, begins at the same point where it ends. This is also called a *cycle* in traditional animation, where artists could shave hours off illustrating a caveman peddling his family home by filming the same cycle of animation cels that describe the beginning-to-end of this action.

The following example uses Fractal Design Painter to create the animated ball. The plot of this movie is the ball bounces down to the bottom of the image window, then bounces back up to complete the cycle. If you don't own Painter, you'll still benefit from reading the steps, because you can use the some of the same techniques in Corel Photo-Paint or many other painting and drawing applications.

Here's how to generate eight frames that describe the motion of a ball bouncing from the air, to the floor, then back into the air to complete the animation loop:

1. Launch Painter, then choose File | New, and create a new image file that's 128 pixels high, 128 pixels wide, with a Resolution of 72 pixels per inch. Choose a Paper color that you don't plan to use in the illustration of the ball. The finished, animated GIF will use the Paper color you choose as a transparency value. In the Picture Type field, click on the Movie With button, type **8** in the Frames Entry field, then click on OK. You now need to name a proprietary type of file format, a Frame Stack, which will hold all your still images.

2. In the Enter Movie Name dialog box, pick a drive and folder for your movie "work shell," name the file BOUNCER.FRM, then click on Save. You'll now have the option of deciding how many Onion Skin layers the Frame Stack displays and the color depth in which the Frame Stack is saved to hard disk. Painter's Frame Stack is a proprietary feature (other applications can't read a *.FRM file) that allows animation cells to be edited as single frames, stored in one compressed file format.

    Onion Skin is an allusion to traditional animation, where a tweener would want to check the amount of difference a design displays between individual sequential frames (not key frames). Choose three layers here, so you can check on the progression of the ball as it moves from the air to the floor and back again in this animation. Also, choose 24-bit color with 8-bit mask before clicking on OK. The finished animation frames will be of significantly lower color depth, but 24-bit color allows you to preserve your work to hard disk in case you need to take a break, and the 8-bit mask allows Painter's Floaters to be saved to disk without merging them into the background image. We'll be using Painter's Floaters (similar to Photoshop's Image Layers and Photo-Paint's Objects) feature to animate the bouncing ball. See Chapter 4, "Working With Models," for more information on transparency masking.

3. Choose the Oval Selection tool from the Tools palette. If the Rectangular Selection tool is currently displayed, click and hold on the Rectangular Selection tool, then choose the Oval tool from the flyout.

4. Hold Shift to constrain the shape of the Oval selection to that of a perfect circle, then click and drag a selection roughly ¼ the size of the image frame.

5. Choose the (Floater) Adjuster tool, click on the selection to turn it into a floating object above the background. Press Ctrl(Cmd)+4 to display the Objects: Floater List. You'll see a new entry to the list after clicking with the Adjuster tool, and by default, a visible bounding box appears around the new floating object (but because the object is the same color as the background at this point, it's hard to see it).

6. Click on the Trim button on the Objects palette. Because Painter adds feathering to all new Floaters, you must either go through this quick step to reduce the "padding" around a floating object, or change the default for this process in Painter in General Preferences. The marquee indicating the size of the circle will shrink.

7. With any of the Artist's Brushes, paint a design on the floating image object. Because you're painting on a floating object, and not the background paper, the shape of the circle will quickly become apparent. In Figure 5-1, I've gone with a slightly different approach to animated character creation. I filled the Floater using KPT Texture Explorer, then used KPT Glass Lens Bright to distort and add a highlight to the circle. You can also use Painter 4's native (Effects | Surface Control) Quick Warp command in combination with the Dodge and Burn paint tools to achieve a similar effect.

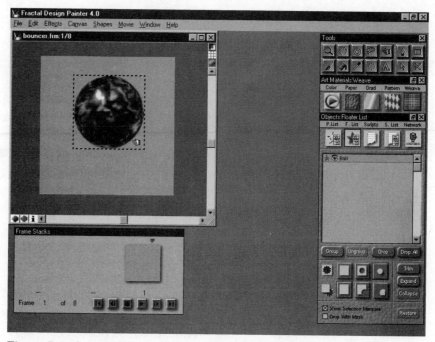

Figure 5-1: *Create an image Floater, then color and shade it to make it look like a 3D ball.*

8. At this point, you're on frame 1 of 8; the Frame Stacks palette confirms this. And the floating ball might or might not be in its first position, the location on the background where the animation loop will begin. With the Adjuster tool, click and drag the Floater so it's in the top third of the frame, centered horizontally. This gives the ball some room to drop and bounce.

9. Click on the Frame Advance button (the second from the right) on the Frame Stacks palette, or press PgUp. This moves you to frame 2 of your animation, and surprise: the Floater appears on frame 2. Part of the secret to Painter's Frame Stack is that you drop a copy of a Floater as you advance frames.

In Fractal Design Painter, you shouldn't go back to a previous frame with a Floater highlighted or visible on the Objects: Floater List. This action will continue to place a copy of the Floater on pages you leaf through, and ruin your design. Painter 3.1 allows you to render a Floater as "inert" when scrolling through animation frames by clicking on the blank area of the Objects: Floater List, but version 4, shown in this chapter, operates a little differently. You need to close the Eye icon on the Objects: Floater List to hide a Floater from view and prevent it from leaving a copy of itself on frames you want to review. You can do this by single-clicking on the Eye icon associated with a specific Floater.

10. Press the keyboard's Down arrow key about 10 times from your view of frame 2. This nudges the Floater by 10 pixels in frame 2.

11. Click on the Frame Advance button on the Frame Stacks palette (or press PgUp). By frame 3, the ball should make contact with the "floor," that is, the bottom of the image frame. And we're going to distort the ball shortly. Pixel-based images progressively deteriorate as you move and reassign pixels in this manner, and you'll want to restore the ball Floater as it rises from the "floor," so choose Edit | Copy with the Floater icon highlighted on the Objects: Floater List, then choose Edit | Paste | Normal. Double-click on the duplicate Floater title on the Objects: Floater List to bring up the Floater attributes box, then type **Copy**, **Spare**, or something that creates a distinction between the copy and the Floater you'll distort next.

12. Click on the spare copy Floater's Eye icon on the Objects: Floater List to hide it.

13. Click on the original Floater's title on the Objects: Floater List, then choose Effects | Orientation | Scale.

14. In the Scale Selection dialog box, uncheck the Constrain Aspect Ratio and Preserve Center check boxes. This is an

interactive editing box, so you can manually adjust the bounding box to scale the image. Click and drag the top right corner of the bounding box around the ball downward until the Vertical Scale field in the dialog box reads about 40 percent, as shown in Figure 5-2. Click on OK to complete the edit. Reposition the ball using the Adjustment tool to make it almost touch the bottom of the image window.

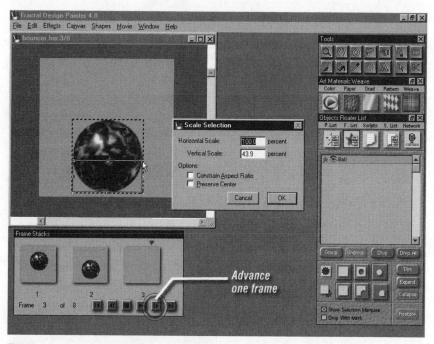

Figure 5-2: *Scale the Floater along only one axis to give the appearance of it flattening as it hits the image window bottom.*

15. Press PgUp (or click on the Advance Frame button on the Frame Stacks palette) to move on to frame 4.

16. Repeat step 14, further flattening the ball Floater by about 50 percent vertical measurement. Readjust the Floater's position if necessary.

17. Press PgUp, and in frame 5, use the Scale Selection dialog box to increase Vertical Scale of the Floater by 200 percent. Reposition the Floater so it's now rising from the bottom of the image window.

18. Press PgUp, then use the Scale Selection to increase the Floater's vertical measurement by about 300 percent. In Figure 5-3, you can see that the ball appears to be dynamically resizing as it pushes off the bottom of the image window. Exaggerated elasticity is a popular animated cartoon convention, and it also works when you only have a few frames in which to convey a graphical idea.

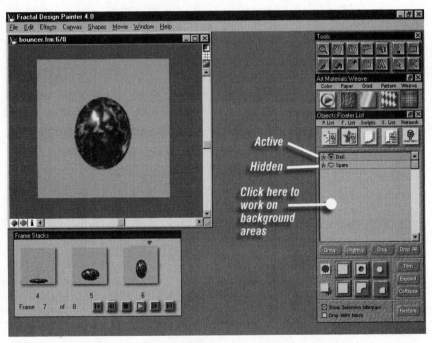

Figure 5-3: *Use the placement of the Floater within the image frame to convey movement and distort the dimensions to suggest the material the ball is made of.*

19. Although these frames will fly quickly by the audience, who therefore won't notice the image *quality* of the Floater, the Floater has been stretched and compressed three times, so the original pixel information isn't what it used to be! Click on the Drop button on the Objects palette, press PgUp to move to frame 7, then click on the Eye icon of the duplicate Floater to choose it and make it visible.

20. In frame 7, use the (Floater) Adjustment tool to reposition the Floater so it's slightly above the top edge of the original Floater you dropped in frame 6. Then, in the final frame, make certain that the Floater is about 10 pixels below the ball's position in frame 1. Drop the Floater in frame 8, then run a preview of the animation by clicking on the Play button on the Frame Stacks palette. Congratulations! You now have a timeless epic!

If anything needs to be tweaked at this point, use the Rectangular selection tool to draw a broad rectangle around the ball in any frame. Then float the selection by clicking on the Adjustment tool, use the arrow keys on your keyboard to nudge the Floater, then click on the Drop button on the Objects palette to merge the Floater with the background.

It should be noted here that a Frame Stacks file can be edited in future sessions of Painter, but Floaters are automatically merged when you close a Frame Stacks file. Additionally, the Frame Stacks file is automatically updated with every edit you perform; that is, there is no Save option under File after you've created a Frame Stack. Your only options at this point are to either export the Frame Stack to a nonproprietary file format or continue finessing the Frame Stack. Because Painter will *not* request through a dialog box whether you want to save changes, don't make any edits to the Frame Stack you don't want saved when you close the file. This behavior is true in Corel Photo-Paint, also.

FILE NAMING CONVENTIONS

There are three processes that sequential image files need to undergo to compile an animated GIF file. First, the original image files should be numbered sequentially: BALL0001.TIF, BALL0002.TIF, and so on is a good naming convention for two reasons: First, the files you created in the previous example can be repurposed in the future; usually, it's not a good idea to color-reduce or crop your original images, because you might want to use them in the future at a higher color capability, and editing the originals removes the possibility of recompiling an animation with them in the future. By numbering the files sequentially, you can easily arrange them in the future. Second, most compilers require that imported collections of files are in a numbered sequence, allowing a three-character prefix followed by four or five digits. Check the documentation of the animation compiler you intend to use for specific naming conventions.

If you created your eight frames in a paint or drawing program, you should manually edit the names of the files as suggested above. Macintosh users should save the image files to PICT format, because we'll show you how to use GIF Builder v. 02 shortly, and GIF Builder seems to work better with the PICT format than other graphics types. Windows users can save in TIF, BMP, PCX, or other image types for use with GIF Construction Set.

If you created your images in Painter, follow the next steps, and Painter will automatically number the files:

1. Choose File | Save As, then click on "Save movie as numbered files," then click on OK.

2. In the Save Image As dialog box, type in a three-letter name, then type **001** directly after your three-letter prefix. Painter will automatically advance all the image file names to produce sequentially numbered files. Uncheck the Save Mask check box and pick a location on your hard disk for the files. Windows users should choose TIFF files (*.TIF) from the Save as Type drop-down list, then click on OK. Macintosh Painter users should choose 15-bit PICT file type.

3. Close Painter, and you're done.

How to Work Around the "Hard Drive Crunch"

If you intend to get into Web animation, CD authoring, or other types of multimedia presentations, hard disk organization is a must. You should create folders on your drive that will store the raw animation still files, and perhaps a subfolder which contains converted images that go into the finished animation.

After a dozen or so animations, you'll also find that you might be running out of hard drive space! Hard drive space offers the quickest access time, because even 6x speed CDs can't compete with the read/write times of today's fast SCSI and IDE hard drives. Therefore, completed animation projects should be archived on either short-term or long-term media. If you know you're not going to use an animation folder for a while, tape backup is okay, but having a CD burned is even better. Personal CD burners that can make a single copy master go for under $1,000 these days, and CD-mastering software is often bundled with the CD burner.

Short-term storage can usually be accomplished with a large media drive, such as the Iomega Zip drives, or the Bernoulli and SyQuest cartridges. *Every* application these days wants as much fast, empty disk space as possible to write temp files, so if you know you'll need animation files you've created in the past month, get them off your hard drive and onto large-media storage. This way, the files don't require unpacking (as do tape backup and PKZipped and StuffIt files), and you can retrieve your work from large-media storage almost as quickly as from your hard drive.

Color Reduction, Common Palettes & Compiling

Now that you have your resource files for the animation, copies of the files need to go through one or two processes before you bring them into a GIF animation compiler.

Animated still frames, like any digital image, use a local color palette to display colors within the bitmap image. As discussed in Chapter 3, "Bitmap Graphics & Special Effects," the smaller the color palette, the smaller the finished image will be when saved to disk and sent across the Web. The images you've created now need to be color reduced and color mapped to one, common color palette. If the images each contained a unique color table, the resulting animation would display color shifts that resemble static or simply a corrupt data file.

GIF Builder v. 02 for the Macintosh is a utility included on the Companion CD-ROM that can map multiple images to a common color table, specify a drop-out color for the finished GIF image, and even time and create a loop from an animated sequence. Here's how to perform the common palette color reduction and compile the finished animation from within one Macintosh program:

1. Install GIF Builder onto your hard drive.

2. Create a folder on your desktop and move the PICT files you created earlier to this folder.

3. Launch GIF Builder, then make certain that the Frames window and the open folder window containing your image files can both be seen on the desktop.

4. If you've experimented with GIF Builder prior to this example, choose Select All, then Clear to empty the Frames window for this example. Drag the first frame image into the Frames window. The name of the file, its dimensions, and other data will appear in list form in the Frames window.

5. Drag the remaining files, one at a time and in sequential order, into the Frames window, as shown in Figure 5-4. If you don't drag the files into the window in order, you can rearrange their order in the window by click+dragging their titles up or down in the sequence of files.

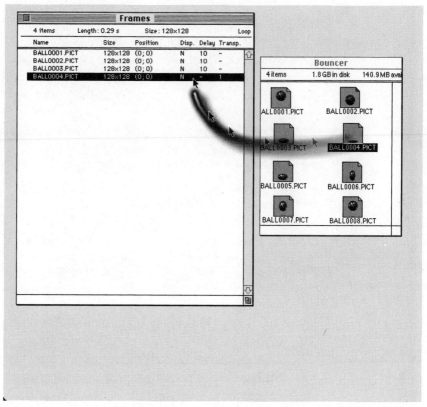

Figure 5-4: *Creating an animated GIF file is as easy as drag and drop with GIF Builder.*

6. If you've accidentally copied the wrong sequence of images to the Frames window, click and drag the image title up or down in the list to change the order.

7. Choose Options | Interlace. This will make the GIF animation begin to appear on a visitor's screen the moment it begins to download.

8. Choose Colors | Load Palette, then choose the Navigator palette 6 X 6 (216 colors). Click on Open to load the palette.

TIP

The Navigator palette is the color palette (lookup table) used by Netscape Navigator. If you work only with Netscape colors, your graphic will not display dithering. And if you color-reduce an RGB image to this palette of 216 colors, you can be fairly certain that the image will display on the Web the same as you see it onscreen.

Although GIF Builder is a Macintosh-only application, the CHAP05 folder on the Companion CD-ROM includes the same color palette in Adobe Photoshop format (file name NCT.ACT, for Navigator Color Table) for Windows users, and the same file as a TIFF image for users who can use a color image as a color table within a specific application. In Photoshop, you can choose Load from the Indexed Color dialog box when color reducing an RGB image to indexed color. You can also specify the NCT color table when exporting an image to GIF89a format in Photoshop.

9. Choose Options | Loop. The animation will now continuously repeat itself from the time the image loads on a page to the next event in Navigator's browser, such as linking to a different page or if the visitor clicks on Navigator's Stop button.

10. Choose Transparent Background | Other, then choose the background color you want to drop out. In our example, solid green was specified in Painter for the Background (R:0, G:255 or 100 percent, and B:0). Choose the color you used in your animation files if you want the background to drop out in the final animation. Alternatively, you can choose Transparent Background | Based on first pixel from GIF Builder's menu. Generally, the first (upper left) pixel is

part of the background of an image. If you created an animation series of files earlier that shouldn't have any transparent color, ignore this entire step.

11. Choose File | Build, then name your file. Read the documentation accompanying GIF Builder, send Yves Piguet, the author of GIF Builder, a postcard thanking him, and you're done.

Windows users can build a GIF animation with a common color palette by using Steven William Rimmer's GIF Construction Set, found at http://www.mindworkshop.com/alchemy/alchemy.html. Install the program, and here's how to color map and compile the animated GIF:

1. Launch GIF Construction Set, then choose File | New.

2. Click on Insert, then click on Loop. This adds an information block after the header of the file that will tell Navigator to play the animation endlessly.

3. Click on Insert, then click on Image. Choose NCT.TIF from the CHAP05 folder of the Companion CD-ROM, then click on OK.

4. A dialog box pops up, as shown in Figure 5-5, informing you that the image does not match the global palette for the file you're creating. This is okay; you're going to delete this file from the list in this multi-image GIF file later—for now, you want it to serve as the color table for all the future GIF images you'll import to make up the animation. Click on "Use this image as the global palette," then click on OK.

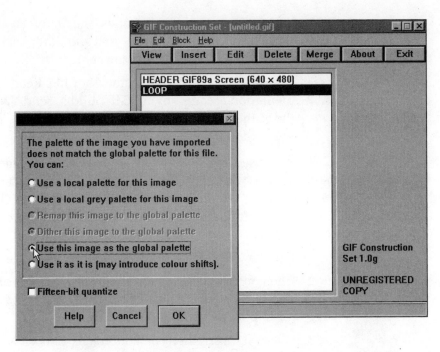

Figure 5-5: *Use the NCT image as a placeholder in your animated GIF file to make the subsequent images you import conform to Netscape's color table.*

5. Click on Insert, then click on Control. A control block is added to the list of ingredients that go into this multi-image GIF file. A control block tells Navigator to erase the previous image, and it can also instruct Navigator to display a color as transparent. A control block must precede an image in the file, and we haven't imported one yet, so we'll fine-tune the control block in a few steps.

6. Click on Insert | Image, then choose the first in the sequence of files you want to be in the animation. A dialog box pops up that tells you that the palette for this image doesn't match the global color palette (the NCT.TIF image). Choose "Dither this image to the global palette," then click on OK.

7. Double-click on the control block that precedes the image on the list. This brings up the Edit Control Block dialog

box, as shown in Figure 5-6. Click on the Transparent colour check box. Click on the eyedropper tool, and the screen will display the image the control block governs. Click on the background color in the image, and you're returned to the dialog box, and the transparency value has been specified for the image. Click on OK to return to GIF Construction Set's list.

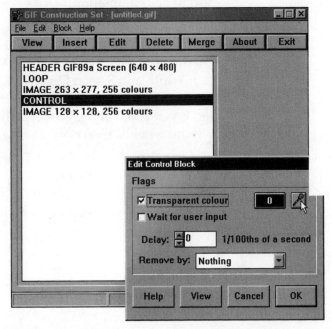

Figure 5-6: *You can choose a transparency color for an image in an animation with GIF Construction Set.*

8. Because it's time-consuming to perform the previous step for every control block for every image you import, press Ctrl+C while the control block is highlighted to copy it to the clipboard.

9. Click on the image title on the bottom of the list, then press Ctrl+V to paste a copy of the first control block to the bottom of the list.

10. Click on Insert, then click on Image, then choose the second file in the sequence of your animation. Choose "Dither this image to the global palette" in the dialog box, then click on OK.

11. Press Ctrl+V to paste the control block to the bottom of the list.

12. Repeat steps 9 and 10 with the remainder of the images you want to add to your animation.

13. Once every image file has a control block preceding it, it's time to clean up the file and save it to its finished format. Double-click on the HEADER block on the list, then type **128** in the Screen Width and Screen Depth fields. 128 was the pixel dimension of the file you created in the Painter example earlier. If you used an image sized differently, enter the values in these fields, then click on OK.

14. Click on the first image in the list (the NCT.TIF image is easily selected from the bunch: it's 263 X 277 pixels), then press the Delete button. GIF Construction Set doesn't use the keyboard Delete key. If your screen looks like Figure 5-7, you're in business.

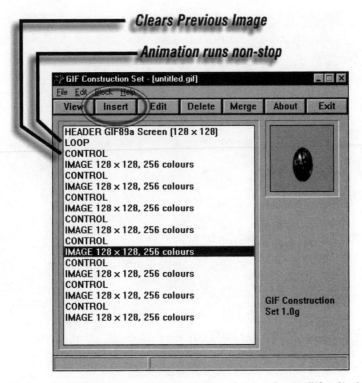

Figure 5-7: *The list on GIF Construction Set is a "recipe" for displaying a GIF animation in Navigator's browser.*

    15. Choose File I Save, then name your masterpiece, and save it to your hard disk. You're done.

The GIF animated image you've created can now be referenced in an HTML document, or it simply can be dragged into Navigator's browser window to preview. In Figure 5-8, you can see the finished animation. Actually, books can't show animation, but Figure 5-8 shows a *single frame* of this example!

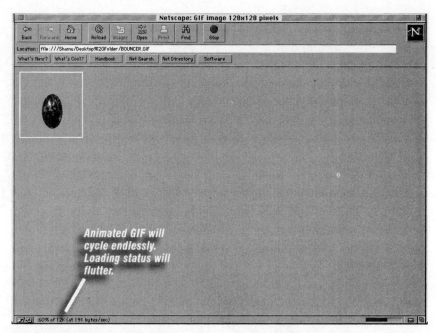

Figure 5-8: *An animated GIF requires no special helper app or plug-in; any viewer with Netscape Navigator 2.0 can see your movie.*

It should be noted here that there are some drawbacks and limitations of the animated GIF construction. First, if you've chosen to loop an animation (which the author recommends for art's sake), there is only one way for the visitor to stop the GIF from animating: They can click on Navigator's Stop button, but this is not an obvious procedure. A smart viewer who grows irritated with an animation could also turn graphics off in Navigator, then reload the page, but don't count on it. The only ways to *conveniently* allow a viewer of your site to turn a looping animation off is to provide a jump to a different page, or to provide information that a click on Navigator's Stop button will halt the action. Bear this in mind when using this new multimedia "weapon!" Additionally, viewers who use older browsers (or non-Navigator browsers) will not see the animation; instead, they'll see the first frame of the animation.

Programmer Royal Fraiser is credited with first discovering the capability of manipulating header information in GIFs to create animations. To date, Unisys, the creator of the GIF file format, has made no claim that the format contains capabilities beyond that of compactness and platform independence. Therefore, no manufacturer has really made an attempt to support animated GIFs beyond those who created authoring tools specifically for designing small animations.

CD-ROM There is a way to reduce the file size of an animated GIF that can help speed your multimedia creation across the wire. If you take the time to dither down your collection of still frames to a very small palette before running them through GIF Builder or GIF Construction Set, you'll save file size. Paint Shop Pro for Windows, and Brenda the Batch Renderer (Windows) are located on the Companion CD-ROM; they and GraphicConverter (Macintosh) can reduce a color palette way below 256 unique colors. Fundamentally, it's a question of speed versus aesthetics: if you design animation stills with a very limited number of colors, color reduction will not produce dithering that distracts from the composition.

OTHER PLOTS FOR GIF ANIMATIONS

I have to admit that a bouncing ball has been done by other HTML multimedia authors, and although it's not a unique animation, it helps demonstrate both a principle and a concept behind small HTML animations. In the CHAP05 folder are finished animations—CAMCORD.GIF and NEWNEON.GIF. These files were designed using the steps outlined earlier, and they have simplistic yet effective story lines you might want to use as a creative springboard.

Here's the trick: Both CAMCORD and NEWNEON are three-frame GIF animations. CAMCORD is a camcorder icon whose Play button blinks on and off and NEWNEON is a neon sign that says "NEW," and it, too, flashes on and off. It has been the author's experience that there is nothing quite as *annoying* as blinking text and icons, but these animations take it easy on the viewer's eyes for a special reason. The changing elements in each animation *fade* on and off. The first frame is that of full illumination, the second frame dims the illumination, and the third frame is completely off. Additionally, each frame is *duplicated* in the GIF animation as a means for slowing the animation down. You cannot depend upon a steady bandwidth, or some of the timing features in GIF animation authoring tools, to keep a steady rate of image progression.

It has been suggested by the creators of these GIF animation authoring tools that viewer download time these days is at an average of 1.7K/second with a 14.4 modem, given optimal line conditions, optimal server transfer rate, consistent ISP throughput, and so on. The worst you can realistically expect is that it takes a second per kilobyte of Web document to download to the viewer. Therefore, if you want your audience to receive a page quickly, keep the total size of your document to under 30K, interlace GIF images (GIF Builder and GIF Construction Set can both perform interlacing), and use progressive JPEGs for graphics if you know your audience uses Navigator 2.0 or later.

PAINTER'S SIDEKICK: POSER

Before we move on to other types of Web animation and compression schemes, it should be noted here that if you have a need to create animations to illustrate actions human beings perform, Fractal Design Poser in combination with Painter, or another animation compiling program, can be your ticket to attention-getting multimedia. Poser offers a collection of 3D human forms you can customize and pose; no modeling experience is necessary, and the renderings can be copied in sequence to the clipboard to make an animated sequence.

If you need to demonstrate online how a piece of machinery is used, express an emotion, or if you simply want to attract attention, Poser makes it easy. In Figure 5-9, you can see a human male figure posed in a sprinting position; the window size has been scaled down to accommodate the throughput of the Web. Once the figure has been rendered to screen, Ctrl(Cmd)+C copies the image to the clipboard. The clipboard image can then be pasted into any application that can handle bitmap-type images.

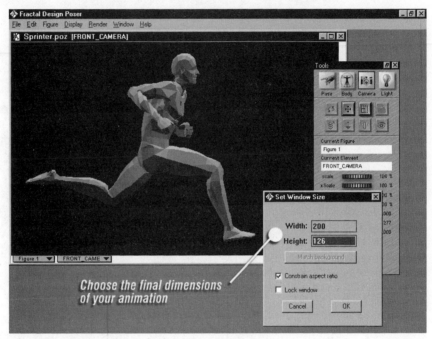

Figure 5-9: *Fractal Design Poser can add a touch of humanity to an animation.*

In Figure 5-10, you can see that Painter has been loaded in the background, and I've toggled between applications to paste a clipboard copy of frame four into a small animation. Once the Frame Stack in Painter has been populated, the file can be exported as sequential still frames, or compiled as an AVI or QuickTime movie.

Figure 5-10: *You can assemble a collection of still Poser figures and animate them in a number of other applications.*

Although an animated GIF file can add interest to an HTML document, animations can also be posted as files that the user downloads and can be played across the Web when the viewer has the right helper application. In the next section, we move from manual "flipbook" animation creation to applications that perform the tweening for you.

3D ANIMATIONS

Specular International has created Specular LogoMotion, a type of application software that can fly, pan, stretch, and otherwise animate a 3D creation. If you read Chapter 4, "Working With Models," you realize that modeling can be as easy or as involved as your graphics requirements. LogoMotion makes it simple to both create and animate a logo, an imported DXF model, or a dimensionalized design you've created in a drawing program.

Reading Chapter 4, "Working With Models," before continuing with the examples in this chapter will help you tremendously if you don't have experience with modeling/rendering applications.

Rendering quality, options, and ease of use aside, LogoMotion is also attractively street-priced under $100. If you upgraded to Corel 6, a Windows version, CorelMOTION 3D, came with the software bundle, and Macintosh users can find LogoMotion included with many software upgrades.

In the following example, we have a fictitious online service in need of a splashy Web site. PartyMakers is a catering service: you provide the crowd, they provide the balloons, music, and refreshments. The first place to gather the materials for the PartyMakers animation is Adobe Illustrator, or a drawing application that can export to the Illustrator format. Although LogoMotion has its own drawing tools and can use system fonts, you might have more creative freedom designing the 2D paths that make up the elements of a LogoMotion 3D scene in a drawing program. In Figure 5-11, you can see the PartyMakers lettering has been aligned and rotated to suggest a festive occasion (URW Candy was the font before converting it to curves), and an eighth note suggests music in a stylish fashion. The resource file for this assignment, PRTYMAKE.AI, can be found in the CHAP05 folder on the Companion CD-ROM if you'd like to participate.

CD-ROM

Figure 5-11: *Use a drawing application's tools to create the 2D paths you need; LogoMotion can import Illustrator format vector drawings.*

Here's how to import and create the 2D elements in LogoMotion (CorelMOTION 3D users may need to perform slightly different steps—the two programs are nearly, but not completely, identical):

1. In Adobe Illustrator (or FreeHand, CorelDRAW, or other drawing application) import (or open) PRTYMAKE.AI from the Companion CD-ROM. You may choose to create your own 2D paths for import to LogoMotion here, too.

2. Copy each of the 2D elements to a new file, name the file, and save it to your hard disk in the Adobe Illustrator (*.AI) format. In this example, the word "Party," the word "Makers," and the music note are collections of paths that have been combined (Compound paths). This means that when they are imported and extruded in LogoMotion, the collection of paths will move and rotate as a single element. We'll get to the creation of the party balloon shortly;

balloon creation requires lathing of a 2D path, and is more easily visualized and dimensionalized within LogoMotion.

3. Close the drawing program and launch LogoMotion.

4. Choose File | Import | EPS, then choose the PARTY Illustrator file you saved earlier. Make certain that the Extrude, not the Lathe button is checked in the dialog box before clicking on Open.

    CorelMOTION users need to "prime" the Scene window with an extruded object before you can import an Illustrator or Corel CMX format file. Click on the Extrude Object tool, click once in the Camera window, then with the Vertical Move tool, double-click on the cube. This sends you to the Workshop View in MOTION 3D, where you can delete the cube path, and choose File | Import | Outline to import the PARTY path. Center the path so that the middle of the path is on the converging point of the X- and Y-guidelines, then click on Done to return to the Camera window.

5. LogoMotion, by default, tends to extrude paths a little deeper than you'd like, but this is easily fixed. With the PARTY object selected, choose Model | Object Info, then type **0.08** in the Dimension | Z: field, and click on OK.

    CorelMOTION users should right-click on the model, choose Transform from the shortcut menu, and on the Scale tab type **20** in the Z: percentage field. For some reason, CorelMOTION creates extruded objects rotated 90° from a face-front view; click on the Rotation tab, type **90** in the X Orientation field, click on Apply, then click on OK.

6. Repeat steps 4 and 5 for the MAKERS path and the music note path.

7. Go to Windows | Window Options, type **200** in the Width field, type **150** in the Height field, then click on OK.

    CorelMOTION users should specify the size of the animation window through File | Scene Setup.

8. With the Vertical Move tool, arrange the elements so that you can clearly see and move them all in the future. Choose Windows | Views | Right View to offer a second

view of the scene; you can more easily manipulate 3D objects from two different perspectives.

9. Click on the Lathe Object tool, then click in the Camera window. Double-click on the sphere in the window to move to the Workshop view.

10. In the Workshop Design window, choose Points | Reshape Outline. (CorelMOTION users: press Delete to remove the current path.) With any of the design tools (the Pencil tool might work best here), design a balloon, as shown in Figure 5-12. As you can see, the 2D profile is spun around its Y-axis to create a balloon in the wireframe preview window at right.

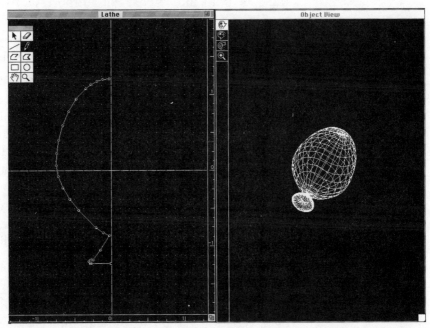

Figure 5-12: *Create a balloon shape by lathing a 2D path around its vertical axis.*

11. Choose Workshop | Exit Workshop. (CorelMOTION users: click on Done.)

12. Reposition the balloon so it fits into the scene. At present, all the objects in the scene are covered with default surface shaders. Click on the PARTY lettering, choose Windows | Surface Floater, then choose from any of the surfaces you think would help convey a party atmosphere. I went with Tangerine for the lettering, and Blue Plastic for the music note and balloon.

    CorelMOTION users should right-click on an object, choose Properties from the shortcut menu, then choose a surface from the Surfaces list.

TIP

This is optional, but you might want to add a bevel to the edges of the lettering and music note. To do this, select the object, then choose Model | Bevel, then choose from the list of presets, and click and drag on the bevel profile in the Preview window to adjust the shape of the bevel.

CorelMOTION users can access the Bevel controls by right-clicking on an object, choosing Properties from the shortcut menu, then clicking on the Bevel Properties tab.

---

13. Adjust the default light in the scene so the scene is illuminated. Work between the Right View and the Camera View window if necessary; click and drag on the light to reposition it.

14. In the Mode drop-down list, choose Shade Better. (CorelMOTION users should click on the Shade Better toolbar button.) If your preview looks okay, it's time to animate the scene. If not, adjust the light, move the objects, and/or specify a different surface for any of the objects.

The plot for the PartyMakers movie, like the bouncing ball, is a simple one: the PARTY and MAKERS lettering will rotate, and the balloon and music note will move up and down. This action will get attention, and the lettering will remain legible as it rotates, acting as an advertisement while it entertains the visitor to the site.

Let's talk about number of frames and time for a moment. Fifteen frames per second is a common animation speed for digital movies; animations for the Web cannot really sustain a higher rate of display without dropping frames. You need to take into account all factors for viewing the file before you animate. The animation frame is a fairly small size and will download fairly quickly with a high-speed connection. Also the total length of the movie governs the speed at which a viewer can see the animation. Let's target two seconds as the total length of the PartyMakers movie, and you'll see in the next example how to use LogoMotion to loop the movie so it will play over and over again onscreen. Compressing the movie as it is compiled will further shrink the broadcast file size, and reducing color depth for the animation helps also.

TIP

You'll notice in the figures in this section that a backdrop has been added to the animation. You can select from LogoMotion's stock backdrops by choosing Stagehands | Backdrops. The backdrop will auto-size to the dimensions of your animation frame. Additionally, if you'd like to create your own backdrop, save an image file to PICT format. CorelMOTION users should save an image to Targa, TIFF, BMP, or PCX format.

The larger the image file, the longer MOTION takes to process each frame, so it's a good idea to create a backdrop image of the same dimensions as the scene window.

Here's how to block the scene, and create the animation:

1. Choose Windows | Sequencer. (CorelMOTION users: click on the Timelines button on the toolbar.)

2. Click and drag the world event marker to the one-second marker on the panel, then move the objects around using the Rotation and Move tools. Use your own judgment as to how the objects should move; the key thing to remember here is that you're describing the scene at one second after the beginning of the movie. LogoMotion will render the in-between frames (14 of them) when you render to file. In Figure 5-13, I've rotated the PARTY and MAKERS objects so they tilt inward, vertically, toward each other. The balloon

has dropped from its original position to the bottom of the frame, and the music note is twirled to its right side across its Y-axis.

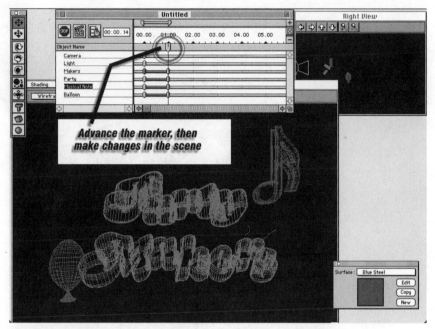

Figure 5-13: *The world event marker advances your scene through time; make changes to the poses of your "stars," and LogoMotion will provide the in-between frames.*

3. Because the finished animation should begin and end at the same place, it's important now that at the two-second time marker, everything in the scene is back at its original frame-one position. LogoMotion makes this easy. Click and drag the world event marker to the two-second position on the Sequencer (Timelines) panel, Opt+click on the first key frame marker of something you've moved, then drag the marker to the two-second position. This action duplicates the first frame (at zero seconds), placing an object in the same rotational angle and relative position in the scene as it was in the first frame.

CorelMOTION users should right-click on the first key frame marker for an object, then choose Duplicate from the shortcut menu. Then, click and drag the duplicate key frame marker to the two-second position. See Figure 5-14.

Figure 5-14: *Key frames for objects can be duplicated and moved along the time line to restore their original position at the end of the movie.*

4. Preview your animation in bounding box display by clicking on the clapboard icon on the Sequencer (Timeline) panel. Correct anything necessary at this point: move the balloon at the one-second marker or rotate the lettering more. The important thing here is not to change object positions at the two-second marker; this would prevent the animation loop from closing in the scene's beginning position.

5. Rendering time! CorelMOTION 3D users should choose 15 frames per second from the Animation tab of the File | Scene Setup dialog box before beginning, and choose Shade Better

from the Shading Mode drop-down list on the Rendering tab. In both programs, click on the filmstrip icon (the Make Movie icon) on the palette. Windows MOTION 3D users will then be prompted for a file location for the rendered movie. Macintosh users will get a series of dialog boxes to specify image quality and frames per second.

6. Choose Shade Better as the Quality option, choose 256 colors from the Colors drop-down list, then choose Frames: From 1 To 29. Because this is a 30-frame animation that begins and ends at the same point, you do *not* want the final frame rendered to animation. Frame 30 is a duplicate, and although its presence in the LogoMotion file is necessary to bring the actors back to position number one, a duplicate frame would make the movie halt for a moment. This is an advanced trick you can use in any of your own future animations.

7. Click on Render and you'll see the options for compression. Highest Quality and final file size are inversely proportional; I've chosen Most Quality in Figure 5-15 (which produces a larger file size), because I've used other means (such as small dimensions and low color resolution) to keep the file small. You need to play with all three parameters in different combinations—dimension, color depth, and amount of compression—to arrive at a small file that animates well and looks good. Your first rendered animation might not look exactly the way you want it. Experiment with it; animations that include different surface shaders and objects will render differently.

And by all means, delete any animation experiments from your hard disk you're not happy with, including the still, uncompressed image frames, if you choose not to compile an animation in MOTION. Resource files can take up an *enormous* amount of hard disk space!

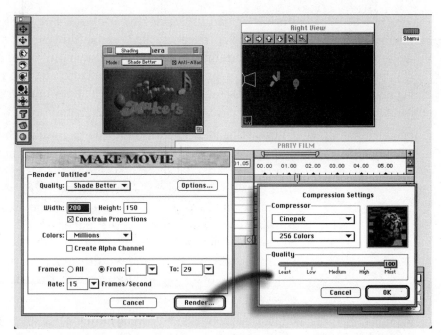

Figure 5-15: *Color depth, compressor quality, and file dimensions all affect the file size of the final animation.*

8. Your choice of compressor also makes a big difference in finished animations. I've chosen Cinepak because I want visitors using Windows and Macintosh machines to be able to view this animation. Cinepak is one of the few codecs (compressor/decompressor) that is platform-independent (see the section on codecs to follow). You cannot write a biplatform animation whose codec is only supported on one operating platform.

9. Finally, choose the file format for the finished animation. Again, this is a platform decision. I recommend the Apple QuickTime file format (CorelMOTION 3D supports this export format)—Macintosh users can read a QuickTime movie, and so can Windows users (with the player designed for Windows installed), but the Macintosh *cannot* read an AVI animation without special software.

10. Click on OK, and find work elsewhere as your machine renders the animation!

COMPRESSION/DECOMPRESSION

Codecs in 1996 are written by a few primary players in the digital video field:

- Microsoft, which offers Video 1, a proprietary encoding scheme that can only be read on the PC platform as of this writing. The quality of Video 1 compression is not tweaked for any specific type of animation; Best Quality generally produces animations of a somewhat greater size and slightly lower quality than Cinepak.

- Intel Indeo Video 3.2 Compression. This compressor is also PC-specific, so if your audience includes Macintosh users, don't use this type of codec. Indeo compression is optimal for movies that contain little motion (such as a digital video of a chairman's speech), but doesn't really offer top-notch quality for animations. Movies compressed using Indeo 3.2 tend to look a little fuzzy, as though viewed though a layer of gauze. Indeo compression does, however, make really small files you might want to post for download on your site.

- Intel Interactive Video for Windows (IVI). IVI is extremely processor-intensive on the client side and is not offered by many animation compilers as of this writing. Things change overnight in this business, however. The QuickTime version of this codec is planned for the fall of 1996, and this codec will install as a standard QuickTime and Video for Windows component by 1997. The thing to watch out for with IVI in the future is that an animation written with IVI compression will intelligently downgrade the movie, as played, depending upon the host machine. This means that if your client owns a Quadra or 486 computer, the animation will play quickly with some quality loss, but the movie will not drop frames (a visually displeasing, Max Headroom-like phenomenon that occurs when your system can't handle the data-transfer rate). IVI also supports a masking channel (similar in principle to the GIF format's transparency color), so an animation using a chromakey effect for making the background transparent can be included within the compressed file.

- **Cinepak by Radius.** Formerly by the SuperMac company, Cinepak compression offers the best compression scheme for movies containing a lot of movement, and is a biplatform codec, which means that Windows and Macintosh machines can play back a QuickTime movie encoded using Cinepak.

  Cinepak is part of the QuickTime extensions, and is a component of Video for Windows on the PC.

- **MPEG (Motion Picture Experts Group)** compression is not the format for broadcasting across the Web because of the hardware requirements for decompression. MPEG is both a compression scheme and a file format. Generally, a few seconds of MPEGed digital video can take hours to compress using software codecs, and hardware compression boards are a faster solution but cost more than your average software solutions. Additionally, the decompression rate on the client side is painfully slow with current technology: your clients would need to own a PowerMac or a Pentium, and these classes of machine are *not* the general Web audience's hardware. However, there is a lot of support for MPEG codec by manufacturers; MPEG compression can take an animation down to $1/100$ of the uncompressed file size, so this technology will help to resolve the speed issue in the future.

STATE-OF-THE-ART DESKTOP ANIMATION

So far, you've seen how a design program and a specialized modeling application can be used to create Web animation. This section gets a little further into the use of a modeling/rendering application—Macromedia's Extreme 3D—to show how visual enhancements can be added to 3D objects in an animation. In Chapter 4, "Working With Models," we discussed how surface properties can make or break the perceived photorealism of a rendered model: opacity and shadows are two real-world properties that are easy to define in Extreme 3D.

In the following example, we'll walk through the steps needed to animate two tropical fish in a fishbowl. Extreme 3D has a built-in, free-form animation engine, so anything you can create, you can also animate. Other applications such as Martin Hash's Animator and Visual Software's Renderize Live can create lifelike animations, and if you want to go through the manual process of creating tweening stills for an animation, almost any modeling/rendering program can substitute in the following example.

The first step in this example is to create fish and a fishbowl. The two fish were created by extruding 2D profiles; eyes were placed in the models (simple sphere primitives) and linked to the parent objects so the eyes will travel when the fish are moved. A fishbowl can be lathed from a profile of a half circle with lips on the top and bottom; floor and wall objects (cube primitives with one dimension flattened by 90 percent) complete the scene. In Figure 5-16, you can see the scene. Extreme 3D allows you to view every object in a scene at different rendering qualities: it would be hard to move the fish if the bowl had an opaque surface (although the bowl will be partially opaque in the finished animation), but because they are displayed in wireframe, you can easily reposition the fish objects for poses in the animation.

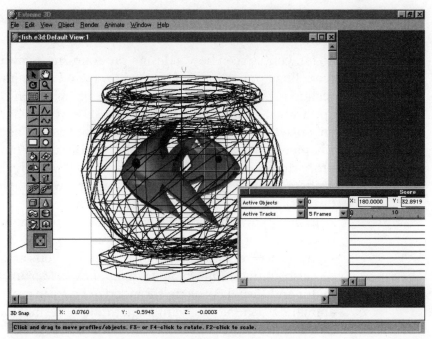

Figure 5-16: *Sometimes you'll find that models can be extremely simple and the animation adds interest to the finished file.*

Because you might not own Extreme 3D, the following example can be performed in LogoMotion, Renderize Live, or another modeling/animation program if you'd like to import the resource DXF files (FISH.DXF, BOWL.DXF, and so on) from the CHAP05 folder on the Companion CD-ROM into the application of your choice:

1. In Extreme 3D, create (or import the DXF files that make up) the scene. You need two fish, a bowl, a background, and a tabletop to place the bowl upon.

2. Let's leave the fishbowl for last; after the fish have been modeled (use the Extrude tool on a path you create of a fish), choose View | Top, and align the fish and rotate them so that the small fish is slightly behind the large fish, and they are facing opposing directions. The animation will be of the two fish swimming in a circle in the bowl.

3. From the Top view, click on the Link tool, and link the small fish to the large fish. Now, the large fish is a parent object, and anywhere you move or rotate the large fish, the small fish will move correspondingly.

4. Switch back to default (front) view, then use the Spline tool to fashion a semicircle with bumps on the top and bottom.

5. Use the Lathe tool to spin the profile of the semicircle in a 360° direction to create a closed, 3D surface. With the semicircle selected, click a point on the top (nonrounded, open) side of the semicircle, click a point directly beneath the first point, then press the Enter key on the number keypad (not the Enter or Return key to the right of the apostrophe).

   With the bowl selected, choose Object | Render Style | Wireframe. The bowl can now be positioned to encompass the fish, and the fish can be selected in future steps "through" the wireframe bowl.

6. Position "slabs" that are the floor and tabletop beneath and behind the fishbowl. Try extruding rectangle paths by a fraction of an inch to create the slabs. If you choose Window | Objects, the Objects palette offers a trackball that can rotate selected objects. I use the number entry fields for rotation; if you type **90** in the X Orientation field, the wall slab will rotate to the intended upright position from your front view.

7. Choose Window | Materials to display the Materials you might want to apply to the surfaces in this scene. You can choose any surface you like for the fish and the slabs, but the bowl should be semitransparent, and we'll show you how to accomplish this shortly.

8. Choose Window | Lights. Click on the Default light title, then click on Edit.

9. Check the Cast Shadows check box, click on OK, then click on Update Scene on the Lights palette.

10. It's time to create the animation. Choose Animate | Score. The Score window operates almost identically to the

Sequencer panel in LogoMotion. Click and drag the key frame marker to the 10-second position in the Score window.

11. Our plot here is to rotate the fish by 360° in 20 frames. Click on the large fish (the parent object), then click and hold on the Point Rotate tool (highlighted in Figure 5-17) to reveal the tool flyout. Choose the Rotate Axis tool, the middle of the three tools.

12. Click the first point of an imaginary axis of rotation for the two fish. Ideally, the fish should be positioned in the dead center of the Working Plane (Ctrl(Cmd)+Y toggles the neon pink Working Plane on and off). If the fish are centered, then your first click should be on the center vertical marker on the Working Plane.

13. Click a second point directly above the first point you clicked. Clockwise rotation is measured in *negative* degrees facing the user in Extreme 3D, and if you don't feel confident about clicking and dragging the fish exactly 180° now, enter **-180** in the Angle field at the bottom of the screen, then press the keypad Enter to finalize the rotation. See Figure 5-17.

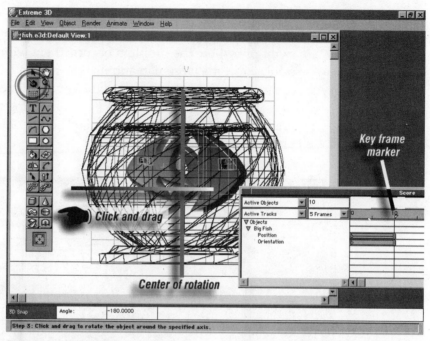

Figure 5-17: *Rotate the grouped fish objects 180° to create the first key frame at the 10-second marker in the Score window.*

14. Click and drag the key frame marker to the 20-second position in the Score window.

15. Rotate the fish again by -180° using the Rotate Axis tool. Extreme 3D remembers the last value you used for the tool, so you needn't reenter the amount if you're using the number entry field to accomplish the rotation.

16. Run a bounding box preview of the animation by choosing Animate I Animation Controls. Type **1** in the Start field, type **20** in the End field of the Animation Controls palette, and click the Loop radio button to continuously cycle through the action. Click on the VCR-like Play button, and

if the fish rotate around a stationary axis, you're home free. If the axis appears to move, go to the frame in the Score window where the problem occurs; then, with the Arrow tool, select the large fish and use the nudge arrow keyboard keys to push the fish to the center of the scene. I have had better luck aligning positions using the arrow keys than manually clicking and dragging objects in an animation. See Figure 5-18.

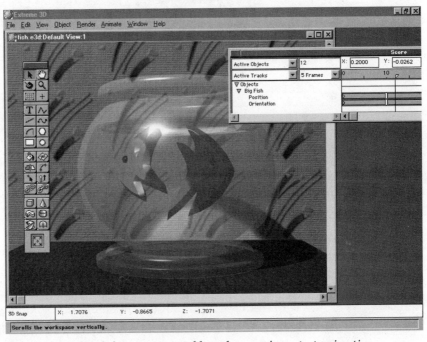

Figure 5-18: *Check for sequence problems by running a test animation.*

17. It's time to color in the fishbowl. On the Materials palette, click on a Plastic shader, then click on the left arrow to add the shader to the current scene. Click on Edit.

18. In the Material Editor window, choose a light cyan from the color picker (click on the Color swatch at top). Then click and drag the Opacity slider for this new material to about .2 (20 percent). Click on OK.

19. Select the fishbowl object, then click on your new transparent Plastic shader on the Materials list, then click on Apply. If you need to do further editing to the fish, hide the bowl by choosing Object | Hide from the menu. The bowl will reappear if you then choose Object | Show, and then select All from the menu.

20. Choose Render | Render Setup, then check the Render Shadows check box, click on OK, then choose Render | Final Render to Screen. This render test is for image quality, not animation. Based on the onscreen preview, you might decide to go back to the Render Setup box and choose a higher render quality. This option doesn't affect the final file size, but does indeed affect the time it takes to render the animation. See Figure 5-19.

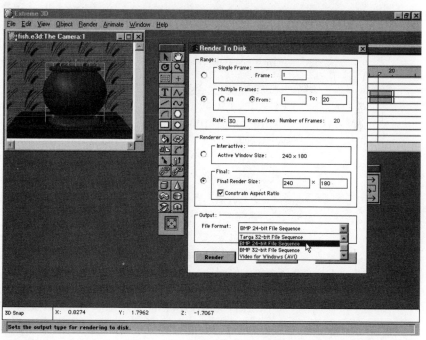

Figure 5-19: *Based upon your test render, you might want to reposition a light or a fish to cast better shadows—or you might decide upon a different material for objects.*

TIP

Danger, Will Robinson! *In Extreme 3D, like in LogoMotion, you can change materials throughout the run of a digital animation. For example, you could specify a glass material in frame 1, assign a brick texture to the same object in frame 20, and wind up with a morphing effect in the animation. This is usually not desired, so you need to make this new material property a consistent one along the timeline in the Score window. As an example, if you want to make the large fish blue instead of purple, move the event marker back to frame 0 of the animation in the Score window. Apply a blue material to the fish. Then clear all other key frame markers for the material associated with the fish in the Score window. Select multiple markers by holding Shift while you select them, then press Delete when all but the first marker is selected.*

21. Now you need to choose a window size for the final render. Choose Window | Window Setup, then choose 240 X 180 Multimedia from the Image Size drop-down list. Click on OK to return to a much smaller image window.

22. Chances are that you won't be able to see the scene now, because the window—your viewport of the scene—has changed dramatically. Choose View | Fit to Window, then, with the Zoom tool, crop into the frame so that the scene is framed more or less as it was originally. This is your final cropping view; take a moment or two with the Zoom tool to get happy with it.

23. It's rendering time. Choose Render | Render to disk. As you can see in Figure 5-20, there are only one or two options you might need to change here prior to clicking on the Render button. Specify the frames you want to render; you don't want to include frame 0 in your animation, because it should be a duplicate of frame 20 (0 to 20 = 21 frames; 1 to 20 = 20 frames). I've chosen BMP 24-bit File Sequence in Figure 5-20, because Extreme 3D doesn't have a QuickTime compressed file format option in Windows. I intend to use a third-party compiler which you'll see shortly. If you own

Premiere or other video editing suite, you might want to consider exporting the Extreme 3D assignment as uncompressed still images. Choose uncompressed frames (PICT for the Macintosh and BMP for Windows), or choose a platform-native file format for the animation, then click on Render.

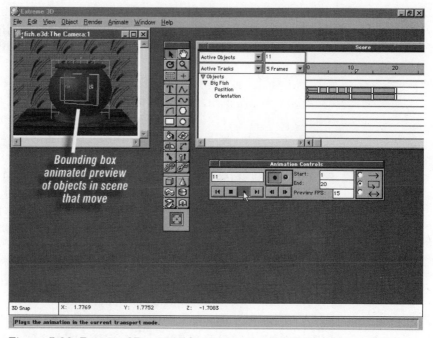

Figure 5-20: *Extreme 3D can render uncompressed still frames or compile a platform-specific animation file.*

24. You're done! Save the project and exit when Extreme 3D is finished rendering.

As mentioned earlier in this chapter, if you render an animation out to still frames, you save time in the long run. If you want to experiment with compression options or different animation formats, the most time-intensive part of the task is already finished.

KEY FRAMES & DATA RATE

Other aspects of a compiled, compressed animation are the Key Frame option most compilers offer and the data rate. If you're using a Macintosh animation package, the default Data Rate is typically set to 90 kilobytes per second (Kbps). This is the bandwidth of the playback on your system, and if you specify a greater amount, playback will most likely drop frames, ruining the animation. Intel-based Windows computers can expect a slightly higher throughput: 150 Kbps is the standard Data Rate in animation programs and compilers.

Key Frames is a commonly found option that can be turned on or off at compression time for your animation. What *key framing* means with respect to an animation compiler is the quality of each frame at regular intervals as the animation plays back. In general, you might want to uncheck this box if offered, because if you go for tighter compression (less quality) in the compiled animation, the key frames, rendered at optimal quality, will stick out like a sore thumb in the animation. Key frame rendering is nice if you're passing along an AVI or QuickTime movie to a client who wants an image still from the animation, but again, playback can get rough with key framing activated during compression.

In Figure 5-21, some readers might see a familiar sight. The animation compiler is called MovieMaker, and came as a utility with PIXAR Typestry II, a font animation program that ceased production in 1995. If you purchased Typestry last year, you might have an undiscovered gem of an animation compiler on floppy disk somewhere! In Figure 5-21, I've told MovieMaker to look for the sequentially numbered files exported from Extreme 3D, to compress the finished animation at 65 percent (a little more speed than image quality), and to use the Cinepak codec so my finished animation can be played back in Windows or on the Macintosh.

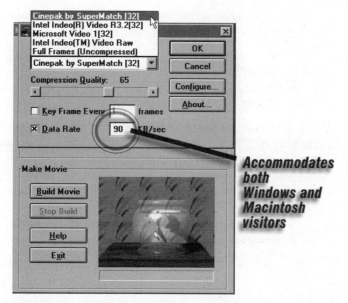

Figure 5-21: *With an uncompressed collection of animation files, you can experiment until you find the optimal compression and video quality.*

TIP

MovieMaker can render to QuickTime format. If you intend to compose animations for a biplatform audience, Intel has a wonderful program, SMARTVID, that can convert AVI movies to QuickTime MooV format. You can download the program from Intel's Web site at http://www.intel.com/.

When moving an animation between formats and platforms, it's important to use a codec (i.e., Cinepak, and Indeo in the near future) that is supported between platforms. Additionally, a converted AVI to MooV file must have its file type edited before the Macintosh OS will recognize the file. After you transfer the file to the Mac, use ResEdit or a similar program to set the file type to "MooV."

Similarly, a QuickTime movie to be played on a Windows machine must be flattened to a single file. Unlike most Macintosh files, a MooV file (the file type associated with an Apple QuickTime movie) contains data-critical information in both the resource fork and the data fork. Flattening the MooV can be accomplished in Premiere, and also with a utility called flattenMooV, by Robert Hennessey. Flattening the MooV is the only way the file can be viewed on both the Macintosh and Windows platforms. Unfortunately, you can no longer edit a flattened QuickTime movie, so you should always perform this on a copy of your original animation.

POPCORN TIME!

The finished animation from the previous example is in the CHAP05 folder on the Companion CD-ROM in both Windows and QuickTime formats. The movie was compressed at 100 percent quality, 50 percent quality, and at no compression. Decide for yourself how this "action film" should best be presented. In Figure 5-22, you can see a composite of the three compression rates on a single playback frame of "FISHBOWL.AVI" (Fishbowl.MooV). Naturally, no compression presents the viewer with original-image quality, but it also takes up 2.47MB of hard disk space. However, the toughest choice you might need to make is whether to lop about 30 percent off the file size, and live with the detail you see in the last frame of Figure 5-22. The texture is gone from the background, and the small fish's eye periodically disappears during the animation. This is because the higher the compression, the more averaging the codec performs on image areas.

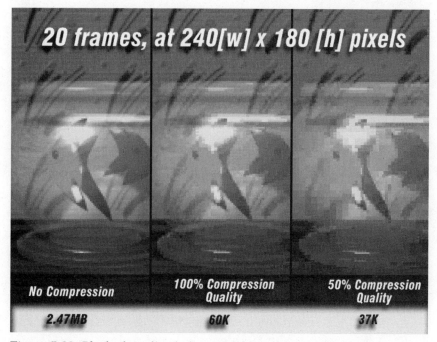

Figure 5-22: *Playback quality declines with compression, so that the aesthetics of the piece are compromised.*

How much compression you use is a very tough call. As a designer, it's unthinkable to allow your work to be compromised, but it's also unfeasible, or impossible, to broadcast the animation at larger sizes across the Web.

Think of your audience, your message, and how you can design a piece that doesn't suffer in image quality *before* you design an animation.

PLASTIC ANIMATION

There is an application made by the Valis Group that Macintosh users might be more familiar with than Windows users. Flo', whose tag line is "freeform plasticity," is a true animation application available on both platforms for about $150 street price. Flo's design tools do one thing: they allow you to push and stretch areas of a still image as though the image were silk-screened onto a piece of latex. Flo' is a great relaxation tool, and at first appears to be limited to doing something really unflattering to a portrait of your boss, but the possibilities for using Flo' as a serious animator's tool are uncovered in this next example.

Flo' offers no native capability to mask image areas, and you're limited to a single image onscreen at a time. However, Flo' can read and write alpha channels; so if you have a little time, you can manually compile an animation consisting of a free-flowing image area against a background that *doesn't* change from frame to frame. There is a series of animation stills labeled KET00001.TGA through KET00030.TGA in the KETTLE folder within the CHAP05 folder on the Companion CD-ROM. Also included is STOVE.TIF, the background image used in this animation. If you'd like to play along with this example, here's how the movie was brought to screen:

First, a scene was created in a modeling program that included a cartoon character teapot sitting on a stove. The kettle and background were rendered as separate images, and the kettle image includes an alpha channel for easy separation of the shape from its background. If you have a modeling program and would like to try this yourself, aligning the poses in the two different scenes isn't hard: You make the complete scene, delete the foreground object, then save the scene under a different name before rendering. You do the opposite with a second copy of the original. Figure 5-23 shows the scenes being rendered in PIXAR Showplace.

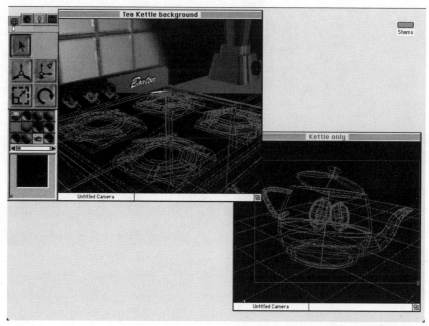

Figure 5-23: *Render the character to be animated and the background as two separate scenes. Make certain the foreground object is in the same relative position in its own frame.*

Here are the steps needed to create animation files of the teapot that include alpha channel information:

1. Launch Flo', then choose Edit | Accept Mask. This command allows Flo' to read the alpha channel (mask) information within any file you import to the workspace.

2. Choose File | Place, then choose the KETTLE.TGA image in the CHAP05/KETTLE folder on the Companion CD-ROM. This is the image rendered from the previous figure.

3. Unlike Photoshop and other image editors, Flo' displays masking information in place; that is, a 50 percent black color surrounds the kettle when it's imported, but the color is actually an alpha-channel view of the unselected areas in the image, and a more conventional alpha channel will be written to the finished files. You have four basic editing

moves in Flo' to distort an image, and the bottom of the
Tool palette contains functions for undoing and reverting
images. Unlike a time-line editor in conventional animation programs, you're supposed to animate images in Flo'
by Undoing and Redoing edits. In Figure 5-24, you can see
that, as a first edit, I've used the Scale tool to marquee
around the kettle's eyes. Once the marquee is closed, a
bounding box appears around the marquee area, and you
scale the bounding box to create the distortion.

Figure 5-24: *Flo' allows you to freeform distort an image or an image area to
create a "plastic" animation.*

4. You're under no obligation in Flo' to select a key frame as you play, but it's a good idea to capture a pose you think you'll want to use before you've created too many variations on the original image. You'll notice as you continue to play with the image that the Undo, Redo, Older, Newer, and Kill buttons become active on the toolbox. These buttons are used to toggle between edits you've made when you compile your animation. The Kill button removes the previous edit from the stack of unseen, saved frames. When you have about three poses you're happy with, choose Animate | Settings. In the Settings dialog box, type **30** in the Total Frames field, and type **15** in the Frames Per Second field. Click on OK.

5. Choose Options | Alpha Out. You will need this feature before Flo' writes the animation files. Alpha Out indicates to Flo' that your file-export format should include alpha-channel information about the selection you're distorting.

6. Go back to the original state of the image by clicking on the Older button on the toolbox.

7. Choose Animate | Start Keyframe.

8. Go to a newer distortion you've created by clicking on Newer on the toolbox. Choose Animate | Add Keyframe. This displays a dialog box.

9. In the Add Keyframe dialog box, type **10** in the Frame Difference field, then click on OK, as shown in Figure 5-25. You now have 20 frames left to play with.

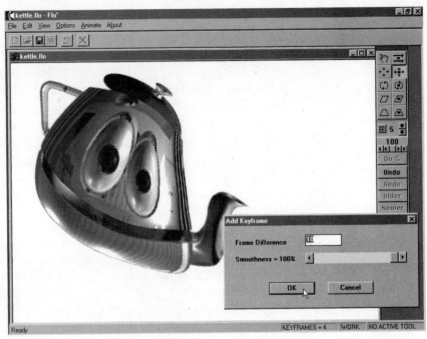

Figure 5-25: *You can specify the number of frames in between key frames through the Add Keyframe dialog box.*

If you'd like to speed up, or slow down the action in a Flo' movie, specify fewer or more than 10 key frames in the Add Keyframe dialog box.

10. Move on to another pose for the kettle, then choose Add Keyframe again.

11. Go back to the original, undistorted image (click on Undo or Older a number of times), then choose Animate I Close Loop. Specify 10 as the Frame Difference in the dialog box, and you've filled the 30 frames.

12. Choose Animate I Create Sequence, then find or create a vacant folder on your hard disk for the finished, rendered files. Be sure to choose TGA (32) from the Save As Type

drop-down list. This is the only file format Flo' offers that can contain an alpha channel.

13. Choose a three-letter prefix for the animation sequence, then type **1** at the end of the default name. This means that your animation stills will be written sequentially to files 1 through 30 (0 through 29 are odd names to deal with later).

You're done! To complete the animation, the files must now be merged with the background image, STOVE.TGA. The easiest way to accomplish this is in Premiere, but Photoshop, Corel Photo-Paint, and other image editors that can read and write alpha channels can be used. We'll show Photoshop in this next example, because Photoshop 3.0.5 retains the relative position of a selected graphic that is copied to a different image of equal dimensions and resolution.

MANUAL COMPOSITING WORK

With many fine video editing suites on the market, it would be folly to propose that you do every piece of compositing work exactly like the following example. The next steps *do* require an investment of about a half an hour and alertness—something that the author is only occasionally gifted with. Nonetheless, I want to show HTML authors here a technique that requires a modest software investment and gives a stimulating visual payoff. Here's how to use Photoshop to composite the "Flo'-ing" kettle with the stove background:

1. In Photoshop, open the STOVE.TGA image from the CHAP05/KETTLE folder, then save it to your hard disk. CD images are write-protected, so saving them back to CD is a little hard.

2. If you're a Windows user, you might want to do a little customizing to Photoshop's shortcut Commands menu to speed up the compositing process. Add Duplicate and Save As to the Commands list (do this from the Edit Commands flyout on the Commands palette). Macintosh users don't have a shortcut menu (it's a Win95 and Win32s

convention), but you might want to keep the Commands palette open, and customize it also to speed up this process.

3. Choose Duplicate (Image | Duplicate), then accept the default name for the duplicate of the stove image by clicking on OK. Windows users can minimize the original STOVE.TGA image, but don't close it yet.

4. Open KET00001.TGA from the KETTLE/CHAP05 folder on the Companion CD-ROM.

5. On the Channels palette (press F7 to display it if it isn't onscreen), Alt(Opt)+click on the #4 channel to load the selection. It's possible that your configuration of Photoshop loads black as selection areas. This is the inverse of what we want here; we want the kettle selected, indicated by white areas in the alpha channel Flo' wrote. So, if the marquee is inverted, double-click on the #4 channel title, then switch Color Indicates to Masked Areas, click on OK, click on the RGB title to move back to the color view of the image, and you're in business.

6. With any selection tool (the Rectangular marquee selection tool is fine), click and drag the selected kettle in one decisive move into the duplicate stove image window, as shown in Figure 5-26. One of the strongest editing capabilities of Photoshop is how it remembers the relative position of selections copied to image windows of identical dimensions and resolution.

Figure 5-26: *A selection from an image window of equal size as the target window will land in its original, relative position in Photoshop.*

7. Press Ctrl(Cmd)+D to deselect the kettle and composite it into the background of the copy of the stove image. Choose File I Save As, then save the image as KETL0001 in the TIF file format to your hard disk. We've renamed the file here, and chosen a different file format, because unlike Flo', many animation compiling programs look for four, not five numbers at the end of a filename to establish a sequence. Conversion from Targa to TIF format is not mandatory here, but Windows users will be able to quickly discern between the Flo' Targa images and the finished TIF images by reformatting them upon saving. Win95 still uses three-character extensions for files, and reformatting the images doesn't change the image information.

8. Repeat steps 3 through 7 with the stove image and the rest of the KETTLE images. You're done! Get a beverage of your choice, kick back, open the KETTLE.AVI or KETTLE.MooV file from the CHAP05 folder, and see what your work looks like compiled into an animation.

PUTTING YOUR ANIMATION SKILLS TO WORK

Like many of the examples in this book, this chapter was assignment-oriented, but we didn't have room to completely document each program shown. You've seen some of their strengths as animation tools, but they are all capable of adding many other embellishments to an assignment.

The more ambitious you become with your multimedia Web documents, the larger the file size might become. As you move from animated GIFs to QuickTime movies, you'll want to provide visitors to your site with an easy means to download the file instead of making them wait for hundreds of kilobytes of information to come across the wire. The author took a chance here, and has referenced the KETTLE.MooV in an HTML document (TWEENER.HTM) on the CHAP05/TWEENER folder on the Companion CD-ROM. This Web site could be posted, but if you notice in Figure 5-27, I provide the instructions for downloading the file in addition to offering the visitor a chance to view the animation online. The file extension, which is required as a three-character element for posting a movie on most UNIX and Windows NT–based servers, is referenced on the page in Figure 5-27. A Macintosh can play a QuickTime movie as long as the file type is MooV, but Windows machines will only recognize and correctly play a QuickTime movie with the *.MOV extension. Shift-clicking on a link automatically downloads a file in Navigator 2.0.

CD-ROM

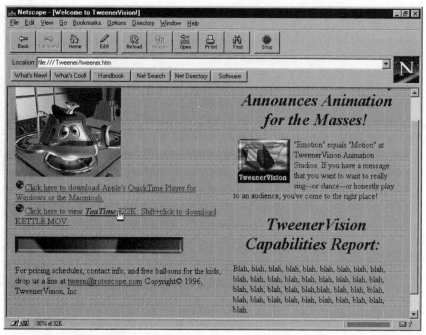

Figure 5-27: *Be a courteous Web author and offer visitors the opportunity to download a large animation.*

A double-speed CD-ROM player has a transfer rate that can be compared to a really good, fast connection on the Web. If you have a 2x speed CD-ROM, accessing the animation by clicking on the linked text in the TweenerVision HTML document will give you an approximate idea of how a 300K file would download. You'll also notice that the ledge separating the Link buttons from the copyright on this page is an animated GIF. You can mix and match animation types on your Web page to create an elegant interplay of media content, or just to draw attention to a certain Web element.

Until Apple or a third party comes up with a Navigator plug-in for QuickTime movies, visitors will have to make do with a helper app for viewing your animations. This means that you have no server-side control over where the helper app pops up in the browser window for the visitor. And you should definitely provide a link to Apple's site on your page to allow visitors to download the latest Windows and Macintosh QuickTime players. Because Apple and many other companies are continually updating sites, it's a bad idea to reference an exact location for a file or other resource with your link. Instead, link to Apple's main page, and let the visitor drill down through the site to get the player. There's nothing quite as frustrating as the display of a dead link because the target site changed.

As a producer, you also have no control over how long the animation lasts, or whether the animation endlessly loops. Controls for animation are hosted by the helper app; you can only ensure that the animation will loop if the visitor specifies this feature in the player. You can see, in Figure 5-28, the process by which the visitor can watch the tea kettle on its uncomfortable perch. The link downloads the file, calls the installed player on the visitor's system, and the QuickTime Movie Player launches. The visitor can resize the Movie Player window and choose from animation controls under the movie menu.

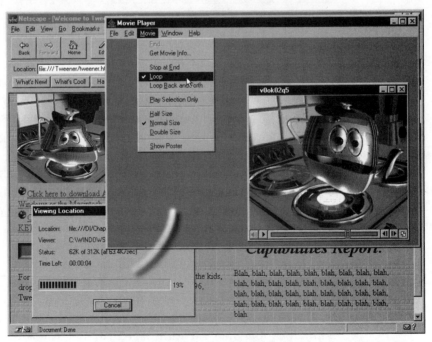

Figure 5-28: *You control the content, but the visitor to your site controls the playback of animated elements on your site.*

BANDWIDTH CONSIDERATIONS

Before you get too heavily into multimedia production for the Web, you should consider the bandwidth you'll eat up, and shop for the most accommodating Internet Service Provider . . . without the last leg of your connection to an audience, your show is going nowhere. Service Providers come in three types: the commercial server who handles only pages, the account server who handles only personal connections to services, and a provider who handles both types of transactions.

You'll be better off in the long run if you go with the provider who only handles Web sites, who has a fast connection, and is located in a remote area of a country with very little online traffic. To check out potential providers, check out sites on their servers during lunch time, after 5 P.M., and after 9 P.M. See how the data-transfer rate goes. This will be the same speed as *your own* site will transfer. Additionally, many ISPs do not allow animations because of the bandwidth problem; this is an issue about which to be up-front with a possible provider.

Finally, you should try to see if a flat rate, or a per page rate, can be established for your site. Many ISPs charge per hit on your site. The number of hits by no means should be mistaken for the number of visitors to your site, however. You can tally up 10–20 hits by a single visitor who simply likes to play your animation—and go broke in the process! Play it fair and play it smart when posting a multimedia page: alert the audience to the file sizes, offer the animations as downloads, and optimize the animation for speed using the techniques shown in this chapter.

See you in the funny pages!

MOVING ON

VRML is an extension of animation, and the creation of virtual worlds is the core concentration of Chapter 6, "VRML." With the modeling experiences tucked under your belt from Chapter 4, "Working With Models," and this chapter, it won't be long before you can offer an audience not only 3D, but *interactive* 3D. Learn how to create an environment where visitors can "reach out and touch something" . . . by turning the page.

6 VRML

By the end of this chapter, you will be able to edit a VRML document, incorporate a VRML document in a Web page, actually *create* a VRML file in a text editor . . . and your head is going to hurt somewhat! The *Virtual Reality Modeling Language* is a compact descriptor language for displaying polygonal objects, shading, lighting, and other 3D qualities you might find in real life. The viewer of a VRML file requires no special computer platform; a single Navigator plug-in and Navigator 2.0 or later will display a virtual world you've created on the visitor's monitor. If VRML sounds like it has commercial, educational, or entertainment possibilities, you'd be right on all counts, and this chapter shows you how to take advantage of a most provocative new digital medium.

VRML WORLDS

Every book on the Web has this section, but I'm only presenting it to quash the possible notion that VRML was created as a frivolous sideshow attraction to a World Wide Web that *already* seems to feature every conceivable type of digital object!

Shortly after the first World Wide Web Conference in the spring of 1994 in Geneva, discussions began as to how dimensional descriptions of graphics might interface with the already established Web hyperlinks. A language needed to be created that is to virtual reality what HTML is to text. Instead of inventing a completely new language, Gavin Bell at Silicon Graphics helped adapt the Open Inventor ASCII File Format (an existing technology) to create the Inventor File Format for VRML, with contributions from a mailing list which Mark Pesce of Labyrinth Group continues to moderate. It was Mark Pesce who wrote the first draft of the specifications to VRML version 1, and Gavin Bell and Anthony Parisi of Intervista Software who wrote the final specifications.

It was the goal of the VRML's creators that the language should be a universal language for interactive simulations. Composed of ASCII text and platform-independent resource files, VRML worlds can be created and posted by Windows, DOS, UNIX, and Macintosh users. The VRML specification also allows for hyperlinks to other worlds and other Web elements; the WWWAnchor node (discussed in this chapter) is the HTML equivalent of a hypertext jump. VRML is also extensible. Although version 1 is a handsome piece of work, version 2 of the VRML specifications includes interactive, real-time behavior, clarifications to certain properties (such as transparency) to ensure conformity to a style of authoring a VRML document, and support for other referenced image formats. So as we are waiting for the new, approved standards for VRML, now is a perfect time to become familiar with the structure for the present and future versions of the Virtual Reality Modeling Language.

THE STRUCTURE OF OBJECTS IN VRML SPACE

VRML files are written as a series of discrete *nodes*; a node is a text-based description of anything in a VRML world. For example, a node can be a reference to a GIF or JPEG image displayed as a surface for a set of connected points in space that describe a 3D sofa—another node in the VRML world.

Like HTML documents, VRML files follow a sequence, a hierarchical order of nodes, as the recipe for building worlds. The hierarchical order in a VRML document can be described as follows:

```
Scene Graph>nodes>fields
```

A *scene graph* is the description of the objects (nodes) in the world, and an object can be anything: a material, a camera, an object. There are three classes of nodes in VRML 1: Objects, Properties, and Groups. What distinguishes one node from another are *parameters* (color, height, and so on) which nest as a *field* within a node. A *separator* is the mechanism that begins and concludes nodes in a scene graph and terminates properties.

As an example, if you want to create a world where there is a green cone and a blue sphere, the *color* of the cone is a *field* which precedes the description of the cone in the node, and both the cone and the cone color are separated from the blue sphere in the scene graph. If a separator was not written to "bracket" the description of the cone and its color, the blue sphere would also take on the color of the cone in the world. Here's an example of what the scene I've described looks like when written in VRML. The pound sign (#) is used for annotations in VRML scripts and is remarked out of files when the scene is read into the browser:

```
Separator{ #Beginning of the green cone
Material { #Material node
     diffuseColor 0 1 0   #Green field
} #End of material node
Cone  #declaration of 3D object
{} #Begin and end of green cone field
} # End of separator
Separator {#Beginning of the blue sphere
Material { #Material node
     diffuseColor 0 0 1 #Blue field
} # end of material node
Sphere #declaration of sphere
{} # begin and end of blue sphere field
} #end of Separator
```

TIP

A field that follows a node can be empty, as shown in the example above. If the VRML browser detects an empty field, the default values for a node are displayed onscreen. However, a node must have a field, even if the field is empty. If you're authoring VRML worlds, and objects don't appear in the browser, try adding an empty open and closed curly bracket after the declaration of the node.

If you're familiar with modeling applications, VRML is very much like the ordered structure of grouped objects that make up a composite object such as an automobile or a mannequin. Users who are familiar with databases might also find a similarity between database *records* and nodes, and database *fields* and the fields within a VRML node.

There are a few things missing from the text above to make it a VRML file that will play in Navigator, but it's intended to give you an idea of the order and the use of separators to describe objects in a VRML world. We'll get to "legitimizing" the above text so that it can indeed be used as a VRML document shortly.

Navigating VRML Space

Without translation or rotation attributes, the VRML fragment outlined in the preceding section would create a green cone and a blue sphere occupying the same space—interesting, but usually unwanted.

The Transform node is perhaps the most useful of the Property nodes to become familiar with at this point, because the correct syntactic use of it can position and rotate objects in 3D space.

In Chapter 4, "Working With Models," we discussed the left- and right-hand coordinate systems. Although many modeling programs use the left-hand coordinate system for defining virtual space, VRML is based upon the *right-hand* coordinate system (although modeling applications capable of writing VRML files can redefine the coordinate system for an individual file). Without an understanding of object space in VRML, objects you create might not be visible to a viewer without panning or flying through the world as they are initially presented from within Navigator.

In Figure 6-1, you can see a planet object in Navigator's browser with annotations for axis direction and a snippet of the Transform node fields for *translation*, which positions the object in VRML space. The planet would normally appear at the 0 0 0 center origin, which is at the center of the screen, but I needed to push the planet off-center to annotate this figure. If you can accept that the convergence of the axes is at the 0 0 0 origin in this figure, a positive number in the first of the three values within the Translation field would move the planet to screen right. Positive Y values move your view of an object upwards, and a positive depth value (the Z-axis), moves the object toward the viewer. Increments are not specified in VRML documents, but if you use a modeling program to build VRML objects, space is measured in meters. X-, Y-, and Z-coordinates are written as values separated by a space; negative values are allowed.

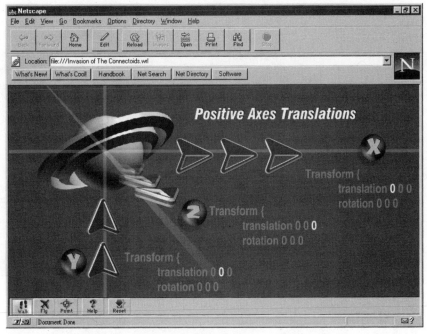

Figure 6-1: *From the center of VRML space, the coordinates for X, Y, and Z translation are specified with three space-separated values.*

You'll also notice in the previous figure that a Rotation field can be written into a Transform node. From the audience's point of view, top-to-bottom rotation (rotation along the X-axis) is specified in positive values to create counterclockwise rotation along this axis. Side-to-side rotation (Y-rotation) is counterclockwise from the audience's perspective when positive values are written into the second position in the Rotation field. Front-face rotation is also counterclockwise for positive values along the Z-axis.

Unlike translations of objects in VRML space, rotation is written as a series of values that refer to the axis of rotation followed by a value for the amount of rotation for any of the axes (see Figure 6-2). Amount of rotation is measured in radians, not degrees, in VRML.

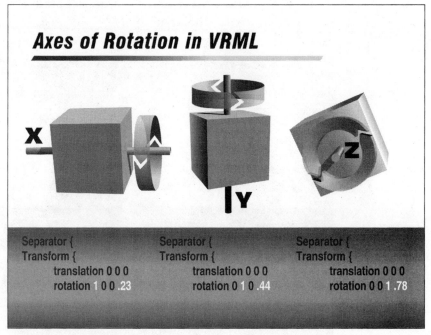

Figure 6-2: *The three axes' rotations and the corresponding placements of entries in the Rotation field.*

TIP

You might *need to resort to a pocket calculator to convert degrees to radians, but there's a fairly easy mnemonic that can help. 180° is equal to 3.14159265 radians; when rounded to two decimal places, this number is equal to pi. If you work backwards, then, 90° can be expressed as 1.57 in the last Rotation field value, and .78 works well to express a 45° positive rotation.*

Now that we have a grasp of some of the fundamental VRML syntax, let's build a small world.

PUTTING BASIC VRML CHUNKS TOGETHER

It should be mentioned at this point that we're walking before we fly. VRML contains native support for classes of objects such as cubes, spheres, and even ASCII text, and although we'll get into using a modeling application as a VRML authoring tool later in this chapter, how much easier can it be than to type **cube** in a text file to generate a 3D cube in Navigator's browser?

It's also necessary to mention as we get into browsing the VRML files on the Companion CD-ROM, that the Live3D plug-in for Netscape needs to be installed on the audience's system (and yours) to view VRML scenes in Navigator's browser window. If you don't have Live3D installed, you can download the latest copy from http://home.netscape.com/comprod/products/navigator/. Live3D is currently available in Windows 95 and Windows NT versions; the Macintosh and Win 3.1x versions of this plug-in are expected shortly from Netscape.

If you're using a Macintosh, you can still view VRML worlds at present by downloading a copy of Virtus's helper application (http://www.virtus.com). The Virtus VRML player will display VRML files in a separate window when Navigator finds an embedded or linked VRML file on a Web site, as all Navigator helper applications do. The setup program for the Live3D plug-in detects Navigator on your hard disk, installs the plug-in to the correct folder, and configures Navigator to the correct MIME type for Virtual Worlds (*.WRL) files.

To create a cube, rotated in space so that three sides are exposed to the viewer, you can use any plain text editor. To better see the relationship between the VRML tags and what they do, refer to Figure 6-3 as we run down the definitions of the VRML components. To begin, every VRML file begins with

```
#VRML V1.0 ascii
```

This line is for easy identification (by users and programs). As you can see, the pound symbol precedes the identifier, here, denoting that the identifier is hidden from the rest of the VRML code as a *comment* (a remark, similar to the DOS "REM" statement). A new line is begun with a carriage return; and nonfunctional white spaces, such as multiple carriage returns and two or more consecutive white spaces, are ignored.

Although in a single-object world it's not required, it's a good beginning to establish a separator for the following cube node in the VRML file. This is sort of like writing tidy HTML code: the more often you practice it, the better you become at authoring more complex documents. Therefore, after a carriage return, type

```
Separator {
```

The curly brace is used to open and close nested objects and fields within nodes. Therefore, after we've written the cube and its properties into the node enclosed by the separator, a closing curly brace must conclude the file.

Next, we need to define the cube's position in VRML space. Zero X-coordinate, zero Y-coordinate, and one meter toward the viewer along the Z-axis seems as good a place in space as any, so let's place the first object, the Transform node, within the separator, and add the field values for the cube's orientation in space, as follows:

```
Transform {
     translation 0 0 1
```

You'll note here that tabs have been used in the text, and that close curly braces are often written to a new line in the examples in this chapter. This is for easy identification, and the extra carriage returns do not affect the structure of the VRML document.

Next, the rotation string must be defined. Because rotation belongs to the Transform node, there is no curly brace separating this string from the translation string, as follows:

```
rotation 1 1 1 .78
    }
```

which, in English, means: all three of the axes about this cube shall be rotated (0 would turn the axis "off"), and the three axes of the cube shall be rotated positive 45 degrees.

Finally, we declare the cube. The size of the cube can be specified using a field after declaring the cube, or, if you choose to leave the curly braces empty (empty braces are allowed in VRML), the cube will appear at an unspecified default size within Navigator's browser.

```
Cube {      width 4
            height 4
            depth 4
            }
```

The order in which the dimensions are written makes no difference in version 1 of VRML. Again, let's play it safe and comply with the specification. Finally, a closing curly brace closes the separator's scene information.

```
    }
```

. . . and that's it; you have yourself a virtual world. Save the file with the WRL extension, load the VRML file into Navigator, and you should see something like Figure 6-3.

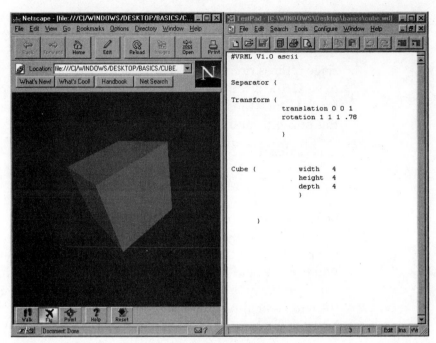

Figure 6-3: *Writing a simple VRML file requires that you follow syntax and keep fields within curly braces.*

TEXTURES IN THE VRML WORLD

Admittedly, a 50 percent black cube against 75 percent black space isn't a thrilling world, and here's where texture mapping comes into play. If you read Chapter 4 on modeling, you understand that a surface on an object can sometimes be more interesting than the shape itself.

Surfaces for VRML objects can be colors or even bitmap images. The GIF and JPEG format are commonly accepted, with limited support for PNG bitmap file types. The PNG format was created as a workaround to the possible royalty issues surrounding the GIF file format, and a PNG bitmap can support alpha-channel informa-tion—which will make bump mapping a possibility in VRML 2.

Basically, there are two ways a bitmap can be displayed upon the surface of an object node: it can be embedded within the VRML file; or it can be referenced, as you'd do with a graphic in an HTML document. Embedding a graphic in a VRML file should be performed by an authoring tool; perhaps only a handful of skilled VRML authors can write bitmap information manually into a VRML file.

CD-ROM   SOL.WRL is available on the Companion CD-ROM in the CHAP06/BASICS folder; and if you'd like to load it in Navigator now, you can see the relationship between the VRML file information and its corresponding virtual world on your monitor. You'll need to copy the entire folder to your hard disk; Navigator is expecting to find all the files in one place because we've specified file names as having a *relative* location to each other, and not an absolute location (a URL) within the VRML document examples.

After the VRML header line, the DEF BackgroundImage Info line calls the LATTICE.GIF file to be displayed as the background to this world. As with HTML documents, if you have a large site that needs to be pathed out to many locations on a server, the URL, within quotes, of the filename must be provided. For example:

```
DEF BackgroundImage Info {
string "file:///D|/mystuff/lattice.gif" }
```

If you simply want to share the VRML document, as we're doing on the Companion CD-ROM, Navigator can find the GIF image because it's located in the same folder as the VRML document; no URL has been specified in the BackgroundImage field.

Background images can also be in JPEG format, and if the physical dimension of the file (at 72 pixels/inch resolution) doesn't fill the screen, the browser will tile the image. In the SOL.WRL document, I'm *counting* on the background image tiling; LATTICE.GIF is an 18K file, and because it was designed to seamlessly tile (see Chapter 3, "Bitmap Graphics & Special Effects"), 18K of pixels provide a background at any viewing resolution.

The proper node to use when texture mapping an image to an object is Texture2. (I've discovered no significance for the 2, but it's necessary when mapping a texture.) Following the Texture2 node is the filename string, which specifies the name and location of the image to be mapped on subsequent objects in the scene graph. An image is mapped to an object a single time without tiling (the browser will stretch or shrink the bitmap to display a surface for covering the entire object), unless otherwise specified by a Texture2Transform node. You might never need to use the Texture2Transform node, but there are four fields available for changing the orientation and size of an image as mapped to a 3D object. In the example below, Texture2Transform comes before the Texture2 node, and annotations explain how the fields are used:

```
Texture2Transform {

    translation 0 0 #moves texture relative to
                    center of object
    rotation 0 #    rotates texture relative to
                    object
    scaleFactor 2 2 #repeats texture twice
                    across surface
    center 0 0      #redefines center of image as
                    applied to object

}
```

Now that the Materials have been defined for the SOL VRML document, let's digress for a moment and incorporate another VRML capability into this composition. A real show stopper of a node to add before declaring the object node is SpinGroup. SpinGroup is the closest thing to a self-running motion world in VRML 1.0. Although the effect is limited to rotating an object, the creative possibilities will be explored in this chapter. Essentially, the SpinGroup requires that three values in a string field specify the X, Y, and/or Z rotation of an object; a fourth value at the end of the field defines the direction of the rotation. Additionally, you can spin an object locally (it rotates around its own axes), or rotate the object globally, creating an orbiting object whose axes of rotation lie somewhere in space. You don't have control over the object when you globally spin it, but it's a neat effect nonetheless.

```
SpinGroup {
rotation 0 1 0 -0.1
local TRUE
```

The preceding code will make subsequent nodes in the scene graph spin about their Y-axis, counterclockwise. As you can see, the node isn't closed with a right curly bracket, because we want the node to affect the following nodes.

The SPHERE node has only one property. If you specify a radius, you can control the overall size of the object. In Figure 6-4, you can see the SOL VRML file as played in Navigator, with the recipe shown at right.

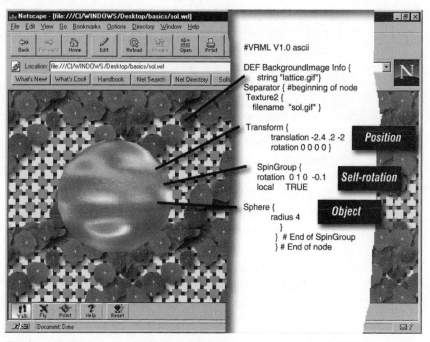

Figure 6-4: *Textures and a little motion can make even a simple VRML world look polished and professional.*

TIP

One of the most definitive papers on the VRML 1 specifications can be found on the VRML forum at http://vrml.wired.com/vrml.tech/ . It contains the latest specifications and detailed descriptions of syntax for VRML. Add this bookmark to your jump list!

USING FONTS IN OUTER SPACE

In the same way a collection of vectors connecting points in space defines the surface of an object, digital typography as we know it today consists of a description of vectors. And text, too, can be a part of a VRML world. The AsciiText node can be used to add text to a world, or even be the main attraction. Because computer fonts are platform-specific in format, the AsciiText fields you can use with this node are confined to SERIF (which generally looks like Times Roman onscreen regardless of your system), SANS (real close to Helvetica), and TYPEWRITER, a monospaced font which Navigator will most likely use Courier to display.

It should be stressed here that the VRML document you build that includes AsciiText nodes—or most any object definition—is completely dependent upon the viewer's VRML plug-in or helper app to provide an accurate description of your world. There are over a half-dozen VRML browsers available; some feature enhancements over the approved VRML specifications, while others don't deliver all the features you might want to include in your world. For this reason, the following example of ASCII text is written "plain." Font attributes are not declared; however, you can rest assured that the text message can be viewed on most VRML browsers.

CD-ROM
TEXT.WRL can be found in the CHAP06\BASICS folder of the Companion CD-ROM. The following is the structure of TEXT.WRL world that produces 3D text against a starry background image:

■ The DEF BackgroundInfo node at the top of the document contains a reference to the background image, SPACE.GIF. SPACE.GIF is a seamless tiling texture that fills the background of the world although the file is only 19K.

■ The Material node in this example defines a color, not a texture, for the AsciiText node to follow. Color is written as a string of three values: red, green, and blue. White text against the starry background helps the legibility of the 3D text, so the string 1 1 1 defines full brightness for red, green, and blue components of the color. *Color triplets*, as this notation for color is called, is based around a 100 percent brightness value for a color channel equaling 1, while 0 percent brightness equals 0; shades in between are written as a fractional decimal value. For example, if you want blue text, you write the values as 0 0 1. It's important that the field for the color is defined as a color attribute (diffuseColor in this example), and that curly braces surround the Material field. See "Material Properties in VRML," below, for details.

MATERIAL PROPERTIES IN VRML

If you intend to use a color instead of a texture for a surface, there are several options that can be used to control the appearance of the surface. The diffuseColor parameter specifies that a Material shall reflect light as a scattered collection of reflections—the Material appears to be rough. This is a good illumination parameter for objects that are small onscreen and need to be mostly illuminated.

There are other Material parameters you can use in combination with diffuseColor. They are:

■ *ambientColor*, which is written with a color triplet (e.g., 1 0 0). The ambientColor parameter spreads light evenly over a surface, as though reflective sunlight strikes the object. You might not want to combine diffuseColor with ambientColor; the two provide similar, although not identical shading on an object.

■ *specularColor* defines the color of the highlight cast by lighting that strikes an object. Here's a neat trick: if you define the specularColor of a Material as a lighter shade of the diffuseColor, you wind up with a metallic-looking surface. Metallic objects often have highlights that are a pure hue of the main surface color. In contrast, white specularColors tend to make a surface look like plastic. The specularColor attribute is defined as a color triplet.

➡

■   *emissiveColor* is written as a color triplet, and can be used to self-illuminate a Material. This is a useful parameter for a surface that you want to appear to glow, such as a star or other object you want to draw attention to in a VRML world.

■   *Shininess* is written as a single-field floating point value (0 to 1), and determines the smoothness of a Material, but has no effect on the faceted look of objects. A high shininess value can help accentuate the specularColor of a Material.

■   *Transparency* is written as a single-field floating point value (0 to 1). This parameter might undergo some changes in VRML 2 specs, because many VRML browsers at present can't handle partial opacity—they read values less than .5 as opaque, and values between .5 and 1 as totally transparent.

In this example, I wanted the headline of the text to float a little in front of the rest of the text, so that viewers who fly through the scene would see more dimensionality to the ASCII text object. Therefore, a Transform node is written within a separator that also includes the first line of text. ASCII text can be translated and manipulated in the same way as other 3D objects in VRML. In Figure 6-5, you can see most of the VRML script and the resulting view of the world in Navigator's browser.

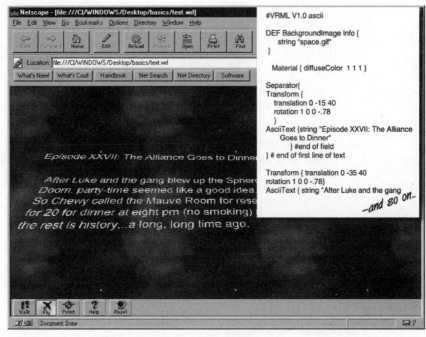

Figure 6-5: *AsciiText nodes can be rotated and aligned to a position in space.*

You can also specify justification of text by adding a field within curly brackets after the AsciiText node is declared. The justification parameters allow any of three single-field values to be used: LEFT, RIGHT, and CENTER. These justifications are made relative to the origin of the text (0 0 0).

There's another property of AsciiText that makes the TEXT.WRL file work: by default, lines of text rendered after the first line are spaced in a negative Y value according to the first font size and spacing. Size and Spacing fields were not used in this example, so the font default values were used. Size is written as a single value after declaring the Size parameter, and Spacing is also a single-field value. You might never need to incorporate size and spacing in an AsciiText node—most of the time, the text will look fine.

You'll notice that the first line of text in this example is translated by -15° from the Y (vertical) origin of object space, and is rotated 45° in a negative, clockwise value, from the viewer. Subsequent lines of text are written outside of the first separator, and therefore can have their own, unique orientation and rotation in space. What is happening here is that the string "After Luke and the gang blew up the Sphere" has a translation of -35° in negative Y space, which places it beneath the first string in the first separator. And this string has the same rotation values as the "Episode XXVII..." string, so in 3D space, the "After Luke..." string appears to advance toward the viewer onscreen. The rest of the lines of text have *the same* Transform values (0 -35 45), yet they appear neatly stacked beneath the "After Luke..." string because the AsciiText node automatically demotes subsequent strings of text along the Y-axis. Rotation fields in the subsequent AsciiText nodes are unnecessary: the rotation parameter is defined in the "After Luke..." string, and because there is no separator bounding this node, all subsequent lines of text are affected by the initial Transform rotation field preceding the "After Luke..." AsciiText node.

BUILDING A MULTIPLE OBJECT WORLD

We hope that you'll take the VRML files from the Companion CD-ROM and edit them to create variations upon the simple themes we're presenting here. For all the explanations based on analyzing finished VRML scripts, the best way to learn how to build worlds is hands-on.

CD-ROM ICECREAM.WRL, in the CHAP06/OG folder of the Companion CD-ROM, is a good example of aligning two objects in VRML space so that they appear to be grouped and spin in the same direction. You'll notice that in Figure 6-6, a sphere of .9 (meters) in radius has been specified, and that its location in space is -2.4 (X), 2.1 (Y), and it protrudes toward the view by one (Z-axis) meter. To place the second object, the cone, so that it rests directly beneath the scoop of ice cream, you need the same horizontal translation value (X = -2.4), and the same depth value (Z = 1), but the cone needs to be lower than the ice cream scoop, so a value of .2 is written into the Translation field. This number was arrived at by trial and error: It's not a bad idea to have your VRML file loaded in a text editor with Navigator's browser tiled alongside the text window. In this way, you can edit the document, reload the file in Navigator, and get immediate feedback.

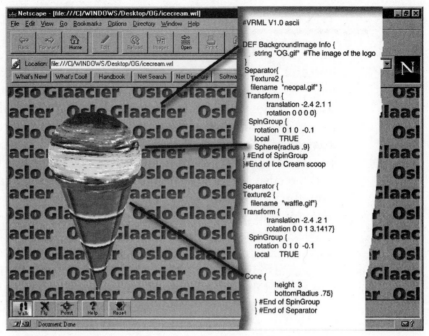

Figure 6-6: *A VRML scene can have motion, textures, and shape, without the use of a modeling application.*

Similarly, the size of the scoop underwent fine-tuning as the WRL file was constructed. A value of .9 as the radius seemed to work when compared to the cone object's bottom. However, in this example, bottom is actually the top from the viewer's perspective. The cone has been inverted: the Rotation field specifies that the cone's Z dimension is rotated by 180° (rotation 0 0 1 3.1417); cone objects written to a default rotation field of 0 0 0 0 appear to the viewer as a dunce's cap.

The SpinGroup nodes apply to both the scoop and the cone, and although they were written as identical nodes, you could easily make the ice cream spin counterclockwise, while the cone spins clockwise. The -0.1 value at the end of the SpinGroup rotation field specifies negative Y-axis rotation—*clockwise* rotation, in plain English!

TEXTURE MAPPING & 3D WORKAROUNDS

There's an interesting property of sphere mapping we should get into at this point, because seams tend to show when a texture is mapped to a spherical object. In totally nonmathematical terms, a square image used as a texture map on a 3D spherical object tends to "shrink-wrap" around the surface; the top and bottom of the image which converge on the north and south poles of the sphere become distorted and squinched. The edges of a texture image on a sphere also meet in the back of the object, the side facing away from the viewer. However, 3D worlds were meant to navigate through, and the SpinGroup node certainly displays the back face of the cone and sphere with regularity.

A workaround to eliminate the seam on the back of textured spheres also works with cones, whose texture projection begins mapping at the back, from an aspect pointing down the Y-axis traveling counterclockwise. The bottom circle of a cone is always mapped linearly: the texture is repeated for the bottom; and we don't concern ourselves with scaling or orientation for the textured bottom here, because it's hidden by the ice cream scoop. However, some methods can be used in an image editing program to ensure that the edges of a texture which cannot be hidden in the scene do not display a visible edge. We have an example to follow that uses Fractal Painter to perform texture-edge disguising.

The waffle texture for the cone object was created by embossing a light brown square in Photoshop, and a pattern that repeats four times was created from the single image to make the WAFFLE.GIF file. Waffles, screens, and other rectangular repeating textures are easy to map, because they end precisely at their beginning point when mapped to even curved shapes such as cones and cylinders.

However, to make a somewhat convincing ice cream scoop texture requires a little ingenuity. Because VRML 1 doesn't support bump mapping (see Chapter 4, "Working With Models"), it's hard to create lifelike, organic textures. However, both Photoshop and Fractal Design Painter can help create seamless tiling images whose appearance suggests a bumpy surface without the assistance of a separate image bump map channel.

Here's how to create an image of a three-flavor scoop of ice cream in Fractal Design Painter 4:

1. Choose File | New, then specify 128 pixels in both the Width and Height fields, and type **72** in the Resolution field. Choose an off-white Paper Color for the New Picture, then click on OK.

2. Click on any linear-type gradation sample in the Gradation drawer of the Art Material palette, then choose Grad | Edit Gradation from the minimenu on the Art Materials palette.

3. The Edit Gradation dialog appears, and it's modeless—you can easily move the focus of the application to other palettes while this dialog box is onscreen. Click on the Color icon on the Art Materials palette to display Painter's color picker.

4. The pins on the gradation strip in the dialog box can be selected and changed by click+dragging the color circle in the color picker around, and by moving the Hue ring on the color picker to a different location. For this example, why not start with a chocolate brown color: click on the far right pin, then click and drag the color picker's target rings to create the brown.

5. Additional pins can be created by single-clicking in the gradation color strip in the dialog box. Click two additional pins to the left of the brown end pin, then specify, from right to left, a lighter shade of brown, then a darker shade for the pin closest to the center of the strip. To delete a pin, press the Backspace key (the Delete key doesn't function as Delete in the Windows version of Painter).

6. You've got the chocolate done; it's time to work on the vanilla portion of the fill. Click to add a pin directly to the left of the last pin you created, then make it a creamy white color. Create a new pin to the left of the last pin, and give it approximately the same color.

7. Repeat steps 4 and 5 to complete the gradation, but choose shades of pink for the pin colors, to suggest strawberry ice cream.

8. Click on OK to exit the dialog box, then click on the Up arrow on the Gradation drawer to access the gradation pattern types and the Save button. Choose the linear-type gradation if you haven't done so already, click and drag the direction control so that the gradation runs at either 90° or 270°, then click on the Save button and name the gradation.

9. Choose Effects | Fill, then choose Gradation from the Fill dialog box, and click on OK. This concludes part one of the assignment; now on to texturing the image.

10. Choose Pattern | Make Fractal Pattern from the Pattern minimenu on the Art Materials palette.

11. Click on the 128 Size radio button. Painter's fractal textures will seamlessly tile across an image whose dimensions you specify.

12. The fractal textures are generated from seed values you choose when you adjust the sliders. There are no absolutely correct ice cream texture settings: experiment with the slider values until you think you have an interesting texture.

13. In the Channel drop-down list, choose Height as Luminance, then click on OK. An Image window now appears that contains the fractal texture.

14. Click on your ice cream gradation image, then choose File | Clone Source, then choose the Untitled image of the fractal texture from the list.

15. With the ice cream image in the foreground, choose Effects | Surface Control | Apply Surface Texture.

16. Choose Original Image from the Using drop-down list. Drag the Amount, Picture, and Shine sliders so that the preview image takes on the semblance of textured, expensive ice cream! Click on OK to apply the surface texture. See Figure 6-7.

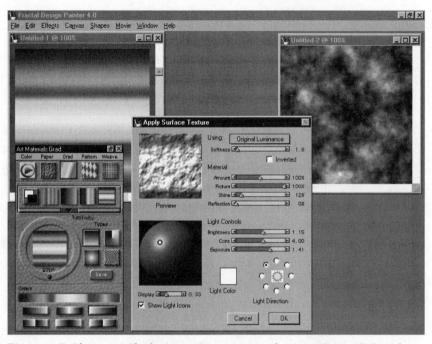

Figure 6-7: *If you specify the same size texture as the target image, Painter's
Surface Texture effect will make the image a seamless, tiling image.*

17. Save the textured ice cream image in GIF, Interlaced for-
    mat, and in the Save As GIF options box, choose 64 colors
    and Dither colors as options. Click on OK. And that is how
    seamless tiling ice cream is made.

We still haven't played out our hand yet for the possibilities of
textures to add interest to a virtual world. In the next section,
you'll see how to *animate* a texture on the surface of an image.

ANIMATED GIFS FOR VRML SURFACES

You might consider using GIF images as textures over the JPEG
format, because it seems like every day people are discovering
new, extended capabilities for the GIF format when viewed with
Navigator. Unlike multi-image animated GIF images discussed in
Chapter 5,"Animation & Digital Video Compression," textures

written to the GIF file format can animate across the surface of a VRML object by simply arranging the image file in a "slide strip" configuration. There are one or two qualifiers to creating an animated GIF texture, but we'll cover the procedure from concept to completion shortly.

CD-ROM

To continue along a theme here of spacey graphics, the SPINCUBE.WRL file and its associated graphics can be found in the CHAP06/BASICS folder. Copy the BASICS folder to your hard disk, then load the SPINCUBE.WRL file in Navigator. You'll see an example of an animated texture on a spinning cube in outer space, as shown, along with the VRML script, in Figure 6-8.

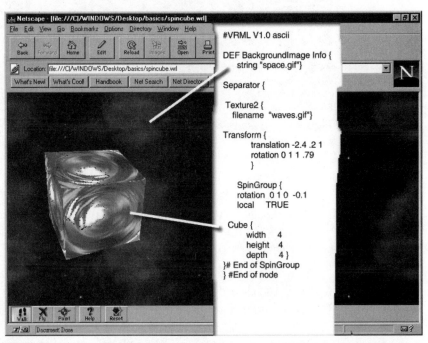

Figure 6-8: *3D worlds can move about in space* and *display surface motion.*

You already know how to define a cube, attach a SpinGroup node, and add a Texture2 node to the background and objects, so that leaves us with discovering how to animate a collection of still images.

One of the common authoring tools, for both the Macintosh and Windows, for animated textures is Kai's Power Tools version 3.0's Interform Designer. KPT 3.0, like previous versions, requires a host application such as Photoshop, Fractal Painter, or Corel Photo-Paint. Although Interform was primarily created for generating Windows AVI files or Macintosh QuickTime movies, it can also render still frames of an animation, and if you follow these steps, you'll learn how:

1. In the host application, create a file that's 128 pixels wide at 72 pixels/inch resolution, and a multiple of 128 as the height. To make the animated GIF a little larger than you should, but also to uncomplicate the math, make the height 1280 pixels; this will give you 10 frames for the animation.

2. Marquee-select the top of the empty image window so that 128 pixels in width and 128 pixels in height are selected. This is the first "frame" of the animated GIF. Photoshop users can specify a Constrained Aspect Ratio Style on the Options palette when the Rectangular Marquee tool is selected.

3. Choose Interform 3.0 from the KPT 3.0 flyout menu in your application's Filter menu.

4. A default installation of KPT 3.0 will fill the keyframes at the bottom of the Interform user interface with images you might or might not want to use in your animation. Alt(Opt)+click on a frame to clear the keyframe as a first step.

5. Choose a texture and type of motion for the Mother and Father fractal pattern by dragging down the drop-down lists beneath each of the preview windows. The actual image you'll write to file is displayed in the center, Offspring window. This window contains a blend of Mother and Father attributes; to specify a blend, click on the left menu arrow beneath the Offspring window, then select Manual Blending. Click in the Offspring window and drag to the left or right to specify the amount of parental influence for the Offspring image.

6. When you think you see an interesting pattern, click in the keyframe box marked with a 1 beneath it. This fills the frame with the pattern, and you can retrieve it at any time in the future by clicking on the keyframe box. See Figure 6-9.

Figure 6-9: *KPT's Interform 3.0 can provide you with the images you need to compile animated GIF texture.*

7. Let a second or two pass, then click in the next keyframe box (number 2). Repeat this process with the remaining keyframe boxes.

8. Click on the number 1 keyframe, then immediately press Enter (Return). Interform 3.0 will close, and the first keyframe will render to the selected area in your new image.

9. Repeat this process by selecting the 128 X 128 pixels directly beneath the first area you rendered, return to Interform 3.0,

select the second keyframe, then press Enter (Return). As you can see in Figure 6-10, two of the frames for the animation have been filled. Eight to go!

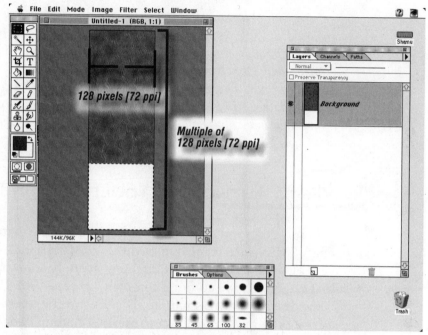

Figure 6-10: *An image to be used as a VRML animated texture has to be 128 pixels in width and a multiple of 128 pixels in height.*

10. Export the file as an interlaced GIF. Photoshop users can use the File | Export | GIF89a filter; other programs might require that you color-reduce the image to 256 or fewer unique shades before saving to the GIF format.

11. That's it. Refer to the file in the string field of a Texture2 node that precedes the object you want to have as an animated texture.

There are advanced methods that can be used to texture an object with different image files on each object facet, but unfortunately, this is beyond the scope of this book. Again, the VRML technical specifications can be downloaded from http://vrml.wired.com/vrml.tech/, and the document on specifications includes parameters for field values of the MaterialBinding node, which can be used to apply different materials to the faces of polygonal objects.

By default, the same texture file is repeated on each face of an object. As with the SPINCUBE.WRL file, you can create some interesting multiple animations on cubes, cylinders, and cones, because by default, a single GIF file tiles exactly once on each face of an object's surface.

VRML AUTHORING TOOLS

Up until this point, we've concentrated upon the manual creation of a VRML world using a text editor. VRML is a little more than a year old, and as of this writing, there are only a few applications that can be used to author a complex virtual world. However, this is the *dawn* of VRML-smart applications, and it's certain that there *will* be programs in addition to the ones highlighted in this chapter you'll be able to use.

All of the VRML authoring tools to date are modeling/rendering programs. If you're comfortable working in a modeling application, it's as easy as File | Export to generate a virtual world from the models, textures, lighting, and camera angles you've specified. The following sections are broken into application-specific techniques for generating VRML documents.

CALIGARI'S FOUNTAIN

Originally designed around the trueSpace modeling/rendering application, Fountain is an inexpensive modeling and VRML authoring tool that features graphical (as opposed to text-based) interface controls, and perhaps generates the "cleanest" VRML files: worlds that can be accurately displayed in a number of VRML browsers, and whose files are small in comparison to other VRML authoring software.

Fountain can import a wide variety of vector graphics, including Illustrator files and DXF files—in case you already have a model you want placed in a VRML world. Additionally, Fountain has polygon tools you can create paths with and then extrude, a Primitives panel that can automatically generate spheres, toruses, and other geometric shapes, and painting tools with which you apply lighting and surface colors and textures.

Although Fountain's tools aren't the easiest to grasp at first, the program makes up for a somewhat steep learning curve by offering WRL *imports* as well as exports. Fountain, unlike its big brother trueSpace, doesn't have a native file format in which you save a creation. Instead, everything is saved as a VRML *.WRL file—which can be read back into Fountain with no loss of geometry or scene detail. In Figure 6-11, you can see the Fountain interface with many of the feature panels opened. I've imported a DXF file of the VRML logotype (which anyone is allowed to model and use on the Web), and completed the logo with a cube, sphere, and cone primitive object. You can view the file in Navigator's browser by copying the BASICS folder on the Companion CD-ROM to your hard disk, then loading the VRML.WRL file in Navigator.

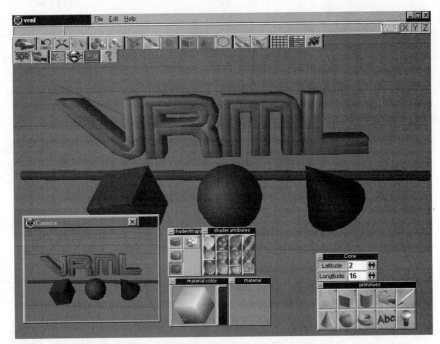

Figure 6-11: *Caligari's Fountain allows you to import DXF files from other applications, and export a VRML WRL file of the resulting virtual world.*

If you're working on a Windows machine, Fountain could possibly be the only VRML authoring tool you need, outside of a text editor for script touch-up work (explained a little later). At this time, no version of Fountain for the Macintosh has been announced.

For all its virtues, Fountain doesn't, and shouldn't be expected to, keep up with the latest VRML enhancements. Live3D supports background images a little differently than Fountain writes them, as an example. You cannot specify a tile size for the background of a Fountain virtual world, and therefore are obliged to use a JPEG image to completely cover the background of the scene. The workaround to this is to hack the file to include DEF BackgroundImage node information preceding the description of the world scene.

If you open VRML.WRL in a text editor, you'll see how the grid background of the virtual world was accomplished. In Figure 6-12, you can see how the world displays in Navigator. Notice also that, regardless of smoothness attributes you assign to an object in a VRML authoring program, the results are always polygon-based. It is much quicker to read and write polygons from point sets—coordinates from which polygon planes are calculated—than to calculate how a curve approximates a surface. VRML is designed for speed, and polygonal surfaces, not spline-based, simulate virtual worlds in VRML.

Figure 6-12: *VRML authoring tools might not provide you with the scene exactly as you envision it. If you're careful, you can manually edit an authoring tool's VRML file to enhance it.*

LIGHTING & CAMERAS

A distinct advantage a VRML authoring tool has—beyond the capability to write a complex world—is that lighting and camera angles, topics we'll discuss right now, are a nightmare for the average designer (like the author) to manually create, but modeling applications that speak VRML make the task a breeze.

VRML specifications allow the definition of one of two different types of cameras in a scene. More than one camera view can be defined for a VRML world, and the audience may toggle between views using the browser controls.

An *OrthographicCamera* node presents a flattened view of a world; navigating through the lens of this camera presents none of the peripheral distortion a narrower lens might produce. The volume described by the point of view of the OrthographicCamera on a scene is box-shaped. The OrthographicCamera node must precede the description of the node that the camera views in the scene graph, but can be modified by a Transform node if one precedes the camera's description. Fields for describing parameters of the OrthographicCamera node are as follows:

- *Position* is the orientation in VRML space. By default, the camera's position is 0 0 1: it points at the X,Y origin of space, and is one meter in front of the scene.

- *Orientation* is how the camera looks upon the scene. Camera orientation is defined by a multiple field containing X, Y, and Z values (ex: 0 0 1 indicates that the X- and Y-axes are not rotated, but the Z-axis is the rotational line), followed by a rotational value, expressed in radians.

- *FocalDistance* is a single-field value that describes the distance from the camera at which objects are rendered to full detail. LOD, or *Level of Detail*, is an implementation of VRML by which objects in the distance are rendered more crudely—with fewer polygons—than objects within the focus of the camera view. You might never need to add this field or allow the authoring application to write it—unless your world is full of objects, in which case it might be too large a file to post on the Web with any hope of people visiting it.

- *Height* describes the vertical viewing limitation of the camera. There exists no corresponding width field for the OrthographicCamera.

Unlike the OrthographicCamera, a more commonly used camera node is the PerspectiveCamera, which does indeed present the viewer with wide-angle distortions as the viewer navigates closer to objects in the world. The fields used in the PerspectiveCamera are the same as the OrthographicCamera, except height is replaced with heightAngle, which represents the total viewing height of the volume defined by the space between the lens and the world. The PerspectiveCamera's volume is shaped like a truncated pyramid, unlike the OrthographicCamera's box-like volume.

Lights for VRML worlds are of three kinds: Point, Spot, and Directional.

A *pointLight* is like a bare lightbulb hanging from a fixture; it illuminates equally in all directions from the center. Fields that can be used with the pointLight node are:

- On (TRUE or FALSE).
- Intensity (a single-field floating point value).
- Color (written as a color triplet).
- Location (floating point values written as X Y Z coordinates with white space separating them).

The pointLight node may be confined to illuminating only selected objects in a scene by placing a separator before the node, and closing it with a curly bracket after the description of the objects to be illuminated.

The *spotLight* node is perhaps the most sophisticated of lighting descriptions, but also the hardest to direct by manually entering information in a VRML text file. (Hint: let a VRML authoring tool provide an onscreen representation that you can more easily direct!) In addition to On, Intensity, Color, and Location fields, the spotLight node also can contain the following:

- *direction*   The target of a spotLight node is directed using a field of three axes coordinates, identical in structure and notation to the Translation field. For example, 0 0 -3 directs the spotLight at the X and Y center of the scene, pointing three meters behind the default depth of the origin point.

- *dropOffRate*   The dropOffRate is expressed as a single floating point value which describes the exponential drop-off of light as it travels from the source to the position it's directed upon in the scene.

- *cutOffAngle*   The cutOffAngle, also expressed as a single floating point value, describes the angle of the cone that the light emitted from a spotLight creates.

The *directionalLight* node is similar to the pointLight, except the light is coherent and parallel to a 3D vector that describes the direction of the light. On, Intensity, Color, and Location are the fields with which you can describe a directionalLight.

Are lights and cameras a challenge to manually define in a VRML script? Yes, definitely, no question about it. However, by understanding light and camera parameters, you can easily edit a camera or light that an authoring application has defined in a VRML file. For example, I had a camera pointing in the 2501.WRL file in the CHAP06 folder of the Companion CD-ROM that was slightly misaligned. Instead of opening the authoring application, repositioning the camera, then asking the application to rewrite the entire file, I moved the camera by changing the rotation amount in the Orientation field. You simply have to know where to look within the file.

VIRTUS WALKTHROUGH & VIRTUS VRML

Virtus WalkThrough has been enjoyed by architects and CAD users on both the Macintosh and Windows platforms for a few years now, and the latest version (2.5) offers the capability to export your virtual world to WRL format in seconds. Although the drawing tools in WalkThrough Pro aren't as robust as those typically found in a modeling program, WalkThrough Pro produces absolutely flawless VRML scripts, and comes with a collection of clip objects in proprietary format that makes peppering a room with lamps, sofas, and even some whimsical, block-like people a snap.

WalkThrough Pro does not allow the import of 3D DXF objects, but will import TIFF images and 2D-format DXF files for tracing over using WalkThrough Pro's native drawing tools. Additionally, it's easy to embed a WWW Anchor node (discussed below) in a VRML world using WalkThrough Pro.

In Figure 6-13, you can see the LANSCAPE.WRL file played in Navigator's browser. This file can be copied from the LANSCAPE folder in CHAP06 of the Companion CD-ROM. LANSCAPE is a simple maze, with linked objects hidden in areas. The idea here is to navigate through the maze until you find a link; if you get bored with the game, there's no roof, and you can easily fly over the landscape to find the hidden treasures.

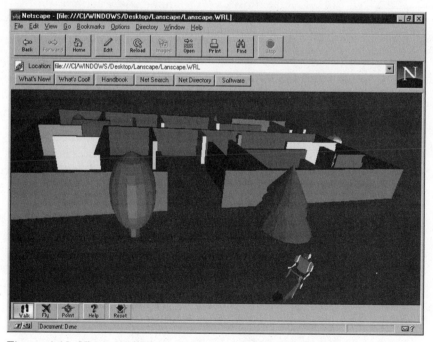

Figure 6-13: *Virtus WalkThrough Pro is a biplatform application that makes authoring rooms and other architectural structures extremely easy.*

The WWWAnchor node is added before the separator to a node (or collection of nodes), and offers onscreen text describing the link if you hover your cursor above the WWWAnchor object in the VRML world. There are three fields you can add (or Virtus can add) to a WWWAnchor node:

- *Name*   The Name field is a *string* (a series of characters that may contain a space, surrounded by double quotes to indicate this special type of field) that represents the URL to which the WWWAnchor object links.

- *Description*   The Description field, also a string field, is your big chance to display onscreen a more evocative description of the site to which the WWWAnchor links. This allows you to make some sense out of URLs for your audience from not-so-obvious URL names. A WWWAnchor doesn't have to link to another world. For example, http://winnie.acsu.buffalo.edu/potatoe/ is *not* easily discerned as the Unofficial Mr. Potato Head Home Page, but you can *provide* this information in the Description field.

- *Map*   The Map field is usually specified as NONE. However, if you find value in mapping a WWWAnchor to a different object in your world, you can specify POINT in the Map field, then use the X Y Z coordinates of a different area in the world (e.g., map 2 .7 -12) as the anchor.

Virtus VRML is an optimized limited version of WalkThrough Pro, like Fountain is a VRML-optimized version of trueSpace. By the time you read this, Macromedia will have an upgrade to Extreme 3D that will write a VRML world from your modeling creations (Extreme 3D is a biplatform application whose files are binary-compatible with Macintosh and Windows machines). Also, Visual Reality, shown later in this chapter, is an extremely powerful VRML authoring tool, and although it's Windows only, is perhaps the most straightforward and most intuitive program to model your worlds in.

INTEGRATION OF VRML WITH HTML

The engineering group at a fictitious company I work with was anxious to provide Marketing with some exciting material concerning a piece of machinery that was still weeks away from prototype. The solution? Send Marketing some enhanced *intra*net (in-office) mail of their work. Figure 6-14 shows the HTML document: some letterhead stationery in the left frame which describes the near-finished product, and a 3D mockup in the right frame. The right frame offers three navigational entry points (three camera choices) from the Live3D plug-in's pop-up menu, and the AsciiText node within the world provides a clear title for the object.

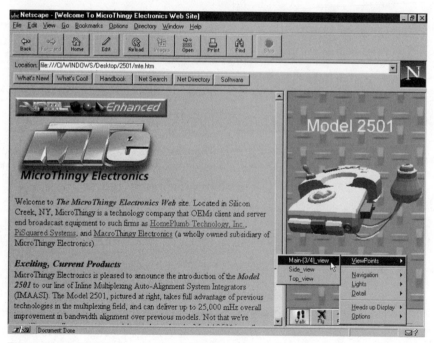

Figure 6-14: *HTML documents can tell a story and provide a picture, but they can also provide complete visualization solutions with links to VRML files.*

The recipe for the memo in the previous figure is an involved one, but fairly straightforward in its execution. The model of the equipment (the Model 2501) was created in a modeling program. It was then exported to Renderize Live (a part of Visual Software's Visual Reality bundle), where lighting was defined, and different camera angles were created. The file was exported to VRML *.WRL format, and a tiling background and the AsciiText node were manually edited into the VRML text file.

To add the virtual world to the HTML document involves the use of frames and named target windows. You can *embed* a VRML file within an HTML document so that it displays as an inline virtual world by using the <EMBED SRC="filename.wrl"> tag, but this can slow the download of any text-based information you might include on the page. Frames were chosen for this intraoffice memo because of the clean style and presentation of the graphic and text information.

CD-ROM If you open the MTE.HTM document (located in the CHAP06/ 2501 folder of the Companion CD-ROM) in a text editor, you'll see that the frameset document is composed of a frame containing MTE-NEWS.HTM, and a frame that consists only of the MODEL.WRL VRML document.

As you can see in Figure 6-14, the camera angles defined in Renderize Live for the model were preserved when Renderize Live wrote the WRL file. The recipient of this document can easily switch between views of the Model 2501 by right-clicking to display Live3D's navigation shortcut menu.

There's always the chance that a part of a Web document won't load when the audience tries to view it. Even when a VRML file that's part of an HTML document *does* load correctly, there's sometimes a wait: VRML files created with authoring tools can be much larger than hand-written VRML files, because complex objects increase file size. Therefore, there are one or two things you might want to consider adding to an intranet document such as the Model 2501 announcement:

■ Let the viewer know that the document contains a virtual world; in the Model 2501 announcement, a small graphic is located above the HTM document in the left frame that tells the viewer that the document is VRML-enhanced. Because, at the moment, there is no Web community agreed-upon method for alerting the audience to how a document is enhanced, this is your big chance as a designer to *invent* a graphic or other device to alert viewers that a virtual world is going to be presented in the document.

■ If you're uncertain that your audience has the latest plug-in for Navigator to browse an inline virtual world, provide a button and/or a text link to download it from Netscape. A good message to precede your virtual world document would be, "This document features a VRML virtual world. For best viewing results, use the Live3D plug-in for Netscape Navigator. Click here to download the plug-in." The link should go to

```
http://home.netscape.com/comprod/products/navigator/
```

Help your audience by providing download links for Web multimedia types you're not certain the audience will have preinstalled.

VRML ENHANCEMENTS

Although we've covered many of the fundamental properties of the VRML structure in this chapter, there are two more enhancements you can create in a VRML document that can help you solve a graphics problem.

Earlier in this chapter, we showed you how to create an animated texture to map to objects in a virtual world. As GIF-type images, any animated sequence displayed upon the surface of an object can also have a transparency color. If you create a GIF animated sequence of text, and specify that the background color should be transparent, you can add floating, *animated* text to a VRML document. Although the animation size must be 128 pixels wide by a multiple of 128 pixels high, you can position the object in VRML space close to a camera, and the image as displayed on the object's surface can indeed display at a size larger than 128 pixels.

Also, alignment to a camera view can help keep a text message or a design mapped to an object, at the same orientation when a viewer navigates through your VRML world. If you fly through the TEXT.WRL document, you'll notice that the AsciiText node disappears as you attempt to peek to the left or right side of the object. This is because AsciiText is two-dimensional. However, try to view "behind" the Model 2501 title in the MTE.HTM document. You can't, because the AsciiText node in this world uses the AxisAlignment node. If you precede an object node with

```
Separator {
AxisAlignment {
 fields    [SFBitMask alignment]
 alignment ALIGNAXISXYZ
 }
```

objects that follow in the scene graph will remain aligned to the camera view, regardless of where the viewer navigates within the virtual world. The viewer can pan away from the scene and fly past all world objects, but the AxisAlignment node will keep an object facing front while it's visible within the browser window.

In Figure 6-15, you can see CRAYONS.WRL, a VRML document originally created in Fountain, then manually edited to include a cube whose dimensions are 1.5 in Width, 1.5 in Height, but zero in Depth. This 2D cube, therefore, cannot display the animated GIF of the rotating star on any other face than the front, because it has no other dimensions. The AxisAlignment node keeps the animation projected upon the 2D surface facing front regardless of viewer perspective, and the transparency for the animated GIF allows the object and the texture to better integrate into the scene. You can view the CRAYONS world in Navigator; it's in the CHAP06/BASICS folder.

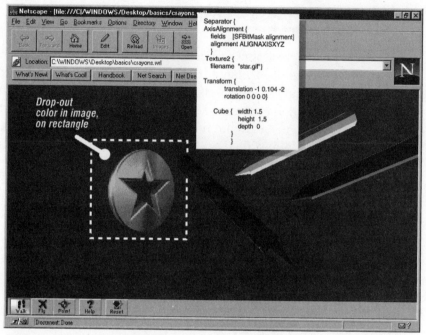

Figure 6-15: *A "persistent" object in a VRML world can be created by using the AxisAlignment node. Such objects are called* sprites.

Depending on the visual content of the animation you play upon an aligned object, you can create any number of special effects. Kyle Sims has some wonderful VRML file examples in the comprod/products/navigator/live3d area of Netscape's Home Page. Kyle created an animation of birds flying, made the background transparent, and mapped the image to an object within a model of a tree. You have the specs; all you need now is a concept to make sprites part of your VRML worlds.

ANIMATED WORLDS

It's important not to underestimate the effectiveness of animated textures as an element of interest in your VRML world. Until the Moving Worlds specifications for VRML 2 are implemented, inter-active behavior and worlds that move upon opening the document are somewhat limited to SpinGroups and animated textures.

If you're skilled with a modeling application, and the application supports animation, you might very well substitute an animated GIF texture on an object for a VRML object of the same model; you have that sort of choice when your authoring tool supports both modeling and animation. In Figure 6-16, you can see Macromedia Extreme 3D's interface. The clown in the first frame of this animation was created using the same tools as described in Chapter 5, "Animation & Digital Video Compression," with the fishbowl animation. The clown animation was originally intended as an AVI file, but the 30-frame animation would be much too large to convert to an animated GIF texture. However, Extreme 3D allows you to scale the actions and events in a saved animation file to create the same visual content in fewer frames.

If you own Extreme 3D and would like to repurpose an animation, open the file, choose Animate|Score to open the Score Window, nest all animation tracks by clicking on the icon to the left of the top object title, highlight the top object title by clicking on it, then choose Animate|Scale Time from the menu. In Figure 6-16, you can see that if a 30-frame animation is scaled by 33 percent, the resulting animation will contain 10 frames, a large, but acceptable number of frames for an animated GIF texture.

Figure 6-16: *You can repurpose existing animation files by scaling the duration of the animation, then writing the scene out as still-image files.*

In any animation package, it's important to render the animation as still frames, *not* MooV or AVI files. You can then compile the animation to conform to animated GIF format using an image editing program, and perform color reduction to comply with the GIF89a's indexed color palette limitation of 256 unique colors.

MOVING BETWEEN VRML WORLDS

Logistically, a VRML world needs to be small: a file over 100K or so will take much too long to download, and if your artistic content needs to be expressed as "large," it would be better to offer the VRML file as a download than as an online world.

However, the VRML content you present as a multimedia component of your Web site can be broken into many small worlds. All you need do is conceptually organize your content into "rooms," or linking gateways, then create links as you'd do in any HTML document.

FreePark is an example of how linked worlds can contribute to an overall experience that suggests a spacious virtual place. The FREEPARK.HTM document in the CHAP06/FREEPARK folder on the Companion CD-ROM is a frame-based document, whose WRL frames change at the click of a button. To view this site, copy the FREEPARK folder to your hard disk, and load the FREEPARK .HTM document in Navigator.

The top page of the FreePark document, like the Model 2501 document, is composed of two framesets: FREEDOM.HTM, the text and link portion of the site, is displayed in the left frame, while different worlds are displayed in the right frame. Figure 6-17 is the top page of FreePark.

Figure 6-17: *A multiworld Web site needs navigation controls. You can create WWWAnchor nodes in the VRML file, but you can also make text and image links in adjacent frames.*

The method used for moving between frames is all HTML-based in the FreePark example. The buttons and accompanying text in the FREEDOM.HTM file link to the WRL files, but the virtual worlds display in the same frame as the kite you see in Figure 6-17, because the kite frame has been named in the FREEPARK .HTM document, as such:

```
<FRAME SRC="kite.wrl" NAME="Kite">
```

Because the frame is named, it can be used as a target frame for links. The underlying mechanism for the first button and accompanying hypertext ("Click here to clown around…") is an *a href* (an *a*nchored *h*yperlink *ref*erence) with a target reference to the frame named Kite in the FREEPARK document:

```
<a href="system.wrl" target="Kite">
<img src="univers.gif" ></a>
<a href="system.wrl">Click here to clown around in space!</a>
```

In Figure 6-18, the hyperlink has been clicked, and the audience moves to a different part of FreePark. The SYSTEM.WRL file was originally assembled in Renderize Live, with models created and imported from Extreme 3D. The starry background (NITESKY.GIF) was manually edited into the finished VRML document, and the spinning cube with the animated clown were also manually added after Renderize Live wrote the initial WRL file.

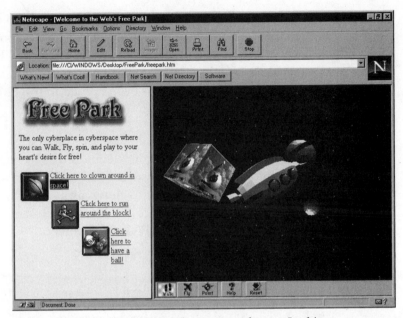

Figure 6-18: *It's a good idea to always name frames. In this way, you can make the frames target windows for other VRML files.*

TIP

When presented with the options of using a VRML authoring tool to create primitive objects or manually creating them, it's better to manually edit the file to include the primitive. In the example of the Clowns in Space world, Renderize Live could easily write the cube object into the world, but not with the economy of simply adding the word "Cube" to the document. Many VRML authoring tools write explicit geographic point position descriptions of geometric primitives such as cylinders and spheres instead of the succinct, simple VRML object node declaration.

While we're discussing the possibilities of good source material for your VRML world, let's not forget that a model in DXF format is completely portable: one file can be accessed by a number of different modeling applications that are capable of parsing a 3D DXF file.

In the final example in this chapter, a chrome cartoon character prances around a 3D block in the CUBE.WRL file, part of the

FreePark site. The chrome character was originally designed as a still frame for an image I used in a book about a vector-drawing application. Because the finished piece contained a model, and not a flat 2D representation of the character, the DXF information could be repurposed as an animation. Extreme 3D made it easy to make a loop of the character strutting (one complete cycle of left, right, then left strutting); Extreme 3D's animation tools don't include inverse kinematics, but if you link different objects together with a proprietary E3D feature, you can achieve almost the same effect.

An animation of this simple motion study wouldn't have nearly the interest value if staged against a solid background, however, so a very wide (128- by 512-pixel) background landscape was created. You can see the complete world, with a frame from the animated texture, in Figure 6-19.

Figure 6-19: *An animated surface texture can make up for VRML 1's limited provisions for auto-playing moving worlds.*

Only a 128 by 128 *section* of the background image is featured in any given frame, however. A *panning background strip* can help convey the sense of motion in any animation that needs to be projected upon a static object surface.

Here are the logistics of creating a motion picture on the surface of the CUBE.WRL document:

1. You need to decide upon the number of frames the animated GIF will be. In the CUBE.WRL document, the chrome guy cycles through a single walking motion in eight frames. The eight frames are rendered to Targa (TGA), because the Targa format is capable of holding alpha channel information about the content of the rendered scene. The static black background in the rendered animation images will be replaced with a moving background.

2. Because the animation is small in dimensions, doesn't last a long time, and needs to support the foreground character without detracting from the "star," a drawing application was chosen to render the background strip. The left and right edges of the image strip need to be identical; this takes a little calculating, but vector-drawing programs allow easy manipulation of paths to align properly in different design areas. You can take a look at the BK-GROUND.TIF image in an image editor to better see how the design is constructed. It's in the CHAP06 folder of the Companion CD-ROM.

   CD-ROM

   The dimensions of the file as exported to bitmap format are 128 pixels high and 512 pixels wide, at 72 pixels/inch. The reason for this width is that cropped sections of the background strip can be taken every 64 pixels to generate 8 different backgrounds for the animated foreground character. A completely different frame containing all new background objects would be a poor decision—objects would flash past the chrome character, and the animation would be very disorienting.

3. Photoshop was chosen for the compositing work because it has an Offset filter that can advance the background strip image, while maintaining the relative position of a crop field designed and called from an alpha channel in the BK-GROUND.TIF image. The process of compiling the animation is detailed in the remaining steps.

4. Create a cropping frame in a new alpha channel that will determine the finished frame size. In Photoshop, you click on the new channel icon on the Channels palette, specify 128 pixels for the Height and Width of the Rectangular marquee tool (do this on the Options palette, behind the Brushes palette), then select an area in the center of the alpha channel in the background strip image, and save the selection to the channel by dragging the new channel icon into the channel # 4 thumbnail (on the channel list area).

5. Create a duplicate of the BK-GROUND.TIF image, then work on the duplicate for the first frame of the animation. Keep the original file on the workspace, however: you'll need to create additional duplicates.

6. Bring in the first frame of the foreground animation. Then, with the selection marquee active in the BK-GROUND duplicate, copy and use the Edit | Paste Into command to place the entire frame within the marquee selection in the background strip.

7. While the copied frame is still a floating selection, click on the new layer icon on the Layers palette, and accept the default name for the layer by clicking on OK in the dialog box. The frame is deselected, and rests on layer 1 now.

8. Activate the saved selection in the BK-GROUND duplicate again by Alt(Opt)+clicking on the channel #4 thumbnail on the Channels palette, then click on the new channel icon to create a channel #5 that's identical to channel #4.

9. Go back to the first frame image, and select the entire alpha channel. Copy it to the clipboard; then from the channel #4 view of the BK-GROUND duplicate, choose Edit | Paste Into.

10. Alt(Opt)+click on the channel # 4 thumbnail on the Channels palette to load the new selection information. The selection marquee should describe the background areas on Layer 1 in the BK-GROUND image. If the marquee is selecting the foreground, press Shift+F7 to invert the selection.

11. With Layer 1 as the active Layer in the BK-GROUND duplicate, press Delete (Backspace), then press Ctrl(Cmd)+D to deselect the marquee.

12. Load channel #5 by Alt(Opt)+clicking on the Channel #5 icon, then choose Edit I Crop.

13. Flatten the image by choosing Flatten Image from the Layers palette's flyout menu.

14. Save the file as MY_ANIMATION01.TIF, and close it.

15. Create another duplicate from the BK-GROUND.TIF image, then choose Filter I Other, then choose Offset. Type -64 in the "Horizontal, pixels right" field, type 0 in the "Vertical, pixels down" field, choose Wrap around from the Undefined Areas field, then click on OK. The BK-GROUND duplicate shifts 64 pixels to the left, however the alpha channel selection of the cropping frame remains in the same location. If you repeat steps 6–15 with the remaining 7 frames (progressively advancing the Offset amount with each new frame), you'll have individual frames that can then be composed into the vertical animated GIF format.

Figure 6-20 shows the Photoshop process of creating the moving-background GIF animation. Like many of the examples in this book, the steps involved to create superior work pose a challenge, but the challenge is more one of following steps exactly than it is a creative or technical hurdle. I recommend as a working environment some quiet music after the kids are asleep, with the telephone off the hook—and you can then successfully complete this 20-minute task.

Figure 6-20: *An attention-getting animated texture does involve concentration and a little time, but the payoff is a completely unique Web-site attraction.*

MOVING ON

We've taken you through the creation and integration process by which virtual 3D worlds can become another element of your Web multimedia events, but like animations and graphics, VRML subsystems on your site are only as result-oriented as the concept you put behind them. They can be a novelty that wears thin, or can continually attract visitors because they provide a visualization solution not possible in other types of media.

In Chapter 7, "Working With Special File Formats," we'll get into other types of objects you can integrate with existing materials. Sound, Java applets, Shockwave movies, and more can allow your production to be as content-rich as a CD-ROM title. And the best part of adding special file formats to your site is that the information can stream to the visitor. Instant access to many types of educational, leisure, and commerce objects helps get your point across, and the how-tos are awaiting you in the following chapter.

7

Working With Special File Formats

Throughout this book we've shown the support Navigator provides for communicating through enhanced HTML support; an idea you can express as plain text can often make a point better when there are other, graphical lines of thought woven into the presentation.

This chapter goes completely beyond the HTML specifications, to the point where you can consider the audience's operating system to be the Internet; Navigator is the graphical interface and you—the multimedia author—write the applications. Navigator plug-in support is here today for the creation of inline enhanced presentations that give all the appearance of interactive television. Let's take a look at how to push the envelope with the addition of special file formats for the Web.

DIRECTOR MOVIES & SHOCKWAVE PRESENTATIONS

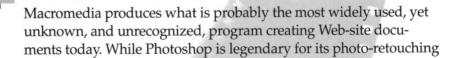

Macromedia produces what is probably the most widely used, yet unknown, and unrecognized, program creating Web-site documents today. While Photoshop is legendary for its photo-retouching tools, and a typical office couldn't survive without Word or WordPerfect, Macromedia Director has been a nonmainstream software tool, whose importance as a Web authoring tool has only recently been discovered.

Director is a creative tool for nonprogrammers that offers a finished product that looks as though it were written in C or Visual Basic. Many branching, interactive presentations and tutorials, animations, and games (*Iron Helix* was produced in Director) are the result of artists who want multimedia richness without the learning curve that programming languages demand.

The Director examples to follow are *not* intended as complete documentation on the program, nor will they provide valuable insights for users who are already proficient with Director. Additionally, the screen figures and steps shown in the following sections relate to Director version 4, not the current version 5. As of this writing, Director 5 projects aren't accepted by the Afterburner utility, an inconvenience that Macromedia is aware of and will correct shortly. Think of the examples primarily as a suggested solution for Web authors who are seeking a specific media-content vehicle, and a tutorial on how Director movies can be converted to Web-ready Shockwave files.

PREPARING CONTENT FOR DIRECTOR

Macromedia would be the first to point out that *Cast members*—the elements used in a Director movie—are best imported, rather than created using Director's native graphics tools. Touch-up work to graphics, application of ink effects (special effects), and other minor edits can be performed within Director, but if you're experienced with other graphics applications, design your resources in your favorite application, then let Director do the animation.

DIRECTOR MOVIE DIMENSIONS

Because of the Internet's current bandwidth, it's not a good idea to create a Director piece to the same dimensions as you would a CD-based interactive title. In fact, the QuickTime movie file dimensions of 160 by 120 pixels are recommended; this option is available in both the Macintosh and Windows versions of Director. 160 by 120 pixels is in the same 4:3 ratio as a computer monitor's display. You'll find that when you compose a multiframe or table HTML document, it's a comfortable aspect ratio to play with among other Web elements that make up a site.

The example used in this section is a Shockwave element within a Web page that solicits programmers to submit resumes to the fictitious LoftySoft software manufacturer. The theme of the page suggests that if you're going nowhere at your present firm, LoftySoft will give your career the wings to allow it to soar (a lofty suggestion indeed). To add imagery to the text content of the page, a simple animation with sound needs to be created. If you spend as little as one hour with Director, you'll find that creating a sound animation file is about as demanding as creating an animated GIF (see Chapters 5 and 6).

Many drawing and paint applications can be used to make a sequence of motion files, but CorelXARA was chosen in this example because of the content of the animation. A hapless cartoon character is stuck on the ground, and no matter how fast it flaps its arms, it cannot get elevated. This animation's "plot" can be accomplished in as little as three frames. If you build a character similar to that shown in Figure 7-1, the arms can be copied and repositioned almost effortlessly, because vector-drawing programs (including CorelDRAW, FreeHand, and Illustrator) allow you to work with design areas as discrete objects. Other qualities that made XARA a good choice for producing the animation resources are that it performs antialiasing on the fly and seamlessly integrates the foreground vector areas of the frames into the bitmap background shown here. Thus, the exported bitmap image doesn't display screen artifacts that are a natural result of combining vector data with bitmap data.

Drawing programs in general do not provide pixel count as units of measurement, owing to the fact that vector graphics have no fixed pixel height or width until they're exported to pixel (bitmap) format. Therefore, in Figure 7-1, you can also see that the 160 by 120 pixel measurements for the finished size of the Director movie are equivalent to 1.67 inches high by 2.22 inches wide, when exported to a bitmap format whose resolution is 72 pixels/

inch. (See Chapter 2, "Vector-to-Bitmap Conversions," for a detailed explanation of pixels versus inches.)

Figure 7-1: *Vector-drawing programs are terrific for producing simple animation files. Objects can be repositioned without the necessity to paint an entire image multiple times.*

The three still image files are exported exactly as they appear in Figure 7-1 to a color depth of 24 bits (a.k.a. millions of colors, RGB color, 16.7 million colors). Director 4, however, cannot accept images whose color depth exceeds 8 bits per pixel, and although color reduction can be accomplished upon export of a XARA file, let's take a look in the next section at how to create the best-looking, color-reduced Director animation.

Color Palettes for Director Files

Director animations use a limited, indexed color palette for the bitmap images you can use for Cast members. Director can handle color reduction of more color-capable files, but you might not be as happy with Director's color down-sampling method as that of an image editing program. This means that imported bitmap files should have a color depth of 256 colors before you import them. Director handles the BMP format (for Windows) and PICT format (for the Macintosh) very nicely, in addition to other bitmap formats. However, here's where the cross-platform issue gets a little convoluted. Although Director files can be played on either system, regardless of the movie creation platform, the Macintosh and Windows machines map system colors differently. System palette (*color table*, or *color lookup table*) color mapping for the Macintosh differs from that for Windows. The Macintosh system palette contains different index color values, and the order in which colors display is different. For example, the first color in the Macintosh system palette is white; the first color slot in the Windows system palette is black.

You can see that there is bound to be a problem mapping colors for playback on either system if a specific system palette is used for the images you import for use in Director. In nonscientific terms, system colors will be mapped to create very unpleasing results on the platform that didn't create the movie. The solution to this problem is to use an adaptive (or custom) color palette when color-reducing original files to be used in a Director animation. An adaptive palette is unique to an image; it's calculated by the frequency of colors that actually appear within an image. In contrast, a system palette consists of fixed color values. Many of these colors may not be found in your image, and if you color-reduce to a system palette, you've wasted space that could otherwise be custom-tailored to contain the colors that most faithfully represent the original image.

Experienced Director users might be accustomed to attaching a color palette to a Cast member to force Director to use a specific color palette. But, if you have access to Photoshop 3 or later, an adaptive, common palette can be used for all animation still files, and the resulting animation can be played back with reasonable color fidelity on either a Windows or a Macintosh system.

Here's how to create the animation source files for a Director movie that will be broadcast on the Web:

1. In Photoshop 3.05 or later, open the first animation still you want to color-reduce to an indexed color palette.

2. Choose Mode | Indexed Color. In the Indexed Color dialog box, choose 8 bits/pixel, select Adaptive in the Palette field, click on the Diffusion radio button in the Dither field if it's not already highlighted, then click on OK. You can also choose a smaller color palette by choosing from 7 bits/pixel, and so on, but depending upon your image files, excessive dithering at such a small file dimension could make your finished piece look harsh and unprofessional. Color depth is a compromise between small file size and preserving original image detail: both are important, and you must decide which you need more.

3. Choose File | Save As, then save the image with a sequence number as the last character in its file name. In terms of file format, you can use GIF, PICT, PCX, BMP, TIF—almost any bitmap format you regularly use. Platform-specific files such as BMP (Windows) and PICT (Macintosh) can be used as part of a Director file to be played on the Web; a Macintosh Director movie compiled using PICT images will play on a Windows system, and vice versa. It's the order of the indexed colors within the image's palette that's of concern here.

4. With the new, saved file open in Photoshop, choose Mode | Color Table.

5. Click on Save, then save this file to hard disk; you'll need it to apply to subsequent images in your animation.

6. Click on OK to exit the Color Table dialog box.

7. Open the second image you want to color-reduce for the Director animation.

8. Choose Mode | Indexed Color.

9. If you haven't processed any other images while in this session of Photoshop, you can simply click on the Previous radio button in the Palette field of the Indexed Color dialog box. This loads and applies the last-used palette. Otherwise, you can click on Custom, click on OK, then find the palette you saved in step 5. Click on the Diffusion radio button in the Dither field if it's not already highlighted. Click on OK to apply the color palette and color-reduce the second image in your animation to exactly the same palette.

10. Finish color-reducing the rest of the images in your collection, and save them to sequentially numbered file names, with the appropriate file type for your operating platform. Director doesn't use the sequential file names, but you will need some sort of handy reference system when importing files to Director (or any type of animation program).

In Figure 7-2, the author has made a futile attempt to graphically convey information about color tables in a black and white screen capture. Photoshop doesn't display two color tables side-by-side (the figure has been edited), but the message I'm trying to convey here is that the system palette for the Macintosh and an adaptive palette calculated by Photoshop for a unique image are both ordered palettes where white is the first of the indexed color slots. And an adaptive palette used on images will display color-reduced converted images very nicely on both Macintosh and Windows systems. The Windows color palette (available in Photoshop 3.0.5 for Windows) maps black to the first color slot. If this palette is used in Director animations to be played cross-platform, it will result in a coarse-looking animation. An adaptive color palette is written by Photoshop to accommodate both audiences' viewing and authoring needs.

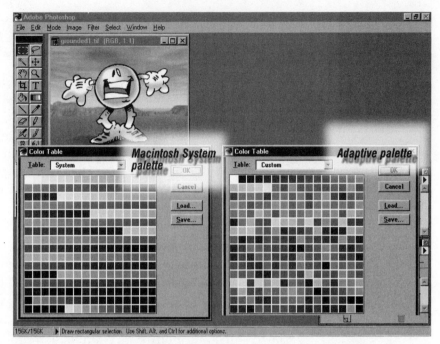

Figure 7-2: *Maintain a common color palette for indexed images that you'll use in Director, and make sure that your palette isn't specific to one system's colors if you want the animation to be cross-platform.*

DESIGNING A HIGH-FREQUENCY ANIMATION

The example of the cartoon character in this section demonstrates the use of low-frequency image resources as the visual part of the animation. High- and low-frequency are terms commonly used to describe a still image and how abrupt color changes within its visual content can affect the success with which it can be compressed using a scheme such as JPEG. However, high- and low-frequency are used in context here to describe how dramatically colors shift in an image as it plays through time.

The cartoon example uses exactly the same colors from frame to frame; in this sense, the resulting Director animation will be low-frequency with respect to color shifts. However, it's more than likely you'll want to design a Director animation with a lot of color changes from frame to frame (like an animated light flashing, or MTV-like color field backgrounds strobing). If your second, third, and subsequent frames do not correspond even remotely to the color content of your first frame, you must use a strategy different from the one described in this section for color reduction to a common palette for all files.

CD-ROM

If you're a Windows user, you can't go wrong with Brenda the Batch Renderer (a utility on the Companion CD-ROM). Brenda can "look" at all the files in a folder and come up with a color palette that's common to all the images. Expect some dithering greater than that produced using adaptive color reduction for each different image; an indexed color palette can only hold 256 unique values. After the common indexed color palette has been created, you can then color-reduce all the images you intend to import to Director.

Macintosh users are familiar with a commercial program, Equilibrium's DeBabelizer Toolbox, that can perform many bitmap conversions, including batch mode color reduction to a common palette.

Alternatively, you can create one composite image of all the sequential files to be used in an animation, then instruct Photoshop or another image editor to create an adaptive palette. This palette can be saved and then applied to individual frames of your animation.

These methods are the best for ensuring that colors don't shift along the play time of your animation. Dithering is a reality with indexed color images, but color shifts are unacceptable and are prevented easily enough with the investment of a few moments in an image editor.

HOW DIRECTOR & SHOCKWAVE WORK THEIR MAGIC

It's important to discuss how Director files are compiled. The Shockwave version of a Director file has a few playback limitations because of the way Director creates a multimedia show.

Through its different versions, Director has undergone changes in the distribution of finished, playable multimedia creations. Currently, when you make an executable (self-running) file from a Director *.DIR piece (a file that runs on a machine without the need for a helper application, like MS PowerPoint presentations do), part of the code of the Macromedia Director program is written into the executable file. At present, if you distribute a Director file for commercial use, you are bound by the End User Agreement (the software license) to display the "Made With Macromedia" graphic in both onscreen and printed presentations.

Director features many user-friendly, intuitive theatrical metaphors for the elements that make up a Director presentation. Cast members are the file resources Director can import. Animations such as QuickTime and Windows AVI files, indexed color images, sounds in AIF or WAV format, and other Director files can all be part of the presentation. Cast members are moved to the "stage" through the Score window in Director; a Cast member is called to stage when the resource is needed to complete the movie. You'll see how this process works shortly in this chapter, when a modest Director movie the author created is compiled and converted to a Web-ready format.

Shockwave, a condensed, optimized version of a Director title, uses a different playing engine than its full-sized parent program. Instead of adding program code to the DIR file when making the executable, self-running, finished movie, a Shockwave movie plays through the Shockwave plug-in for Netscape. The player is *external* to the movie.

Director titles traditionally have been as large and intricate as the author's need and energy. Much of the strength of Director as a multimedia tool lies in *Lingo*—scriptable code that provides time-based, host-based, dynamic interactivity between the movie and the user. Lingo is a scripting language rather than a programming language, but Lingo does require some time to implement correctly in a script that can change the movie according to user input. The most common uses of Lingo are to retrieve items that will be used in a movie, to make buttons and forms, and to keep the display of the movie smooth by loading and unloading Cast members.

Because of security issues (custom Lingo scripts can read and write data to and from the user's hard drive) and the reality that the Internet is not a CD-ROM, certain modifications and restrictions to Lingo commands must be made for the DIR file to qualify as a candidate for condensing to a Shockwave file. If you're an experienced Director author, Lingo Network Extensions can be used as replacement commands for:

- Getting Cast members from a specific Net site to be added to Cast members in the movie the user is currently viewing (StartGetNetCast).

- Reading specific text from a remote site (StartGetNetText).

- Preloading a resource file for a movie into local cache (NetPreload).

. . . and several other commands that require a Universal Resource Indicator (a URI is a superset of a URL, which also uses the HTTP scheme) for locating files across the Net.

It is beyond the scope of this book to provide advanced documentation on Director's Lingo code. It's an invaluable feature for multimedia authoring to any type of delivery system—kiosks, Apple Pippin systems, CDs, and now the Web—but the attraction of Director to designers is two-tiered. Lingo is a Director enhancer in the same way that Visual Basic extensions are an MS Excel or Access enhancer. You can indeed create fascinating Web work without Lingo commands, and the basic, introductory tier (Director sans Lingo code) will adequately serve the discussions that follow on integrating movies with HTML scripts.

TIP

For complete, detailed discussions of how Lingo extends the power of Director, pick up a copy of The Comprehensive Guide to Lingo, *by Gary Rosenzweig, published by Ventana.*

CREATING A SIMPLE DIRECTOR MOVIE

Compared to programming languages, Director's scripting language (Lingo) is easy; however, compared to a GIF animator or paint program, Director demands more user experience to get the most out of the application. Nevertheless, Director is one of the few programs that a designer with intermediate skills can get commercial-quality results from within an hour. As mentioned earlier, this section is an introduction to—an exploration of—new Web media-creation tools. In the following example, you'll learn how to create a Director animation with sound and how to convert your work into the Shockwave format. The example will also serve as an introduction to digital sounds you can post on the Web.

Here's how to make a Director movie that can be incorporated into an HTML document:

1. In Director, choose File|Preferences, then choose QuickTime 160 X 120 from the Stage Size field.

2. The Stage Location: options determine where the Stage displays onscreen, and its location is fixed until you specify a different option in Preferences. To work in Director efficiently, you must have at least three panels open (and the Score window is fairly large). Therefore, if you choose Left, at 0 pixels from the Left and 0 pixels from the Top of the interface, you'll have plenty of room in which to work with an unobstructed view of the Stage. If you're running 800 X 600 video resolution, you might want to place the stage at about 50 pixels from the Left and 100 pixels from the Top of the interface. You can change these options at any time.

3. Click on the Save Settings Now radio button if it isn't already highlighted, then click on OK.

4. Press Ctrl(Cmd)+3 (Window | Cast), then choose File|Import and select the first frame of your animation from hard disk. If you have a well-organized hard disk and keep resource files for assignments in discrete folders (hint: make this a practice before you get too many assignments), you can choose to Import All from the Import File dialog box, and save some time here. The imported file(s) will load in the Cast window as thumbnail images.

5. Choose Window|Score (Ctrl+4) to display the "blueprint" of your movie's architecture. You'll notice that the cells are empty upon creating a new movie.

6. Click and drag the first Cast thumbnail into the Score window. You can use as many tracks as you need for Cast members, but animation sequences must be built along a single track. Therefore, you can think of these animation stills as being Cast members who play the same role along the timeline of the movie.

7. Click and drag the second Cast thumbnail into the second cell in track 1.

8. Click and drag the remaining Cast members into cells following those you've placed on track 1 in the last two steps.

9. Choose Window|Control Panel (Ctrl(Cmd)+2). This is the playback panel for your movie; it's similar to the panel in Extreme 3D shown in Chapter 5, "Animation & Digital Video Compression."

10. Unless you were extremely ambitious in the earlier example, you should now have about 3 still frames populating the cells in track 1. At 15 frames per second (the default animation speed; this is a good value to keep here), the animation will run $\frac{1}{5}$ of a second. This would produce a file of the right size, but of inadequate content, for the Web. Click, hold, and drag from left to right to highlight the cells marked in track 1.

11. Press Ctrl(Cmd)+C to copy the frames to the clipboard.

12. Highlight a number of cells—to the right of those you selected (empty cells)—that corresponds to the number of frames you copied (e.g., you highlighted three frames, so highlight the next three empty cells).

13. Press Ctrl(Cmd)+V. Duplicates of the frames you copied are placed in the empty cells. Here's the trick with Director: Cast members are used as a resource *once* in a completed movie. But their presence in an animation is an *instance*—a reference, an occurrence where the copied file is read into the completed animation as many times as you specify without significantly increasing the saved file's size.

14. Repeat step 13 with empty cells to the right of ones you've populated until you have filled about 30 cells. Alternatively, you can copy all the cells you've created in a previous step to paste the multiple (3 cells, then 6 cells, then 12) of Score window instances more quickly.

15. Save your work as MYFILE.DIR to hard disk. Macintosh users can skip the file extension convention here, but a Shockwave file needs an extension, as do most Web media, so it's a good practice to get into the "dot-plus-three" convention of naming files.

A Brief Interlude With Sound

Sound is discussed in more detail later in this chapter, but its relevance to Director titles needs a little explanation before you add sound to your saved work.

Sound, used as a Cast member in Director, can be prerecorded and imported, or it can be directly recorded if your system supports recording and playback. The Macintosh operating system has a slight advantage over Windows when it comes to Director's support of sound.

Basically, you have your choice of Windows WAV files or Macintosh AIF sound files to use when you import sound. The Macintosh version of Director doesn't recognize Windows WAV files (because there is no Macintosh data type for a WAV file, and WAV files simply don't play natively on a Macintosh), but the Windows version of Director can import and use either AIF or WAV files. In terms of file structure, there is very little difference between WAV and AIF files; the distinction lies mostly in the file's header information.

The Macintosh format for stored sound file types can have an impact on successfully making a Director movie for the Web. Windows users might find the information that follows useful, especially for cross-platform authoring. Apple has historically avoided the distinction between a system sound file and an AIF sound file. System sounds (the Quack, Sosumi, and so on) are compressed sounds with the sfil or snd data type written into the resource fork. Although system sound files—and the sounds you can save through the Simple Sound utility—present most applications with perfectly legitimate sound data, Director will not read a file of this type into a Director movie. Director will tell you that it cannot import compressed sound and will offer to link the intended sound file instead. This creates no problem with CD-ROM-based Director movies, but Afterburner, the utility for making Shockwave movies from Director titles, will not accept data linked in this way to the file.

SoundApp, a freeware, drag-and-drop utility that can be found at ftp://mirror.apple.com/mirrors/info-mac/gst/snd/sound-app-151.hqx (the unoffical location for SoundApp, which might be subject to change), can automatically change a compressed-system sound into an AIF file that can be used as a Director-imported sound, or can be posted on the Web as a free-standing media object.

The alternative to imported "canned sound" is to record it yourself, live, from within Director. Most Macintoshes today support the recording and playback of sound natively, and Windows PCs can be outfitted with a sound card capable of recording sound for as little as $100. In the following example, you'll see how to add sound to the Director animation:

1. With MYFILE.DIR loaded in Director's workspace, choose Cast | Record Sound. If your system doesn't support the recording of sound, you can import GROUND.WAV or GROUND.AIF (see the CHAP07/LOFTSOFT folder on the Companion CD-ROM) using File | Import. The file will appear in the Cast window to the right of the last-occupied thumbnail pane.

2. Depending upon your system, a dialog box or mini-interface will appear within Director's workspace. Record your sound, keeping it under 2 seconds (the example in this section is only 30 frames—or 2 seconds—of animation), click on Stop when you're done recording, then click on OK. The name of the file and a tiny speaker icon will appear in the Cast member thumbnail frame.

3. Click and drag the Cast member thumbnail into the Score window. Director will gently guide the Cast member to a special, appropriate position in the first cell of an audio track.

4. Double-click on the sound thumbnail in the Cast window, then click on the Looped check box, and click on OK. Unlike animation Cast members, Director will play back sound across the Score without an instance of the sound Cast member occupying all of the cells that correspond to the animation. This is true provided the sound file is shorter than the total play time. If the animation plays out before the sound file, the remainder of the sound file is clipped—the excess amount won't play in the finished movie. If you want a short sound to play continuously, regardless of the total animation play time, checking this box makes it happen.

5. Preview the animation by clicking on the Play button (shown in Figure 7-3) on the Control Panel. The Cast menu has been pulled down in this figure to show you where you will find the recording option for systems equipped to record sound.

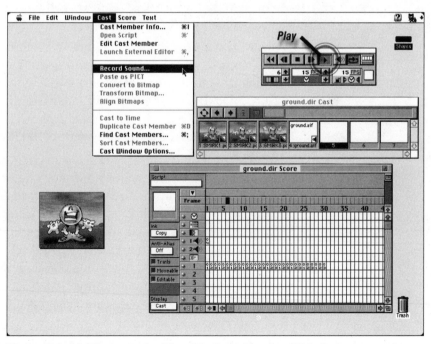

Figure 7-3: *Melding sound with animation to create a Web element can take only five steps in Director.*

6. Save your file to hard disk, and you're done. You can close Director now.

We hope you've seen how easy it is to use Director to accomplish a significant task. If you're serious about multimedia production for the Web, it's unlikely that you'll outgrow Director as a suite of tools.

AFTERBURNER & SHOCKWAVE

Afterburner is a Director post-processing utility for the Macintosh and Windows. It provides one-step compression and conversion of saved Director movies to DCR (Director Compressed), Web-ready format. As of this writing, a late beta of Afterburner can be downloaded from Macromedia's site free of charge. A price has not been fixed for the final shipping version of this utility, but it is included in Director version 5.

Shockwave is the Navigator plug-in that lets visitors to your site view your Director title. Like most of Navigator's plug-ins, the Director Internet player (Shockwave) should be located in the plug-ins directory of Navigator to be properly called when Navigator encounters a Shockwave file on an HTTP server. The plug-in is about 37K.

If you've downloaded Afterburner and run the installation, here's how to convert a copy of the Director file you saved in the last example to Shockwave format. Watch carefully; this is the world's second-shortest list of steps!

1. Double-click on the Afterburner icon (or its alias) to launch the utility. Upon opening, Afterburner will ask you to choose the Director file you want converted. Click on the file name, then click on Open.

2. Afterburner will display a status line indicating the progress of the transformation. Upon completion, it will ask you to name the file. Use an eight-character name followed by a period, then the extension name DCR. Click on Save, and see Figure 7-4 for a view of the two dialog boxes in Afterburner.

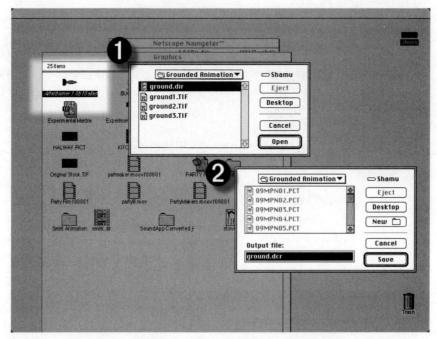

Figure 7-4: *"Burning" a Director file requires only that you select a file, a finished filename, and a folder in which to store the Shockwave file.*

Because of a proprietary encoding scheme, and the fact that the burden of playing the Director movie is now placed on the Navigator plug-in, you'll find a dramatic reduction in the Shockwave file size when compared to a self-running Director movie. For example, the GROUND.DIR file—the file containing the original Cast member information—is about 288K. When the self-running movie, called a *Projector file*, is created from the animation, the saved file size is 480K. Additionally, Projector files are platform-specific: you have to create a Projector file for the operating platform your version of Director supports. (Uncompiled Director projects, however, can be shared between platforms; they're binary compatible.) The Shockwave file compressed by Afterburner from the same 288K Director file weighs in at about 92K. Not only are Shockwave files smaller, but they are also platform-independent.

ALTERNATIVES TO SOUND-ENABLED ANIMATIONS

Because Director files can be recompiled again and again for tweaking and tuning, there's no reason why you can't also compile a Shockwave file without sound, to accommodate the hard-of-hearing or audiences that have no sound capability on their systems. There are still many Windows users who've yet to invest in a sound card. To communicate successfully with any audience that can't receive sound, there's a creative solution to be found in Director.

Director ships with auto-animating text Cast members. You choose the font size and style as well as the duration of the effect. You can automatically add typewriter-text additions, sliding letters, banners, and other animations onscreen. In the following example, let's suppose that you want to use the same animation as created earlier, but with the sound message replaced with onscreen banner-style text. Here are the steps to let Director do the "hard" part of making an "MOS" (*without sound*—from the corruption "mit out sound," affectionate slang from 1930s Hollywood when German directors were prevalent) version of the animation:

1. With the Director file loaded in Director, highlight frames 1 through 30 in an empty track. If you chose to make the animation shorter or longer in the previous example, highlight only the number of cells in the vacant track that corresponds to the length of the longest track in the movie.

2. Choose Score | Auto Animate, then choose Banner.

3. In the Banner dialog box, type in the phrase you want to animate across the screen. In this example, because the cartoon character's sound file says, "I can't seem to get off the ground!" the typed line, "I'm grounded!" would serve well here.

4. Click on the Text Style button, then choose the font you want to use from the list of installed fonts. In terms of font size, this can lead to text that's too large unless you understand the relationship between points and pixels. They're roughly equivalent: 72 pixels to 1 inch. Because the frame size in this example is only 120 pixels in height, you can

get away with 30-point type—it will take up only $\frac{1}{4}$ of the total available screen height, will be legible onscreen, and won't overpower the animation.

5. Click on the Transparent Text check box. This is an important one: Transparent text means that areas outside of the text will appear as clear, allowing the background of the animation to show through. If you leave this check box unmarked, a solid banner with text will scoot by in the animation, covering up more of the background animation than necessary.

6. Click and hold on the foreground color swatch and choose a color for the text. Your choice of both font and color is important for maintaining the legibility of the banner text against the background image. I chose a bright yellow for the text in this example because the cartoon character is primarily a faded violet, and the background scene lacks any colors in this area of the color spectrum. Additionally, my choice of font, Dom Casual, is bold, a little on the whimsical side, and is easy to read as it flashes by onscreen. If you intend to use a solid (and not transparent) background for the animated text, click and hold on the background swatch to select a background color now, then click on OK.

7. Finally, you need to set a speed for the text banner, in frames per second. This should be the same speed as your animation (15 frames per second). Decide whether you want the text to immediately scroll across (Initial Delay value), and how many times you want the text to scroll. This last option isn't really necessary for a 30-frame animation; scrolling more than once in 30 frames (2 seconds) would make the text hard to read. Click on Create, and Director fills the highlighted cells with your new text animation.

8. Because Director is object-oriented, the text you will now see in the Stage window can be repositioned if it interferes with the display of the animation behind. All the cells you selected before choosing Auto Animate should still be highlighted; simply click and drag the text object to the

place you like on the Stage, and the animation will be moved within the time frame of the highlighted cells in the Score window (in other words, for the complete animation). If the cells were accidentally deselected, highlight all of them on the text banner track in the Score window *before* repositioning the text on the Stage. See Figure 7-5.

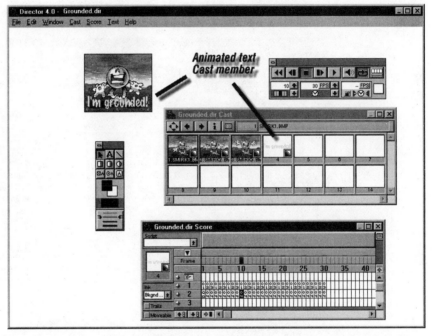

Figure 7-5: *Text can be auto-animated in your movie; use any font installed on your system and reposition the text after it's been created by Director.*

9. Save the project when you're done, then pass it through Afterburner to create a variation on the original movie.

INTEGRATING A SHOCKWAVE FILE INTO YOUR PAGE

Shockwave files can be referenced like any other Web object. When you put up a site with Shockwave content, the file must end with the DCR extension (e.g., GROUNDED.DCR), and the server on which the Shockwave file resides must be configured to send DCR files with the MIME type of application/x-director. In Figure 7-6, you can see the LoftySoft Opportunity/Education Web Page. The document is a frameset, and one of the documents displayed in the upper left frame is replaced by the Shockwave movie when a visitor clicks on the graphic in the original frame. You can copy the contents of the LOFTSOFT folder (in CHAP07) on the Companion CD-ROM to your hard disk to play it in NavGold.

Figure 7-6: *A Shockwave movie is as easy to call in an HTML document as a graphic or a VRML document.*

Here's how to create the LoftySoft Web site and how to create the mechanism by which the graphics document is replaced by the Shockwave file:

1. Create the frameset container document in a text editor. Depending upon the dimensions of the Shockwave file,

you should specify the first FRAMESET COLS width as the pixel width of the Shockwave file. For example,

```
<FRAMESET COLS="190,*">
```

used in the LOFTFRAM.HTM document specifies that the two columns that make up the topmost frames shall be divided into a frame that's 190 pixels in width and a frame whose width is the remainder of the screen space. By doing this, the left frame will always be 190 pixels wide, regardless of the visitor's monitor resolution. The 190-pixel width gives the Shockwave file a small amount of padding around it when it appears in the frame. Save the file to hard disk; we need to create a page element so that its dimensions can be referenced in this frameset document.

TIP

If you're new to this frame stuff in HTML, put a bookmark right here and go back to Chapter 1, "Composing in HTML & NavGold," where the construction of a frameset document is covered in detail.

2. Create a graphic that the Shockwave file will replace in the frame. In Figure 7-6, you can see that a still frame was used as the original graphic in the frame, and a button and a legend have been added beneath the graphic. The graphic was converted to transparent GIF89a format using Photoshop (Paint Shop Pro and GraphicConverter can also perform the task), so that the graphic, the button, and the legend are nested within a transparent area of the GIF image and appear to float in front of the background image. You don't need to create a background GIF image in this example; it's a nice embellishment (CIRCUIT.GIF in the LOFTSOFT folder), and the

```
<body background="circuit.gif">
```

body attribute is used to display the background image. The STILL.GIF image is 160 pixels wide by 152 pixels high.

3. As long as we're creating graphics, let's create one to serve as a billboard advertising the company name. The LOFTLOGO.GIF file, called within the LOFTLOGO.HTM document (the bottom, left frame in Figure 7-6), is 200 pixels wide by 300 pixels high. It's unusually tall because, at different viewing resolutions, the LOFTFRAM document will show more of the height of the lower, left frame. The LOFTLOGO.HTM file uses the LOFTLOGO image as a background, not as an image source. It will repeat as many times as the frame dimensions allow, and it will appear without padding within the frame. This is because the image you see is a background image, and not a foreground element that inherently "pushes" slightly away from the browser window edge. (See Chapter 3's example of the SPECIALS Web document for a detailed explanation of this workaround.) The "extra" area to the right and bottom of the LOFTLOGO.GIF image is defined as a transparent color. The background image shows through if a viewer displays the frame document at resolutions higher than 640 X 480.

4. The main frame playing inside the frame document contains the text portion of the site, and a graphic was used instead of text to display the headline. It's noteworthy here that text as a graphic can help convey a feeling or make a point in a way that text as ASCII text cannot. HTML has no specification for displaying a condensed style of text; Garamond Condensed is used in this example as the font in the graphic (Kabel Light, an unobtrusive, sans-serif font, is used as the subheadline). The choice of font within the graphic allows for a slightly lengthy headline (the condensed face allows more characters per line), and Garamond works nicely with the default font for Navigator's browsers across platforms (Times Roman doesn't "fight" with Garamond Condensed in font style).

USING TEXT AS A GRAPHIC

David Siegel, the creator of the Tekton font and several others, has a wonderful home page (at http://www.best.com/~dsiegel/home.html) that contains detailed explanations of how to use graphics as text to augment default font styles in an HTML document.

If you've ever wanted to place an em dash within a sentence or use an authentic trademark or copyright symbol on a page, check out Mr. Siegel's site.

5. To get back to the frameset document, open it in a text editor, and add

   ```
   <FRAMESET ROWS="180,*">
   ```

   beneath the FRAMESET COLS attribute. This will make the top, left frame display at the previously defined 190-pixel column width, and at 180 pixels in height (the graphic is 152 pixels in height, and will display a little vertical padding around it). The asterisk tells the browser to use the remainder of the browser window height to display the bottom, left frame.

6. Define the Frame Sources for the document. The LOFTFRAM.HTM document calls three documents for display: GROUNDED.HTM (the still graphic to be replaced by the Shockwave file), LOFTLOGO.HTM (the logo for the company), and LOFT-DOC.HTM (the text content of the site). The frames for the left side of the document are:

   ```
   <FRAME SRC="GROUNDED.htm" SCROLLING="No"
     NORESIZE>
   <FRAME SRC="LOFTLOGO.htm" SCROLLING="No"
     NORESIZE>
     </FRAMESET>
   ```

The SCROLLING="No" and the NORESIZE attributes prevent the visitor from resizing the frames (which, in turn, prevents the text frame from resizing), and state that the frames shall display no scroll bars. It's important here that you carefully measure the contents of each frame window when using the SCROLLING="No" attribute, and allow for a little padding around the graphical contents specified within the HTML documents. If you don't, the nonscrolling window will clip part of the contents, and the NORESIZE attribute prevents the visitor from manually exposing the clipped areas.

7. In the LOFTFRAM document, you then end the first column of frames with </FRAMESET>, and begin the second row with <FRAMESET>.

8. This right pane in the frameset document occupies the entire column width, and because it is a single row, the <FRAMESET ROWS="100%"> is used to define the remaining space in the window.

9. The contents are specified and this nested frame is closed with

```
<FRAME SRC="loft-doc.htm">
</FRAMESET>
```

10. The "master" frameset needs to be closed with </FRAMESET>, and the LOFTFRAM document is closed with the standard </html>.

There is nothing special happening within the LOFTLOGO and LOFT-DOC HTML documents. With the exception of a link out to Macromedia's site in the text portion of the frame document (which we'll explain shortly), these two frames are static containers for content that the user cannot interact with. However, the GROUNDED.HTM document uses a table to center the graphic, and the graphic links to the Shockwave file through an anchor href tag.

Because the padding that Navigator's browser puts around the edge of the window is unpredictable in the number of pixels that "push" the contents of the document, the table containing the graphic is three columns by three rows, with the center cell containing the graphic. If you check out the GROUNDED.HTM document in a text editor, the table looks like this:

```
<tr><td></td>          <td></td>          <td></td></tr>
<tr><td></td>      <td>graphic</td>       <td></td></tr>
<tr><td></td>          <td></td>          <td></td></tr>
```

In this example, the spaces between cells do not need to be written into the HTML document. The table has been arranged in a way that's easy to visualize on this page, and two consecutive white spaces are usually discarded by servers when the document is broadcast.

The cell that contains the "graphic" placeholder in the table above is where the anchor and href in the GROUNDED.HTM document is written.

```
<a href="grnd-MOS.dcr">
<img src="still.gif"
border=0 height=152 width=160
align=abscenter></a>
```

In English, the cell contents above mean, "The attribute for this cell is an *a*nchored *h*yperlink *ref*erence for the image "still.gif" to display "grnd-mos.dcr" when clicked on. There shall be no border around the hyperlink (even though this sometimes helps the visitor discern that the image is a link). Here are the dimensions the image source should be displayed at (so Navigator doesn't have to do the calculations and slow down the broadcast), and the image should be aligned within the cell to the absolute center. End of anchor."

In Figure 7-7, you can see that the image has been clicked on, and the Shockwave file plays in the frame. Afterburner places a very brief display of the "Made With Macromedia" billboard before the Shockwave movie plays. This eliminates the need for the author to comply with the license agreement for Director and manually add the billboard to the movie.

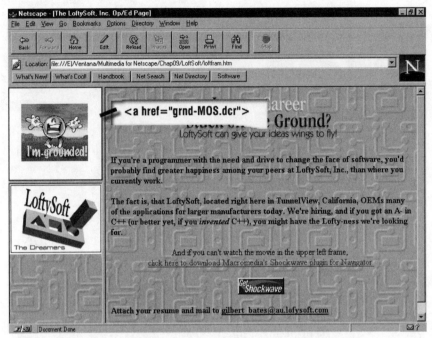

Figure 7-7: *Include a link in your opening page to the Shockwave file, and allow it to play in a frame within the document.*

It should be noted here that Shockwave movies, like Projector files, play against a white background that surrounds the Stage (the live area). If you want to eliminate much of the white space surrounding your content, a frame is a good solution.

TIP

The Shockwave example in this chapter auto-plays only once within the HTML document. It begins playing after it is loaded, and the last frame is a persistent element on the page. The element can be played again if the visitor clicks on the Back button on Navigator's toolbar. If you'd like to offer the visitor timing controls—when the movie begins, how to pause the Shockwave movie, and so on—you need to use Lingo commands.

CROSS-PLATFORM SOUND COMPATIBILITY

Unlike the many inline Web objects you can include in a multimedia production, sound, at present, requires Navigator to load an external player to execute the sound file. To make a sound a universally accessible object, the sound file has to be of a type that a server can dish out to users working on Macintosh, PC, and UNIX platforms. To pursue this line further, sound has as many qualities as graphics have: sounds can be tinny, full-bodied, large, small, compressed, and stereophonic.

The following section details the porting of sound files to a common format and how Windows and Macintosh authors can provide a visitor to your site with exactly the sound they need to play on their computer.

SOUND CONVERSION & COMPRESSION

Like graphics files, sound files need to be small to pass quickly from the Web server to the visitor's machine. There are three basic ways to make small sound files:

- Make the sound short in play time. You don't have the luxury of posting a three-minute song on the Web for playback. Such a file would be better for downloading. In general, keep your sound files to under four or five seconds. You'd be amazed at the information you can include within this time frame. Many Macintosh and Windows start-up sounds are only two or three seconds in length. Use sound creatively to accent a multimedia piece. Sound effects can enhance an animation, for example, and have a play time of only a fraction of a second.

- Limit the bandwidth of your sound file by resampling the original to a lower sampling rate. This might seem like a ham-handed, unartistic thing to do, but think about what you do with 24-bit images you want to display on the Web; even JPEG images suffer slightly in visual quality because original information has been removed to make the file smaller in size.

- Use compression on the file. The Web supports a *specific* type of compression, so don't use a proprietary or plat-form-specific compression scheme on a file until you read further in this chapter.

In general, the quality of digital sound has been broken into three classes of sampling rates that Navigator's playback utility can read. The following list gives a definitive explanation of the quality of digital sound depending upon how many times a second the sound file is sent or received (measured in hertz, generally written as 20,000 Hz, for example, to express twenty thousand hertz) from an audio device or playback utility:

- *CD-quality sound*   Music (from the lowest subtones to the upper-harmony frequencies) is faithfully reproduced from the source sound in a 44,100 Hz range. The sampling rate can be compared to the color depth of computer graphics; this is the playback speed of the sound. Because the breadth of tones that can be captured at 44,100 Hz is more or less the same as those present when the human ear hears a natural sound, CD-quality digital sound can be thought of as the TrueColor (24-bit, RGB, millions of colors) of sound.

- *Music-quality sound*   This sound quality can faithfully reproduce only half the audio range of CD-quality digital sound. 22,050 Hz is an adequate range in which music tones and speech can be captured and played back, but this quality of sound won't provide the listener with the subtle overtones and harmonics found in natural sounds or audio CD music. 22,050 Hz can be compared to an indexed color image such as a GIF.

- *Speech-quality sound*   At 11,025 Hz, the breadth of tones is so narrow that the original instruments in a composition are hard to distinguish: a clarinet might be confused with an oboe, for example. Musical notes can be distinguished in speech-quality sound, as can different types of voices such as a child's, man's, or woman's voice. Speech-quality sound can be compared to the sampled rate of a 4-bit or 1-bit per pixel image. Speech-quality sampling makes it apparent to the listener that the sound is recorded (not natural in origin), but this sampling rate can be used effectively as Web content if you choose your source sounds carefully.

Working from high to low quality, the Macintosh has defined sounds of lower sampling rates than speech-quality sound as telephone-quality. Telephone-quality sound operates within a range of about 8,000 Hz, and is generally as acceptable a range for capturing symphonic sounds as a personal-dictation recorder would be. The Macintosh and Windows descriptions of sound quality differ slightly: the Macintosh system considers Windows speech-quality to be of telephone-quality, but you get the general idea here as to how lower sampling rates affect sound quality. In the final analysis, the hertz level of sample rates is used to compare sounds, and not the fanciful analogies to telephones and CDs.

Once you've sampled a sound, it needs to be stored for playback. Like any other type of computer media, digital sound is stored in bytes of media space. Sound can be organized in 16 bits or 8 bits for posting on the Web for playback. Although 16-bit digital sound files introduce (and play back) less noise, they take up twice the space on hard disk. Also, stereophonic sound files are twice as large as monaural (mono) files; each sample has to be interleaved when saved to file format (e.g., channel 1 sound, channel 2 sound, channel 1 sound, etc.). If you do a little math here, the bytes that a saved sound file takes up are approximately equal to the sampling rate when saving to 8-bit format, and twice the sampling rate for saving in 16-bit format.

Here's a reference guide to sound quality and sound size when saved to 8-bit and 16-bit formats:

Quality	Sampling rate	Sound type	Saved format	Saved file size
CD	44,100 Hz	Stereo	16-bit	172K/second
CD	44,100 Hz	Mono	16-bit	86K/second
CD	44,100 Hz	Stereo	8-bit	86K/second
CD	44,100 Hz	Mono	8-bit	43K/second
Music	22,050 Hz	Stereo	16-bit	86K/second
Music	22,050 Hz	Mono	16-bit	43K/second
Music	22,050 Hz	Stereo	8-bit	43K/second
Music	22,050 Hz	Mono	8-bit	22K/second
Speech	11,025 Hz	Stereo	16-bit	43K/second
Speech	11,025 Hz	Mono	16-bit	22K/second
Speech	11,025 Hz	Stereo	8-bit	22K/second
Speech	11,025 Hz	Mono	8-bit	11K/second

The table could go down as far as from 8,000 to 5,500 Hz sampling; at 8,000 Hz, the only types of sounds that can be played back with any recognizability are sound effects such as a cork popping or glass shattering.

All of which leads us to the musical question: what type of sampling and format should I target for my Web sound file? The patience of your audience, the speed of the connection, and the processing power of the visitor's machine should all influence your decisions regarding the file size and whether to compress a sound file. For example, a 2-second, 11,025 Hz mono, 8-bit sound file is 22K in file size and would transfer to the visitor's machine in about 6–7 seconds on a 28.8-kilobytes-per-second connection, given a clear connection with light Internet traffic, and a sustained transfer rate of 3K per second or better. It's important to understand that conventional digital sound doesn't stream to a visitor; it requires a helper app, and the file must be completely received before it's played back from system cache. RealAudio files can stream to a visitor's machine, but RealAudio requires a proprietary file format and proprietary server software to dispense sound to your visitors. Your visitors, in turn, must also have installed the RealAudio plug-in to decode the sound.

Before we discuss the methods available to you for compression of "generic" digital sound types, you need to know what types of sound formats can be downloaded from a Web server.

SOUND FORMATS & CONVERSIONS

The most common formats for sound that you'll encounter on the Web are the AU and AIF types. The AU format is native to the Sun operating system, and AIF files are native to the Macintosh. If you're a Windows user and you want to reach the broadest audience with your multimedia message, forget about the WAV sound format. Macintosh users cannot play a WAV file until it is converted into another file type, but Windows users can indeed access an AU and AIF file type if a sound card is installed. Navigator is configured upon installation to handle MIME types of audio/x-aiff and audio/basic through the NAPlayer utility (a sound plug-in that ships and installs with Navigator and NavGold 2.01 or later) when AIF and AU media objects are referenced in an HTML document. Additionally, the WAV file format is supported as the audio/x-wav MIME type, but a WAV file will not play to the Macintosh audience, or to a Windows audience that doesn't have a sound card installed.

The most useful utility for converting Windows WAV files to AIF, AU, or other sound formats is GoldWave, a Windows shareware program engineered by Chris Craig, which can be found on the Companion CD-ROM. GoldWave is a sound-shaping, editing, and conversion program, and is about as feature-rich as a commercial sound editor. It's also highly accessible to novices who simply want to convert sounds they've recorded. In the following example, you'll see how easy GoldWave is to use when a sound file example, HAPPY.WAV, needs to be converted to the AU format. HAPPY.WAV is a component of the Happy Birthday Home Page, an example in this chapter that also works with Java applets. HAPPY.WAV was sampled at 22,050 Hz and saved in 16-bit mono format. At 8 seconds long, HAPPY.WAV is 347K—a ponderously large file, and needlessly so, because the audio content of the file doesn't need the dynamic range that a recording of a symphony might. HAPPY.WAV is simply a recording of a boisterous crowd shouting "Happy Birthday" with glasses clinking and party favors buzzing in the background.

Here's how to use GoldWave to resample and convert the WAV file to a format supported by NAPlayer:

1. With GoldWave installed, choose File | Open, then choose HAPPY.WAV from the CHAP07/HAPPY folder. A spectrograph of the sound file appears in a window in GoldWave. By default, GoldWave zooms in to maximum resolution of the sound wave; click on the 1:1 button on the toolbar to get an idea of the true sound amplitude at which the file was recorded.

2. Choose Effects | Resample. A dialog box appears, as shown in Figure 7-8.

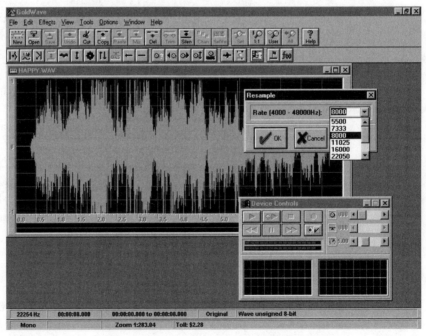

Figure 7-8: *Resampling a sound removes some of the original information—and sound quality—but it also dramatically reduces the size of the sound file.*

3. Choose 8000 from the drop-down list, then click on OK. Goldwave resamples the sound, and you'll probably see no apparent change in the spectrograph.

4. Click on the Play button on the Device Controls panel (the button with the smiley next to it). The sound plays back with little or no discernible loss of fidelity. In actuality, much overhead has been removed from the file, and it will be saved at a fraction of its original size. Using 22,050 Hz, 16-bit format for party sounds is akin to saving a black-and-white image into 24-bit RGB image format. The extra room is unused and unnecessary.

5. Choose File | Save As, then choose Sun (*.AU) from the Save File as Type drop-down list, and choose "μ-Law, mono" from the File Attributes drop-down list. See Figure 7-9.

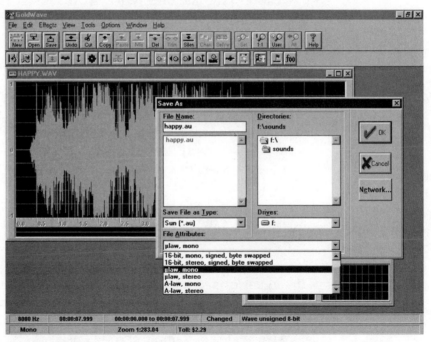

Figure 7-9: *The Sun sound file format is a Web standard that you can easily convert WAV sound files to using GoldWave.*

Depending upon the operating platform, sounds are encoded in a way, with or without compression, that obliges a sound editing utility to read the sound data in as raw information. GoldWave is one of the few sound utilities that can write an AU sound file correctly, in addition to importing different platform sounds as raw sound data.

In the previous example, the "room" within the file format was decreased when the μ-Law compression encoding was used to create a smaller AU file. And when you downsample audio files, two things generally happen in addition to acquiring a smaller copy of the sound:

- Noise is introduced to the sound. This is a reality that can only be coped with (but not entirely eliminated) by using a noise gate on the sound before saving it to hard disk. GoldWave holds sound information in RAM while you work on a file and offers a feature to remove noise in sound areas that fall below a specific volume. You can effectively remove unwanted noise before you write the file to a specific format.

- Original sound quality is lost with most encoding/compression schemes for digital sound. *Lossy compression* might be a familiar term to those who save copies of images to JPEG; a good lossy compressor will intelligently remove from a file sample portions that it calculates the human audience won't miss. In sound files, data is lost from the extreme upper and lower ends of the original sound. This makes good sense, and good compression, because as we grow older, the extreme high and low receptors we have for sound diminish.

The saved HAPPY.AU file should be about 62K on your hard disk if you performed the previous example; the file can be played with only a short delay on a visitor's machine that has a fast connection.

Before we get to an example of sound used as a stand-alone element on a Web site, let's examine a method for Macintosh users to provide Windows WAV files for site use. Although WAV files are not universally understood, you might be a Macintosh author who needs to put up pages for an office intranet consisting of Windows machines, or you might want to provide different native sound types for downloading from your site.

SoundApp: A Multilingual Sound Converter

SoundApp is a freeware drag-and-drop utility created by Norman Franke that addresses the need for Macintosh users to port SimpleSound files, AIF files, Sound Suitcases, and Resource Sounds to other formats. Sounds you create, for example, using the SimpleSound recording utility can be saved as Alert sounds (snd files) or as AIF files. Snd files are completely illegible to Windows playback systems, and AIF files need to be read (by a program such as GoldWave) as raw data to then be converted to WAV format.

In actuality, there is very little difference between the structure of AIF, WAV, and Macintosh snd files; the primary difference lies in the header information in the file, which indicates how the decoding scheme works. SoundApp can create an AIF file from System 7 files, suitcase sounds, and translate the data to Windows WAV format with complete authenticity and accuracy; UNIX and Windows machines play the sounds as though they were created on the native platform.

In the example to follow, the Happy Birthday Home Page offers visitors a choice: they can play the birthday cheers from the HTML document or choose to download a copy of the file for continued listening pleasure all day long. Your assignment, then, is to create a WAV version of the original AIF file on your Macintosh. A copy of SoundApp can be downloaded from ftp://mirror.apple.com/ mirrors/info-mac/gst/snd/sound-app-151.hqx, and the HAPPY.AIF sound file is in the CHAP07/HAPPY folder on the Companion CD-ROM. Here's how to perform the conversion:

1. After downloading SoundApp (it's about a 140K transfer, and 300K when expanded), install it and create an alias on the desktop for it.

2. Double-click on the SoundApp icon to launch it.

3. Choose Options | Preferences, then make sure the Auto Quit When Done check box is unmarked. In subsequent sessions of SoundApp, the program will remain open after playing a file you've dropped upon the Program icon on the desktop. This allows you to convert a file you've played.

4. Click on the Conversion icon, and choose "Prompt For folder" from the Output Location drop-down list. Select a folder on your hard disk for the converted sound files, then click on the Select button to return to the Preferences box. If you need to translate sound files in the AU or AD-PCM compressed format (more on this shortly), this Conversion preference can be checked in this box at any time in the future. All the converted files will reside in this folder in the future. Click on OK to close the Preferences box.

5. Choose File | Convert, then choose the HAPPY.AIF file from the CHAP07/HAPPY folder on the Companion CD-ROM.

6. Choose Windows WAVE from the Convert To drop-down list, then click on Open. See Figure 7-10.

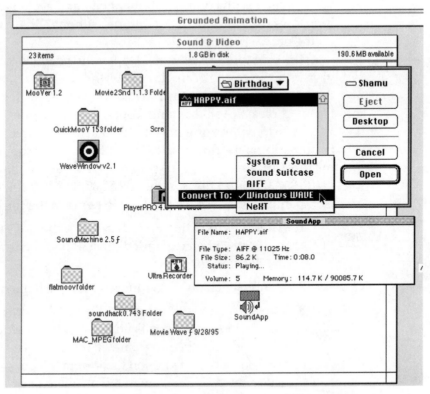

Figure 7-10: *Choose the format for a single file—or a folder of files—you want to convert using SoundApp.*

7. A Directory dialog box will appear requesting that you name the folder to be created that will contain the converted file, which will be located in the folder you specified in Conversion Preferences. Name the folder, then click on Save.

8. The HAPPY.AIF file is now converted to Windows WAV format. Close SoundApp. You're done.

You can test your work simply by dragging the converted file onto the SoundApp icon. SoundApp will read WAV and other files not directly supported by the Macintosh OS as raw sound data, and you can indeed play back Windows native sounds through the use of this program.

There are one or two things you need to do after converting a sound file to WAV format that will ensure that the Windows visitor can easily download the file from a Web site. Windows files use the *.WAV naming convention for sound files: SoundApp doesn't convert filenames, so type HAPPY.WAV (capitalization isn't important here; all versions of Windows will change filename uppercase and lowercase letters to suit the specific version of the operating system) as the filename to make the converted sound a true Windows sound file.

Additionally, ZipIt, a shareware program authored by Tommy Brown, can create ZIP archives on the Macintosh. ZIP (PKZip) is the standard compression scheme in Windows and DOS machines; users will easily be able to uncompress and play the converted file.

> **TIP**
>
> *StuffIt Expander for Windows is a shareware program that can uncompress a *.SIT file in Windows. SIT is the format for StuffIt files on the Macintosh—equivalent to PKZipped files. StuffIt Expander for Windows can also Zip files and decode HQX files (BinHex-encoded Macintosh archives).*
>
> *Because the compression code file format for zipping files was openly published by Phil Katz, inventor of PKZip, many software developers have ported the zipping format of archiving to various platforms. There is no user difference between a file zipped by PKZip, ZipIt, WinZip, or other programs, and we refer to PKZip here as a generic procedure of zipping and unzipping archived files.*

WHEN IS A WAV NOT A WAV?

Sound Driver for PC-Speaker, a software sound driver, has been very popular since Windows 3.1x because it can be used to play sounds directly through an Intel-based machine's speaker without requiring the purchase of a sound card.

Sound Driver for PC-Speaker still works, sort of, under Windows 95. If you downloaded this file from Microsoft's BBS, or if a copy of it was installed with ICON HearIt or another animation/sound utility, you're better off removing the file and buying a Sound Blaster or compatible card.

Serious multimedia authoring cannot be accomplished with the PC-Speaker driver; the file can play back, but cannot be used to record sound WAVs. Additionally, this file can interfere with other drivers (such as mouse drivers) when running under Win95.

Sound Driver for PC-Speaker also cannot be accessed by Navigator's audio player (NAPlayer). In Figure 7-11, Control Panel has been opened, and Multimedia has been selected in Win95. This is where you can turn off Sound Driver for PC-Speaker if a program installed it. If you encounter a multimedia sound file in an HTML document, NAPlayer will try to load and you'll then get the message shown in Figure 7-11.

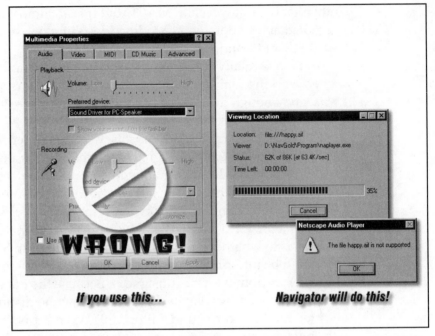

Figure 7-11: *A software sound driver alone cannot provide quality sound or the recording features you need to produce digital audio for the Web.*

COMPRESSION & SIGNED AUDIO FILES

If you decide that audio will play an important part in your multimedia authoring for the Web, there are a few things you should know to get your ideas off to the right start.

Audio compression is an effective means for shrinking file sizes that need to travel from the Web server to the host machine, but there are a limited number of formats that can be easily accessed by you, or by Navigator's audio player. One type, MACE compression, is very fast (it decodes on a machine almost instantly), it's very dirty (it adds noise to compressed audio), and decoding this format can only be accomplished automatically on a Macintosh, and only with 8-bit sound files. MACE-encoded files must be read into a sound editor as raw sound information, then saved to μ-Law compressed Sun AU files, or to compressed (or noncompressed) AIF format. IMA/ADPCM encoding, on the other hand, is slower than MACE, but it is an almost universally accepted and understood encoding/decoding process: it works on AIF, AU, and Windows WAV files.

You'll eventually run across the terms "signed" and "unsigned" when working with different files and sound editors. Chris Craig was kind enough to explain this one to me, and here's the user-friendly author's version.

Individual sound samples must be decoded (interpreted) by the audio device as the digital signal is converted to analog for playback. And the header information in an audio file needs to tell the playback device whether the information shall be interpreted as a straight binary combination of values (unsigned) or as a "2s complement" form (signed). If the distinction is not made in the header as to whether a file is signed or unsigned, an 8-bit sound file could be interpreted as having values from -128 to 127 (signed), or from 0 to 255 (unsigned). Because the data is ambiguous to the decoding (playback) device, allow the distinction to be written to file by the sound editor: GoldWave supports signed and unsigned formats, and can convert between the two. Typically, 8-bit sound files from a Macintosh are signed, and audio files that are a product of Creative Labs' Sound Blaster (the standard for PC-Windows sound support) are unsigned.

 ## SOUND WITH A HINT OF JAVA

Integrating different media elements can make your Web site an irresistible attraction. Earlier in this chapter, you saw how to sample and convert sounds for use as Web elements, and this section takes you through how to hook up all the pieces on your Web page to create a true multimedia event.

IF JAVA IS TOO STRONG, TRY A LITTLE "DECAF"

Java is a programming language that is streaming, multithreading, and small, among its other attributes. Perhaps the reason why there are so few after-market books published on Java to date is that, as a multimedia author, you do need a programming background (which would be in C++) to make effective use of Java. Most experienced graphics and desktop publishing users don't currently have these skills, and this book would be about 15 inches thicker (and have a different author) if the knowledge of how to write Java code was contained herein.

JAVASCRIPT

Fortunately, you don't have to know how to write Java code to take advantage of its capabilities. JavaScript is a scripting language, not a programming language. If you're handy with Director Lingo or another scripting language, the words and syntax can be found on Netscape's home page—commands are continually updated and additions are made, so if there's something you can't do today with JavaScript, wait about a week. JavaScripts can have the capability to load pages, ask viewers if they have a specific plug-in, then direct them where to download it if they don't, read a host's system clock and then display a "Good Morning" or a "Good Afternoon" message, and perform other interactive tasks. JavaScript might become a close relative to HTML in the future. Because the script is not hidden (as is a compiled program such as a Java applet), visitors can download, examine, customize, and emulate JavaScripts created by others. This is the way HTML pages were first created when no one knew the syntax, attributes, or other HTML specifications.

APPLETS

The best news to date is that a number of gifted programmers have created Java applets—compiled code, whose parameters can be changed in a simple text editor to customize whatever it is the

Java applet performs. And many of the programmers are willing to share their applets with you for use on your Web site. Ahmed Abdel Hady of ITSolutions of Egypt (also the Webmaster of the unofficial Egypt Tourism site) has created a very small "ticker tape" Java applet that users can customize with their own message. You guessed it: NavigatorTicker.class can be found on the Companion CD-ROM (in the CHAP07/HAPPY folder), and the following example shows how Java applets that offer user-defined parameters can be added to a Web site.

> **TIP**
>
> *Visit Ahmed's site at http://163.121.10.41, and if you like what you see, feel free to contact him at ahady@idsc.gov.eg.*

Here's how to create a Happy Birthday home page for people whose family and friends aren't into tossing them a party, or for folks who like to celebrate more than once a year:

1. Copy the HAPPY folder in the CHAP07 folder on the Companion CD-ROM to your hard disk for starters. We'll refer to the BIRTHDAY.HTM document throughout this example, and the site can be played from your hard disk in Navigator.

2. Create some festive background imagery for the site using any of the techniques shown throughout this book. BLOONS.GIF, the example file in the Happy Birthday site, was created by defining a nozzle of balloons in Fractal Painter. The image area was selected and defined as a pattern, and this is why the balloon GIF image tiles endlessly without seams showing. Alternatively, you can convert any of the TEXTURES files in the BOUTONS folder on the CD to GIF format, and these, too, will tile across the document without detectable image edges.

3. Using NavGold's Editor, in the HTML document, choose Properties | Document, click on Use Custom Colors, then click on Image File in the Background field and Browse for the GIF image you intend to use for the Web page.

4. Type out a headline, make it a +2 or +3 font size, and give it a color that stands out from the background GIF image (white will probably work here). Highlight the text, click on the Font color icon, and choose the color. Additionally, you might want to bold and italicize the headline for emphasis and to make it stand out from the background image.

5. Save the file as MULTI.HTM, close the file, and open it in your favorite text editor. The NavigatorTicker.class applet is customized through the use of specifying attributes within parameters; you don't actually touch the Java applet to make changes to what it does.

6. Check out the TICKER.TXT file in the HAPPY folder. You can highlight and copy the text into your HTML document to make the Java ticker run, but the following explains how you can tweak each parameter value:

   - Following the Center attribute, which centers the ticker onscreen regardless of the visitor's monitor resolution, you must have the <applet code=...> line that tells Navigator that an applet is coming its way. The name "NavigatorTicker.class" specifies that this is a Java applet, and that Navigator should go and find the file in the same location as the HTML document unless pathed to an absolute URL.

   - The Width and Height attributes, measured in pixels, define the size of the ticker.

   - The first parameter is the number of slogans you want the applet to display. I've got three in the TICKER.TXT file, so the line following the applet code is: <param name="count" value="3">.

   - <param name="msg0" value="Happy Birthday! Your horoscope for today, YOUR day, is splendid! \\No Link"> is the tag that follows the parameter for the number of messages. You name the first message "msg0," and subsequent messages increase by one in their name. In the value string that follows the NAME, you type your text in quotes. Ahmed built a secondary feature into this ticker: you can place a URL after two backslashes. When the visitors click on the scrolling ticker text, they go to the defined URL. In this example, I've used NO LINK to specify that there is no URL in the text string. You must use the two backslashes and close the tag before typing the next line. You can also put more than one space between the last character of your slogan and the backslashes. This separates the following scrolling message from the first.

■ The appearance of the text and the frame of the applet can be specified by using <param name="speed" value="9">, where the speed can be changed by a single value (hint: 9 is good for average Internet traffic). <param name="bgco" value="50,0,200"> specifies the background color of the ticker. The value in this parameter is a color triplet, with each primary color having a range from 0 to 255. The <param name="txtco" value="250,250,0"> parameter specifies the color of the text. You cannot change the font because the font choice is determined by the visitor's operating platform.

■ The applet and the center tags are closed. Check out the TICKER.HTM document in the BIRTHDAY folder for Ahmed's documentation on the NavigatorTicker.class applet.

   Copy the NavigatorTicket.class file in the HAPPY folder to your own site folder if you're building a new site in this example. Java class objects have to be located in the same folder on a server as the HTML document that the Java applet plays within.

7. Create a graphic that looks like a birthday present, with a button on its side. The GIFT.GIF file measures 207 pixels in height by 207 pixels in width. Including the ticker and the headline, the very bottom of the gift might be cropped off at 640 X 480 viewing resolution, resulting in document scrolling. This is acceptable in this example because the

visitor can still see the message "click here to hear…," and as you'll see shortly, the entire graphic will be a link, so there's plenty of exposed area for the visitor to click on.

8. Create a second graphic that will serve as an image map; the visitors click on the sound and platform of their choice to download the sound file in addition to, or as an alternative to, playing from the document. INSTRUCT.GIF is the image used in the Happy Birthday page, and it was image mapped using Fractal Painter to HAPPY.ZIP and HAPPY.SIT.HQX. See Chapter 1, "Composing in HTML & NavGold," for the details on creating an image map.

9. Open in NavGold's Editor the MULTI.HTM document you saved in step 5. You'll notice that tags display in the Editor window: these are the tags you wrote for the ticker applet—*do not accidentally touch them!* Insert your cursor after the applet, and choose Insert | Image.

10. Browse for your own creation, or use the GIFT.GIF image here. After choosing it, click on the Original Size button on the Properties | Image menu. Click on the Alignment Top button, then click on the Link tab to display the Link menu.

11. In the "Link a page location or local file" field, type **HAPPY.AIF**, then click on OK. HAPPY.AIF is in the HAPPY folder on the CD-ROM, so if you're creating your own site here, you must copy the file to your own site folder to make the link.

12. Add the INSTRUCT.GIF image (or use one of your own), using steps 10 and 11 here. If you look at this file, you'll see that information about downloading the Windows and Mac versions of the sound are offered. This image now needs a map reference in the HTML document.

13. Close Navigator, then open Mapedit or Fractal Painter to get the coordinates for the image map. Mapedit, a Windows-only utility included on the Companion CD-ROM, is a little easier to use, because it will write the image map information to the BIRTHDAY.HTM document, while

Painter only writes the coordinates to hard disk. See Chapter 1, "Composing in HTML & NavGold," for information on how to manually edit the coordinates Painter provides into the HTML document. You're done!

In Figure 7-12, you can see the Happy Birthday Home Page. If a user clicks on the gift button image, the HAPPY.AIF sound plays through Navigator's NAPlayer, or through a helper app the user might have specified in Options | General Preferences in their own copy of Navigator.

Macintosh users can specify SoundApp as the sound helper app in Navigator, and play many different types of sound files on the Web, not simply AIF and AU files.

Figure 7-12: *Sounds and animation can present the visitor with a content-rich sight, without a lot of bandwidth.*

When Navigator encounters a file type it doesn't understand, it pops up a query box asking you how you want it to handle the file. If visitors to the Happy Birthday page click on the Windows HAPPY.ZIP button, Navigator gives them their choice of downloading the file or having a system program read the file. You've accomplished your goal.

VDOLive

If we think about it for a moment, there's a competition going on right now between the capabilities of a computer and a television set for playing back media. Indeed, a television isn't burdened with digital to analog conversion (DAC), and an animation played back on videotape is inherently less choppy than a computer's display of animation. However, the personal computer is likely to win in the long run as a home media player because of its capability to play many different kinds of media types, in addition to providing a place to *compose* multimedia.

Therefore, if the television isn't going to offer the same level of interactivity and control that the PC does, it seems natural that the computer would try to engender more of television's qualities. VDOnet Corp. has taken this idea and made it a reality with VDOLive, which gives, quite literally, cable television service to your audience.

VDOLive is a state-of-the-art technology that requires video equipment in addition to server software and proprietary authoring tools. Because of the significant start-up expenses, a working example of how to create online video will not be provided in this chapter. However, the following is an overview of this exciting technology: what it does, what you'd require to be a "net-network," and what you can expect from VDOLive as part of a multimedia presentation.

VDOLIVE IS A WEB OBJECT

The VDOLive movie resides on a server. The special VDOLive Server software establishes a connection from itself to the visitor's machine when the host document is called. The visitor must have an Internet connection active when an HTML link is made to a *.VDO file.

There are two basic components to VDOLive: the VDOLive Player plug-in for Navigator and the VDOLive Server, a software program which currently can run under Windows NT, Windows 95, Sun, SGI, and other UNIX-based workstations. As of this writing, a Macintosh version of both the client Navigator plug-in and server software is not yet available, but has been promised for 1996. If you have the server software and the video content, you can embed VDOLive objects as inline components within an HTML document. To embed a VDOLive object, place the following code in your HTML document where you want the video to play:

```
<embed src="http://www.mysite/epic.vdo"
autostart=false stretch=false width=160 height=120>
```

Everything that follows the URL for the video on your server is optional, but the parameters might come in handy if you want to autostart a video or offer resizing of the video frame. (Height and width are generally good to specify—it takes Navigator a shorter time to compose the page when you are specific.) *Stretch* and *autostart* are true or false attributes. Stretch=false keeps the VDOLive object centered within the area specified by the width and height attributes; when Stretch=true, the video object will automatically zoom in to a 100 percent greater viewing resolution, but only if the width and height attributes allow resizing to twice the object's size within the document. Autostart=true will automatically launch transmission of the video, and autostart=false requires that the visitor right-clicks (Macintosh: click and hold) on the VDOLive object and chooses Play from the pop-up menu.

VDOLIVE REQUIRES VDOLIVE MEDIA

VDOnet offers the plug-in Player free of charge from http://www.vdolive.com; the download includes a stand-alone version of VDOLive Player for non-Netscape browsers. VDOLive content never resides on the user's hard disk; caching is not performed due to security reasons on the Web, and you cannot save a VDOLive video to play back at a later time.

VDOLive is a highly compressed video and audio format (you need a sound card to listen to as well as see a video); at present, you need to use VDOLive Tools to convert existing analog video (videotape) to the VDOLive format. VDOnet plans to release a version of VDOLive Tools in the future that will allow authors to port digital media (Director, Premiere, and After Effects files) to the VDOLive format. To give you an idea of the compression VDOLive offers, let's use a 160- X 120-pixel frame, displaying 24-bit color, at 15 frames per second. Uncompressed, 1 minute of digital video would take up 52MB of hard disk space. VDOLive can offer anywhere from 180K to 1MB per minute, depending upon the amount of compression you specify, for the same video. MPEG compression, although it's getting better as the technology advances, can only offer about 5:1 compression for the same amount of uncompressed video.

In Figure 7-13, you can see the VDOLive connection to VDOLive's server. If you make this connection yourself, you'll be better able to see that the video frame features the play time on the lower left, and the *reception* (how efficiently the data is being passed, and how clear and fast your Internet connection is) on the lower right.

Figure 7-13: *VDOLive is video-on-demand for the Internet.*

VDOLIVE REQUIRES A PROFESSIONAL INVESTMENT

Like any type of digital media, VDOLive requires that you invest in additional hardware to make this technology a permanent part of your multimedia suite of tools. At least two video decks, a camcorder, a two-way video capture board, sound- and video-mixing equipment, and long- and short-term storage devices (measured in gigabytes) would be a fair place to begin your video shopping list. To be fair, VDOLive will first impact on traditional video editors who seek distribution channels for smaller works. Video houses already have the recording equipment, and with VDOLive Server and Tools, these firms can make a fairly painless migration to Web video.

But for the rest of us, VDOnet also offers a limited, personal edition of server software and tools. You'll still need video content and a video card to get the content into your machine, but for a limited time (check their site on this one), you can download a personal edition of VDOLive Server and VDOLive Tools free of charge. You can only run 2 lines on your server, and videos are limited to 60 seconds, but this is a terrific way to try before you buy. Server software begins at about $1,000 for 5 "stations" and goes up to $10,000 for 100 simultaneous broadcasts.

THE STRENGTH OF VIDEO AS A WEB TOOL

You can see the quality of VDOLive's product for yourself by visiting their site. Depending upon the speed of your modem and your ISP's connection, you can expect transmission rates of about 2 frames per second with a 14.4-kilobits-per-second modem up to 20 frames per second with an ISDN connection. Because of the unique nature of broadcasting video across the Internet, you'd be well advised to notify your audience that running other applications isn't a good idea while watching video from your site. The clarity of the video depends upon how much compression is used to encode the media. Already, there are more than 20 "channels" you can choose from on VDOnet's home site—CBS News, PBS, and others have already seen the potential of VDOLive and the Internet as a communications tool.

Like any new medium, there is most certainly a fascination with the technology; many might argue that "serious" motion pictures weren't conceived of until the newness of this "moving-picture nonsense" had been in the public eye for more than a few years. Entertainment is a perfectly legitimate reason for adopting VDOLive; if you run an intranet at the office, or need to present content on the Web that's already in video format—the solution is already here. In Figure 7-14, you can see NYE's "booth" on VDOnet's home page. VDOnet has assembled a collection of titles for visitors to play that is a little reminiscent of the octoplex movie theaters that have sprouted in shopping malls. The only difference in VDOnet's site is that you don't have to buy an extra ticket if you want to see what's happening in another theater.

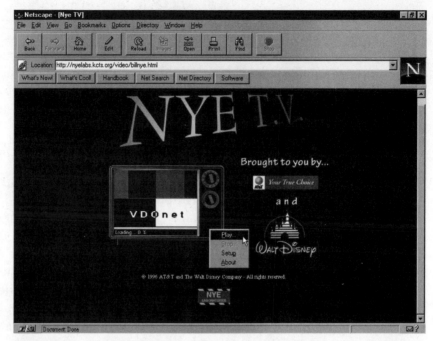

Figure 7-14: *VDOLive can be a component—or the main attraction—of your Web site.*

ACROBAT AMBER

Adobe Systems introduced a platform-independent technology three years ago that revolutionized the way traditional publishers conceived—and executed—magazines, newspapers, and any other type of printed material. Acrobat is a portable document format that allows the creator of the document to distribute a file (along with a browsing utility to UNIX, DOS, Macintosh, and Windows users) that is reassembled onscreen almost exactly the way the creator composed it. Fonts, graphics, margins—everything you put into a document—play on the recipient's system, even though the recipient doesn't have the authoring tools or fonts on their machine.

Adobe has taken this technology a step further with Acrobat "Amber" Reader; this plug-in for Windows and the Macintosh can be downloaded from http://www.adobe.com. The Amber Reader offers inline display of PDF (Portable Document Format) content in Navigator's browser window; whenever a PDF file is linked to an HTML document, a full complement of zoom, panning, and selection tools surrounds the edge of the window.

There are three components to the Acrobat publishing system:

- The reader. Acrobat Reader is an application that can decode a PDF file, and Amber is the Navigator plug-in. Both are free of charge and are upgraded regularly to take advantage of new features supported in the creation programs.

- The conversion utility. Acrobat files can be created using almost any graphics or DTP application in Windows or the Macintosh. There is no document-composing program per se for making a PDF file. In Figure 7-15, you can see a page layout being designed in Adobe PageMaker 6.01. When finished, the file can be written to PDF format directly through a software driver called PDFWriter, or the document can be written to a PostScript file saved on disk that can then be optimized using Acrobat Distiller, which comes in Adobe Acrobat Pro. Many PDF files you've seen posted on the Web never passed through Distiller. Distiller's worth as a conversion utility over the PDFWriter is that the resulting PDF file can be as much as 20 percent smaller in file size. Distiller can also embed fonts and check for page errors. Distiller is an optional purchase; Adobe Acrobat 2.1, discussed next, comes with the Exchange and PDFWriter software conversion utility.

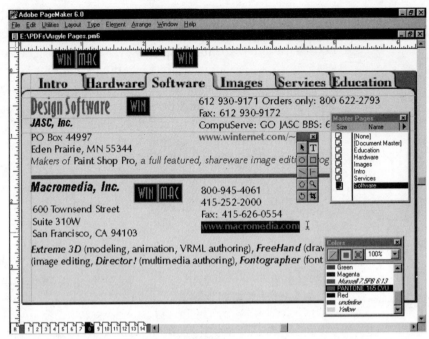

Figure 7-15: You don't compose a document in an Acrobat program; you use Acrobat to convert existing graphics and DTP files to PDF format.

- The post-processing editing application. Acrobat Exchange handles any PDF format enhancements you want to make to the document. Exchange doesn't allow you to copy, paste, or place new elements on a page; cosmetic changes must be made in the native file before conversion to PDF format. What Exchange provides are links within the document, links outside the document (you can jump from one PDF file to another by making a link), and the ability to crop pages, rotate them, and create a table of contents (which also supports links).

The most significant enhancements Adobe has made to version 2.1 of the Acrobat publishing system have been increased loading speed for the reader and the capability to embed a URL as a link within the Acrobat document. The example document in this section is *The Argyle Pages*, a directory of resources for graphics and

publishing professionals. ARGYLE.PDF is in the BOUTONS/
ARGYLE folder (on the Companion CD-ROM), and we'll use it

shortly to demonstrate the power of Acrobat as a *Web* publishing
system.

If you own, or intend to own, Acrobat Pro, the complete suite of
viewing, converting, and post-processing tools, the steps are very
simple for getting a document into PDF format:

1. In the application of your choice (PageMaker, Illustrator, or
   CorelDRAW are good choices), compose the document.

2. Choose File I Print, then choose Acrobat Distiller from your
   list of installed print drivers. Here's where printing to
   PostScript gets a little ambiguous. Depending upon the application, you may or may not need to check any Print to
   File check box. In PageMaker, the decision is obvious—you
   click on the Print to PostScript button and name the file to
   a folder of your choice. However, in applications such as
   MS Word and CorelDRAW, you need to check the Print to
   File check box, print the file, then hunt down a file with the
   .PRN extension and change the extension to .PS (e.g., Paris
   in the Spring.PS). For some reason as mysterious as why it
   costs more for an unlisted telephone number, many applications insert the .PRN extension in Windows by default,
   and won't let you change it in the Print dialog box. Without the .PS extension, Distiller cannot recognize the file
   you want it to distill to PDF format.

3. Close the creation application and launch Distiller. Distiller
   can be configured to watch a specific folder, and will automatically convert files it finds there upon opening. Also,
   you can specify that PostScript files are deleted upon successful conversion of the work. PostScript files are text-
   based descriptions of a page; they can be 10 times the size
   of the PDF document, and you'll usually want to trash
   them after the conversion to PDF format.

4. Before you choose File I Open and select the PostScript file
   for conversion, you might want to choose Distiller I Font Embedding from the menu. Big tip here: although you can embed font outline information in a PDF file, you shouldn't

embed font information about fonts *not used* in the original document. Make a mental note of the fonts you've used in the document or pause Distiller while you go back to the original document and check. Every font embedded, used or not, takes up additional space in the PDF document. Before continuing, move fonts that aren't used in the document out of the Always Embed list in the Font Embedding dialog box. Font embedding allows Acrobat Reader (and Amber) to display fonts exactly as they appear in your document; this is the closest thing to date to being able to specify a font in a Web document. If you don't embed fonts, the document will display with a close, but not accurate match (e.g., Optima might look like Helvetica).

5. Choose the PostScript file you want distilled, and Distiller will then prompt you for an output name and directory. Fill in the field in the Specify PDF File Name box, click on OK, and Distiller will process the file, usually at about a page every five seconds for a graphically dense page on a Pentium or PowerMac.

6. Close Distiller, then open Acrobat Exchange. Choose File|Open, then open the new PDF file that was written to disk.

7. PostScript is funny, in that page orientation is usually presumed to be portrait, even if you clearly specify landscape in the creation program. The browser window in Navigator is landscape in orientation, and I'd suggest that you compose PDF files in landscape orientation. The first thing you need to do in Exchange, if your document is lying on its side, is to press Ctrl(Cmd)+Shift+O. Click on the Left button in the Rotate Pages dialog box, pick All Pages, click on OK, click on OK to confirm, and your document will thank you for this simple step.

8. Ctrl(Cmd)+Shift+C brings up the Crop Pages dialog box, and it is here you can trim the excess space off the sides of your document (if needed). For original page size in the creation program, I recommend 6.25 X 3.5 inches; this size fits nicely within the browser window in Navigator after Amber's toolbox loads, and the smaller the physical dimensions of your document, the smaller the file size will be.

9. To create links in the document, click on the Link tool, as shown in Figure 7-16. To keep the Link tool selected in case you need to make a lot of successive links, hold Ctrl(Cmd) while you click on this button. Click and drag the Link cursor around the area you want to be the button for the link. The Create Link dialog box then pops up, and you can choose to make the link invisible (an excellent option), or you can choose colors and widths for the rectangle you've drawn.

10. The Action the link provides can be a link to another page (you'd turn to the target page before clicking on Set Link in this case), a link to an external file (Open File, from the Action drop-down list), or a link to the Web. In Figure 7-16, you can see that choosing this latter action pops up another dialog box in which you type in the complete URL for the link. It's important to understand here that the area the link surrounds need not be the complete address; it could be a graphic of a chicken or text written in a foreign-language font. *The Argyle Pages* lists several URLs in user-friendly terms, but the Base URL name in the dialog box must be a complete one.

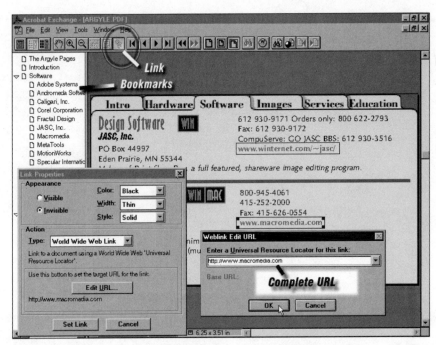

Figure 7-16: *Enter the full URL of the location you want to provide to visitors in your Acrobat document when you make a WWW link.*

11. Another user-friendly gesture you could include, depending upon the content of your PDF file, is a Bookmark list. In Figure 7-16, you can see that *The Argyle Pages* is organized according to category of services (also, the background graphics with the tabbed folders link to each part of the document according to topic). To make a text bookmark for the user, first click on the Bookmarks icon on the toolbar, go to the page you want bookmarked, highlight the main text topic with the Text tool (e.g., highlight "trucks" if the page's content is about trucks), then hold Ctrl(Cmd), and press C, B, then V. The bookmark is copied from the text and pasted into the Bookmarks area of the document. You can edit the Bookmarks text by simply retyping into it, and you can arrange nested bookmarks by click+dragging a Bookmark beneath a different one.

12. When you're done with the links and the bookmarks, choose File | Document Info, then Open. Choose Bookmarks and Page to make the document open in Amber Reader (or from Acrobat Reader outside of Navigator) with the Bookmarks displayed. It's a nice table of contents for a long document. You'll also notice that the Document Info provides commands for entering author or owner name, for locking the document, and for choosing a default display resolution upon opening. The security features are good for preventing visitors from copying text and graphics out of the file, but 72-pixel-per-inch graphics can't be reproduced with any quality, and you might find that you want visitors to copy information such as URLs, prices, telephone numbers, and other data from the document.

13. Always choose File | Save As, and overwrite the original document on your hard disk if you've done substantial editing in Exchange. This recompresses the document; PDF files take on slack when more than 10 or 20 links and bookmarks have been added. You're done! Close the file, and let's see what this masterpiece looks like in Navigator.

TIP

Because the Acrobat publishing system is designed for both traditional printing and screen display, you need to decide which is more important before you prepare elaborate graphics for the original document. Increasingly, commercial printers are encouraging advertisers to bring them a PDF file instead of camera-ready art. If you need to create a PDF document for physical output, use the same rules for image resolution as you'd use for conventional PostScript output (e.g., a 133-line-per-inch printing requires the bitmap images in the publication to be 266 pixels per inch in resolution).

However, if you intend to use the PDF file primarily for Web display, and printing the document on a personal laser printer is merely an afterthought, make your bitmap graphics 72 pixels per inch, the same as monitor resolution. You'll dramatically decrease the size of the PDF document, and it will load more quickly. All the bitmap graphics in The Argyle Pages *were placed in PageMaker from original images of 72 pixels per inch resolution.*

HOW PDF FILES WORK ON THE WEB

Given the artistic latitude the PDF format provides, if you're heavily into traditional publishing, you might well forgo the HTML route for document conversion, create a simple HTML top document, and link to a collection of PDF files on your site. Alternatively, you could create dual formats of presentations on your site: offer HTML versions of text for quick scanning online and a PDF version with sumptuous page composition and graphics for downloading. An Acrobat document can be repurposed as a file to be printed, a vehicle for interoffice training, the README file for an application, or conference information that would waste paper if too many copies were printed (and as an impromptu "print-on-demand" resource on diskette if too few pieces were printed).

The Acrobat Amber Reader comes with an installation routine that locates Navigator on the user's system and places the program kernel in the plug-ins directory. It also creates a Fonts directory on the user's system within the Navigator folder that contains special Type1 fonts the reader program uses to simulate fonts that are not embedded and not available on the user's machine.

When a PDF file is called from an HTML link, the visitor first sees the Amber splash screen, and then the browser window is customized to resemble Acrobat Reader's interface. The visitor can access the links you've provided in the document, zoom in or out of the document, and use the toolbar to show or hide bookmarks (to maximize the display size of the document). The order in which an Acrobat file assembles onscreen is as follows: the text first appears at low-resolution, then the text resolves to the true font specified in the document (a little like interlaced GIF images progressively increasing in resolution), and finally the graphics are loaded behind the text. The process is a fairly quick one, but at present, you cannot count on the loading order to present a neat, finished document immediately from within the browser.

If you have Amber installed on your machine and would like a first-hand look at Amber's display prowess, load ARGYLE.PDF in Navigator from the ARGYLE folder on the Companion CD-ROM. Figure 7-17 shows the first page of the document; a small hand icon appears when a user is over a link. You can't see the original bitmap image for the front page (it's still in my PageMaker document), but rest assured that the image as displayed in the PDF file looks as good as the original file.

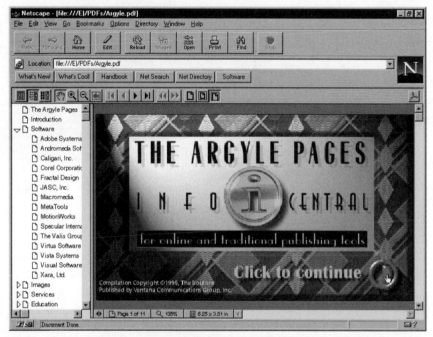

Figure 7-17: *Handsome graphics and an easy way to organize pages are compelling reasons to try out the PDF format as a Web element.*

In Figure 7-18, you can see what it looks like when a visitor hovers the cursor over an embedded URL in the PDF file. The cursor changes to a pointing hand with a tiny "W" on it (for Walter. Okay, for Web), and clicking on the link takes them to whatever place on the Web the link defines.

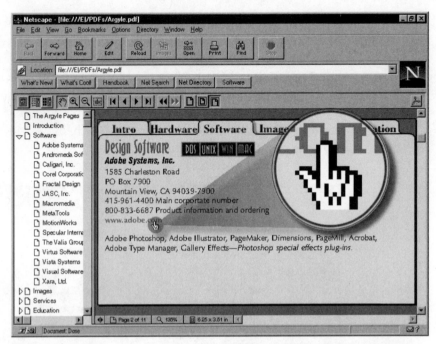

Figure 7-18: *URLs can be embedded in VRML documents, HTML documents, graphics, and now Acrobat documents. Let this freedom become an element of your multimedia presentation.*

In Figure 7-19, the link in *The Argyle Pages* has taken the Acrobat visitor to Adobe's home page. To get back to *The Argyle Pages*, the user could click on the Back button in Navigator; *The Argyle Pages* could also have a link on Adobe's home page if Adobe provided one, and if *The Argyle Pages* document was on a server. There's a sort of plasticity you, the Web author, can find in the bending, homogenizing, cross-pollinating, linking, and transforming of data before the visitor's eyes that makes the new art forms supported by Navigator both a challenge and the ultimate thrill.

Figure 7-19: *Take the time to decide which links help support your own Web site the best. Your site can become an attraction in and of itself if you provide the most interesting ways on and off your page.*

The author feels that Adobe's sentiment, as expressed in the previous figure, is an excellent one to adopt personally. However, they might have emphasized the wrong word: If you can dream it, you *can* do it. You can become a virtuoso on several instruments, not just by playing on the computer application you first started with, but with the programs discovered in this book, and with the ones yet to come.

MOVING ON

If you're the sort of individual who reads a book from cover to cover, beginning at the beginning, Chapter 8, "Putting It All To-gether," is the happy ending. We take all the pieces of profundity, discovery, and a little goofiness found in previous chapters, and put them to work making over the *Digi-Toons* home page in Chapter 1's example. Didn't you think the buttons were too small or the wrong color? Wasn't that link out to a cartoon gallery a little flat, and couldn't it use an animation playing in it? Bring your suggestions and the new tools you've found in this book into the next chapter, and let's put the pride of your progress into action.

8

Putting It All Together

The example files throughout this book often include a little "something extra" that is an integral part of the example site's execution. This something extra has many names—foundation, planning—but is most commonly called a *concept*. This chapter takes you from the concept of a working multimedia Web site to its completion. We'll put into perspective how everything works together—the ideas, the economics, the tools, and the elements.

In Chapter 1, "Composing in HTML & NavGold," you saw how to take a traditionally published document and port it to HTML format with some additional Web elements. However, an article on digital cartooning can contain a much bigger concept when its format is online and electronic. This chapter takes you through the procedures and creative processes by which a good idea becomes a continuing, growing, multimedia event on the World Wide Web.

SITE CONSTRUCTION FROM THE OUTSIDE IN

This chapter's example, the Digital Cartoon Home Page, is a fully functional, multidocument, multimedia site. The only quality that separates the Cartoon site from an actual online site is that links are made relative to the Companion CD-ROM; "true" URLs are not used. The Webtoon folder in the CHAP08 folder contains the site. If you copy the folder to your hard disk, it'll be easier for you to see what's going on (and why) as the site is examined in this chapter. The total file size of this site is 1.8MB. To break this number down, which might seem a little large, the site contains:

- Two Zipped files for downloading; 709K.
- One BinHexed file for downloading; 40.6K.
- Two QuickTime movies; 142K.
- The graphics, HTML documents, a response form, and a VRML file that together make up the interactive part of the site; 267K.

In the following section, we'll get into the head work that determined the components of the laundry list above. Every great piece of art, digital or traditional, begins with a concept.

WELCOME TO WEBONOMICS 101

Unless you're independently wealthy, the primary reason for putting up a multimedia Web site is to create a source of continuing revenue. This can be accomplished by taking any number of routes, but they all lead to the same place.

If you're a multimedia author of CD titles, your motivation for creating a mini-masterpiece on the Web is that a sampler of your craftsmanship will lead visitors to purchase a commercial title. And purchases can be made on the Web.

If you're an accomplished artist—an author, illustrator, programmer, or other professional—a multimedia Web site can be used as an advertisement for your trade. A multimedia site is a production, and as such, is more than likely a capable vehicle within which to express your talents. If you use the right elements, multimedia presentations can display many levels of thought and personal expression that strike the visitor in obvious—and subliminal—ways. In contrast, a simple text-and-graphics home page gets only a single opportunity to impress the visitor.

Even if you're not an author, and have no personal product to sell, a well-designed multimedia site can be offered as a service to others. Web designing, in and of itself, is a talent that commerce is actively seeking.

All of the preceding scenarios imply that a product is the central content of the multimedia Web site. Not so obvious is what constitutes a good product.

Who's Your Market?

In this chapter's example, let's suppose you have an affinity and a talent for creating cartoons using the computer. This was the author's original reason for the *Digi-Toons* article you saw in Chapter 1, "Composing in HTML & NavGold." The computer offers the capability to express one's fondness for a particular topic in a multitude of ways. Cartooning can take the form of animations, still image files, articles on how to create digital cartoons, even digital fonts composed of cartoon characters all tied in to a central theme.

> *Profound Realization:* If you keep the theme of your multimedia site general enough, then the site is capable of expansion, is extensible to accommodate new technology, and can be updated more easily.

Because the Web site's topic is of general appeal, it invites a broader audience, than say, the Low-Sodium Ketchup Home Page (if this site actually exists, I apologize for the slight). Let's ask ourselves right now what we can do to motivate the potential audience to continue visiting the site and spread the news of the site's existence. All motivational ploys should be addressed as a separate issue from outside advertising or corporate sponsorship of the site.

Give It Away Today, Charge a Little Later

If you're success-oriented, you should plan on what your multimedia site will be a year from now, before building the first element for the site today. It has become a common practice, for instance, to give limited, "time bomb" versions of fully functional software away on the Web. This is one route you might take from the beginning of your Web site offerings; everyone loves to download stuff from a site—it's the premium in the cereal box. If you're a programmer, you most certainly would want to remove a few key features from the application you've worked so hard on before posting it on your Web site.

However, there is another approach we can take to cyber-goods that are slightly less prized by their creator. The Digital Cartoon Home Page contains an area where the visitor can download, free of charge, a copy of the most recent issue of the Digital Cartoon Gazette, along with a free cartoon Type 1 font. Is this an attraction? You bet—it's free!

Also calculated into this free offering is the slick production value of the e-zine; the content is identical to the *Digi-Toons* article featured in Chapter 1, but it's been converted to Adobe Acrobat PDF format with handsome graphics and text formatting that cannot be accomplished in HTML format. Symbol fonts are also not that time-consuming to create. An experienced illustrator with a copy of CorelDRAW, FontLab, or Macromedia Fontographer can build a workable, attractive font in less than two hours.

Therefore, at the same time we appear to be "giving away the store," the download area contains goods that can be replenished without a lot of effort, and as your own site grows in popularity, you can start adding items that are not free for download to the downloads area. Wherever possible and feasible, it is much more attractive to offer free goods without strings and to clearly label goods that cost something, than to offer a 2MB download whose contents expire in 30 days. You'll see shortly in this chapter how to design a download jump site to your top page, and we'll discuss the methods you can use for vending files.

GET A CORPORATE SPONSOR

An additional source of revenue from your site, and one that would be most welcome at the site's infancy, is a corporate sponsor. You've seen persistent *ledges*—narrow frames within a frameset document whose contents can't be moved—on home pages practically everywhere on the Web. This is advertising space, and as with traditional roadside billboards, clients pay a monthly fee for its use.

There are two approaches to garnering a corporate sponsor. You can approach it from the economic position that a sponsor will be your main source of revenue for the site. The impact on your Web site's content from this decision might lead you to continue offering free downloads, or your sponsor might have goods to vend that come at a premium. To count on a sponsor for 100 percent of the income on the site also can change the dynamics of your business relationship to a point where it becomes a partnership. At this point, you're then providing a service, the same service as other Web authors do for clients, and you might have less control over the content and the future of your multimedia site.

Another factor to consider when soliciting a corporate sponsor is how much you should charge for posting an advertisement. There are no fixed rates so far for Web advertising as part of a site, but you should decide upon a weekly or monthly charge based upon how successful you or your Marketing Department can convince a client your site is. A *counter* of hits to your site is a CGI (Common Gateway Interface) script that is generally offered as a basic option from most commercial site Internet Service Providers. Although a counter is one of the CGI scripts an ISP is least likely to refuse you (many providers will not allow a Web author to implement their own CGI script), counters are an information source only trusted by the most naïve of clients. Why? Because you, or your friends, could "war dial" your site for about an hour or two, and you could then claim to a potential sponsor, "My site averages 2,000 hits per week. Go and look at the counter for yourself."

If you're ambitious enough to grow a commercial multimedia site, you should also take the time to contact an audit bureau, get their software installed on your host server, and offer an authenticated account of your site's traffic to a potential sponsor.

> **TIP**
>
> *There are several firms whose specialty is site verification and auditing. Check out the Internet Audit Bureau's site at sponsor@internet-audit.com, or try any of the following addresses for more information on site audits:*
>
> *The Audit Bureau of Circulations:* http://www.accessabc.com
> *The Nielsen I/PRO I/AUDIT:*
>   mailto:interactive@nielsenmedia.com
>
> *. . . and yes, the Nielsen service is part of the same company that performs "sweeps" for television networks.*

On the Digital Cartoon Home Page, I've taken an alternative route to corporate sponsorship. My tack is to charge a monthly fee for advertising space and calculate the cost of renting the space as a percentage of my monthly ISP charges. The prestige of being sponsored by the famous (fictitious) Draftman's Sidekick pencil company has its own rewards. If your sponsor has a Web site (which is fairly common), a link might be arranged so that their site links to yours. Links are another commodity of exchange on the Web that you shouldn't overlook. They get an audience to your site, and from your site to others; as you build traffic, you then have the option of clearing away additional top page space for other client advertising.

> **TIP**
>
> *The ledge on the top page of the Digital Cartoon site is a background graphic with a completely transparent GIF placed within the ADSPACE.HTM document. Background images cannot include an anchored href tag, but a transparent foreground GIF image can. If you hover your cursor over the address on the pencil, the status line in Navigator will tell you that this link takes you out to (the nonexistent example site) www.draft.com.*

If you need to establish a link from a page that you want to include only tiling background graphics, create a GIF image with a two-color palette, fill the image entirely with one color, and specify this color as transparent when you save it. You can then assign a link to it, and visitors will only see the background graphic on the page.

REGISTERING WITH AN INDEXING FIRM & META NAMES

Yahoo, Xcite, Lycos, and other companies you'll find on Netscape's home page are all in the business of indexing sites on the Web. Using custom software, sometimes called Web crawlers, companies in the business of providing comprehensive site listings automatically search sites for keywords and other site content, making listings available whenever anyone clicks on Navigator's Net Directory button.

The best, most straightforward method of getting your site on the map is to register your site with as many of the indexing firms as you can. You can jump to their sites from Netscape's Net Search page at http://home.netscape.com/home/internet-directory.html.

There is an additional way to ensure that Netizens in search of specific site content can easily locate your work on the Web. The META NAME tag is an approved HTML standard, and even Web authors who don't own NavGold yet can manually enter meta names in a document. The meta name can be used to identify the author of a site to people who run search engines as well as by people who use indexing services. Meta names can also include a brief description of the site, a keyword list, and a classification for the site (provided by an indexing firm). In Figure 8-1, you can see the Document Properties menu displayed in Gold's Editor. On the General tab are numerous fields you can use to describe your site.

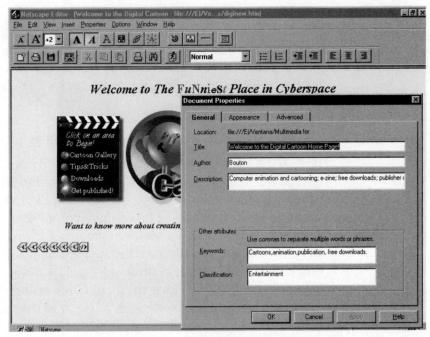

Figure 8-1: *Meta names* Author, Description, Keywords, *and* Classification *are entered through NavGold's General Properties tab under Options.*

If you want to manually edit the HTML code for a page that contains meta names, or if you don't have access to NavGold, the syntax for meta names is:

```
<meta name="Category of meta content" content="actual
content">
```

Meta names should be opened and closed in HTML tag style, and should appear directly after the TITLE tag in your document. NavGold offers the meta name categories that most search engines look for. Meta names include Author, Description, Keywords, and Classification. Because meta names are enclosed in quotes to signify literal text (as opposed to HTML tag or attribute text) to the browser application, the use of spaces and punctuation is allowed in your meta name descriptions. So if you want a Web search engine to easily locate your home page, an attraction for yachting enthusiasts,

```
<meta name="Description" content="Boating information, best
places to sail in North America, storm warnings posted
hourly">
```

. . . would be a fair, attractive, and accurate description of your site. People who use a search engine for topics relating to serious sailing would find your site easily.

MISUSE OF META NAME TAGS

Although meta names have helped many indexing firms offer a wide range of connections to sites, the meta name tag is currently misused by a few misguided Web authors. The following is not a trick or a tip, but instead it's a suggestion that could save you a lot of headaches in your professional career as an electronic publisher.

Without mentioning names, a car dealership recently posted a Web site whose Description meta name consists of "girls, sex, hot," and other similarly evocative phrases. Clever? Perhaps, if the dealership is prepared to handle the flames and spamming that are a response—not to the sexual content of the meta name, but to the inaccuracy that thwarts the organization and self-government under which the Web currently operates. If you play this misleading name game in your own work, you give additional cause to conservative factions all around the world to ban certain sites—or access to the Web altogether—for political, religious, and/or moral reasons. At the very least, you make fine search engines fail to perform because the data they accumulate is flawed. Indexing firms are also wise to the misleading meta name scheme, and search engines are being programmed to ignore Keyword and Description attributes that appear to have no sentence structure. For instance, that car dealer's meta name would be dumped by a "smart" search engine because the description is not a sentence.

Search engines generally will accept the first 250 words they find in a site. Your meta name tag is your best calling card to search engines, and to the world. Keep it relevant, and keep it honest.

A FINAL THOUGHT ON WEBONOMICS

Before moving into the following sections on how to orchestrate the Web elements for the Digital Cartoon site, it's necessary to stress here that the Web is, in a very real way, one large HTML document. A link will most likely bring your audience to your site, and you should provide links to other cool sites as a matter of courtesy to your audience.

Beyond courtesy, providing links to other sites is also good business. Web search engines, in addition to looking for keywords, also look at the number of links the engine has collected that lead to a specific site. The more points a site acquires, the more prominent it becomes, and goods and advertising premiums can be scaled to a fee in line with the site's traffic. If you are diligent and spend some quality time corresponding with the really cool sites, telling them how often folks link to their page from yours, it won't be long before they offer a link to your own site. And the more links to your page that you can negotiate, the more often a Web search engine will record the link. This is perhaps the smartest use of the medium of advertising on the Web, and the best part is that it can come free of charge.

EXPANDING FROM PAGE TO SITE

As mentioned earlier in this chapter, the Digital Cartoon Home Page offers an e-zine, downloads, and a small ad for a corporate sponsor. Given that exciting Web multimedia elements come at a price of extra processor cycles on the visitor's part, it would be discourteous (in addition to cluttered) to offer all the goodies on a single, scrolling page. Instead, the Cartoon site is composed of five documents, with each component page offering links to locations within and outside of the site. Here's the structure we'll work with and explore in this chapter:

- The top page is a frameset document, CARTFRAM.HTML. Within the frameset is a mostly persistent item, ADSPACE.HTML, the ad for the pencil company. The ADSPACE document necessarily must disappear when certain linked pages are called, due to a limitation in the frameset attribute when certain types of Web elements are called. We'll get into this a little later in the chapter, but for the most part, Mr. Pencil will be happy that, wherever you link to on this site, the ad remains in the top frame.

The bottom frame of the frameset document is the area that continually changes according to which places within the site the visitor would like to see. There are four documents that will play in the bottom frame of CARTFRAM.HTM, three of which are links to the top document, MAINTOON.HTM. Here is the relationship and contents of the four bottom-frame HTML documents:

- The MAINTOON.HTML document can be called from the top document. It's an animated cartoon gallery, and the visitor can play animations and return to the top page.

- The TOONVOL1.HTML document is the Gazette in HTML format. As mentioned earlier, this document is a simplification of the *Digi-Toons* document found in Chapter 1. Controls have been added at the top of the document to go to an Acrobat view of the document, to go to the top page, or to go to Adobe's site (so the visitor can download the Reader plug-in to view the Acrobat document).

- The DOWNLOAD.HTML document is a collection of image map graphics that link to files the visitor can copy to their system. Additionally, the Home button will take them to the top, the CARTFRAM document.

- The DIGIFORM document is a form document that you might want to consider if you want feedback from your site, or if you simply want to collect names of visitors. Conceptually, if this is to be a site that has growth potential, I'll need contributors to the gazette. So this form is a call for entries on the Cartoon site. The site now has potential to self-perpetuate, and this lets the author concentrate on expanding other areas of the site.

As you can see in Figure 8-2, the top page is an active one. From the time the visitor hits the site, everything in site (sic) is in motion; the menu (the clapboard) is an animated GIF, the main graphic of the comedic pair uses LOWSRC image animation (explained shortly), and a very modest 3K VRML inline object provides a catchy banner for the top page.

Figure 8-2: *If you tap into the different ways a Web element can be animated, your top page can remain small in download size, but contain a number of separate, moving graphics.*

There are a few techniques used to build DIGINEW.HTM that haven't been covered in this book. In the following section, you'll learn some new multimedia techniques that are supported directly through Netscape Navigator.

It's a Small WRL After All

In Chapter 6, you saw how both a text editor and a modeling application could be used to build a virtual world—a VRML file that Navigator calls with the .WRL extension. Although there is artistic merit in using a modeling program as a VRML-authoring tool, it is unlikely that you can generate a world in a modeling app that's smaller in file size than a world designed in a text editor.

The purpose of the TOONBALL.WRL is not to be a virtual world to explore, however; in fact, unless visitors are sharp, they might not realize that the spinning banner is a VRML file. The TOONBALL.WRL file was created in a text editor using the Sphere node, the SpinGroup node, a Texture2 node, and a camera definition. All of these nodes (virtual world elements) are described in detail in Chapter 6, "VRML."

The only texture called for in the TOONBALL world is an embossed-style lettering and cartoon figure; this is the main content of the VRML world—the message to the visitor. Because the SpinGroup node is specified in negative rotational degrees, the sphere appears to be rotating clockwise. The direction of the sphere's spin definitely has an influence on the composition of the DIGIBALL.GIF graphic, seen in Figure 8-3. The cartoon silhouette appears to run to the left, because the sphere is rotating to the left. The lettering also animates from the left because it's hard to read English when it's spinning to the right.

I used CorelXARA extensively in this chapter for many reasons, but its primary benefit for this example is its ability to perform antialiasing on the fly as it exports vector shapes to bitmap format. This eliminates the need for a second application to perform the conversion. As you can also see in Figure 8-3, an emboss effect can be created very quickly by duplicating vector objects, filling a copy with black, filling a second copy with white, and then slightly offsetting the three groups of shapes. If you load the CARTFRAM.HTM page in Navigator's browser, you'll be able to better see the relationship between the graphics elements in Figure 8-3 and how they are displayed on the sphere within the embedded VRML file.

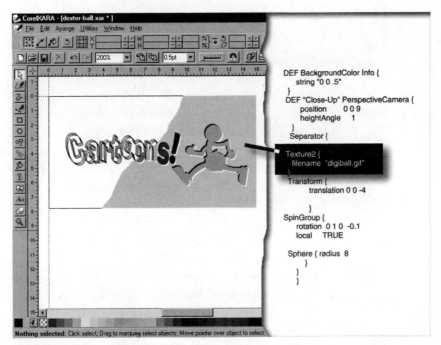

Figure 8-3: *A graphic and a text editor is all you need to create a spinning, eye-catching Web element.*

In previous chapters, we've shown VRML worlds as objects in a frame and as the main content of an HTML document. But you can also use the EMBED tag to place a VRML world within a page as an inline object. In this example, the DIGINEW document has the line:

```
<embed SRC="toonball.wrl" width="112" height="112">
```

The positioning of the virtual world was accomplished by simply placing the tag after the animated GIF clapboard and main graphic of the comedic pair. The width and height attributes were invaluable in this embedding operation for two reasons. First, by default, a virtual world plays as an inline object at a very small size when the parent document is played from within Navigator. Second, this top document was composed to be viewed the best at both 640 X 480 and 800 X 600 viewing resolutions. Through experimentation, I found that a height and width of 114 pushed the embedded object onto the next line, spoiling the viewing experience of the Cartoon site when viewed at 640 X 480 screen resolution. It's usually handy to have a text editor open alongside Navigator, and to experiment with width and height attributes for graphics and virtual worlds as you compose.

In the WRL file, the PerspectiveCamera node's attributes were also arrived at through experimentation. Without a camera definition, Live3D, the Navigator plug-in for viewing WRL files, would create a default viewing angle, which would place the view of the spinning ball much too far away from the viewer. In the previous figure (8-3), you can see that the Z-coordinate for the camera position is a high positive value (9), which means that the camera is quite close to the contents of the world.

Finally, something that helped keep the spinning WRL file's size to a minimum was the use of a background color definition instead of a background image. If you refer to Chapter 6, "VRML," you'll see that BackgroundColor attributes can be written as a string value that specifies individual color amounts of red, green, and blue. The background is half-intensity blue, written as 0 0 .5 in the WRL file.

HOW DO YOU HANDLE PROPRIETARY, INLINE OBJECTS?

WebFX is the firm that Netscape acquired to create the Live3D plug-in for viewing virtual worlds and to make future enhancements to the viewer plug-in as the VRML specifications advance to version 2. As of this writing, WebFX has not made a plug-in for the Macintosh version of Netscape, but has announced plans to make one.

Deciding whether to include a Web object as a self-playing inline Web page element requires a little foresight, and perhaps plans for a workaround. I chose to offer the WRL file in this Cartoon site example, because I have high confidence that by the time you read this, a plug-in will exist for the Macintosh for viewing virtual, VRML worlds.

➡

Because the WRL file in this example is called as an embedded tag, at present, the world will display as a broken link on the page when viewed on a Macintosh computer. If you need to get a site up tomorrow that features a virtual world, it's best to use an anchored href tag to display the file instead of embedding it. This will cause Navigator for the Macintosh to ask the visitor which application on his machine should be used to view the file. In this scenario, it would also be helpful to your Web audience to provide a link to Virtus's home page (http://www.virtus.com). Virtus VRML player is a helper app for Navigator; it pops up as a separate window when a Macintosh visitor (who has Navigator configured properly to call the helper app) hits a VRML file on a Web site.

It should be noted here that Apple's own WHURLPlug and certain other 3D-type Web browsers *do not* play VRML files as specified by the VRML Architect's Group (VAG) standards for virtual worlds (WRL files). Yes, they play 3D worlds, but not VRML worlds. Apple's WHURLPlug depends upon proprietary technology, Apple's 3D metafile format, and cannot browse a file written to VRML specifications.

Stick with the approved standard when writing Web objects, and the browser support will surely follow.

CREATING AN ANIMATED IMAGE MAP GRAPHIC

As you saw in Chapter 1, "Composing in HTML & NavGold," the imagemap attribute doesn't belong to a graphic; instead, it is a series of referenced coordinates that lie in the parent HTML document. However . . . and here's the big secret in this section, the image editing programs and image mapping utilities mentioned in this book cannot take coordinates off an animated GIF image. You'll see a totally black image in the application instead of the graphic, or the graphic won't load, because the file is a special GIF structure that holds more than one bitmap image.

No problems here, only solutions. CLAPPER.GIF is the image used in the DIGINEW.HTM document. The highlights, which periodically cast off the buttons on the clapboard, were created in Photoshop using the Lens Flare plug-in filter. This is not a unique solution for creating highlights or stars, but we'll go through the steps used to create the animated GIF for reasons of aesthetics and overall Web site presentation quality.

Like puns, animated GIFs can sometimes be appreciated only by the creator; depending upon the graphical content of an animated GIF, they can be perceived as surprising, or really obnoxious. Candidly, I experimented with a number of animations before settling upon the clapboard. I had wondrous marquee lights strobing around the menu, and buttons flashing on and off . . . and I was also giving *myself* a headache previewing them! Photoshop's Lens Flare filter offers levels of brightness, so the glimmer of a lens flare can be—in a word—subtle. For additional control, you can also use Photoshop 3.0's Layers feature to control the amount of opacity with which the Lens Flare is written to file. Here's how to create an animated GIF menu for the home page that balances with the amount of animation of the top page, and suggests illumination from afar instead of a flashbulb:

1. Create the main graphic you want to animate. It's best to keep this graphic small, but in RGB 16.7 million color mode, programs such as Photoshop won't offer filter effects with indexed color mode images. The CLAPPER.GIF file measures 130 pixels in width by 162 pixels in height. This is a medium-sized graphic for the Web. The reason I was able to pack 6 animation frames into it and still get a file of only 25K is that I color-reduced all the finished component images to 5 bits per pixel color depth (32 unique colors; 2 to the 5th power) before compiling the animated GIF. Color reduce to a common color palette if you want to achieve the same, optimized, color-consistent animation. See Chapters 5 and 7 for more information on color palettes.

2. In Photoshop, click on the new layer icon on the Layers palette, choose Screen from the Mode: drop-down list in

the dialog box, check the "Fill with Screen-neutral color (black)" check box, then click on OK. By default, you're now working on Layer 1 in the image.

3. With the rectangular marquee tool, select an area around the button that you want to apply the Lens Flare effect to. Make this a loose selection (the selection area will contain the Lens Flare effect) and limit it to a small area of the image.

4. Choose Filter | Render, then choose Lens Flare. The Lens Flare dialog box appears.

5. Choose a Lens Type (50–300mm is good), click and drag the crosshair in the proxy window until the Lens Flare preview is where you want it, then click and drag the Brightness slider to about 65 percent. Click on OK to execute the Lens Flare effect.

6. Press Ctrl(Cmd)+D to deselect the current selection, then click on the new layer icon on the Layers palette to add a layer to the image.

7. Repeat steps 2–6, but increase the brightness of the Lens Flare effect.

TIP

If you press Ctrl+Alt+F (Macintosh: Cmd+Opt+F), you can reenter the last-used Filters dialog box without going to the menu.

8. Figure 8-4 is a screen capture of the process described in this example. A layer equals a frame in your animation. I've got a highlight increasing over one button while a second high-light fades in the CLAPPER image, but you can choreo-graph the highlights any way you choose. Quit these ex-ample steps when you have five layers in the image.

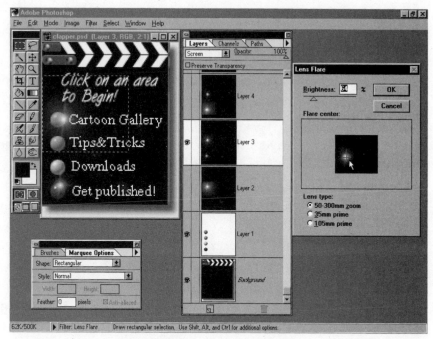

Figure 8-4: *Adobe Photoshop's Lens Flare effect simulates photographic patterns caused by light reflecting at an angle into a camera lens.*

Now, you'll want to export every layer after it's been melded to a copy of the background graphic:

1. Choose Image | Duplicate, and accept the default name for the new copy of the layered image.

2. Click on the eye icon to the left of every layer thumbnail on the Layers palette *except* the one directly on top of the Background thumbnail (probably labeled 'Layer 1' unless you specified a unique name). Click on Layer 1's title to highlight the title to make it the current active layer.

3. Choose Mode | Indexed Color. Photoshop will pop up an Attention box asking whether you want to discard hidden layers and flatten image. You do, so click on OK.

4. In the Indexed Color dialog box, choose 5 bits/pixel in the Resolution field, Adaptive in the Palette field, and make sure that Diffusion is chosen in the Dither field. Click on OK.

5. Choose Mode | Color Table, then click on Save. Save the color table for this indexed image as MYPALETTE.ACT, or something equally evocative.

6. Choose File | Export, then choose GIF89a Export.

7. Click on OK, then save the file to disk as CLAPPER1.GIF.

8. Go back to your original, layered image, and click on the Layer 2 icon on the Layers palette. Click on the eye icon on Layer 1 to make Layer 1 invisible.

9. Choose Image | Duplicate, and accept the default name for the new image.

10. From the Layers palette's flyout menu, choose Flatten Image. Click on OK in the attention box that asks if you want to delete the hidden layers.

11. Choose File | Export | GIF89a Export.

12. Choose 32 from the Colors drop-down list in the GIF89a Export options dialog box.

13. Click on Load, then select the MYPALETTE.ACT color table you saved in step 5. Click on OK, then save this file as CLAPPER2.GIF.

14. Repeat steps 8 through 13 for the rest of the layers.

 Quit Photoshop, and use GIF Construction Set (Windows), or GIF Builder (Macintosh) to build your animation. (GIF Builder is on the Companion CD-ROM.) See Chapter 5, "Animation & Digital Video Compression," for directions on how to use these programs. You can safely delete the resource files for this animation afterwards, except for one—you need one GIF frame in "plain vanilla" format to use with an image map utility.

If we think about it for a second, this makes absolute sense. Fractal Painter, Mapedit, and other image map programs only look for coordinates within an image that you specify. The coordinates are then either automatically or manually added to the HTML document to create the multiple URLs. Check out Chapter 1, "Composing in HTML & NavGold," for the details on how to create an image map file, and use a saved copy of one of the animation resource files to perform the mapping. Then specify the multi-image GIF in your HTML document instead of the "dummy" GIF file used to take the image map coordinates.

REPURPOSING A "CONTINUING CHARACTER" GRAPHIC

In television advertising, those 30-second slices of activity can often become more effective sales tools if a character from the commercial is also the star of the next commercial. Occasionally, these *continuing characters* become a cliché, and many folks actually begin to *like* them! Mr. Whipple, Mssrs. Bartles and James, even the Poppin' Fresh Doughboy are continuing characters that people immediately identify with a product.

In a similar way, the Digital Cartoon Home Page has continuing characters: "a skinny one and a fat one," as audiences used to describe many popular comedy duos. There's simply something funny about physically contrasting pals. In Figure 8-5, you can see my synthetic comedic pair as rendered in Extreme 3D. The two are a collection of spheres, cylinders, and other geometric primitives. See Chapter 6, "VRML," for some basic lessons on how to use a modeling program for Web element creation.

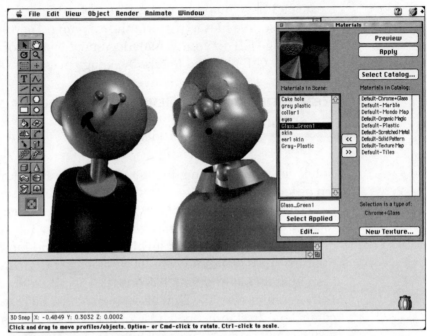

Figure 8-5: *Continuing characters who greet a visitor to your site don't have to be paid actors. You can model them yourself!*

We need to digress for a moment and ponder a few details of why computer models are a good choice for a Web site pertaining to cartoons, and how the time invested in their development and creation is time well-spent. First, the models shown in this chapter are distinctive, and they serve as an element that the visitor can relate to. They look familiar, and yet there is something unreal about them. It's this dynamic, cognitive tension that will attract and maintain attention, but it is the *reuse* of these characters in different areas of the Digital Cartoon Web site that helps tie the site together thematically.

A modeling program can usually render a scene to different file dimensions, but I chose to perform a quick render in Extreme 3D, then move the finished file into a drawing program, to then accurately trace over the characters. Why? Because through experience, I've found that if you invest some up-front time illustrating over a rendered model, you can then scale the model to any dimensions without loss of image detail. In short, I could spend a few hours rendering the models to bitmap format at half a dozen sizes, which requires careful measuring and preplanning for the site . . . or I could spend the same time manually converting the rendered model to vector format. By choosing the latter, I've got my models "on tap" at any resolution for future use.

The point is that a vector design program can provide you with many versions of the same image at different sizes. The choice to illustrate over a rendered model is an incidental issue, and if you have a good art background, you may choose to create a vector design without using a rendered model as an aid. For myself, modeling provides computer-accurate perspective, shading, and surface highlights, qualities of a realistic design that I find take too long to calculate mentally.

The tracing process took about four hours, and the original image I traced over took about five minutes to render to bitmap format. In Figure 8-6, you can see the beginning phase of the work: the bitmap image is imported into CorelXARA (Illustrator, CorelDRAW, or FreeHand could also be used); geometric shapes are created, then filled with gradient blends that accurately represent areas in the original image.

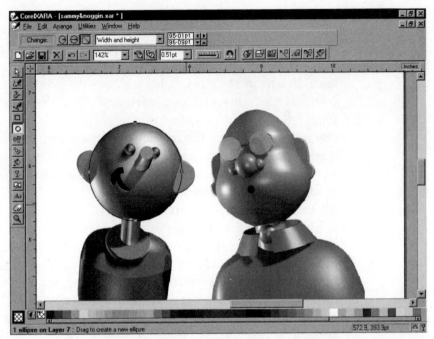

Figure 8-6: *Bitmap images cannot be scaled without blurring and distortion of original information; vector designs are flexible and resolution-independent.*

In Figure 8-7, you can see the finished design, along with variations on the design. After the initial tracing work, duplicates to different sizes were made in about two seconds by copying, pasting, and then scaling. Notice the outline version in Figure 8-7. We'll talk about how this simplified version of a graphic can be used along with the LOWSRC attribute to create an animation in the next section.

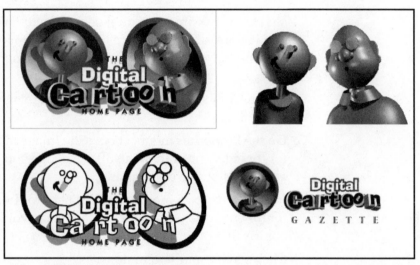

Figure 8-7: *Accurately tracing a bitmap image to produce a vector drawing can save you hours of editing or rendering time if you need multiple copies of such a design at different dimensions.*

The LOWSRC Attribute

A provision went into the HTML specifications that allows an alternate image to be quickly displayed while the final image to be presented in a document is loading. The two images, the low resolution one and the final image, have to be of the same file type, and it's a good idea if they are of the same dimensions, but with a little thought and planning, you can treat this feature as a limited form of animation resource.

Many sites already use the LOWSRC attribute to replace a monochrome image with a color one of the same design, and if your site is in need of a dramatic, or even humorous effect, here's how to work with the LOWSRC attribute:

1. Create the two images you'll use; make them of equal size, and it's probably good here to save them to interlaced GIF 89a format instead of JPEG, because some non-Navigator browsers don't read JPEG files.

2. In NavGold's Editor, click on the Insert Image button on the toolbar.

3. On the Properties menu, choose the Image tab, and browse for (or enter the path name of) the image you want to appear last in the document.

4. In the Alternative representations field for Image, browse for (or enter the path name of) the image you want to appear first onscreen.

5. Click on OK, and you're done.

In HTML code,

```
<img src="final image.GIF" lowsrc="first image.GIF">
```

describes the load order for the graphics. You should also specify the height and width attributes, and a border, if any, within the tag (NavGold lets you do this without touching the actual HTML code, in the Properties box).

In Figure 8-8, you can see the top document as it's partially re-placed the LOWSRC image with the final one. If you use this trick and find that the first image is being replaced too quickly (not likely if your audience uses 14.4K modems), you can slow the loading of the first image by making it larger in file size. For example, if you saved the first image at a resolution of 4 bits per pixel, try making a copy at 5 or 6 bits per pixel to increase the color capability. This also increases the size of the file as it downloads, which is a tad wasteful when thinking about conservation of bandwidth, but then again, graphics themselves increase Internet traffic.

Figure 8-8: *Create a slow fade between two images by using the LOWSRC attribute.*

TIP

> *Most of the images shown in the Digital Cartoon Home Page do not use the GIF89a's transparency feature. It wasn't necessary to make the graphics appear to float above the pale cream background.*
>
> *To perform this integration of foreground image with background color, red=255, green=255, and blue=128 was the chosen color in Navigator for the Web site's background. These same values were then specified in Photoshop and XARA for the backgrounds to the graphics. The graphics were cropped very tightly so not much of the background color in the graphics shows. Occasionally, using a graphic with a background color that's a close, but not an exact, match to the background you specify for a document creates a visible edge in the HTML page. Use the NCT.ACT (Photoshop color table), or the NCT.GIF image in the CHAP05 folder on the Companion CD-ROM to accurately match design colors with those Navigator uses to specify background and text colors.*

LIGHTNING-FAST ANIMATION CREATION

The MAINTOON page, which links from the top page through the clapboard image map, features two small animations. Unless you know of a continuing resource for animation files, you might need to get inventive and dream some up yourself for a site such as this. The author was faced with a decision when creating the Cartoon site: should the cartoons offered for viewing on the site be of the static, still image type, or would animation contribute to more overall interest?

If one considers that traditional animation began as a very primitive art—in black and white and with typically slapstick humor—the following solution I went with isn't a bad idea. In Chapter 1, you saw four cartoon illustrations peppering the *Digi-Toons* article. Instead of taking hours to make new illustrations for animation stock, I thought about the ways the still cartoons could feature animated elements.

One possible route you can take to add the inherent interest of animation to a still design is to use Fractal Design Painter's Nozzles or Floaters features in combination with Painter's capability to export AVI and QuickTime movies. (Chapter 5, "Animation & Digital Video Compression," contains a good example of how the Frame Stacks feature works.) Animating a Painter Floater simply involves moving a Floater a little in any direction for each sequential frame in the Frame Stack.

Moving from the ridiculous to the sublime with the cartoon of the flying camera was easy. I created a Painter Frame Stack of 10 frames, and copied the cartoon camera drawing to each frame. The camera image was then merged to the background of each frame by clicking the Drop button on the Objects: Floater List palette. To then add the animation, follow these steps:

1. Press Home to return to the first frame of the animation Frame Stack.

2. On the Objects: Floaters List palette, choose Floaters from the F. List menu. This pops up the Objects: Floaters palette, where you have a selection of premade floater objects that can be added to the animation.

3. Click and drag any icon on the top row into the first frame of the animation. For additional Floaters, click on the Drawer button on the palette to extend the palette and display more icons.

4. When you drag and drop a Floater into the Frame Stack, the Floater Adjuster tool is automatically selected. Use the tool now to reposition the Floater in the first frame by clicking and dragging. Before you turn the Frame Stack to the second frame, make sure the Floater is where you want it within the image.

5. Press PgUp to go to the next frame in the Frame Stack. Although you can't see it now, the Floater has dropped a copy of itself into the first frame. The second frame still contains the Floater as a floating object above the background image.

6. Click and drag the Floater to its second position in the movie. In this example, I used a public domain image of a NASA astronaut. Painter 4 has a new collection of premade Floaters which feature a dartboard, a plastic pig, and other elements that make ideal characters in whimsical animations. See Figure 8-9.

Figure 8-9: *Move the Floater object by a few pixels in each frame to create an animation.*

7. Press PgUp and move the Floater to its third position in the movie. Repeat steps 5 through 7 for the remaining frames in the movie. If at any time you want to go backwards in the Frame Stack, click on the eye icon on the Objects: Floater List to hide the Floater. This prevents the Floater from dropping a copy of itself in frames you've already finished. When you reach the final frame in the animation, click on the Drop button on the Objects: Floater List to meld the Floater to the last frame and clear the Frame Stack of floating objects.

8. Choose File | Save As, then you have your choice whether to save the movie as a platform-specific, compiled movie, or as numbered frames. Windows users can now create an AVI movie, and Macintosh users can create a QuickTime movie. If you want to address the largest audience, choose to render to still frames in this dialog box, and compile the movie in an application that can write either QuickTime or AVI movies. You're done.

QuickTime movies can be played on either a Windows or a Macintosh system, but AVI files for Windows cannot be read on a Macintosh without special software. For this reason, you'll see more QuickTime movies on the Web than AVI (Video for Window) files, but Windows users can use Intel's SmartVid utility (go to http://www.intel.com for a copy) to convert AVI files to QuickTime's *.MOV format.

With a little practice, you can add an element of animation to any still image using Painter in less than a half-hour. In the following section, you'll see another technique for animating single frame graphics.

REPLACEMENT ANIMATION TECHNIQUES

In traditional animation, a shortcut that has been used for decades is called *replacement animation*. As the name suggests, an element of the animation frame is replaced with another to create motion while the background remains the same. In Figure 8-10, you can see the WEB-GUY graphic originally featured in the *Digi-Toon* HTML document. Three different arm poses were created for the character, and the main graphic shown at right is exported with different arms added to make a simple animation.

Figure 8-10: *You can replace areas of a still image with different character or background elements to make the necessary frames for an animation file.*

CD-ROM   If you take a look at the WEB-GUY.MOV in the WEBTOONS folder, you'll notice that an additional element of animation has been added. I used Flo' (described in Chapter 5, "Animation & Digital Video Compression") to make the modem and the bottle in the cartoon image move around before using replacement animation to move the arm. Twelve frames were rendered out of Flo' as single, uncompiled frames. The images were brought into CorelXARA to add the arms, and the frames were then written to sequentially named files for the animation compiling program to turn into a QuickTime movie.

PLAYING THE GOOD HOST ON YOUR SITE

All the multimedia events in the world on your Web site won't amount to an exciting time for visitors to your site if they don't own the necessary plug-ins for viewing special Web objects.

Specific to animation files is Apple's QuickTime MoviePlayer; the Macintosh natively supports playing QuickTime movies, but Windows systems need the PLAYER.EXE file to be able to view QuickTime pieces.

Don't count on your audience having this file; although it ships and installs as part of many graphics, modeling, and animation programs, the chances are slim that every visitor to your site will be a graphics designer or own the file. A good solution to this problem is to offer on your page a download link that contains the animations. In Figure 8-11, you can see that the MAINTOON page is made up of two images that link to their respective animations, and a note is also featured that tells Windows users how to install PLAYER.EXE and configure the MIME type in Navigator. A text link is even provided to Apple's site, where the file can be downloaded.

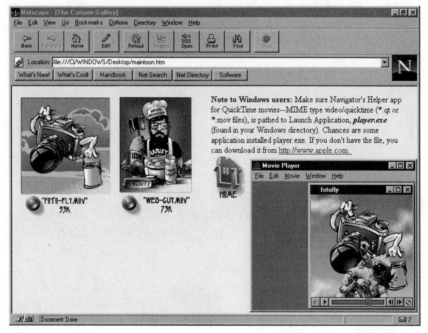

Figure 8-11: *Make it as easy as possible for your audience to experience the sum total of your multimedia creation. Provide links for the necessary plug-ins and helper apps.*

Although it's an optional thought here, you might also want to provide information on how to make animations play in a loop. If you've created an animation whose beginning and end wind up on the same frame (both the animations on the Cartoon site do), you might offer:

"If you're viewing this in Windows, choose Movie | Loop from the Movie Player menu before you click on the Play button in the QuickTime movie window."

Similarly, you can advise a Windows 95 audience viewing an AVI file with Media Player (the Win95 stand-alone movie playing application) to go to Programs | Accessories | Multimedia | Media Player, and choose Edit | Options | Auto-Repeat. This will make every AVI file loaded into Media Player repeat until you uncheck this setting at any time in the future.

Multimedia on the Web is a new phenomenon, and it would serve you well as an author to provide detailed instructions wherever necessary to make the event as effortless as possible for the visitor.

TRADITIONAL PUBLICATIONS PRESENTED AS MULTIMEDIA

The term "multimedia" has yet to be successfully defined save through example, and "interactive" is usually the buzz word that follows "multimedia" when describing CD content or the Web. This lack of definition can lead to some perilous escapades for Web authors, because the use of what multimedia *does* can often overshadow the use of multimedia for what it *is*. The author's personal definition of "multimedia" is:

The display of information in a related sequence of different media that can help explain the content, where the use of a single medium cannot.

The whole reason why the world doesn't publish physical documents as ASCII text is because text formatting, font styles, and graphics serve as more than embellishments to a thought. A well-laid out document adds content through its formatting—folks are familiar with the structures of magazines, books, and other physical literature, and can assimilate them quickly. The vehicle for the content becomes a part of the overall event.

If you accept my reasoning up to this point, it's logical then that the second component of the Cartoon site–the Digital Cartoon Gazette–should be offered from different media views, to better appeal to a market that has different ways of looking at things. The writing in the Gazette is identical in both the TOONVOL1.HTM document and the Acrobat PDF document that visitors can view if they click on the corresponding Web page button (and have a copy of the Acrobat plug-in installed in Navigator).

In Figure 8-12, you can see the TOONVOL1 document; this HTML page contains a bare minimum of graphics and can be downloaded for reading quite quickly. On the other hand, I've also provided the option to view the document in Acrobat format, including a button for jumping to Adobe Systems to download the Acrobat plug-in. The Acrobat document will download more slowly from the server to the visitor's machine because it's a 700K file. However, more experienced surfers understand that there's usually something special contained within an Acrobat document, and the graphics and text formatting I've used in DIGI-1.PDF make for a more complete, leisurely reading experience. You, too, can appeal to the graphically oriented audience as well as those in a hurry, by offering a work in multiple formats on your own site.

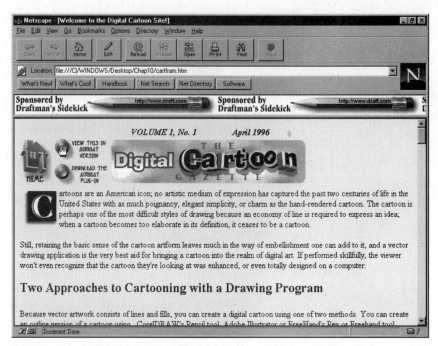

Figure 8-12: *Offer your audience more than one way to view document content, and you've got a multimedia event.*

MULTIMEDIA & THE ACROBAT FORMAT

As described in Chapter 7, "Working With Special File Formats," the Acrobat portable document publishing system consists of a PostScript-to-PDF converter, a viewer for PDF files, and a linking and formatting program called Acrobat Exchange. If you own the Pro edition of Acrobat, the Exchange program can be upgraded by a trip to Adobe's site to get the WEBLINK files, which enable the program to add Web links to any PDF document.

Although the obvious advantage of a PDF document with URLs is that it allows someone who views or downloads your document to access the Internet links you've provided, there's also a perk we'll explore here that makes a PDF document an integral part of a site. In Figure 8-13, you can see the Acrobat Exchange workspace with the DIGI-1 document being edited. After you install the

WEBLINK update, Exchange offers World Wide Web Link as a type of Action in the Link Properties dialog box. However, a URL can have many different *access methods* on the Internet, and the URL you see in Figure 8-13 will link back to the top document in the Cartoon site.

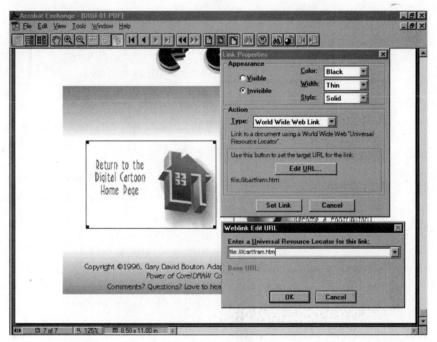

Figure 8-13: *The structure of a URL allows Web authors to link to a site, a file, or other approved Web schemes.*

We've shown different types of links throughout this book, but as a brief recap, here are four access methods—types of Uniform Resource Locator (URL) names—that can be used to provide different Internet services.

■   The http:// access method is the HyperText Transfer Protocol, and is used to link to another place on the Web. For example, http://www.netscape.com is the URL you'd use in an Acrobat document or HTML document to link to Netscape's home page. Note that the colon and two forward slashes are part of the HTTP scheme.

- The ftp:// access method is the File Transfer Protocol used to point the visitor at a location on a file server on the Web. We haven't used this scheme extensively in this book, because the Companion CD-ROM's contents are not on a file server, but if you need to offer a download, you should use the FTP access method for your URL.

- The mailto: access method is for the transfer of mail messages. You can use the mailto: scheme of URLs to allow Navigator to pop up its mail window with your return address when you want some response from a visitor to your site. The mailto: scheme contains no forward slashes. An example of a mailto: URL you could put in an HTML document or an Acrobat document would be:

```
mailto:petesmith@author.com
```

- The file:/// access method generally isn't used for transferring files, but instead references a local link within a system—it displays files, it doesn't download them. In this example, the file:///cartfram URL you saw typed in Acrobat Exchange's Weblink Edit URL dialog box will return the visitor to the top frameset document on the Companion CD-ROM, or on a Web server. It's important to understand that this is a legitimate scheme, but not a (uniform) URL because there is no absolute location for the frameset document. Instead, it references a file in the same folder as the Acrobat document. So if you need a local link from within a PDF file to an HTML file within the same directory, the file:/// access method is your ticket.

As you can see in Figure 8-14, when the visitor to the Cartoon site clicks on the "View this in Acrobat Version" button on the TOONVOL1.HTM page, the Acrobat Reader plug-in fills the browser window with the document and its own navigation controls.

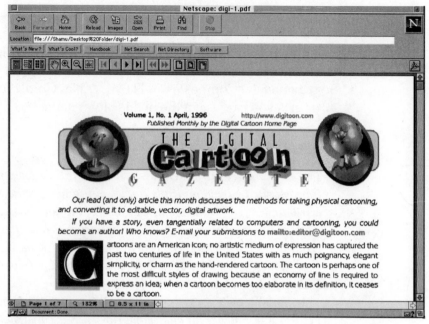

Figure 8-14: *The Acrobat plug-in offers its own document navigation controls when a link to a PDF file has been clicked on.*

You'll notice in this figure that the Draftman's Sidekick ad is gone from the browser window. There's a reason for this, even though your corporate sponsor might not like it. Acrobat documents played on the Web are unaware of the frameset tag in HTML documents (as of this writing; things change daily!). Any kind of link you make in an Acrobat document will fail to load if the Acrobat document is called from a frameset document. Therefore, to make the link to the Gazette's editor on the front page (hint: this is a dummy link and won't connect you to anything), the mailto link, and the Home button on the last page work, the TOONVOL1.HTM document uses a magic target attribute to clear the browser window of frames. If you open the TOONVOL1.HTM document in a text editor, you'll see the image map coordinates that specify a link in the "View the Acrobat Version" area of the GAZSHTML.GIF image:

```
<area shape="rect" alt="View the Acrobat version."
coords="67,1,175,45" href="digi-1.pdf" target="_top">
```

The href in the line above tells Navigator to display the PDF document in a browser window that clears the window of framesets. See Chapter 1, "Composing in HTML & NavGold," for the various attributes you can use in the magic target name.

TIP

The magic target attribute is also used in the link documents for the Cartoon site to avoid multiple frames piling up. The target="_parent" attribute is used for the Home buttons on the download and form pages because if the reference alone were specified to the top page, the Draftman's Sidekick advertisement would also "come along for the ride" from the previous document, and the main Cartoon page would then have two advertisements.

In your favorite text editor, check all the documents you find in the WEBTOONS folder for additional tips on link construction.

By displaying the PDF document in its own browser window without frames, all the links to URLs can function correctly within the document. The file:///cartfram.htm URL will return the visitor to the top of the site (the CARTFRAM.HTM document) as shown in Figure 8-13 (or on the last page of the DIGI-1.PDF file, if you'd like to load this document and check it out firsthand), and the file:///digiform.htm URL takes the visitor to a forms page, which we'll get to later in this chapter.

In Acrobat Exchange, you can also make bookmarks for long documents (see Figure 8-15). Decide whether or not, upon opening, the document displays the bookmarks (which take up space in the browser windows).

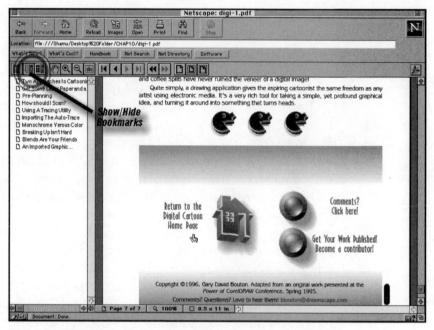

Figure 8-15: *Use an Acrobat document exactly like an HTML document; include document links, mailto: addresses, and links to files.*

TIP

You can also include a link to a movie within an Acrobat document using Acrobat Exchange 2.0 or later. This capability can come in very handy for Intranet communications such as training manuals.

DISPENSING GOODIES FROM YOUR SITE

As mentioned in the previous section, an FTP server is an important service your ISP should provide to put up a commercial site such as the Digital Cartoon Home Page. With monetary transactions, the Secure Sockets Layer (SSL) is an open standard that should be implemented on the host server to assure the visitor that credit card information, names, addresses, and so on, are a private affair between the visitor and the site.

However, if you're dispensing files free of charge, as in this example site, and the files are small in size, as you begin your venture, you can use a somewhat primitive but effective strategy for file transfer. It's called, "Compact the files so Navigator is forced to query the visitor about how the files should be handled."

There are two almost universally accepted means for archiving files: the Zip procedure originally created by Phil Katz for DOS, and the StuffIt compactor for the Macintosh, a product of Aladdin Systems. Most types of Macintosh files are saved with both a resource and a data fork. These types of files cannot travel successfully across the Internet. A *sit* (StuffIt-compacted) file only contains a data fork, and therefore can be downloaded successfully. It is common, however, for a StuffIt file to be packaged with an additional layer of compression—BinHex—to ensure the data's integrity.

In Figure 8-16, you can see the screen of a Macintosh visitor who has clicked on the download button for the Macintosh version of ElephantsAndBears PS, a cartoon font on the Companion CD-ROM that has been Stuffed and BinHexed. Because this visitor has StuffIt on their hard disk, StuffIt configures itself upon installation to take the BinHex file, remove the contents, UnStuff the archived file, and place the uncompressed file on the desktop. Windows users can also configure Netscape to automatically launch WinZip (a shareware utility on the Companion CD-ROM) when a *.ZIP file is downloaded. It might be more convenient, however, to allow Navigator to query visitors as to what they'd like to do with the file, and to which location on their system they would like the file copied. This query is an automatic one that requires no explanation, and is the default configuration for Navigator.

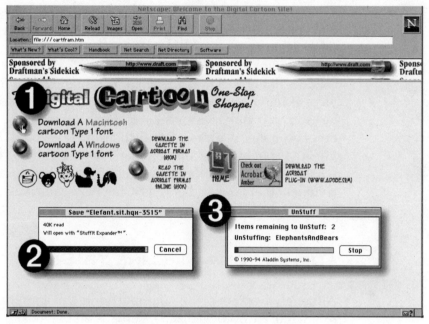

Figure 8-16: *An archived file can be used as a vending method for your site.*

The download HTML page also contains a link to Adobe Systems, so the visitor can easily download the latest version of Acrobat Reader. If you decide that archiving files is a good method for dispensing goods from your site, you should also take into account the compression rates of different files. For example, PDF files do not compress significantly because their format is innately an economical one. I've compressed the PDF document linked to this site for reasons other than speedy download. If, in this example, the DIGI-01.PDF document were not compressed, the trick of forcing Navigator to query the user about what to do with the file would not work. If left uncompressed (I saved a whopping 2 percent in file size by compressing this file), the Acrobat plug-in would address the link by playing the document, and, in this example, that's unwanted.

You also might want to offer advice to your visitors on how Navigator can be used to automatically download any Web object on your site.

"To download this file, Shift+click here"

... does not make for as elegant a presentation of your site's services as renting access to an FTP server, but if your downloads can be estimated in the tens weekly instead of the hundreds, this is another economical approach to dispensing free goods. Shift+clicking is a Navigator-specific command, as is the dialog box that asks what a visitor wants Navigator to do with a linked file, so if you're confident that your audience is using Navigator, you're home free with this technique.

FORMS: YOUR PIPELINE TO SITE FEEDBACK

Although there are plenty of opportunities in a multipage Web site for mailto: URLs to be placed, perhaps you're looking for *structured* feedback from your site—a neatly categorized collection of information you can sift through and analyze at your leisure.

Forms are an approved specification in HTML, and with Navigator and a program that can write forms, a form page can look as clean and professional as the rest of your site. Unfortunately, at this time there really isn't a forms authoring tool for the Macintosh, but there are many shareware forms databases for the Macintosh that can retrieve and sort data generated by a form page. Commercial databases such as Microsoft Excel can also be used to sort data formatted by a forms page.

Basically, the way a forms document works is that your form, written in HTML, contains INPUT tags, with parameters (attributes) that specify what sort of information should go in a form field. For example:

```
<input TYPE="checkbox" NAME="Questionnaire" VALUE="Did you
take a shower today?">
```

would return information from the site that the visitor either checked the check box (true) or else didn't take a shower or didn't care to answer this personal information (false). There are many attributes you can specify in a form document: size of field, type of input—and because a form is in HTML, *other* Web elements such as a background image and graphics can be added to the form.

The real trick to form responses lies not in the creation of the form, but in how the data is returned to you. Generally, a form requires the use of a CGI script to take in the information, sort it into a database, and return the information to you. Many ISPs offer CGI scripts for forms, but if you intend to retrieve lots of information from your site, you should consult with your ISP and find out how they can implement a CGI script. If they don't use one, there are several online resources for CGI scripts (see following tip). These online resources are typically free of charge or modest in price; the scripts are approved by many Service Providers, and you might convince your own ISP to set your site up with one.

TIP

If you need a CGI script to perform automated routines from your site's sever, check out these locations:

CGI.pm, a Perl5 CGI Library by L. Stein:
http://www-genome.wi.mit.edu/ftp/pub/software/WWW/

Selena's Public Domain CGI Scripts, by Selena Sol:
http://www.eff.org/~erict/Scripts/

Matt's Script Archive, by Matt Wright:
http://worldwidemart.com/scripts/

However, if you can manage a modest amount of data, perhaps less than 100 responses a week, you can collect data all by yourself—without the need for CGI intervention—through the use of a shareware program such as WebForms. WebForms is a Windows utility that is both a forms authoring tool and a database. The Professional Edition allows users to batch import responses to a form, and provides a database from which you can view your responses or export the responses to a database program. The Standard Edition, shareware version of WebForms can be found at http://www.q-d.com.

WebForms, shown in Figure 8-17, offers a step-by-step tabbed menu for the creation of a form. You enter the parameters, such as name, e-mail address, text fields in which the visitor can enter long comments, and multiple check boxes, then move on to the next tab as WebForms generates the HTML code that makes up the document.

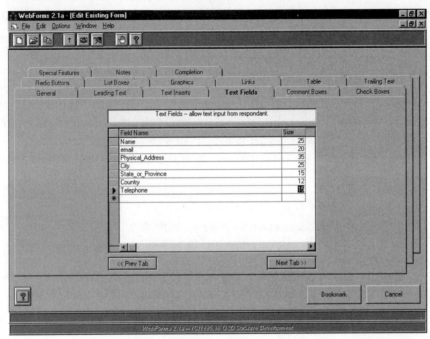

Figure 8-17: *If you want information from your site returned to you in an organized manner, WebForms is a solution for medium-traffic sites.*

David Verschleiser and Q&D Software Development have implemented JavaScript as part of WebForms to make the transportation of a completed form, the organization of the responses, and the return of the information to you as effortless as writing e-mail. The technology is as sound as a CGI script, but is decidedly easier. If you take a look at the DIGIFORM.HTM document in Navigator's browser, you'll see that this particular form was intended to draw out potential contributors to the Digital Cartoon Gazette. Forms, however, can be used for any purpose you might have in mind for your site. Simply keep the site friendly and inviting, and folks will sign your guest registry, your purchase order, or other form-based creations.

In Figure 8-18, you can see an example of what the responses from the DIGIFORM document would be like if this document were actually posted on a server. The procedure for getting returns from a WebForms document is a simple one: WebForms is capable of importing responses directly from a POP (*Point of Presence*) mail server, the type of service that is basic to Internet accounts. In WebForms' Import Setup window, enter the information you're prompted for. The next time you fetch your e-mail, WebForms will perform a smart sort of mail. Regular e-mail is returned to you as e-mail, but specially formatted mail will go into WebForms' database.

Figure 8-18: *WebForms displays responses to your site in the order in which you specified the information on your form page.*

Unlike the Acrobat document shown earlier, an HTML form can indeed share a frameset document. And this is bound to please potential corporate sponsors because they might want you to post order forms of their own. In Figure 8-19, you can see the top of the form as it will display in Windows. On the Macintosh, the graphics and basic structure of the document will be seen as identical, but the font, the check boxes, and the buttons in a form document are all native to the version of Netscape that the visitor is running.

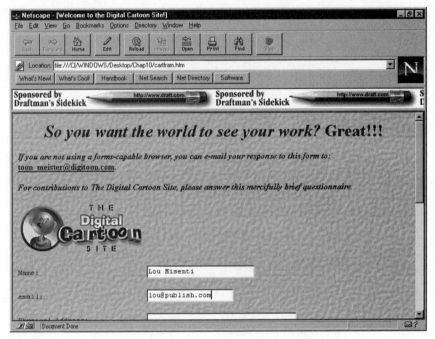

Figure 8-19: *You can decorate a form with visual elements that tie your site's look together when you use WebForms.*

TIP

For Macintosh users, there are several good shareware programs that can make form-sorted e-mail arrive at your machine in neatly organized table or database format. Web authors will still need to create the HTML forms, but the following applications can make data retrieval a lot easier:

E-forms is a script that handles data sent to you via e-mail from HTML forms. E-forms requires Eudora (as the mail handler), FileMaker Pro, and AppleScript. Write to rcanetta@micronet.it for more information on E-forms.

Send File *is an auto-reply script for Eudora. This script is useful for sending one or more files to people who request them. Write to Casgrain@ere.umontreal.ca.*

The INFORMer *is a HyperCard stack for the Macintosh, that will parse several e-mail message files into a database format. Go to http://www.phoenix.net/~jacobson for the INFORMer.*

As you saw in the previous figure (8-19), a form doesn't have to be all business. To relieve some of the tension a visitor naturally experiences when conducting business and offering information on the Web, you can provide reassurances and a conversational aside or two within the form. In Figure 8-20, the Submit button has been clicked, the underlying HTML tells the JavaScript to return a confirmation, and the tone of the dialog box's text—which is specified by the author in WebForms—is light and personal.

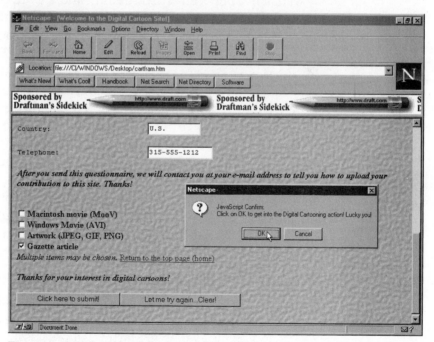

Figure 8-20: *You can perform light polling on your site without the use of a CGI Script when you have a program such as WebForms e-mail the responses to you.*

WRAPPING THINGS UP: SET YOUR SITES HIGH

If you perused all the examples in this chapter, you most likely had to refer to previous chapters, but that was the intention—to get a routine going that integrates what you've learned with what it is you want to say to the world. And while thumbing, you might have noticed that there aren't many pages to follow under your right thumb. It's the end of the examples, but not the end of your experiences with the concept work, the specialized applications and authoring tools, and the logistics of putting a full-featured Web site on the Internet.

Although a summary might be appropriate here, let's leave you instead with some key thoughts as you go off and build your Ultimate Web Site:

- Make it a practice (as the author occasionally does) to strike a balance between artistic quality and HTML pages that can download to a visitor within a lifetime. This is a hard thing to do because artists are growing quite accustomed to generating 150MB images on machines with 250MB of RAM ever since prices fell on memory and disk storage. This is fine for desktop publishing, but thwarts your prime goal: attract visitors to your site with quality graphics that are as small in size as possible. With a little work, you can convert copies of large pieces to Web size. Many image editors offer an unSharp Mask filter that can bring a large graphic that's been resampled into crystal clear focus. I personally choose the largest thumbnail size on Photoshop's Layers palette when I load a big graphic, then take a screen capture. The thumbnail is often the perfect size for a Web graphic, and I don't have to alter the original image by a single pixel.

- Offer alternative representations of an idea with a medium that best expresses the thought, not simply because the technology is available. Martin Guitars has a splendid site on the Web that offers sound clips of their classic line of instruments. This is a good use of sound. A *poor* use of sound would be a recital of a corporate annual report by the chairman. Unless the chairman was also a gifted jazz singer and knew how to belt out the year-end figures and the letter to the shareholders.

You have animation, sound, video, graphics, embedded objects, and many more media of creative expression waiting around technology's corner. Sometimes, a technology will inspire you; other times, you'll come up with an inspired use of a new technology. The point is, don't throw a technological "wrapper" with no content at your audience. Firecrackers come and go in a moment, but pyrotechnics that are well choreographed make the event an experience to remember and one to come back to again and again.

■ Test your site privately for at least a week before you go on the road. This is a point that we couldn't demonstrate in this book because the examples are all on CD-ROM. But believe me, I revised and revised these example documents until everything looked like alphabet soup, specifically HTML soup! A misplaced bracket in a VRML world text file will result in a black hole, not a virtual world. A link won't load because there's a typo in a path. There are 40 files that make up the Digital Cartoon Home Page, and this is by no means a complex site.

My best advice to help you build a bulletproof multimedia Web site is to invite friends to test your site on a server for a week. In software beta testing, manufacturers ask sites to "Bang it, and bang it hard." This is the only way to see whether something can be broken, or whether it doesn't work to begin with. When it runs as expected at least a dozen times in a row, your site is ready to go public.

■ Politics are for Washington, DC, not for the Web. You'll notice that very few popular entertainers make a career out of criticizing a faction of society. The Web is a society also, composed of users with different types of machines. Appeal to all types of users, and you've got yourself a large audience. On the other hand, if you want to practice "platform chauvinism"—offering platform-specific goods or attractions—then you limit yourself by shunning part of the available audience. Mac users need to brush up on the way Windows users browse and surf, and Windows users should be aware of what a Macintosh audience might expect from your site. There is very little difference between the Macintosh and Windows 95 systems (you'll notice that the screen captures in this book are biplatform, but mostly look the same while in an application), and the Internet operates largely as a UNIX-based system. You grow as a Web author when you learn foreign languages, and your site can benefit from your knowledge.

- What was impossible five minutes ago is now commonplace. Don't get frustrated if you can't place a hologram as an embedded object in an HTML file, because Netscape will announce a hologram plug-in tomorrow. Or next week. The Web is an evolving place; treat change as a thing you simply place on top of your present expertise, and you'll have the best of new and existing technology at your disposal.

- Get to know one or two applications well enough that you feel free to deliberately do things in them that the documentation tells you can't or shouldn't be done. I achieved an interesting texture once by running the "wrong" video driver with an application.

  Neither Ventana nor the author will reimburse you for allowing an elephant to perch on your flatbed scanner or for similar stunts, but *do* push your applications a little for the results you think you can get. There's a wealth of innovative techniques at your fingertips with a personal computer. See what's in there.

Finally, share what you've learned with others. Artists tend to live a solitary existence, but no one's a stranger for very long on the Internet. Netizens are renowned for offering good, solid, and often advanced advice. Reciprocate in kind, and subscribe to as many graphics and HTML lists and discussion groups as your ISP has to offer—and your hard disk is able to hold. It's like getting a second education in your spare time, with resource documents that are as fresh as tomorrow's news.

Appendix A

About the Online Companion

Information is power! The Netscape Press Online Companion is all you need to be connected to the best Internet information and Netscape resources. It aids you with understanding the Internet and Netscape's role in the technology.

You can access the special Web site for purchasers of Netscape Press products at **http://www.netscapepress.com/**. Some of the valuable features of this special site include information on other Netscape Press titles, Netscape news, and Navigate!, the magazine for Netscape Press.

Navigate! is the official electronic publication of Netscape Press. Netscape Press is a joint effort between Ventana and Netscape Communications Corp., and serves as the publishing arm of Netscape. Navigate! is a monthly online publication that offers a wide range of articles and reviews aimed at Netscape users. Navigate! will also feature interviews with industry icons and experts, as well as articles excerpted from upcoming Netscape Press titles.

The *Official Multimedia Publishing for Netscape Online Companion* also links you to the Netscape Press catalog, where you will find useful press and jacket infomation on a variety of Netscape Press offerings. Plus, you have access to a wide selection of exciting new releases and coming attractions. In addition, the catalog allows you to order online the books you want without leaving home.

The Online Companion represents Netscape Press's ongoing commitment to offering the most dynamic and exciting products possible. And soon netscapepress.com will be adding more services, including more multimedia supplements, searchable indexes, and sections of the book reproduced and hyperlinked to the Internet resources they reference.

Free voice technical support is offered but is limited to installation-related issues; this free support is available for 30 days from the date you register your copy of the book. After the initial 30 days and for non-installation-related questions, please send all technical support questions via Internet e-mail to help@vmedia.com. Our technical support staff will research your question and respond promptly via e-mail.

Appendix B

About the Companion CD-ROM

The CD-ROM included with your copy of *Official Multimedia Publishing for Netscape* contains valuable software programs and example files from each chapters.

To view the CD-ROM:

- **Windows 3.1/Windows 95/Windows NT:** Double-click on the viewer.exe file from your Windows Explorer or File Manager.

- **Macintosh:** Double-click on the Viewer icon on your Macintosh hard drive. You'll see a menu screen offering several choices. See "Navigating the CD-ROM" below for your option choices.

NAVIGATING THE CD-ROM

Your choices for navigating the CD-ROM appear on the opening screen. You can exit from the CD, get help on navigating, learn more about Netscape Press, browse the Hot Picks, or view the Software and Chapter Examples.

The Chapter Examples are broken down by each chapter. To see what is in each chapter, click on it in the box on the left-hand side of your screen. You can choose to copy all of the examples from a chapter to your hard drive at one time or you can copy one example at a time.

The Software section lists all of the software programs that are on the CD-ROM. You can choose to copy the programs one at a time to your hard drive or you can copy all of the programs at once. A complete listing of the programs follows in Table B-1.

Program	Description
BBEdit Lite (Mac)	The freeware "cousin" of BBEdit, the popular and critically acclaimed text editor.
BBEdit Demo Version (Mac)	The demo version of BBEdit.
The Black Box Filters (Win 3.1x and 95)	A set of 10 Photoshop-compatible filters.
BRENDA*The Batch Renderer (Win)	A batch-oriented image processing utility, developed primarily to create VGA-friendly palettes and to efficiently remap images to VGA-friendly palettes.
Compact Pro 1.5.1 (Mac)	A shareware file compression and archival utility.
DropStuff with Expander Enhancer (Mac)	Allows you to create plain or self-extracting StuffIt archives, or BinHex files.
FontLab (Win)	Gives you special tools to edit and transform existing fonts as well as to create new, quality typefaces.
Fractal Design Painter 4.0 Demo (Mac and Windows)	A leading paint and image creation program.
GIF Builder 0.3.2 (Mac)	A Macintosh utility for creating animated GIF files.
GIF Converter 2.3.7 (Mac)	A graphic viewing and conversion program.

Program	Description
GoldWave (Win)	A great audio processing tool.
KEYview (Win)	This 30-day demo version of KEYview must be installed in order to use the KEYview plug-in, which is also on this CD-ROM.
Mapedit (Win)	A utility for creating image maps.
Paint Shop Pro (Win)	A shareware product with a wide variety of useful features for manipulating images.
StuffIt Expander (Win and Mac)	A utility for expanding compressed files.
TextPad (Win)	Provides the power and functionality to satisfy your most demanding text editing requirements.
WebTools (Win and Mac)	Artbeats Webtools contains an extensive library of decorative elements, including icons, buttons, bars, sounds, and tiles.
WinZip (Win)	A compression utility.
ZipIt 1.3.3 (Mac)	An unzipping utility for Macintosh.

Table B-1: *Programs on the Companion CD-ROM.*

There are two folders on the CD-ROM that are not referenced by the viewer. You can open both of the folders from your Windows Explorer or File Manager if you are using Windows or from your hard drive if you are using a Macintosh.

The first folder is labeled Boutons. This folder contains fonts and textures that the author has referenced in the book.

The second folder is Plug-ins. You can copy each plug-in folder to your hard drive and install it. A list of the plug-ins follows in Table B-2.

Plug-In	Description
CoolFusion (Win)	A streaming Video for Windows (AVI) plug-in.
Crescendo and Win)	A MIDI plug-in that lets users listen to MIDI (Mac files embedded in Web pages.
Envoy (Mac and Win)	Allows you to read Envoy 1.0/1.0a files and Envoy files published with Tumbleweed Publishing Essentials.
Formula One/NET (Win)	Provides powerful spreadsheet functionality in reusable component form.
Fractal Viewer (Win)	Enables the inline use of fractal images on the Web.
KEYview (Win)	Lets you view and convert over 100 file formats without needing the original application that created them.
Lightning Strike 2.5 (Mac and Win)	A wavelet compression/decompression program that is designed to increase the graphical content of the Web through higher compression ratios and improved image quality.
Sizzler (Win and Mac)	A stream-based multimedia software plug-in that allows Web users to play live, real-time interactive animation and multimedia.
Talker (Mac)	Allows Web pages to talk and sing to Macintosh users, using Apple computer's text-to-speech software.
VDOLive (Win)	Compresses video images while maintaining the same viewing quality.

Table B-2: *Plug-ins on the Companion CD-ROM.*

Technical support is available for installation-related problems only. The technical support office is open from 8:00 A.M. to 6:00 P.M. Monday through Friday and can be reached via the following methods:

Phone: (919) 544-9404 extension 81

E-mail: help@vmedia.com

FAX: (919) 544-9472

World Wide Web: **http://www.vmedia.com/support**

America Online: keyword *Ventana*

LIMITS OF LIABILITY & DISCLAIMER OF WARRANTY

The author and publisher of this book have used their best efforts in preparing the CD-ROM and the programs contained in it. These efforts include the development, research, and testing of the theories and programs to determine their effectiveness. The authors and publisher make no warranty of any kind, expressed or implied, with regard to these programs or the documentation contained in this book.

The authors and publisher shall not be liable in the event of incidental or consequential damages in connection with, or arising out of, the furnishing, performance, or use of the programs, associated instructions, and/or claims of productivity gains.

Index

S

Explore the Internet

Internet Business 500

$29.95, 488 pages, illustrated, part #: 287-9

This authoritative list of the most useful, most valuable online resources for business is also the most current list, linked to a regularly updated *Online Companion* on the Internet. The companion CD-ROM features the latest version of *Netscape Navigator*, plus a hyperlinked version of the entire text of the book.

Walking the World Wide Web, Second Edition

$39.95, 800 pages, illustrated, part #: 298-4

More than 30% new, this book now features 500 listings and an extensive index of servers, expanded and arranged by subject. This groundbreaking bestseller includes a CD-ROM enhanced with Ventana's WebWalker technology; updated online components that make it the richest resource available for Web travelers; and the latest version of Netscape Navigator along with a full hyperlinked version of the text.

Quicken 5 on the Internet

$24.95, 472 pages, illustrated, part #: 448-0

Get your finances under control with *Quicken 5 on the Internet*. Quicken 5 helps make banker's hours a thing of the past—by incorporating Internet access and linking you directly to institutions that see a future in 24-hour services. *Quicken 5 on the Internet* provides complete guidelines to Quicken to aid your offline mastery and help you take advantage of online opportunities.

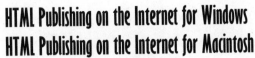

HTML Publishing on the Internet for Windows
HTML Publishing on the Internet for Macintosh

$49.95, 512 pages, illustrated
Windows part #: 229-1, Macintosh part #: 228-3

Successful publishing for the Internet requires an
understanding of "nonlinear" presentation as well as
specialized software. Both are here. Learn how HTML
builds the hot links that let readers choose their own
paths—and how to use effective design to drive your
message for them. The enclosed CD-ROM includes
Netscape Navigator, HoTMetaL LITE, graphic viewer,
templates conversion software and more!

The Web Server Book

$49.95, 680 pages, illustrated, part #: 234-8

The cornerstone of Internet publishing is a set of UNIX
tools, which transform a computer into a "server" that can
be accessed by networked "clients." This step-by-step in-
depth guide to the tools also features a look at key issues—
including content development, services and security. The
companion CD-ROM contains Linux™, Netscape
Navigator™, ready-to-run server software and more.

The Windows NT Web Server Book

$49.95, 500 pages, illustrated, part #: 342-5

A complete toolkit for providing services on the Internet
using the Windows NT operating system. This how-to guide
includes adding the necessary World Wide Web server
software, comparison of the major Windows NT server
packages for the Web, becoming a global product provider
and more! The CD-ROM features a hyperlinked, searchable
copy of the book, plus ready-to-run server software, support
programs, scripts, forms, utilities and demos.

 Books marked with this logo include a free Internet *Online
Companion*™, featuring archives of free utilities plus a
software archive and links to other Internet resources.

Web Pages Enhanced

Shockwave!

$49.95, 350 pages, illustrated, part #:441-3

Breathe new life into your Web pages with Macromedia Shockwave. Ventana's Shockwave! teaches how to enliven and animate your Web sites with online movies. Beginning with step-by-step exercises and examples, and ending with in-depth excursions into the use of Shockwave Lingo extensions, Shockwave! is a must-buy for both novices and experienced Director developers. Plus, tap into current Macromedia resources on the Internet with Ventana's *Online Companion.*

Java Programming for the Internet

$49.95, 500 pages, illustrated, part #: 355-7

Create dynamic, interactive Internet applications with Java Programming for the Internet. Expand the scope of your online development with this comprehensive, step-by-step guide to creating Java applets. Includes four real-world, start-to-finish tutorials. The CD-ROM has all the programs, samples and applets from the book, plus shareware. Continual updates on Ventana's *Online Companion* will keep this information on the cutting edge.

Exploring Moving Worlds

$24.99, 300 pages, illustrated, part #: 467-7

Moving Worlds—a newly accepted standard that uses Java and JavaScript for animating objects in three dimensions—is billed as the next-generation implementation of VRML. Exploring Moving Worlds includes an overview of the Moving Worlds standard, detailed specifications on design and architecture, and software examples to help advanced Web developers create live content, animation and full motion on the Web.

Macromedia Director 5 Power Toolkit

$49.95, 800 pages, illustrated, part #: 289-5

Macromedia Director 5 Power Toolkit views the industry's hottest multimedia authoring environment from the inside out. Features tools, tips and professional tricks for producing power-packed projects for CD-ROM and Internet distribution. Dozens of exercises detail the principles behind successful multimedia presentations and the steps to achieve professional results. The companion CD-ROM includes utilities, sample presentations, animations, scripts and files.

Internet Power Toolkit

$49.95, 800 pages, illustrated, part #: 329-8

Plunge deeper into cyberspace with *Internet Power Toolkit,* the advanced guide to Internet tools, techniques and possibilities. Channel its array of Internet utilities and advice into increased productivity and profitability on the Internet. The CD-ROM features an extensive set of TCP/IP tools including Web USENET, e-mail, IRC, MUD and MOO, and more.

The 10 Secrets for Web Success

$19.95, 350 pages, illustrated, part #: 370-0

Create a winning Web site—by discovering what the visionaries behind some of the hottest sites on the Web know instinctively. Meet the people behind Yahoo, IUMA, Word and more, and learn the 10 key principles that set their sites apart from the masses. Discover a whole new way of thinking that will inspire and enhance your own efforts as a Web publisher.

Books marked with this logo include a free Internet *Online Companion*™, featuring archives of free utilities plus a software archive and links to other Internet resources.

To order any Ventana title, complete this order form and mail or fax it to us, with payment, for quick shipment.

TITLE	PART #	QTY	PRICE	TOTAL

SHIPPING

For all standard orders, please ADD $4.50/first book, $1.35/each additional.
For software kit orders, ADD $6.50/first kit, $2.00/each additional.
For "two-day air," ADD $8.25/first book, $2.25/each additional.
For "two-day air" on the kits, ADD $10.50/first kit, $4.00/each additional.
For orders to Canada, ADD $6.50/book.
For orders sent C.O.D., ADD $4.50 to your shipping rate.
North Carolina residents must ADD 6% sales tax.
International orders require additional shipping charges.

SUBTOTAL = $ _____

SHIPPING = $ _____

TOTAL = $ _____

Name _____

E-mail _____ Daytime phone _____

Company _____

Address (No PO Box) _____

City _____ State _____ Zip _____

Payment enclosed ___VISA ___MC ___ Acc't # _____ Exp. date _____

Signature _____ Exact name on card _____

Mail to: Ventana • PO Box 13964 • Research Triangle Park, NC 27709-3964 ☎ 800/743-5369 • Fax 919/544-9472

Check your local bookstore or software retailer for these and other bestselling titles, or call toll free: **800/743-5369**

All technical support for this product is available from Ventana. The technical support office is open from 8:00 A.M. to 6:00 P.M. (eastern standard time) Monday through Friday and can be reached via the following methods:

World Wide Web: http://www.netscapepress.com/support

E-mail: help@vmedia.com

Phone: (919) 544-9404 extension 81

FAX: (919) 544-9472

America Online: keyword *Ventana*